BRUTUS BEEFCAKE

Struttin' & Cuttin'

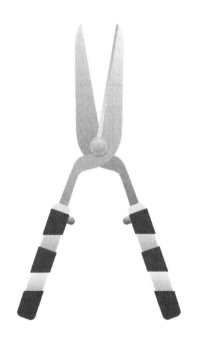

Brutus Beefcake
with Kenny Casanova

Brutus Beefcake: Struttin' & Cuttin'
Copyright © 2017 by Walking on Hot Waffles Publishers
in conjunction with Kenny Casanova & WOHW.com

ISBN: 978-1-090610-02-7

Printed in the USA

FOREWORD - WADE BOGGS

When I was young, my family lived in several different places, due to my father's military background. I lived for a short time in both Puerto Rico and Savannah, Georgia, before finally settling down in Palma Ceia; a little neighborhood located southwest of downtown Tampa, Florida.

Being the new kid, my father thought it was a good idea to get me out there to be social, so he introduced me to little league baseball. It turned out that I was pretty good at it at a young age and because of that, right away, I loved it.

Now, if I had had a bad team, I can't say whether or not baseball would have become my passion. One of the reasons baseball was so enjoyable to me at this time was because of who I was playing with and how they brought the best out in me. One particular teammate that I was playing with who really stood out above the rest was a tall skinny, wiry, and somewhat awkward kid named Edward Leslie. He may not have looked like much yet at such a young age, but boy, could he play ball.

Now, we didn't play on the same team at first. He lived on the other side of town, so he wasn't on my neighborhood team. We actually played against each other on opposite teams quite a bit. We knew each other well though, and we were very competitive against each other. However, when it came time for the big "Tampa Little League All-Star Series" we all had to set our differences aside.

For our All-Star team, the coaches put the best players of all the area's teams together to take on other regional All-Star teams. That is when Ed Leslie and I finally found ourselves on a field together wearing the same jerseys.

I played shortstop, and Ed was first base. We practiced and worked together a great deal after school, and we always made it a point to team up for drills. Most of the other players on our team had some skills, but they were really just "okay." Ed, on the other hand, was very athletic and a good ball player. He pushed me to play even better, and I did the same to him. We really hit it off.

Seeing what he could do out there on the field was great. I really thought he would make it on a big team one day and make to the next level. He just had that extra "It Factor" that you couldn't really teach, if you know what I mean. We had a great time together learning and perfecting our game.

As time went on and we had graduated from little league, Ed continued to challenge himself with various endeavors. We kept in touch a little, but it eventually happened. I went on to Plant High School in Tampa, but Ed went to Robinson High, which was one of our biggest rivals. Once in a while, I would hear what Ed was up to. I heard he started getting into sailing and racing boats. I also heard he got into running - *running after girls that is.* I knew though that Ed was no longer into baseball as he once was back when we played together. And because baseball was my life, I guess I eventually lost touch with him.

During my high school years, baseball was everything. For a time, I also tried football and even became the team quarterback. However, because baseball was my first priority, I had to make the conscious decision to step aside from playing that position to avoid injury. I needed to take the bullseye off my back in football in order to protect my future in baseball. In the end, that turned out to be a good gamble. When I graduated from Plant in 1976, I was selected by the Boston Red Sox in the seventh round of the MLB draft. Life got very busy after that.

In 1984, years after already establishing myself with the Sox, I found myself attending a dinner banquet out in Rochester, NY being thrown by the legendary MLB Umpire Ken Kaiser. People were there from all walks of life. I sat down and got to talking with another athlete, and surprisingly found out that I had quite a few things in common with a professional wrestler. Since we had had a number of similar interests outside of our games, eventually, I went fishing with a guy named Curt Hennig. The rest was history.

Our love of nature and the hunt developed into a terrific friendship. Whenever we both had time off, we would go out on hunting trips together be it local, or further away like British Columbia. On one of these particular journeys, Curt Hennig would even save my life. I was climbing over a broken barbed wire fence as I had many times before and slipped. The barb ripped right through my pants and severely cut my leg deep. We were out in the middle of nowhere and I was worried about bleeding out. Finally, Curt caught up with me and was my savior that day. He carried me over a mile out of the wilderness out to the road to safety. If he wasn't there that day, I probably would have died.

Curt was wrestling for the AWA when I first met him. Around 1988 or so, he got a call from New York to work in the major leagues for Vince McMahon in the WWF. He had been there before in a smaller capacity, but this time, he was about to hit a home run. They were all set to debut him as a new character to their world by the name, "Mr. Perfect." Some of you may recall that they aired a number of promos to help get over his new gimmick. These videos illustrated that Mr. Perfect excelled in every sport, not just wrestling. As a favor to Curt, I appeared in one as a cameo to help Mr. Perfect display his perfect baseball abilities. (We remained good friends until the very end. In 2007, I would get to induct the late Mr. Perfect into the WWE Hall of Fame.)

Soon after, Curt invited me to come backstage to a show in Tampa. I was all about it. See, I was already a huge wrestling fan. I used to go to Tampa Armory as a kid with my father. I loved to watch guys like Buddy Colt, the Brisco Brothers, and Dusty Rhodes. So, later on when my son was born, I started taking him around to any of the shows that I could around Tampa so he could experience the same thing. I bought him the event programs, just as my father did for me, so he too could see all the big monsters of the ring on the pages. For him, there was even more merchandise available. I bought him the big pillow wrestling buddies and also a whole bunch of action figures. The Undertaker was one of his favorites.

Walking around backstage was great. Curt brought me around to meet some of the guys, and then all of a sudden, a big jacked grappler came up to me wearing bright colored animal print spandex.

"Hey, Wade!" he said. "Do you remember me?"

Now, I had gotten this question a number of times in my career. Normally, the outcome was that the person asking the question had some random, trivial interaction with me that no normal person could really remember, like waiting a table on me at some diner. However, this guy looked familiar, so I paused to try and figure it out.

"Wait a second," I said. "I do feel like I know you."

"You do," he said.

His face looked like someone I knew, but I didn't know who. I inspected him up and down a little, then at his eyes. Finally, it clicked. "Ed Leslie?"

"You remember me?"

I hadn't seen him since we were 14. Over 25-30 years, you could safely say that he had changed maybe just a little! Back then, he was a tall skinny kid, but the man standing before me was probably now 265 pounds and ripped. I hadn't seen Ed in forever, then just like that, he was back, standing there backstage with me and, man, he was bigger than life. He had taken things to the next level, only I didn't know it.

"Ed Leslie! Long time, man!" I said shaking his hand. "Wait a minute, YOU are The Barber?"

He nodded.

"My six-year-old son, Bret - he has your doll!" I said. "All along, I had no idea this was you!" That's right, Ed Leslie, the very same guy I used to play baseball with, was also Brutus Beefcake, the toy Bret was playing with in the basement just the other day. I never made the connection. Brutus Beefcake had been on our television set for quite some time up until that point, and I had no idea who was playing the role.

I knew the gimmick and liked it, but I liked it even more once I knew it was him. The concept for his character was great. Brutus Beefcake had the flashiest clothing. He had the bowtie. He had the long gloves. He had all that long flowing hair, but yet he wanted to cut everybody else's hair. It was just awesome, and he blew my mind on that reveal.

After reconnecting with Ed, it wasn't long before I would see him again. I used to throw these very famous Christmas parties with my wife, Debbie. There were sometimes 250 to 300 guests at these shindigs, and it always got crazy. The wine sipping quickly turned to beer guzzling when Curt Hennig showed up with a couple of Florida's best wrestling residents. In no time at all, I was looking at Jim "The Anvil" Neidhart, one of the Nasty Boys, and my former first baseman, Brutus "The Barber" Beefcake.

It was great to catch up with Brutus again. It was funny, too. Brutus being the thoughtful individual that he was came prepared with a Christmas gift for me. The present was all wrapped up. When I opened it, I found a beautifully framed picture of our little league team with my father right in the middle and two shots on either side. One side was his picture, and the other side was mine. On the bottom was an inscription that read "Two famous guys out of Tampa."

"This is the best present anyone has ever given to me," I said, and I meant it.

Not too long after that, I met up with Curt again for a hunting trip, and he told me about Beefcake's horrible accident on the beach.

"Oh no!" I said, after just hearing the tragic news. "Is he okay?"

"He's in bad shape."

"Oh my God."

"He was lucky enough to survive," Curt said, "but he probably will never wrestle again."

There were countless operations and hours of therapy. After that, I learned even more of who Ed Leslie had become. The fact that Brutus Beefcake had survived that crazy accident alone was inspirational in itself. However, he wasn't going to let it set him back. He worked long and hard until he recovered, then actually made a comeback to the ring. Then, he continued to travel around the world just the same as he had before like nothing had ever happened. That is incredible. It really says something about his toughness and his character.

Brutus Beefcake is what professional wrestling is all about.

For a living, I swung a bat at a ball. These guys swing steel chairs at each other's skulls. I never heard a steel chair sound like a powder puff as it crashed over another man's head.

They may say wrestling is staged, but make no mistake about it, these are legitimate tough guys. For those of you who think that wrestling is fake, they can take a real beating for real and Brutus Beefcake is a testament to this fact.

In this book, you will read about his life-threatening accident. If something of this magnitude were to happen to a normal man, it would probably kill him. But because it happened to a fighter like Brutus, it brought the fight out in him - and the will to survive. I don't know how many people in the world could have made it back after that to a normal living, let alone make a comeback to the wrestling ring like he did.

I've had the privilege to meet a handful of exceptional people who the very first moment they sit down around you to tell a story, everyone in the room is pulled in and captivated. Stories like the ones in this book are priceless. I have a short list of extraordinary people I have met over my life including some musicians and athletes. When these people, especially certain wrestlers, give you a little peek of their lives behind the scenes, you can see how larger-than-life they really are. Brutus Beefcake is one of these people.

I look forward to reading about his cat and mouse games, the practical jokes wrestlers played on each other to make life more interesting, the camaraderie, the good-versus-evil, - *all of it.*

Wrestlers seem to have the best stories, and I'm sure that Brutus Beefcake will have one story after another.

DEDICATED TO MY
BEAUTIFUL WIFE, MISSY...

TABLE OF CONTENTS

CHAPTER ZERO

Right as I turned to see where she was, there she was. I never saw her coming.

FUMPPP!!!

The girl on the rope panicked. She pulled her legs up into a cannonball formation and both of her knees rammed me in my face.

The impact ripped me right out of the water. I did a full gainer. My entire body flipped in the air, with my heels straight above my head. Then, I dropped back to my feet in a crash.

The entire world shook.

Time stopped.

I fell to my knees in about two feet of liquid, but I had no idea where I was. There was a ringing in my ears. I was seeing flashes of light, but that was it.

My body broke out into a cold sweat and I felt nauseous.

The people around me had no idea what had just happened to me. There were no lacerations, at all. There was no wound, or bleeding. My head was a bag of broken glass. My skin held the fragments in, but most of the bones in my face had just been pulverized into hundreds of pieces.

I tried to scream for help.

"Mrph! Mrrrrrrumppphh!" Nothing would come out.

Dammit! I can't open my mouth! My teeth are stuck together! What just happened?!

I tried to open my eyes, again. I touched my eyelids and realized that they were in fact open, but the eyes weren't working. I couldn't see anyone. I couldn't see anything.

I shook my heavy head to figure out what had happened. My neck hurt when it turned like pins and needles. My face felt sunburnt. Then I heard the water. I heard water splashing and the sound of the motor dying off in the distance. Someone started coming my way so I tried to call for them, and I started to choke.

"Mrph! Mrrrrrrumppphh!"

Still nothing.

I can't breathe. I CAN'T BREATHE! Help!!! Oh my God, what am I going to do?

My face felt like it was falling off. It burned on the inside. It was as if it was melting. My lips were like dried rubber. When I tried to scream, it felt like there was a sweat sock in the back of my throat. Something in there felt like it was choking me out so hard that with every gasp, it became harder and harder to get air. It got worse and worse until finally, I couldn't inhale at all.

It's over. It's really over. I am a dead man!

I had no idea at the time that the obstruction was actually the complete collapsing of the upper inside of my mouth. The area that separates the oral cavity from the nasal cavity was broken, forcing bone shards and tissue down my windpipe.

I tried to open my mouth, but it wouldn't work. My jawbone was smashed shut. I tried to suck in as much air as I could, but realized there was blockage. I had to get my hand in my mouth somehow, or it was going to be all over.

I was light-headed. I took both of my hands and tried to force my mouth open, but it wouldn't work. In a final act of desperation, I took my thumb and shoved it between my upper and lower teeth.

Using my finger like a pry-bar I pushed it hard through my swollen, tire-like lips. I forced it between my teeth and wiggled it up and down, tearing the skin off under my nail. Once I made it in, I jammed it upwards as hard as I could.

To my amazement, there was no foreign object in my mouth. It was all my own flesh, and bone, and meat hanging downwards. I pushed up the roof of my mouth in the back. It opened the airway and allowed just enough space to breathe.

I gasped like a fish out of water. I sucked in metallic oxygen and filled my lungs with air and blood.

What if nobody saw? What if nobody knows how bad this is?!

I coughed and tried to stabilize my breathing. I collapsed into the water for a moment, but got back to my knees. I didn't know if help was coming, but figured that if I wasn't upright, they wouldn't see me.

I reached for my nose. It was hanging off the side of my face. Then, I poked my cheeks with the fingertips of my other hand.

My face! IT IS GONE!

The skin was still there, but it felt like rubbery mush with no structure.

Waiting for what felt like an eternity, people were finally coming closer. I couldn't see them, but I heard the hysteria around me.

No pain meds.

The ambulance hit every bump in the world, and then it dumped me off like cargo. The medics thought it was only a broken jaw, so they barely took my injury seriously.

They wheeled me in on a gurney, but I wondered if it was my coffin. Invisible hands started to work all around me. The poked, padded and probed. Someone checked my blood pressure. It was way, way up there. *They thought I was having a heart attack.* They rushed me to the ICU. The doctor angled my body around for a bunch of x-rays. I tried my hardest to move into the right positions, but my head felt 100 pounds.

They realized that much of the bone around the center of my face was concaved. My facial bone matter was practically powder.

After some time, a new faceless voice came to my bedside.

"I don't understand how you are still alive," he said. "Hang in there, my friend. I will do my best for you."

They cut me ear to ear, like Walkman headphones sit on the top of your head. They peeled my face down below my nose. I saw pictures. Without the skin, it looked like a bowl of spaghetti with two eyes on the top instead of meatballs. My face was a hollow mess. Everything from my cheekbones to my eye sockets was gone. All of the bone matter was shattered to splitters.

The doctor needed to totally reconstruct my face in a highly risky surgical procedure that had never been done before. But to keep me alive, it needed to be done.

Sixteen hours later, it was done.

The doctor gave me a new face. The frame was like Papier-mâché and sheet metal. They used 32 screws, 8 strips of titanium, 100 feet of wire, and more than 100 hundred staples.

My jaw was wired shut.

There were dozens of stitches in the roof of mouth.

Oh yeah. My eyelids were also sewn together.

I felt like freakin' Frankenstein.

CHAPTER 1 - RIGHT PLACE, RIGHT TIME

I grew up in Tampa. I was living in a smaller, middle-class household, and I was the middle child of five kids. I had three sisters; two older than me and one younger. I also had a younger brother. We all had a very happy childhood. My parents worked hard to "keep up with the Joneses." We grew up in a very nice neighborhood where most of the people had more money than we did, but we put up a good front and just didn't let anyone know.

My parents did okay though. My mother was an operating room nurse at Saint Joseph's hospital in Tampa. My father worked in the post office pretty much his whole life. While the post office was probably more of a boring, same-shit-different-day type life, he made up for that outside of work. To have some kind of creative outlet, my dad took up the saxophone and the clarinet. He became a really great musician, so much so that he became the president of the musician union in Tampa, Florida.

My dad played the saxophone for a local group called the Tampa Police Dance Band. He wasn't a cop or anything, but a lot of the other members were so they played for a lot of police functions. They were really good. They traveled around the state with bookings all the time. I remember quite often, I wouldn't see him all week. He would be off playing somewhere and I would get mad.

I did, however, like to hear him play. Quite often, they would have these little concerts set up by the city down at the Lowry Park Zoo by the hospital where my mother worked. On Fridays, we would grab some food in a cooler and go watch daddy play at the "Extra Concert Series," Tampa's oldest tradition, showcasing the best local musicians free to the public. People would come from everywhere and park all over the place. It was like the city stopped for a bit in the name of music. We would usually park a little bit away to beat the traffic and then walk a couple blocks. I remember my sisters and I would haul all these lawn chairs down with my mom. Then, we would just sit there and eat bologna sandwiches, watching dad play.

My parents were cool. My earliest fondest memories all include my parents going out of their way to give us a childhood they were proud of. We always had family vacations in summer. Like a scene out of Chevy Chase's movie "Vacation," our parents would load us all into a station wagon, and we would begin the journey. Being a little younger, I don't know how safe it was, but my dad used to make a little bunk out of towels and blankets in the back of the station wagon. If we were traveling late at night, my sisters would be dozing off in the middle, but I would lay up across suitcases in my special bunk and fall asleep watching the world spin by out the side window.

We would drive to Atlanta and hit various campgrounds and have all kinds of fun. Then, we would swing up to the Carolinas where we would visit some family friends. One of my earliest memories is me on vacation wandering around a farm. I remember climbing around in the barn and falling asleep in the hay. I remember riding in the tractor, smelling the fuel burning and cutting hickory. We had all kinds of hickory-smoked barbeques.

One time, I remember I was almost barbecued myself. They say you always remember one of your first traumatic experiences as a kid, and I remember one well at the age of probably 4 or 5 years old. At the tail end of vacation, we were at the farm and they had one of those electric fences there to keep the pigs and cows in. I remember grabbing it and getting jolted with a little bit of electricity. It wasn't enough to do any real damage, but just enough to make you want to keep away from it. For whatever reason, I grabbed a hold of it, and couldn't let go.

"Argh! Arghhh!" I cried. "Please help!"

I started crying and screaming, but my hand wouldn't open and I couldn't seem to break free. Eventually one of the farmers came running to see what the racket was.

"Are you okay?" he asked. No answer. I just kept on screaming. He tried to pry open my hand, but it wasn't happening. He quickly ran around the back of the barn and shut off the fence.

"It's okay, buddy. You are all right," he said, looking over my apparently unharmed hand. "I just don't understand why you didn't just let go of the fence, is all."

One would think I would have just let go of the fence, but for some reason, I just couldn't.

The farmer led me back to the house. When I got there, my sisters made fun of my hair and said it was sticking straight up in the air from all the electricity. There is no way that was true, but they kept teasing me about it the whole rest of the vacation.

BASEBALL

During the school year, Mom and dad were always working overtime to put food on the table. We had a modest little house with two bedrooms for five kids. From oldest to youngest, there was Karen, Mary, myself, Virginia (aka Ginger), and John John. My parents didn't even really have their own bedroom. What they did was they had a big pull out couch that they pulled out every night after we went to bed, and slept off to the one side of the living room. The hideaway was just off to the right of a cast iron, old-school oil burner, which was great when it got cold. If it weren't for that nice warm heater in the winter, us boys probably wouldn't have had our own room!

Florida nights in the summer were rough with no air conditioning. It got hot. Unlike some of our more well-off neighbors, without central air, there were a lot of sticky nights. We did have a big attic fan that pulled air in from the windows.

Our parents spent everything on their children's education. Their biggest concern was always having enough money to keep all the kids in private schools for grade school and middle - and they did just that. Though they didn't have a lot, we were able to attend the same private schools that all our neighborhood friends did.

Back when I was around eight years old was the first time I laid eyes on who would eventually become known as the immortal Hulk Hogan. My parents started me off in Little League baseball probably when I was 7 years old. By this time, Terry was already a legend on our field.

I had already heard all the rumblings of Terry playing in the upper-age divisions of our little league. All the teams protested against him. The coaches on his opposing teams hated him. People thought he was older than his actual age, because, at 11 or so, he was already taller than most of the parents! All the parents said that it wasn't fair that he played against their children. However, none of that mattered. Terry wanted to play ball, and he was going to play it.

Terry truly was the biggest kid ever in the whole little league. He was a beast. At 11-years-old, Terry was 6 foot tall and 200 pounds. He was just so much bigger than everyone that all opposing team players cowered in his shadow. Terry's dad, Pete Bollea, was one of the coaches. By 12, Terry was already bigger than his own father.

Being three years younger than Terry, I remember watching him in awe. The first game I saw him in, I remember Terry hitting the fence covered in all those sponsor signs. He hit it so hard, he broke the wood. The ball left a crater in it! The next time up, I watched him hit the ball so high over the trees, that if he was in the big leagues, he would have been clearing a 400-foot stadium fence. The ball was out of sight, and so was Terry.

Terry was so powerful, powerful beyond his years. However, he was a little clumsy at 12 years old and ran awkwardly to first base. He just couldn't run great yet because he was so big. But it didn't really matter. If he hit a home run, he could take all the time in the world walking around the bases. That happened a lot.

I wanted to be like Terry, but make no mistake about it; our team rocked. We were the best in our age division. All of the teams had like one of the player's fathers as coaches. Most of them were businessmen and had some pretty serious jobs to attend to. They would practice a little during an hour or so before the games, but as far as real practice was concerned, none of the teams ever really practiced. None of them, except our team.

Our coach was a baseball fanatic. He breathed and ate baseball. Because of this, we practiced regularly and became ridiculously disciplined by Little League standards. We could do things that the other teams didn't even understand. Not often did you see Little League player hit a double, or even a triple play! Because of all of our practicing, we would go out there and just murder all of the teams. Because of our team's record, the league had to instate a special "Ten Run Rule." This rule stated that if we made ten runs unopposed, after four innings, they would just call the game to stop us from brutally torturing our opponents.

Because of this rule, we almost never played more than 4 innings.

From 7 to 11 years-old, I have very vivid memories of leaving the fields and looking over at the losing team's players on the benches, with all the kids crying their eyes out. So as you can imagine, just like the monstrous Terry Bollea, nobody wanted to play our team the entire four-year stretch I was there.

Members of our team went on to big city tournaments every year. I remember, at 10 or 11 years old, I made the All-star team. There, I met and got to play with Wade Boggs. His dad was one of the All-star coaches, and I played on his team.

I loved baseball. It was a huge passion of mine, and I could do it all. I was a decent hitter, a good pitcher and catcher. If I had stayed in it, I am pretty sure that I would have been in pro baseball.

THE THRILL OF THE HUNT

My buddy Nat's parents had a maid who practically raised me. She was a real nice lady named Janie. With my dad always out and about and my mother working at the hospital, it was Janie who bandaged us kids up and did a lot of the motherly things that we needed. I was like an adopted kid there. She always took good care of us, so we always tried to return the favor.

I did a lot of fishing off of Bayshore Blvd. in Tampa with my friends. For those of you who are not familiar with it, Bayshore has a long continuous sidewalk along the sea wall. We fished up and down the whole 6 mile stretch of it and caught tons of fish. We got pretty good at it, too, though some of it wasn't the best to eat. Sometimes we would catch some Yellowtail Jack and had to bleed them out and put them on ice before cleaning. But as Janie said, "Everything tastes good deep fried." Janie had something like twelve kids, so that was a hell of a lot of mouths to feed. Being poor, she really appreciated it. Anything was a help. In the summer, we would just catch as many fish as possible, and then they would have a big ole' fish fry.

At one of the fish fries, Nat and I were both out at Janie's home having a good time. We got to working on an old mini bike. Janie figured it was no good, but if we could fix it, it should have been worth something, right? Well, sure enough, we got it working and took it out for a spin.

The two of us were driving all around, off the main road. Eventually, we took it out to the state highway. We were really tearing things up when all of a sudden, we heard sirens behind us. It wasn't long before a police car came up to us and pulled us over on the highway.

The policeman walked over and asked us for our names. I told him mine, and my buddy said his.

"You know, you shouldn't be out here driving like this," he snapped. I can't let you ride it out of here, either. We will probably have to put the bike in the back of the car."

The cop disappeared and called in our names to the station, then came back to us from his car. He had a whole different tone. It was obvious they knew who my buddy was. He was the son of a pretty well-off political dignitary. Someone back at the station must have told the officer, "Don't mess with those kids."

"Be careful, guys. You are free to go," he said. He didn't take the bike or anything. Because of this, I could get away with practically anything.

BIT BY THE BUG

I was just an average student. I never studied at all. I never did much homework and got mostly B grades. This was before the time of video games and cell phones. I didn't even watch very much TV. My parents did. They watched the Honeymooners on a black & white TV that was more wood than screen. I wasn't a huge Jackie Gleason fan, but I did like the Star Trek. For the most part, if I was not in school, I was playing "Kick the Can", cork ball, or Wiffle ball, but no matter what I was doing, it was outside.

When I got a little older, all I wanted to do was hunt. Every weekend, I would tag along with people from our area. We would head off to some of the most remote areas Florida had to offer for some very adventurous camping trips. We would often pack up and head north of Tampa to the Cypress Swamp. We would hit up fields that during wet seasons would fill with water and then dry out in the offseason. These were perfect for attracting all kinds of birds, doves, ducks and wild turkeys.

It was a real good pack of guys. I learned a lot from them. Most of the time, our trips were more like safaris than hunts.

We would all go out to appreciate the wildlife, more than for seeking the thrill of a hunt. One thing that we liked to do was put out grain to attract doves or ducks to the field. While it was illegal to do this as a baiting for shooting, we would often just feed them so we could watch them flock. I could seriously watch them for hours. The birds would roost in swamps and trees in Cypress, but once word got out to the rest of them that there was some free dinner below, thousands of them, seemingly millions would swoop in. Another way we would get to interact with the wildlife by feeding was to drive the Jeep down into about a foot of water in a lake and watch from the window. Watching ducks feed was incredible.

As a kid, I remember hiking for hours through palmettos and pine needles just to feed turkeys. The way we would track them was by finding a disturbance in the fallen leaves. It would be all crazy on the ground from scratching.

Sometimes, Nat and I tried to get his older brother Jeff to go with us, but he never would. However, his little tomboy sister, Terryl, was a savage maniac hunter, and she was always with us. We would get up at 4:30 in the morning before school every day, and rush out to the woods to go "hunting." Mostly, we would just go down to the water and feed our ducks and turkeys, then haul butt to get to school. Once school and any of the sports we might be playing were over, we would eat dinner and then go right back to hunting at night.

One would think that this didn't sound safe. By today's standards, younger kids shouldn't be out hunting alone, but this was a different time. We could be out and about, and our parents never worried. We would hear about the dangers of alligators, but we never saw it. We spent so much time jumping off boats, but never even really thought about gators in lakes, or sharks in the gulf. On our hunting expeditions, we would often talk about hunting one down, however. There was this one big ranch we would often go to. It was a huge open area that some rich guy owned who was like never there. There was this one old groundskeeper who lived there named Gus. They let him live there for free since he worked there.

Gus was pretty cool. He was an older black gentleman with no teeth and always smelled like whiskey. Wearing his same trademark overalls, we would see him some in our travels. He took a liking to us and let us wander around the ranch for our hunts. One night, he crept up on us and startled Terryl and laughed.

"Hey, you guys," he said. "You catch anything yet?"

"Not yet," replied.

"Well, I gotta warn you," he said with a toothless grin. "You ever seen how my cattle go down to the lake?"

"Sure," my buddy said. "We've seen them."

"Well, they used to love to go down and eat the vegetation, by the water. But they don't go down there none anymore," he said, dropping his voice and looking over his shoulder nervously for dramatic effect. "You wanna know why?"

"Why?" she asked with her eyes open wide.

"Lilly pads. They used to love eating that shit, but one day," he said looking around all cautiously again. "One day, they done learned their lesson. I watched in horror as a 15-foot alligator came right out of the water and grab a decent-sized cattle."

"Oh my!" Terryl said.

"Yep. Pulled her right in the water by her head. The tail went flipping this way and that. Next thing you know, she was gone. Pulled her way under and made hamburgers for all her demon babies."

"He's just teasing," Nat said.

"Believe that if you will," Gus said. "But I seen it with my own eyes."

Gus disappeared. He put the fear of God into Terryl and she stopped going hunting with us for some time after that. If we wanted to ditch her, all we had to say was we were going to the ranch and she would find something else to do.

One morning before school, we went out to feed our ducks and turkeys with Terryl. We were throwing all kinds of grain out to them and doing our own thing. We didn't even notice that Terryl was out of our sight when we heard a scream.

The gators got her!

We went running over the paths in the dark looking for her, fearing the worst.

Finally, we made it to his sister. She was lying on the shore and was half in the water.

"Terryl!" we yelled.

We rushed through the brush and she looked up at us holding her arm.

"Something bit me!"

Man, I wish I had brought my pellet gun with me! We had only really planned to feed the birds on this morning. I had no idea that we would be battling alligators. Her brother made it to her first and pulled her up. Her legs weren't working. She was holding her arm and crying.

No gator bites. But she did get bit by either a Brown Recluse, or Black Widow spider.

Out of the over 20,000 different species of spiders in America, only 60 of them bite humans. Only four of those are poisonous; the Brown Recluse, the black widow, the Hobo spider, and the Yellow Sac spider. Then, out of those four, only the Brown Recluse and the Black Widow have ever been associated with death. It was just dumb luck. Out of all of them, it was one of the two deadly ones that had to bite her.

I had heard the warnings before. I was always in barns with horses and all. The farmers always warned that you could go to grab up a handful of hay and grab a handful of spiders that could kill you. They were why we always had to be careful and fumigate any spiders out of all the camping gear after trips. It was then we learned why.

We rushed the girl to the hospital for anti-venom. She started puking. She complained of being cold and dizzy. Fortunately for her, we got her there in time and they gave her the antidote. Aside from muscle cramps, vomiting and a nasty mark on her forearm, everything turned out alright.

TOES IN THE WATER

I was a tall, skinny, and wiry kid. I remember one summer, I took up playing basketball.

Because they didn't have a court at school, my basketball court of choice was only a few miles away. It was right across the street from my old grade school, Saint Patrick's. It was really a concrete skating rink that they doctored up. They added a few baskets to it so it could also double for basketball. My sister Ginger loved to skate and dance, so sometimes I went down to the rink with her.

I was playing one day, and I remember getting really roughed up by two other kids. They were probably twice my size. They started innocently enough, just pushing a little too hard, but then it got obvious.

"Sorry, man," one would say, as he knocked me over.

"Whoa, sorry again, man!" the other would say laughing, as I picked myself off the concrete.

After three of four times, I knew I was going to have to man up. When it was totally clear that they were crossing the line, I decided to let them know that I had had enough. I had to let them know they weren't going to push me around. After one more accidental knock over, I got up off the ground. I dusted myself off and then fired the ball as hard as I could at the one kid's face.

"Hey I got - what the hell?! Oh shit!" His friend looked down as the ball bounced off his buddies face and rolled back to my feet. "Oh no, you didn't!"

His friend came at me.

I rebounded the ball and immediately whipped it at his charging partner's eyes.

"Umphhh!" he said.

As they say in wrestling, he got color the hard way. I'm pretty sure that I broke the second guy's nose. I knew I was either going to have to fight them now, or they would chicken out and take off. Hoping for the latter to happen, I took a deep breath and moved forward at them.

"Arrrggghhh!" I yelled like a madman.

It worked. They thought I was crazy. They both got up and ran off like they had seen a ghost.

While waiting for my friends to make their return home from that long summer vacation, I was also mowing some of the neighbor's yards for dollars. I had collected some good money for the day. I was pushing the lawnmower down the sidewalk to blow grass off the walkway, when I saw their familiar car come down the street.

The car passed me. My buddy waved from in the car. He pointed down the road where he lived about 4 blocks away, as if to signal to run and catch up with him. I nodded. I started pushing really fast and ran to catch up with him. In doing so, I tripped and fell backward. The mower went up a little hill, then rolled back at me and rolled directly over my foot.

The car stopped.

I got up to my knees and pushed the wheels off of me to see the mess.

The blade cut right through my tennis shoe. The white toe of my Converse was completely red. My eyes welled and I bit my lip. I peeled back what was left of the rubber and I could see my second toe was missing.

They took me right off to the Tampa General Emergency Room. Tampa General was the closest facility, but probably in hindsight, not the best. It was considered more like the poor people Emergency Room with just enough to get by, and not a whole lot else. Most importantly, it was not my mother's hospital.

To their credit, I didn't wait long. They cut my shoe off and went right to work trying to clean everything up. It was a disgusting mess and looked worse than the Piper/Valentine dog collar match.

The blade had severed my big toe in half right down the center, like a snake's tongue. I mean my big toe was filleted in half, with the whole toenail hanging off, like two pieces of meat with the whole center chopped out.

The mower also had completely cut off my second toe, leaving a stump that looked like a little spiral ham. Fortunately for me, they found the missing toe in the sneaker and immediately put it on ice.

In the meantime, someone had the good sense to call my mother, who immediately took off from work. By the time she got there, my foot was bandaged up. She ran in, grabbed me and my severed toe and got the hell out of there.

We went straight to her hospital, Saint Joseph's. I sat for only a few minutes, while my mother went on a frantic search, looking for the best plastic surgeon she could find. Her efforts were not in vain.

The guy she got a hold of was good. He quickly took a skin graft from my leg so he had enough material to replace the missing tissue from my big toe. He also retrieved "the little piggy who stayed home," from somewhere else and sewed my second toe back onto the bloody stump.

If the operation didn't take, I wouldn't have been able to walk well, let alone think about running. That big toe is really needed for balance. Sports would have been altogether out of the question, as well. What a horrible, dirty wound you get from a lawn mower. There was a lot of worry that if they didn't get all the junk out of my toe tissue, it could have meant gangrene. The infection could have caused a loss of my entire foot.

Thank God the operation took.

I was in the hospital for weeks, a wheel chair for about a month, and up and hopping around again on crutches in a half a year. It was during this time I lost some of my enthusiasm for sports.

COME SAIL AWAY

My other friend, John Garth, was a year younger than me, but a year ahead of me at our private school because of how smart he was. He got that trait from his dad. His father, Doctor Garth, was a great heart surgeon in Tampa who would eventually treat my own father's heart attack years later.

John was the man. He had the newest Hobie Cat 14 sailboat with one sail, and he also had the 16 with two sails. With a bum foot, I was unable to play baseball, so I started hanging out with John some at the Tampa Yacht Club. That place was insane. You had to be a millionaire to be a member there. I remember one time, a guy who owned a 120 foot yacht parked there. The thing must have been worth millions!

So once again, I was in the right place at the right time. I found myself rubbing elbows with the very elite. Eventually, I became a life guard at the pool at the club, and I got to network with people I would have never have even met. It was crazy.

Hanging around with that bunch, people tipped me huge to help dock their boats. People bought me incredible dinners at the restaurant. People taught me literally everything there was to know about sailing. To this day, I can prepare, sail, and take down a 60 foot boat like a master boatsman. I am better than the Skipper and Gilligan put together, because unlike them, I never crashed a boat.

I soon started training with John to be his partner for races. His parents were very supportive. We had all the equipment we needed for our boat to be successful. Money was no object. His parents spared no expense to make sure we got it right. We practiced in very rough conditions to get ready. We practiced in storms working the sails and handling the wheel, so we would be ready for anything. We got really good at sailing and finally started to compete professionally in big races.

We started winning races. John's mom would take us everywhere to race, and we would always be in the top 5 of finishers. Then we got even better. It was funny for most to see that a 16 and 15-year-old kid became good enough to beat out all competition in some of the top races in the world. We were hot. Super hot. We even beat the actual guy who invented the boat we were sailing in, Hobie Alter, in a race.

My life has really been blessed. I was in the right place at right time for so many things. I also learned how to water ski at the club, and I learned how to do things that many don't get to ever do in a lifetime.

Come high school time, private school ended. I continued to compete with John, but all of us went to the same public high school, Robinson High. A few other famous wrestlers, incidentally, also graduated from Robinson. There was Mike Graham, Dick Slater, and even someone else who would be very instrumental later on in helping my wrestling career.

CHAPTER 2 – COMING OF AGE

Come high school, most of my friends got their driver's licenses, and I got jealous. Gas was only 19 cents a gallon then, but that wasn't the concern. The freedom that a set of wheels could bring was. Wanting to save up enough money to get my own ride and be free like my friends, I decided to join the wonderful world of part time jobs.

At about sixteen, I got my toes wet in the workforce. One of my first real jobs was earning $5 an hour landscaping. Yes, that's right. I got back behind the mower even after that accident. But believe me, this time, I was wearing steel toe boots.

I found a ton of landscaping work while I was still in high school that I would continue with after I graduated. I worked on-call with a high-end nursery planting and taking care of trees. I learned a lot about landscaping and got real good at it. I remember working for them on $50,000 jobs on luxury homes. We also had the Terre Verde account, a real rich hotel near Saint Petersburg. They would pay nearly a million dollars just in landscaping for that hotel in a year's time. One time, I remember having to dig up and deliver some palm trees to that hotel. We had to actually move them on giant flatbeds, and then lift them off the trucks with forklifts and raise them with cranes.

There was this one kid in high school named Barry Borden. He was a year older than me and was the stud of the school. Big guy. Big arms. He was in all the sports. He was the only dude our age in our town who owned a Corvette. I, on the other hand, was a tall, awkward skinny punk and wanted to be just like him.

His dad worked for the Air Force and wasn't around a whole lot. My father was always out and about with his band, so we had something a little in common. That being said, we also had some similar interests, and I decided to try to befriend him. We hit it off pretty good. It turned out, his mother had a housekeeping business, and Barry got me a job.

I would go in at night and clean the floors with a buffer machine in businesses that were closed. One night, I was in a law office somewhere and that's when I saw Barry's sister, Jessie.

Jessie was in eleventh grade with me. She was also working for her mother. She would dust and clean up things as I waxed the hallway. I remember for weeks before I had the nerve to say, "Hello," just watching her, drooling like a dog on the floor that I just cleaned behind me.

Man, do I want to wax that.

I would zone out many a night, wearing my Sony Walkman. My mind would drift off just as any high school kid's mind would at that age. My hormones would kick in, and she would instantly transform into a scantily-clad French maid, with the ass-less outfit and everything. I swear, I could even hear the cheesy nWo theme porno music in my head and everything!

Now, this was years before that dog, the lady-killer Brutus Beefcake existed, believe me. If I had known then what I know now, we would have been off in a closet somewhere the whole night. We would have been making things dirty, rather than clean up in those offices, if you know what I mean. I was still young though, and had no idea how to approach girls well and be discrete.

One night, I was buffing the floor and checking her out from behind with my headphones on. She was all bent over with a feather duster, and I was loving it. All of a sudden, she looked directly at me in a mirror wall and I was caught. Eye contact. She knew I was checking her out. She had to have.

She knew I was looking at something way more groovy than my work.

Oh, shit! She saw me look directly at her ass! My life is over! She will tell her mom. I will lose my job. Barry is going to kick my ass and everything!

She turned around and faced me. She started yelling something, but I couldn't hear what she was saying. She rushed around a file cabinet, shook her head, and stormed right at me. She raised her hand and I thought she was going to hit me, so I cowered.

"Hey dumb-dumb!" she said loudly, actually pulling one of the headphone speakers off my ear. "What the hell are you doing?"

"Man oh man. I'm sooo sorry," I said. I got all choked up. "Well, I… You see… I was just cleaning and…"

"Just cleaning?" She put her hands on her hips and looked at me like she was pissed. Then, her face changed, and she started laughing hysterically. "Look."

Behind me was a wet line of freshly cleaned floor that went right over a runner carpet.

After that, Jessie became my high school sweetheart.

Barry was cool about me dating his little sister. On top of making $5 an hour with the housekeeping job, I also picked up some work after learning mechanics from Barry. He was making great money as a senior working on three or four cars a day. He showed me the ropes and I got a job with him at the body shop. They had a deal with Greyhound Rent-A-Car, and we did all their fleet work. When they were done with cars, we would fix them all up and detail them. Then Greyhound would just auction them off.

CHAMPIONSHP WRESTLING FROM FLORIDA

With a little bit of extra spending money, every Tuesday night I was off to the Fort Hesterly Armory. The armory is a historic building that still stands at 522 North Howard in the West Tampa section of Tampa, Florida and was well-known for its "Championship Wrestling from Florida "shows.

In an era before Vince McMahon's WWE dominated the wrestling business, individual states and cities hosted territorial promotions. Promoters would have their mapped out little areas that they would run and nobody would really come into their areas to oppose them.

From the mid-1900s to the 1980s, Championship Wrestling from Florida became one of the most popular wrestling territories, and it was right in my home town of Tampa.

Back then, I was checking out Eddie Graham's promotion for whoever might be keeping score. He was also working closely with Georgia and North Carolina territories at the time and even some with NY. That meant as a kid, I was seeing some really cool talent. Some of the biggest names ever would make their way to the promotion, stay a little while and then move on. Switching talent around back then was a good money-making technique and kept the shows fresh.

I remember seeing Wahoo McDaniel, Jose Lothario, Hiro Matsuda, Buddy Colt, Dusty Rhodes, Superstar Billy Graham, Jack & Jerry Brisco and Harley Race. Most of the industry's big names worked for Championship Wrestling from Florida at some point and performed at the armory.

I also remember seeing my first matches with Johnny Valentine there. I remember he was big, rugged and mean and I hated him. Who knew that I would one day be a world tag team champion with his son, Greg?

JOHNNY VALENTINE

One thing I now know about Johnny is that he was a crazy ribber. I mean, he would play pranks on his own son, Greg, that were just ridiculous. One thing I remember he would do is call Greg like something terrible had happened, "Hey kid, you gotta get over here!" He would describe all the symptoms of a heart attack without actually saying the words.

Greg would then hop in the car, fearing the worst not knowing exactly what was wrong. He would jump out of the car and rush right to the front door. He had no idea that there was a large glob of shit smeared under the doorknob, just waiting for him to put his hand in it.

Another rib Johnny was the innovator of was hotel desecration. What he would do was turn the heat up in a guy's hotel room full blast, even in the dead of summer. Then, he would shut all the windows and take a huge steaming dump in the middle of the bed and wipe with the sheets. After that, he would make the bed up again perfectly, nice and smooth, so that you couldn't tell where the smell was coming from until it was just too late.

Johnny also broke new wrestlers in the hard way on the road. One time, there was a rookie who was trying to get over with him. He would follow him around and annoy the shit out of him. He would constantly sit down to shoot the shit with Johnny at the worst possible times and bum his chew off him to try and look cool. It was obvious to everyone that this kid didn't like chewing tobacco. Not really knowing who Johnny was, he had no idea how literally "shooting the shit" was soon going to be.

Tired of sharing his chew with someone who didn't even appreciate it, Johnny devised a plan. He went out into a cow pasture and collected up some nice choice mounds in a shopping bag. Then he pounded those turds out and spread them in the sun to dry on some stones. The next day, he cut the dung up the best he could and put the shredded goodness into some of his old chewing tobacco bags that he saved just for the occasion. For the finishing touch, he sacrificed a small bit of real chew to mix it into the mash to make it look legit.

Back on the road, the kid came by and watched Johnny chewing his tobacco.

"You want some?" he asked. The kid nodded. He reached into his suitcase, grabbed the little bag, and handed it to the rookie. He watched with great delight as the newbie began to chew and suck on the poop-juice. "Pretty good, aye?" Johnny asked, spitting his tobacco spit into a cup.

Man, oh man. The new kid's eyes watered up like he just ate the world's hottest pepper, or something. Then, his face shriveled. "Yeah. Mmm. Good," he said, trying to kayfabe the horrible taste in his mouth and look cool.

"You can keep that bag. I got more."

For the rest of the week, whenever the new kid saw Johnny around, he would take out his pouch and pack a huge dip in his lip of "dip-shit." He would just sit there and rough through it, chewing on that bag of cow poo and smile, still trying to get over good with Johnny.

What a shithead.

THE SPORTATORIUM

After going to a wrestling show on Tuesday night, sometimes I would get to catch a television taping the next day, if I was lucky. Every Wednesday afternoon, the wrestling matches were recorded at a place called "The Sportatorium" for broadcasts set to air throughout the state on Saturday nights.

The Sportatorium was literally a hole in the wall. It was a little shithole of a venue that barely sat 50 people on each side of the ring. The place was a real dive. A wrestler named "Cowboy" Clarence Luttrall was the original owner who opened the place up for operation in the 1940s. By the look of things, nobody had done any real upkeep on the place ever since the doors opened, including after Luttrall sold it and his promotion to Eddie Graham in the early 60s, years before I walked in as a fan.

With maybe 150 wooden folding chairs on three sides of the ring, I remember squeezing in once, sitting by the fourth and final side. There, there were only a few chairs set up for the fans, because of the interview stage and the announcing table which was home of the legendary Gordon Solie, the voice of Championship Wrestling from Florida. It was surreal to see the voice behind the microphone in action.

I remember it was also funny how everything looks bigger on TV. The walls in the Sportatorium were painted black. The ring had spotlights on it and the rest was dim. This created the illusion on television that the building was actually an arena. In reality, it was probably only two thousand square feet. Dory Funk says today that the Sportatorium was really "more like a television studio" than it was an event venue, and he was right.

"We made magic in that Sportatorium every Wednesday afternoon," said Gerald Brisco in a recent interview about that place. He knows. He held the Florida Heavyweight Championship in 1974 when I was there watching.

One time as the show was letting out, I remember sneaking up to the second floor to have a look, hoping to see Dusty Rhodes. There was a door, and I creaked it open. To my surprise, there wasn't a wrestler in sight. It was all editing equipment and cameras. They also had shelves and shelves of tapes up there, too, and audio equipment.

"Hit the road, kid!" an invisible voice bellowed behind the door, scaring the shit out of me, and sending me running. "The show's over."

Later on, I would learn that those TV tapings were not about a show for the fans at all. They were really an hour long commercial. The commercial they shot there was ultimately to get people to buy tickets to big arenas, like the armory, where they could sell more seats and really make money.

The booking was much different from what we would see on Tuesday nights. Most of what I remember seeing in the ring at the Sportatorium was what people today call "jobber matches."

A few big names might be there, left over from the armory show from the night before. But they would never face each other. They would just get in the ring and annihilate some no-name, enhancement talent wrestlers – some guys I had never heard of before. People would see that on TV and then would obviously want to pay to see the two big names wrestle each other. Eddie Graham was smart. He didn't give that match away on free television.

This formula worked and I paid for tickets to the armory. But seeing the TV taping was also a treat for me as a kid, even if the matches weren't as good. If I could get a ticket to that, I was there.

On one Saturday morning, there was a special Sportatorium TV taping. I woke up my oldest sister, Karen, and begged her to take me over so I could get in line for a ticket. Karen was a good sport. She got out of bed and we got into her first real hotrod car, this kickass Mustang.

Karen just threw whatever she had laying around on, and we hoped in the car. I was excited to see who was fighting on the card, and we really couldn't get there fast enough. There was one obstacle, however. Have you ever heard that big sisters pick on little brothers before? Well then, just to mess with me for waking her up early on a weekend, my sister decided that she wasn't going to drive straight to the Sportatorium. Nope. Not happening. Karen took a detour and made a pit stop off to the empty Tampa Dragway racing track.

"Wait, why are we here?" I asked. "This isn't it. I wanted to see the wrestling, not a race."

Karen didn't say anything. She just laughed. Karen got out of the car, pulled open one of the gates to the track, and started driving.

"What are you doing?" I asked again, angrily as she started to drive laps around the track, torturing me and my patience. "WHAT ARE YOU DOING?!"

"Oh, just going for a spin," she said laughing. She would spin around a few more times to waste time and make me feel like I was possibly missing out on purchasing that last ticket for the show. I knew that seats were always limited.

When my sister was done torturing me, we finally made it to the Sportatorium. I remember stepping out of the car slightly dizzy and slamming the door. I ran to the now long line of people in front of me and started counting them in my head, trying to do the math to see if I would be getting in.

As I was counting people, I noticed that one head near my spot in line was sticking way up above the rest. I recognized that head. I had seen it some, sitting at the Armory on Tuesday nights and also long ago back on the field. It was some kid named Terry Bollea, aka "The Little League Legend." Terry was bigger than ever. He ate more than the average teenager. His typical breakfast could include 10 eggs, a pound of hamburger meat and a quart of orange juice — all the protein and vitamin C needed for a giant growing boy.

At this point, Terry was probably about 19, and far since graduated from our baseball days. He was driving so he pretty much seemed like an adult to me. He was playing in a band and seemed way cool. Seeing him in person was something else, for a young guy like me. Like Jessie's brother, I even more so wanted to be like Terry.

I walked up to him. He was much taller than I had remembered, and even bigger. He reached 6'7" by the end of his senior year of high school and tipped the scales at 300 pounds. Now, seeing him again a year or so later, he looked even bigger. It was obvious that he was hitting the gym now, instead of just hitting a baseball.

"Hey man," I said to him, trying to make small talk. "I've seen you at some of the shows."

He nodded.

"I didn't know you were into wrestling," I said to the guy in the line who looked bigger than half of the wrestlers we were about to see.

"Yeah, it's okay," he said, trying not to look as excited as I did.

As we waited, I told him I admitted that I always liked watching him play ball. I liked the way he just kicked everyone's ass no matter what the parents said. He seemed to like the compliment. We talked more about baseball, and then about some of our favorite wrestling stories.

Our conversation was cut short. The line started to move.

"Listen Ed," he said. "Nice talking to you. A bunch of us are going to the beach tomorrow at about 10 o'clock. Why don't you come by and hang out?"

Awesome! It will be pretty cool to hang out with him and the guys.

"Sure thing!" I said, then trying to look cooler, "I mean, sure. I'll see you there, then."

The Sportatorium TV taping was good, but I barely watched it. I was so excited to be invited into the circle of the popular "cool kids" that I was thinking more about that than the actual matches.

The next morning, I rolled up onto the beach around 10 am, just as we had planned. To my surprise, Terry and his friends were all done. They were already toweling off and making their way back to their cars. It was obvious; they had gotten there at 8 or 9 am.

"Sorry brother," he said. "We got an early start. Why don't you come by next week, same time? We will be here around 10."

"Okay, no problem," I said, just happy he was talking to me.

The next week came and it was déjà vu, all over again. Same scene, same story. I got there just as they were leaving. I must have fallen for that same stupid joke five or six times or more, before I finally realized that they were just messing with "the young kid." You see, Terry and I had gone to the same high school, but he was three years older than I was and looked at me as being just some goofy boy. Come graduation time, I was 17, but Terry and his circle were like 20, or 21. He was already playing in a band and going to bars. He was also lifting weights like a demon.

Nat was more into football at this time, and he got a full scholarship into Florida State for it. I mean, I had tried to keep up with Nat, but around sophomore time, my knees blew up like two balloons practicing with the line. Football was not really my thing.

I still stayed good friends with him, though. I remember driving up four hours to visit him in Tallahassee on the weekends and hanging out with him as a freshman and a sophomore in college. I didn't have a big ball team paying my way, so I just went to Hillsborough, a small community college in Tampa Bay.

TRAINING

I continued to work hard at my jobs and I also started weightlifting. I was tired of being the scrawny kid. I wanted muscles and I wanted women. I started going to Hector's Gym on Pratt Street. Fresh out of high school, I was 6'1, but by 21, I was almost 6'4. All the weight lifting stimulated even more height growth. At this point, I would run into Terry again some, who was finally looking at me a little differently. He could see that I was training hard, and I started getting a little respect.

We talked a little at the gym. He said he was still into wrestling, and thought if things didn't go well with his music career, maybe he could wrestle for a living.

"That would be awesome," I said.

Some of the other guys at the gym gave me some pointers and supplement advice. I worked harder and harder and it eventually paid off. Soon, I was bench pressing around 450 pounds – almost double my bodyweight!

One day, I ran into Mike Graham at Hector's Gym. He was the son of wrestling promoter Eddie Graham. He went to high school with me back in the day. He remembered me, even though he was a few years older. I was still a big wrestling fan and wanted to talk with him, so I brought up the only link I thought could maybe keep him talking.

"Did you know a guy named Terry Bollea?" I asked, trying to make small talk. "Wasn't he in your class? He goes to this gym, too. Do you know him? People here think he should be a wrestler."

"Yeah, I didn't really hang with him though," he said. "He was in my 7th period gym class, along with all the high school football players. Terry was good, but he did his own thing, I guess. "

"What was that like?"

"He just beat everyone's ass because the teachers didn't give a shit. They didn't bother to teach a regular class at the end of the day. It was anything goes. Terry didn't know his own strength and like clotheslined and steamrolled right through everyone."

"I'm surprised he didn't play football then," I said.

"Apparently all the jocks hated him. They felt he was a traitor to his school and a waste. He could have played some great football, but he was too lazy. He only wanted to play music after school, not sports." He was right. Terry's focus was rock 'n roll. He kept up with his love of music, too, after he got out of school. When he returned from college, he formed his own band, Ruckus. They were now playing a few times a week at a number of clubs around Tampa. They played a lot of hard rock covers like Aerosmith and Tower of Power, and built up quite a following.

I could tell right away by his tone that he was not too keen on Terry, so I dropped the subject. That subject was not getting me over with him, it was actually getting me heat.

After Mike Graham left, one of the guys at the gym named Scott had heard us talking.

"Awe, he is just jealous."

"What do you mean?"

"He just wishes he was as big as Terry, is all," Scott said. "He's got little-big man syndrome."

I laughed. I knew the type all too well.

"I didn't know you were into the wrestling," Scott said. "A lot of the wresters have been stopping by the Imperial Room after the show, where Ruckus is actually playing, too."

Scott and I decided to go over.

The Imperial Room was a happening place. It was packed with ladies and loud music. I got in with a fake ID that Nat helped me get somewhere. I grabbed something to drink.

The band was rocking. I saw Terry up on stage pounding away on his bass guitar. He had a really neat style, playing on a bass with no frets on it. Everything was very slide and slap and fun to watch. Scott patted me on the shoulder and pointed at the door. There, by the bouncer I saw a familiar bearded face with long locks of red flowing hair. He made his way through the sea of humanity and moseyed up, belly to the bar.

Shit! There is that manager, Oliver Humperdink!

Next thing you knew, Jos LeDuc was walking in, then the Briscos, and then even Dusty Rhodes. Eventually, the club was full of wrestlers. I felt like a kid again. During the band's break, I rushed over to Terry to tell him about the wrestlers.

"Brother, now is your chance!" I said. "Usually the wrestlers put on a show for us, but tonight, they are here for yours. You should go up and tell them you want to wrestle."

"You are right," he said. He rolled up his sleeves and walked over to Bob Roop who was hanging out, drinking with Bob Orton at a table.

"Hey, Bob. Do you like the music?"

Bob nodded, but didn't say much.

"I just wanted to let you know I am also a big fan of you guys, and I would love to be a wrestler myself, one day."

Roop and Orton looked him up and down and nodded. I saw them talk for a few minutes. The next thing you know, Terry was taking down a number. The band played another set, and then Terry went up to get a drink at the bar. There was Mike Graham. The both walked out of the bar for a bit and then Terry came back in elated.

I rushed over to see what had happened. "So, what happened man?" I asked.

"Brother, Bob Roop hooked me up with Mike, and Mike is going to set me up with Hiro Matsuda! I'm going to go and train with him tomorrow!"

After my talk with Mike at the gym, I was surprised that he was going to help Terry out. It sounded to me like they had heat, but I figured they must have worked through it. "That's awesome, man! Congratulations!"

A few days passed. There was no sign of Terry at the gym. Finally, he returned with a huge cast on his right leg. He shook his head and told us his story.

"Matsuda met me at his tailor shop, right down the street from Briscos Body Shop. In the back, there was a decent sized area where he put out some mats. Matsuda made me exercise for 3 hours, until I was almost ready to faint. When he finally started to go over some wrestling moves, I took him right down and just held him there. Matsuda laughed a second, sitting there between my legs. But then he jammed his elbow into my shin, grabbed my toe and snapped my leg in half."

He said he couldn't even drive off the lot because he couldn't bend his foot even enough to step on the gas. He then had to call his dad to pick him up, and tell him what had happened. His father was pissed. I felt horrible. Along with the other guys in the gym, we decided to push him to train to better heal his wounds. That lasted for the next 12 to 13 weeks. We all gave some positive talk to him, and convinced him to keep training hard to return to Matsuda. He agreed that he was going to finish what he started.

Just like the other guys, I wanted to fight Matsuda for what he did. We all did. Someone hurt one of our pack. The brothership of the gym was pretty strong. We pushed Terry very hard, and it worked. Once he got the cast off, he was right back over to Hiro Matsuda again, to get his teeth chipped and his face mashed into the canvass. Probably afraid of possible retaliation from Terry, Matsuda didn't immediately go back into grappling with him. One guy, Gordon Nelson, was a real shooter. He went in some to work on him and beat the dog shit out of him. A few other wrestlers also came to help with the Terry beatings.

This was my first connection to the wrestling world. I never much thought about being a wrestler myself, but seeing someone else almost making the breakthrough made me think I had a chance. Even though I was getting into the best shape of my life, I still saw myself in the mirror as being the tall scrawny kid that liked to feed birds in the woods.

I started training even harder.

During his almost a full year of torture, Terry would still work out at the gym and tell us of his progress. He felt that his treatment was far worse than anyone else's. He watched as other new guys were walking in and out of Matsuda's classes without a scratch. None of them got beat up like he did.

Then one day, he said it happened. Matsuda wasn't there. The Briscos came in. Gerald said, "We think you have had enough. Tomorrow you are going to go to the Sportatorium, and you are going to work out with Eddie Graham."

Terry went to the Sportatorium in Tampa the next morning. He got in the ring with Eddie and attempted to work with him the same rough way he had with Matsuda. That was when Eddie decided to smarten him up and let him know that professional wrestling was a work. Eddie taught him how to lock up, hit the ropes, and do everything, the right way – working with your opponent, not against him. It blew his mind. Terry told me that he excused himself to the men's room and actually started crying. It freaked him out so much when he realized that he had been worked for almost a full year. When he returned, Eddie told him they were very impressed that he didn't quit after everything they did. He passed the test. That meant he had paid his dues, and they thought he was going to become something very special.

Eddie started him up the next week in the Sportatorium. He decided to have Terry wrestler under a hood so that if he was horrible, he would have time to get better and not hurt his name. So with a pair of Jack Brisco's boots dyed black and a mask, Terry became the "Super Destroyer."

Terry started wrestling his first matches in Miami and Tallahassee. He was still paying his dues, however. Mike Graham was not going to allow another local boy to outshine him on his turf. He was going to be the local hometown boy, nobody else. The rides to his shows were murder. They only paid him around $25 for a 500 mile trip, 7 or 8 hours to Tallahassee. Guys like Rocky Johnson and Gordon Nelson would all pile into his car, drinking and partying the entire way. His girlfriend's brand new Ford Trio was getting trashed. He didn't know anything about charging guys for transportation, so the boys took advantage of him. They would hit him in the head and screw with him while he was driving. If he would stop off at the side of the road to urinate, they would sneak up behind him and piss on the back of his legs.

Eddie said that he was going to use him at the armory locally, but it never happened. Terry couldn't make a living wrestling two days a week for peanuts and not even getting enough to pay for the gas. He had to rethink things.

After about two months, he came to me and told me that he quit again.

LEFT: Here I am as "The Beefcake Kid," sporting my groovy cowboy hat at my best friend Bobo Sellers' birthday party. Even at a young age, note the boy/girl ratio.

BELOW: Looking sexier than Erik Estrada from CHiPS, this is one of my first real means of transportation.

CHAPTER 3 - COCOA BEACH

The owner of one of the clubs, Whitey Bridges, was an older guy from the gym that we all liked. He had long blonde hair and big arms and was fun to work out with. He had been talking about revamping his bar with a hard rock theme, and he wanted one of his boys at the gym to take up the job.

Terry was the obvious choice. He had played in a number of bands on the Tampa scene, but he was hesitant at first, because Whitey's bar was about two hours away over at Cocoa Beach. That meant he would have to leave Tampa behind, a number of his friends, and the gym which was pretty much his life. He was torn, however, because he really needed the money. Whitey said that if he took the job, he wouldn't have to worry about leaving the gym behind. They would build their own gym right on Cocoa Beach, to run in conjunction with the bar. He also promised Terry that if he ever wanted to get back into wrestling, he could do everything he would to help.

Terry asked all of his friends and weightlifting buddies to go to Cocoa Beach with him for his new endeavor. He was also taking on a management role at "The Anchor Club" and could hire his friends to help. Make no mistake about it, the Anchor was no sailor's club like what you would see in the movie *Philadelphia*. It was anything but a gay bar. I mean, *Steppenwolf* was even booked to play there.

As cool as it may have sounded to him, none of Terry's close friends wanted to give up their jobs and run away. I was Terry's absolute last resort. So finally, Terry called me, the kid he kind of picked on, and asked me to go to Cocoa to help set up the bar and run the gym with him. We got to talking and I put the idea of wrestling back into his head. Our plan was to make the club do well so it could run itself, then just shift our efforts over to the gym. There at our own gym, we could train huge and hopefully look good for a return to the ring. So, with Terry agreeing to a new focus back at wrestling, I dropped everything to go off with him and to try to become famous.

The Anchor was a hard rock club, right on the beach off of 5 and 20. We took over and started the first steps to make it into "the place to be." Once the bar was reset and restocked, it re-opened. Terry became the bartender, and I worked the door at night. My role was important. I stocked the place with the best customers I could and made sure to weed out the riffraff. Being the guy at the door was good for me and my game, because it meant I had the absolute first shot at the hottest girl in the club as she was walking through the door. I flirted with the girls and talked locker room filth with the boys. It helped make me into the social butterfly I am today.

We worked long and crazy hours for a number of weeks, but it all paid off. Eventually, it was the "in" place to be.

Right next door to the bar, Whitey rented a little building that used to be an insurance agency. During the day, I transformed myself into a contractor to make sure that the gym would be everything we wanted it to be. We gutted it out completely and started to build our ideal gym, brick by brick, piece by piece. It turned out that Whitey was a real good welder. We cut, created, and painted all of our own exercise equipment from scratch. We loaded up the Anchor Bar's van at the York Barbell company probably a dozen times so full of weights that it sat probably a foot lower, with its frame almost scraping the ground!

Sometime in 1976, our Olympic Gym was finally open to the public. We had our own t-shirts that read, "Bodybuilders have more meat & stay harder longer." Yes. We were pigs. We had very few members at first, but that was because we were selective. Whitey still made decent money in the bar, so he didn't care either way. The gym was more a project of passion and a way for us to get ring ready.

We would train hard at the gym for like a year, but it never really brought in any money. The real reason it didn't grow was *we didn't really let it.* The one rule of our gym was, "no girls allowed." That's right. We wanted it to be a hardcore, bodybuilding, iron-pumping, real weight-lifting gym like you would see in that Arnold Schwarzenegger film, *Pumping Iron*. We wanted it to be gritty. We wanted it to be smash-mouth. We wanted guys swearing up a storm and getting jacked. This formula, however, didn't equate to dollars and cents. It was a very specific member that we were looking for.

There was one girl that would make a gym appearance from time to time, however. She was the one who sold us our cash register, but we mostly just saw her at the bar. The boys called her "Bahama Mama." She was connected to all of the fishermen in the area, which meant she could get anything you wanted from anywhere in the world. She could get any kind of herbal tea, supplement, or drug that you could imagine. That wasn't really our scene at the time though. We weren't much into drugs. There was a little pot around, and maybe some hash here and there, but we would never get too crazy back then.

Bahama Mama was funny. She would come into the bar with a big bag that had everything in it, and I mean everything. She had everything from Rolex watches, to rare thimbles, to Cuban cigars, to hardcore narcotics. One time, a very rich businessman at the bar ordered some weird exotic drink. Terry didn't have the right booze for it, but Bahama Mama did, and it was right in her bag. Terry bought the bottle, mixed it up and then split a pretty good tip with Bahama.

We only worked at the bar for a short time. While we were working at the Anchor Club, we rented an apartment just two miles down the road in Cape Canaveral. Bahama Mama helped us furnish the whole place for pennies on the dollar. It wasn't very fancy, but it was a good place to crash and bring an occasional date to from time to time, not like that was happening all that much, wink, wink.

The Anchor Club was happening. Whitey's plan had worked and we had a very popular place on our hands. We had bands and dancing. The hard rock music went hand-in-hand with the whole "sex, drugs and rock 'n roll" vibe that we created and that made us very big on the singles scene.

People would go to our bar if they were looking to hook up. That made it really easy for me and Terry to find chicks. After all, we were the rockstars of the bar.

THE BET

One night, when Cocoa Beach was throwing their annual Surfing Contest, a bunch of girls came in after a bikini contest. The bar was already packed, shoulder to shoulder with some of the hottest girls around, but then in came these contestants. These girls were ridiculous. They were the hottest girls you ever saw in town just for spring break, and they would do just about anything for attention.

There was a tall blonde that really had my eye from the moment she walked through my door. She didn't have big boobs or anything, but she was smoking hot. She was probably about two years younger than me or so. I would say she was 18. She had blonde hair with just a tint of red. Perfect lips. She was a real knockout. We got to talking and she explained to me what she did to win the bikini contest, hands down.

"Could you show me the move," I asked. We positioned in the corner a little as to not give the whole bar a show.

Boom. Two scrumptious boobs, right in my face.

"Hey, Terry!" I shouted. "We have a problem over here." Terry was mixing someone a drink, but when he looked up, he knew exactly why I was calling him. He was over to our corner in probably less than 30 seconds.

"You don't mind showing my man that move, do you sweetheart?" I asked.

Boom, boom.

It was obvious. Terry's eyes bugged out of his head. He had to be excited. I know that I was "hulking up" in my pants probably 7 or 8 years before Hulk Hogan would even be invented. She was a knockout.

She was great. She was a pretty girl just starting college and she loved to mix it up with the boys. She became a bit of a celebrity there for winning the contest. She started coming back every night or so and became one of our regulars for a time. She was a big-time flirt with everyone, but really poured things on thick with me and Terry like you wouldn't believe.

"Listen, Terry," I said one night closing up, after having a few drinks myself. "She is my girl."

"No, no," he said, laughing, wiping down the bar with a white towel. "I think you are mistaken."

"Oh, you think I'm wrong?" I joked, picking up leftover bottles and cups off a table. "I bet you $20 that she ends up with me."

"You are on, brother." Terry pulled the string on one of the lights. "Twenty bucks."

"Twenty," I said, with a big Mega Powers handshake to seal the deal. It was official; $20 was on the line to see who could pin the Cocoa Beach Champion first.

She seemed to always show up when the place was packed. Whenever she came into the bar, everyone and everything would stop because she was so gorgeous that their dicks all got hard. Terry would be bartending, and couldn't always give her the attention she craved because of all the customers. Whenever I saw her, however, I was working the door, so I would just work her too with small talk. Terry would try his hardest to pick her up, but of course, she liked me just a little bit more because I was able to put the time in with her that she demanded.

One night, it was late. The place had pretty much cleared out, but the Cocoa Beach Bikini Champion was still running wild, burning the midnight oil with the last 20-30 people left in the bar.

Just before closing time, she started getting extra frisky. She was both grabbing my ass and running behind the bar to mess with Terry while he was mixing drinks. Eventually, she let us know her intentions. She said she wasn't going to leave until she got what she wanted. She was greedy, too.

"I want both of you," she whispered in our ears.

Now, I was totally into pro wrestling, but there was no way I was tag-teaming with Terry. That wouldn't come until later, and then it would be in a ring somewhere, not with some chick in the back of the bar. I only have two rules in life; one never engage in a devil's threesome, and two, never order double pickles at Subway from Jared, if you know what I am saying.

As it turned out, taking turns was totally acceptable to her, so then in my mind, the game was on; *whoever could get her first.*

There were a few last drink stragglers on hand. Terry and I quickly started to shut off all the neon beer lights and close down the fort. Because there were still customers paying their bills, and because I was much sexier than Terry (let's face it), she took me by the hand. We disappeared out of sight – me first!

"Dammit!" Terry yelled, holding up his hand in a fist, while cashing out someone at the register.

I laughed loudly. The door closed behind me but then other things immediately opened up. Now, I was no angel. I had been with girls before, but this one was different. Very different.

She was very vocal. When we started fooling around, she started moaning, real loud. She was practically screaming before I had even really touched her. I stopped.

"Is everything, okay?" I asked, worried that she was going to call the police, or something.

"Couldn't be better," she said.

That was just it. She was a screamer. That was her thing. Shouting at the top of her lungs was supposed to, "intensify her sexual experience." She must have really wanted to optimize our session, however. I practically needed earplugs before I even got to second base.

When we were finished, she told me to go out to get Terry, because it was his turn. I couldn't wait to see his face and bust his chops. I shut the door behind me and walked back over to the bar to tag out.

"Terry?" I called, looking around the bar. "Umm, Terry?!"

It had only been about ten minutes, but now the whole place was a ghost town. The lights were off. The stools were on the tables. The floor was swept. There was not a soul to be found. I walked over to the window. Terry's van was gone, and I would be walking back home that night.

It turned out that Cocoa Beach Bikini Contest Champion was such a screamer that, come Terry's turn, he must have heard us through the door and tapped out. The screaming was almost too intimidating for even me to be on my game, so I understood why he was gone. As I turned around to head back to the room for a rematch, I noticed something funny and had to laugh.

There was a twenty dollar bill on the table.

THE DREAM

One night, I practically had to bodyslam some rude asshole out the door, who refused to leave after having one too many. After all that working out, it turned out it was actually much easier for me to do than I thought it would have been. That is when I decided even more so that I wanted to wrestle.

Besides working at the Anchor, I was also working at the gym and getting in the best shape of my life. The possibility just started to formulate in my head that maybe I should really go and take a shot at it. I guess I had built up a lot of confidence talking to the ladies, and also bouncing at the bar.

During our downtime, I asked Terry if he could show me how to do some wrestling moves. He had no problem doing so, because he was grateful of the hard work I had been putting in. I had already taken Judo. I knew how to do some judo throws and some basic moves. We set up some mats in the back of the gym and we were ready to go.

First, I learned the basics. Locking up. Hitting the ropes. Taking a slam. Then, I made him show me how to throw an arm drag and grab a hold. I had him show me how to do a headlock. I would watch things on TV, then ask for lessons. That was all I really needed.

So a new plan emerged. I took about a full year to train really hard and get bigger than ever. I was excited about networking and tapping some contacts to eventually try to make my own debut in the squared circle. I also pushed Terry to do the same, right at my side. My new found career path got me excited, and I think that my excitement at the idea also started to restore Terry's faith in wanting to pursue his dream, once again. It was a good thing we had wrestling as a backup plan.

As the saying goes, all good things come to an end. One day, Whitey Bridges got married. You see, Whitey was about twice our age. When he tied the knot, everything changed. His priorities went in a whole different direction. Even though he was a weightlifter too, the moment he said, "I do," his wife was saying, "you don't." We were no longer his main priority, and we played second fiddle to his bride. She started pressuring him not to hang out with us. The writing was on the wall. The gym wasn't making any money and it was the first to go. After that, the Anchor Club was next.

As another saying goes, when one door closes, another opens in front of you. As we were packing our bags to head back over to Tampa, I told Terry he should entertain the possibility of wrestling again. He admitted that he was getting the itch again and made some phone calls.

Eventually, we got a call back from Harley Race who talked about having us go to Kansas City. Harley enjoyed smashing beer cans on Terry's head in a bar when he was working for Eddie in Florida. Harley liked the idea of doing so again.

"So what do you think? Should we go?" Terry asked.

"Absolutely, brother," I said.

That is when we came up with the best idea in the world; *we would tell everyone that we actually were brothers.* We figured if we had each other's backs, maybe we would be taken seriously. No getting pissed on. Nobody breaking your leg. If someone wanted to mess with one of us, they would know they would have to deal with the other brother. It made perfect sense.

Before we accepted Harley's offer, we made yet another call to Jerry Jarrett in Memphis to see if we could play the two promotions for some better money. It worked. Jerry gave us the best offer. The only condition Jerry had was he wanted us to go polish the gimmick up some with some smaller promotions, before bringing us into Memphis.

We agreed. I quickly realized that I needed to start working on my look. Terry already had it. He was tanned and had his blonde hair back growing out. He was jacked. I knew that if I was going to sell myself as Terry's younger brother, Eddie Boulder, I was going to need to look the part. Therefore, I immediately started taking as many vitamins as humanly possible and started shaving differently.

That's right. I began to cultivate my own lady-killing, handlebar mustache, brother!

About the time I had the look down, Terry finished showing me pretty much everything he had learned. He was working a little here and there, but ready to debut our tag team gimmick. The ball started rolling very fast, after that. Terry talked to Bob Roop, again, who he had seen in the early days of the school. He got us meeting with Jim Barnett, who was a well-known NWA affiliate promoter in Georgia, the early WCW.

We showed up to an Atlanta show in gear as "The Boulder Brothers," Terry and Eddie Boulder. We were all jacked up and tanned with the blonde hair and matching mustaches.

Now, Jim Barnett was gay. Very gay. He took one look at Terry and saw a Greek god. He took one look at me and thought boy toy. He took one look at our facial hair and pictured mustache rides. That was just how he was.

"My boys," he said in what almost sounded like a bad Charles Nelson Reilly impersonation, "You really got something here."

He looked us over and over again, and then nodded. His face lit up like a pinball machine. There were dollar signs in eyes and a roll of quarters in his pocket. Barnett agreed on the spot to some future dates with us and asked us to practice in some smaller territories to try it out. First stop, Pensacola.

Oh, my boy... Jim Barnett was a wrestling promoter in Georgia, Indiana, Australia, and other territories for many years. He was also a treasurer for the National Wrestling Alliance.

CHAPTER 4 - PENSACOLA

Hitting the road, we knew we needed a good ride that we could crash in, and also turn heads with, in style. Before leaving Cocoa Beach, we sold our two cars to get a van from Whitey. Whitey knew he was whipped. He gave us the van for a great price as a bit of severance pay reparation, probably feeling guilty about having to shut things down after all of our hard work.

Whitey's van looked like a Matchbox car from the 70s. It was a big brown Winnebago with custom airbrushing. It had a pimpin' ocean scene of a seashore, a boat, some seagulls overhead and a giant anchor in its sky, painted there as a commercial for the club. It had four chrome zoomie pipes all along the side that turned and went up over the back wheels. Those shiny pipes gave it power and a real throaty sound.

The back was already gutted, because we used it for hauling shit for the bar and the gym. So what we did was put a bed in the very back from side wall to side wall with a little elevation, and some space with another roll-away cushion under it. Usually, Terry would sleep in the bed and I would sleep the long way, with my feet under it. The design was kind of like a sideways capital T, kind of like Robert Fuller's silhouette. (If you didn't get that one, that joke will make more sense later on.)

When I started wrestling for Southeastern Championship Wrestling owned by Ron and Robert Fuller, Louis Tillet was booking the Southern territory. This area included Pensacola, Panama City, Northern Florida, Dauphin, New Brunswick, and Mobile, Alabama. The way that or SECW ran may be confusing to some. Southeastern Championship Wrestling had almost like two different promotions running under the same name; the Northern area was Knoxville, and the Southern area was more like Alabama. The Fullers took turns overseeing the two different areas and Louis Tillet pretty much managed the south for them.

Pensacola was perfect for us. We were pretty much brand-new, working in a territory with many shows only a few hundred miles away from each other. It was a great way to break in, because you had at least a little time before shows to breathe. Pensacola was very unlike Bill Watts Mid-South territory, where you were constantly on the run, having to drive all day and night to get to the next town.

The first show we did with the promotion was Panama City. We were there on a Thursday night, walking in all excited to be finally showing off our new personas. Some of the wrestlers you may have heard of in this territory were the Honky Tonk Man, David Schultz, Don Fargo and the Wild Samoans.

In my very first match, I didn't team with Terry just yet. They put Terry out in a singles bout, and they had me tag with a guy named Ron Slinker, an ex-police officer turned wrestler. Real nice guy. We worked against the tag team combination of Eric the Red & Ox Baker.

The next night, we finally debuted as our tag team. In Alabama, we wrestled as Terry and Ed Boulder, known as The Boulder Brothers. I remember coming to the ring. The people ate it up. We had a bunch of choreographed double-team moves and really good chemistry. Very few people actually knew our real names outside the promoters we worked for. These early matches working as "The Boulders" were so memorable to diehard fans that a rumor started later on that "Hulk Hogan and Brutus Beefcake were actually brothers."

Speaking of actual brothers, we got to be real good friends with the Samoans, Afa and Sika. They were not the crazy monsters like they were depicted on TV. They were two big teddy bears. They were in the same boat as we were; new and broke. None of us had any money back then. We couldn't afford motel rooms like the other guys. We didn't need one. We had the no-tell motel on wheels with us, everywhere we went. Every night, Terry and I would sleep in his finely airbrushed van on the beach in Pensacola, and the Samoans slept in their vans too, right next to us.

For the beginning, it was just survival mode. It kind of reminded me of going on those long vacation trips with my family as a kid. Every morning we would get up, and one of us would maybe pound on the side of the Samoan-mobile. They would roll out the van and we would all go find something cheap to eat at a diner. After that, we would grab our towels and head down to the public beach showers to clean up. After the showers, we would do whatever we wanted for a bit, then we would leave together to drive to the towns.

Since I was still pretty green, I liked to go to the shows a little early to get some practice in. Some of the guys would take me in the ring and give me some training. The show would go down and could practice some of what I had learned live in front of a real audience to perfect my craft. After the matches, we would drive back to Pensacola, if it wasn't too far.

When we couldn't stay at Pensacola beach, we would try to park outside a nearby wrestler's house after shows; one who lived in the area. One parking spot was outside David Schultz's apartment. He was cool. He let us come in whenever we wanted in case we had to poop. He even let us use his shower every once in a while, if we were in a hurry.

When there was no local wrestler in the area, we would leave the arena and then just sleep in our vans in a random parking lot somewhere. Sometimes we would get up in the morning and drive over to one of the local gas stations that had one little room you could lock. We take turns using the bathroom to poop and brush our teeth or whatever, and then and then drive back to Pensacola. Eventually, we would always circle back to Pensacola beach and start everything all over again. Pensacola was home base.

SAMOAN LOVE

We would be tanning, or in the water and then smell barbeque. The Samoans quite often would pull out a little grill and be cooking out in front of their van on the sidewalk. Man oh man, they fed Terry and I a bunch. They were really generous and great.

To pay them back, sometimes we would go to this buffet place called, Moms. It was a little buffet style joint off the main strip and they had the best fried chicken in the world.

The moment we walked in, we would transform into savages. All manners were out the window. We wouldn't even sit down at the table, as the waitress showed us to our seats. We would walk over and acknowledge it, don't get me wrong. We would nod to our assigned eating headquarters, but then rush right over to the plates and immediately go up to the food.

Let me tell you, the Samoans and the Boulders could eat. We would each grab a heaping plate of fried chicken and make quick work of it in little time. All four of us would pound the poultry and toss all the bones on a few empty plates in the center. Then we would get right back up and do it again. The amount of chicken bones left when we were finally done was ridiculous. It was always like a huge mountain. It was just wrong.

The people at Mom's just hated us. It got to the point that when we showed up, you could see the anger in their eyes because they knew we were just going to eat everything in sight. If we were able to just pull our seats up to the buffet tables themselves, we probably would have done that.

The nights were relatively peaceful sleeping on the beach. I do remember one night, I had checked in early. I was already asleep when all of a sudden, it felt like I was on a boat. I was out of it. I shook myself awake and looked out of the window to see if we had been hit by the tide, or something. Then, I realized that the motion was coming from within the van. Someone had snuck in the back.

It was late, and the bars had all closed. Terry had just come back from drinking and had a girl with him, and maybe a six-pack. Now, I don't think he was necessarily trying to get it on with her. The really wild days would more come from our next territory, Memphis, after we were more widely known. But either way, I didn't want to cock-block, or be there first hand to see what was going to happen. That would be breaking the bro code, so I decided to take off. Before I shut the door, I saw Terry out of the corner of my eye. He just barely gave me the thumbs up.

I rolled out, knowing damn well that I shouldn't return anytime soon, as to let them have their space. Terry wasn't a big player like me, but either way as a bro, you knew you had to follow the unwritten universal gentlemen's rule that states, *"If the van is a-rocking, don't come a-knocking."*

Tired as hell, I ventured out for what I figured would be a long night. I walked down a few spots over in the parking lot to the side of the Samoan's ride to look for shelter. A light drizzle was hitting my face, as I was hitting the van.

Bump! Bump! Bump!

Nothing. I pounded a bit harder.

BUMP! BUMP! BUMP!

Finally, a dazed Afa slid the side door open. A stale cloud of dank Samoan tobacco smacked me in the face. I grimaced and pulled my blanket up over my shoulder and nose.

"What, what? Is it morning yet?" he asked, looking to see that it was still dark.

"No. Just wondering if you mind if I crash in the front?" I asked in a chuckle. "Terry has some company in the van, and I can't get any sleep."

Afa started to laugh, and he shook his head. "Too much sound from Terry?" he asked.

"No, I don't think so, but didn't want to stick around to find out."

"Ok. Get in." Afa pointed to the front. He slid the door closed, and then I saw his forearm unlock the front. I crawled into the passenger side. The seat was back pretty far already, but I leaned it back some. The head of my chair pushed back this drapery thing that they used to keep the light out of the back. I heard Afa say something to Sika from the back, and then I passed out.

About 20 minutes later, I awoke again. This time, however, my makeshift bed was not moving around. The thing that woke me from the dead this time was the curious sound of wood being sawed.

I laid there for some time and listened to the wood-sawing storm in full force. I tried covering my ears with my blanket, but it was no use. I waited it out. After about 10 minutes, I heard Sika, I think, tell his brother to roll over. Finally, the snoring subsided.

I closed my eyes again. I thought about the day and some of what I had learned in the ring. A peacefulness came over me. Just as I started to drift, I heard the gentle blast of an earth-rattling fried chicken fart and then the sawing started up again, in its entire splendor.

Then to make matters worse, out of nowhere, it became a duet. Yes, another saw chimed in, in perfect harmony. It was magical. A full on wood-sawing, Samoan symphony in stereo was being performed just for me, right there in that shitty smoke-filled Dodge ram.

It wasn't worth it. Some wet socks and a couple of sand flea bites were far better than hearing that, so I rolled out of van number two. I wrapped up in the blanket and fell asleep on the beach.

A younger shot of The Wild Samoans, Afa & Sika.

Days were easy. Terry and I would go to Pensacola health club and work out, or maybe I would go swimming with the Samoans. We might hang out on the beach until late in the afternoon and then maybe drive to New Brunswick, or Mobile, or Montgomery - wherever we were wrestling that night.

Sometimes, Ox Baker would show up to our vans hang out. Ox and I worked a lot of matches together. He was very helpful with me training early on in my career, and we hit it off pretty well. When he stopped by, he would just sit down next to me on a stoop, maybe and eat some Samoan barbeque. Other times, he would bring sandwiches to share. I liked eating with Ox. He always had interesting stories to tell.

Ox didn't care about kayfabe at all, in a time when we had separate everything for the heels and the babyfaces. From our cars, to our hotels, to the locker rooms, good guys wouldn't be seen with the villains anywhere in order to protect the business. But Ox didn't care about any of that. He would come out swimming, or even lay down right next to me to tan in the sun, even when we were set to work against each other that very night.

Terry absolutely hated this. If he strolled up on us on the beach and saw me drinking with Ox, his face would go sour.

"Awe, Ox," he would say, disgustedly. "Come on. Kayfabe brother! Get out of here."

So it became a weird kayfabe struggle rivalry between Terry and Ox. I was wrestling Ox and so was Terry, so I get why he didn't want us to be seen together, but we always set up camp in the middle of nowhere.

Ox knew it bothered Terry and thought it was funny. So he would wait until like Terry was asleep on the beach working on his tan, and he would come over and sit right down next to us. Terry would wake up, look to his left and yell, "God'dammit, Ox!" Then he would run to the van. Sometimes Ox would actually chase after him.

Ox cared about Kayfabe, but he just liked me and Terry more. I was good friends with Ox right up until the time he died a short time ago.

One Friday night after our TV tapings at the farm center in Dauphin, Alabama, I snuck out to drive Ox over to a bar with the van, but Terry would have none of that. After the show, Terry instead hopped a ride over to one of the hotels where some the wrestlers were staying for a swim.

He says that he got changed in Don Fargo's room and then headed down to the pool. When he got there, he couldn't believe his eyes. Apparently some nudist beach, exhibitionist, hippy-type conference was there and they were all out in rare form. Everyone was naked and swimming.

Just as he was about to turn around and leave, he looked over and there was Robert Fuller, aka Col. Rob Parker, who owned the territory with his brother, Ron. He was standing on the diving board in all his glory, completely naked.

Surrounded by tons of wasted drunk people cheering him on to dive, someone reached over and handed him the Southwestern Heavyweight title belt. He put it on like a champ and the crowd went wild. It was dangling off his waist, as well as something else he was very known for; about five pounds of Fuller man-meat.

Now, I don't know if you have ever heard the legend of Col. Rob Parker's massive penis before, but it far surpasses anything he ever did in the ring. His penis really was bigger than his career. He wasn't shy about it either, let me tell you. He would just whip it out with no notice anywhere and swing it around like a pocket watch on a chain. He would take it out in the locker room, in the grocery store, driving next to a car of nuns, it didn't matter.

I guess on this particular night, he was in his element, in full exhibition mode. He started bouncing up and down on the board, getting the proper momentum going enough to spin his cock around in a complete circle. Once it looked like a propeller of an airplane, he was ready for lift off. He took three steps and jumped.

Low and behold, he didn't drop like a bag of shit. His spinning penis actually helped him finally take flight like a helicopter. Everyone's hair blew back. They watched in awe as he elevated ten to fifteen feet in the air! Robert Fuller flew around the entire room three full times before he dropped into the pool gracefully like a big beautiful swan (with a big massive dick), still wearing the belt. That's no lie, either. A whole room of people saw it with their own eyes!!!

CHAPTER 5 - MEMPHIS

"I remember, back in day Memphis days, Brutus came in with Terry as "The Boulders." I hooked up with those guys and we rode up and down the Kentucky and Tennessee roads in his big old Lincoln. We slept in that car. We went to the gym together in it. We camped out. It was like our motel. That is where I got a chance to really know them.

One night at the Coliseum, I heard how the promoter was skeptical about Boulders skills in the ring. He knew they looked good, but he didn't want to take any chances with them being green. The promoter told Beefer all he wanted him to do was to, "pick up your opponent and slam him." Only one move. Just bodyslams from him and that was it. Pick him up again, and slam him down again. Now for Terry, the promoter said, "All I want you to do is bear hug our opponents. Keep doing over and over." That's it.

After the show, I said you have to do more than that. I took them both up to a little old place in Divesburg, Tennessee to a barn to show them how to really work more than just the basics. Beef wanted to learn dropkick. Hogan wanted to learn more big man stuff. We worked out in that barn for hours and hay was flying everywhere! That's when we became great friends.

Years later when I finally came to WWE in 1996, Beefer saw me walking into the arena. He ran to me and picked me up like a little kid. Eddie Boulder. I still think a world of him today. He's like a brother to me. Never had any cross words at all."
- "The Birdman" Koko B Ware

From July- September of 1979, I wrestled in the famous Memphis territory. The Boulder Brothers were not signed to any type of contract with a non-competitive clause like you might see today. Back then guys moved pretty freely from territory to territory. Keeping faces fresh was all part of the business. So we took a match wrestling a one-off show for Continental Wrestling Association (CWA) in Memphis for Jerry Jarrett. Memphis was a huge wrestling town and the fans had done their homework. They all knew who we were, and we got a huge response from the crowd.

This promotion was a major NWA territory during the 1970s and early 1980s that operated out of Tennessee and Kentucky. Working for them and getting a great response was huge for us. The promoter was impressed. He approached us after our last night and offered us a job in Memphis for $800 a week. We didn't even need to talk about it. The offer was far more than the $175 a week that we were making for Tillet and the Fullers. We quickly accepted the offer and left Pensacola.

Things changed immediately. We could now actually afford to stay in hotel rooms. When we got to Memphis, the first thing we did was we sold the Anchor van and bought a new long green Lincoln in anticipation of the extra money we would be earning. We would travel around in it for several more years to go. It really was a status symbol.

After a month or so waiting to officially debut us to the roster as fulltime members of the locker room, they decided to start me out first.

I was still pretty green, but found myself in a high-profile match at the Mid-South Coliseum. I walked out and couldn't believe my eyes; *I was in a Memphis ring*. It was the biggest match for me exposure-wise that I had seen to date. The Memphis shows aired everywhere. They got massive press and they were in the NWA.

They put me in the ring as "Eddie Boulder" in a tag team bout, but not with my brother, Terry. Not yet. I was tagging with another guy named Dallas Montgomery. My first appearance on the Championship Wrestling show was against Ron Bass with his lackey Pete Austin, with their manager Danny Davis. The idea is that I would be the catalyst to start a feud with Ron and Terry.

Immediately, Bass started targteting me. When I turned my back, he attacked me before the bell. Referee Jerry Calhoun started the bout but the fans knew it was too late for me. I didn't know how to "get color" yet, but it was going to happen.

Some wrestlers back then taped a small blade to the side of their finger with a protective flap over it. When the right moment came, they would flip it back and cut a small incision in their hairline. Before the match, they would take a bunch of aspirin to thin their blood and get their heart pumping. This would make a guy bleed like a stuck pig. Other guys didn't like to tape the blade to their finger. They would either hide the blade under the ring some place, or have the referee pass it off to them at an opportune moment during the match. Getting color was really an art form and one I hadn't yet mastered, so Ron said he would help me out.

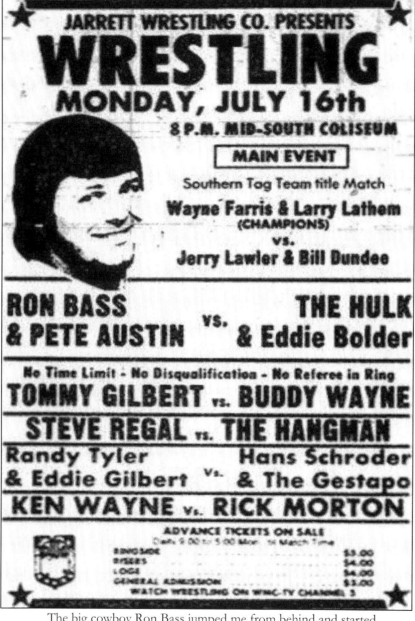

JARRETT WRESTLING CO. PRESENTS

WRESTLING

MONDAY, JULY 16th

8 P.M. MID-SOUTH COLISEUM

MAIN EVENT

Southern Tag Team title Match

Wayne Farris & Larry Lathem
(CHAMPIONS)

vs.

Jerry Lawler & Bill Dundee

RON BASS & PETE AUSTIN vs. **THE HULK & Eddie Bolder**

No Time Limit - No Disqualification - No Referee in Ring

TOMMY GILBERT vs. **BUDDY WAYNE**

STEVE REGAL vs. **THE HANGMAN**

Randy Tyler & Eddie Gilbert vs. **Hans Schroder & The Gestapo**

KEN WAYNE vs. **RICK MORTON**

ADVANCE TICKETS ON SALE
Daily 9:00 to 5:00 Mon. 'til March Time

RINGSIDE	$5.00
RISERS	$4.00
LOGE	$4.00
GENERAL ADMISSION	$3.00

WATCH WRESTLING ON WMC-TV CHANNEL 5

The big cowboy Ron Bass jumped me from behind and started stomping a Texas mud hole in my back. I was green and honestly, I was scared to death. "Here it comes, kid," he said. He nicked me a little high on my forehead and I barely felt anything. I thought it was going to hurt far worse than it did, but it really was a little bit of nothing. But then the blood started to come. He cut me too deep. There was so much blood that he must have poked right through a vein in my head.

This was TV with the big guys. I couldn't just run out and cry for a Band-Aid to put over my boo-boo. My first Memphis match had to look good, and that's just what I was going to do even if I had to die in the process. I made Bass look like he was murdering me, and I sold it like I was dying.

My heart was racing. Blood was squirting out everywhere. My long bleach blonde hair was the perfect white canvas to compliment all the red. It was spraying out like a hose. It was so nasty that it looked like someone had cut a deer open. There was a puddle in the ring. There was so much juice that the place actually smelled.

They had to back the cameras off me at the end of the match, because I was such a bloody mess.

I went back to the locker room and everyone congratulated me. I took some pictures for their program and the magazines. Then headed to the back. I took a shower and watched all the blood go down the drain, just like that movie Psycho. The medic put a couple of stitches in me and butterfly bandaged me up.

The next day, we went over to Jerry Jarrett's house to shoot some promos for TV. They had me explain that my brother wasn't planning on following me to Memphis, but when he saw what Ron Bass did to me, he decided it was time to avenge me.

They shot Terry's first vignette, starting on his boots. Then, they slowly panned up. They panned up until it reached his torso. His chest hair was shaved and cultivated to look like a tornado.

HULK

During this time in Memphis, Terry appeared on a local talk show that also coincidentally was featuring Lou Ferrigno, the star of the comic book adaptation television series, *The Incredible Hulk*. The host was supposed to get a few plugs for Memphis wrestling, then a longer interview with Ferrigno to plug his show which had been suffering a little in the ratings.

Terry was a great talker, but Lou maybe not so much. Lou was hearing-impaired and didn't make for a great interview. To get more out of the interview, the host started to actually pit the wrestler versus the body-builder. He commented on how Terry stood 6 ft 7 and weighed 295 pounds. He was that and with Terry's 24-inch biceps, he was actually dwarfing "The Hulk."

"That's because I'm the real Hulk," Terry said. "He only plays one on TV."

Watching the show backstage, Mary Jarrett noticed that Terry did look bigger than Ferrigno and told Jerry they had to play off it. Whether it was just Terry's medium sized shirt, or the fact that Lou Ferrigno was wearing something a little less revealing, Terry did come off looking much bigger than Lou. As a result of the show appearance, Terry Bollea began performing in the ring as Terry "The Hulk" Boulder.

Jerry Jarrett gave him the name. When we were on the road, we would hit different gyms and all the guys would yell, "Hulk," when they saw us enter. People everywhere said that Terry looked like a bigger Lou Ferrigno and that the new name was perfect. Terry started to get national exposure in the weightlifting magazines, as well as the gyms, which led to appearances outside of wrestling.

Guys like Robbie Robinson in California paid "The Hulk" to come workout at his place and sign autographs. Mike Katz who owned a big gym in New Haven CT also paid for an appearance. Even though the big name weightlifters called him that, there was no heat from Lou. Lou loved being able to have had a hand in Terry's success. We hung out with him quite a bit back in the day, and even today he sees me and gets giddy about remembering the good old days back when they were gods.

BLOWING OFF A MATCH

Once we started to really catch on, we could get away with a little bit more in the shenanigans department.

Bill Watts' territory, Mid-South Wrestling, wasn't doing so well and he didn't know why, so he asked Jerry Jarrett and Jerry Lawler to come up for a show for some feedback. After the show, Watts took them out to a nice Italian restaurant. They were eating, and Watts asked them what they thought was wrong.

"Where are all the blowjobs?" Jarrett said, nonchalantly pounding some pasta.

"What the hell does that mean?" Watts asked.

"All your wrestlers are big, ugly, tough guys who only appeal to your standard wrestling audience," Jarrett replied, taking another big bite of spaghetti. "If you get younger wrestlers and push them properly, you'll get more girls and kids to come to the shows."

He was right.

Eventually, promoters everywhere in the early 80s started to discover that babyfaces were supposed to look good to the girls so they would sell more tickets. When Jarrett learned the idea that sex sells, he saw his ticket sales immediately go up. Jarrett explained to his younger talent to be flirty and make all girls think they had a chance with them. He actually encouraged them to go out with as many different girls as possible. This way, his fan-favorites seemed "getable" and would be desirable like real sex symbols. None of the better-looking part of the locker room seemed to mind meeting this standard. The boss' request didn't always come without recourse, however. The boys in the locker room often ended up having to cover for each other, because with sex often comes violence.

One night before a big show, a girl started following Terry and I around while we were shopping to kill time. She looked a little bit like Daisy Duke with short cutoff jeans and had that farmer's daughter appeal.

When you are in the spotlight or have any sort of fame, it is easy to tell when someone is watching you. You develop like a sixth sense. You can feel a hole burn in your back from their eyes, even if you haven't spotted them yet. Terry and I were in a shopping center somewhere, and this same girl was always about 50 feet behind us. I started to get that feeling we were being watched.

Fresh off of the Ferrigno appearance, I figured she wanted to meet Terry. While Terry was looking at a wrestling magazine at a newsstand, I turned around and made eye contact. She smiled. Used to playing wingman, I pointed at Terry and then pointed at her.

She nodded no. Then, she pointed at herself, and then she pointed at me. "I'll see you at the show," she shouted, as she disappeared.

I immediately became aware.

"Who was that?" Terry asked, distracted a moment from his reading.

"Oh, just some fan."

I was a single guy. I had come up with some extra filthy plans for the farmer's daughter, if she was serious. I thought about her for the next few hours. I finally told Terry on the way over to the show and he laughed.

"You'll probably never even see her," he said.

Before the show, I looked around for Daisy Duke where the fans hung out. She was nowhere to be found. I also looked out from behind the curtain a few times to scan the audience and still no dice.

"Told you, brother," Terry teased. "You should have gotten her number. You might as well just forget it, now."

The crowd was hot. During the match, I finally spotted the girl a few rows back from ringside. She was better looking than I remembered. I waved at her. She pointed at me and then pointed at herself again. Then, she added a new gesture to the formula; the international symbol for blowjob.

I became aware once again. I nodded at her. Wearing spandex was not the best for concealing the way I was feeling at that very moment. I conveyed to her to meet me after the match. I had to look away from her after that and immediately think of baseball.

After the match, she met me over by the curtain near the locker room entrance.

"Wait here a second," I told her. Terry was off talking with someone, so I grabbed the keys to the Lincoln. I met back up with the Daisy-girl. I went to speak again, and she shook her head "no" and put her fingers over her lips to indicate her rules, "No speaking allowed."

Kinky.

We snuck out the back to the lot with no words. I backed the big green pill up to the furthest, darkest part of the lot.

Make out session. The only thing you could hear in the car was the smacking of lips. My window was open. Because the arena was more like a huge pavilion, I could still hear all of the bodyslams and the reaction of the crowd coming through the openings around the entire structure. There was a little rustling sound from the spandex, and then the country girl started to go to town.

I couldn't believe it. Everything was perfect. I felt a little bit bad though, because I was all sweaty. I just finished wrestling and it is possible I didn't smell the best. So I felt a little bad... BUT NOT THAT BAD! Trying to be impressive, I was holding out thinking about baseball again. Then, all of a sudden, I heard the announcer begin to announce the next match.

"And coming to the ring... from Tampa, Florida... weighing in at a total combined weight of 535 pounds... here are Eddie and Terry, The Boulder Brothers!"

I sat up in my seat.

Wait a minute? What?! I'm positive they called my name, again. That doesn't make sense. I just wrestled! Why are they calling me out again?

Then it hit me. About a month ago, the same thing happened when the show was going to end early. A few of the guys had to wrestle again to stretch things out because they said, "one of the matches finished too quickly."

No more baseball. I need this match... to hurry up... and "finish too quickly!"

I thought of every filthy thing I could think of. I went through my whole raunchy Rolodex and finally hit her with my finisher. Then, I gave her a high five and started running back to the ring, pulling up my tights.

When I got back into the dressing room, it was clear that everyone knew what had just happened. Terry must have seen me heading out to the car with the rizzat, and he told everyone. That is why they picked us to tag team, *just to rib me.*

Jerry Jarrett and everyone gathered around. They roared laughing.

"Alright, kid! It's time for your third match of the night!" one of the boys said, roughing up my hair. "Now, get out there!"

I rushed down the aisle a little frazzled. The audience had no idea why I was late, but it felt like they were all "in the know" when they started clapping. When I climbed up to the apron, I saw Terry take one look at me and practically lose it. He was in the ring getting beat up by our opponents and taking the heat for me, but biting his lip all the while not to lose it.

He looked at me and shook his head, laughing. "Just horrible," he said, as he tagged me in. "You have lipstick on your face and everything."

I wiped my cheek off, stepped between the ropes, and went to work.

SHERRI MARTEL

One night, Terry and I met up with Sensational Sherri at a strip joint, long before she became a wrestler. We watched her dance, and our eyes were bugging out of our heads. Man, she was a really good dancer! Terry and I watched her for a long time, and we tipped the hell out of her. Later on, she came up to us and told us that she knew who we were. She loved the sport and really hit it off with Terry. After that, she never really went away. Not many people know this, but she was really good friends with both of us, and I think she kind of considered dating Terry for a short time.

One night, Terry and I were both sharing the same hotel room. We got a call, and Sherri said that she wanted to come over with her friend and have some drinks with us. Now, who is going to turn down two beautiful women asking if they can come over to your room, with alcohol in the mix, right? We were both single at the time, so we were down with it.

The girls came over as planned, and they were all dressed to the nines. Sherri introduced me to her friend, who she wanted to hook me up with. Cold beers and hot bodies allowed one thing to lead to another. Terry was on his side of the room with Sherri, and I was with her friend in the other. Now, let me be clear, this was by no means about to ever turn into a crazy orgy scene, or something. (Not that I am opposed to orgies - I just was not going to engage in one with my good buddy the Hulkster in the mix, if you catch my drift… brother!) My girl was very forward. She practically attacked me. I knew that stuff was soon to happen on my side of the room.

I turned the lights out. I remember kissing my girl, then hearing what sounded like Sherri making ridiculous crazy noises across the way. Now, the

room was big enough and dark enough that I couldn't see what was going on over on Terry's side of the room. I don't know if she was faking noises to make us laugh, or if what I was hearing was legit – but it didn't matter. I am a competitive guy, and I wasn't going to let Terry outshine me in any athletic event.

Sherri started breathing hard and making more outlandish noises, so I worked my girl and hit her with a couple of stiff potatoes. She knew how to work, so she sold it good. Then, the other side of the room followed suit. It was on. Five minutes later and there were all kinds of moaning, groaning and slapping sounds going on. The cheap bed springs were working overtime. It sounded like the three stooges, only there were four of us in the room.

The next morning, we met up to get breakfast. We looked at each other and laughed, but we didn't say a word about it. We both thought it was weird, and I guess we just decided to never to do that again.

CATCHING ON

After a while in Memphis, we could only go so far with the big brother avenging the younger brother storylines, and they wanted to split us up in the end. See, I knew it. They wanted to put Hulk by himself, and not have me there just to serve as his lackey, or whatever. Looking back, it would have better served him to put him out there as a singles competitor, but the problem was we were traveling around together. We still liked the idea of watching each other's backs and pushing each other to do better.

Terry became my brother. I mean we did everything together. We trained, ate, traveled, we had become family.

Hot off the new name, Terry "The Hulk" Boulder, in around May of 1979, Jim Barnett made good with his promise. He gave Terry a great booking for a shot against the NWA World Heavyweight Champion, Harley Race.

This was one of the highest honors in wrestling and really increased his stock. Terry ended up winning the Northern Division NWA Southeastern Heavyweight Championship, which was recognized in Alabama and Tennessee. At the same time, he was working for Georgia Championship Wrestling under the name "Sterling Golden."

We wrestled around a bit, but things were a little tough and the cash just wasn't coming in.

Terry decided then again to quit wrestling again for a time, bummed out that he wasn't making very much money. Not knowing what to do, I suggested we go back to the docks in Tampa where we "could really make some good cash," pouring concrete and loading big cargo ships.

The money was good. We went from making something like $120 a week wrestling to $700, or $800.

I kept pushing Terry as much as I could in both the gym and wrestling. We pushed each other into a lot of hard work that we hoped would eventually pay off in the long term with success.

CHAPTER 6 – WWWF & MID-SOUTH

After our brief run there in the NWA as the Boulder Brothers, their Champion, Terry Funk, took a liking to me. He likened my naive rookie ways and my beautiful flowing hair to that of a ditsy blonde, so he called me "Dizzy." The boys in the back thought it was funny, so I went with it.

Playing off the idea that we were truly brothers, I sometimes wrestled as Dizzy Boulder, Dizzy Hogan, depending on what our last name was, whatever town we were working in. I can even be seen from time to time in results or videos online around 1979, perhaps, wrestling under the name Dizzy Golden.

Terry wrestled as "Sterling Golden" for Jim Barnett who was fascinated with his golden tan. When he wrestled with that name for the Fullers, I also took the surname, as his "brother" in the territory. In Pensacola, Sterling Golden defeated Bob Roop for the NWA Southeastern Heavyweight title in the Northern Division. Even though he dropped it a month later to Bob Armstrong, it was great exposure for us as a team.

After this run, we had a little dry spell, so we took to some of the odd jobs that I used to do back in Tampa. Terry Funk heard that we were moonlighting and figured manual labor was a waste. That is when he introduced us to the New York territory promoter, Vincent J. McMahon, Senior, who was the father of the Vince McMahon you see on TV today with the WWE. Terry got his bags together and took a flight to New York.

McMahon himself was Irish and wanted to bring in an Irish wrestler to attract more of that ethnic fan base in the Northeast. That is why he suggested that Terry "The Hulk" Boulder take on the Irish surname, Hogan. McMahon asked Terry to dye his hair red, and he said he would. But Terry told me he had no intentions of ever doing so. Just before he took off for a Japanese tour, he poured it down the drain. He said that his hair was starting to fall out, and that dye would probably just melt the rest away.

On November 17, 1979, Terry wrestled his first match as Hulk Hogan as a villain. The fans ate it up. During his initial run as a heel, Hogan was paired with "Classy" Freddie Blassie, a wrestler-turned-manager who could really guide Hogan and show him the ropes. After that, Hulk made his Madison Square Garden debut, defeating Ted DiBiase. McMahon next put Hogan with Bob Backlund and then started his first big run with the legendary André the Giant.

During this time, I was also working for Vince. I did some shots with the WWWF in New York wrestling in tag team matches. I still played Hogan's younger brother, Dizzy Hogan, but not really for any sort of exposure on TV. I was still a little less experienced, than Hulk, but that didn't matter to everybody. There was one guy who took a liking to me, and that was Pat Patterson.

Pat Patterson was a one of the best bookers out there. Many of the greatest matches you have ever seen had Pat there to help make the magic behind the scenes. However, Pat also had a reputation of booking younger attractive guys to have some eye candy around because, he was gay. Pat decided he wanted me as a job guy on TV, meaning someone who would lose all the time to make the other guys look good.

"No, no, no," Hulk said. "We can't start him out that way. There is no upside to that." He didn't want me type-casted and to destroy any future potential I may have had with the promotion. "Let's just get him more experience, and then call him up again later."

Patterson agreed. He said they would try their best to find something for me, after I got a little more experience under my belt. So I was off to hit the road alone, betting on myself.

MID SOUTH

While Hulk Hogan was beginning to make waves in the WWWF in singles competition, I was set to pick up more experience wrestling as Dizzy Golden in Mid-South. I had been in and out of the promotion some with Terry at first, but at this point took on more dates on my own between September of 1979 and February 1980.

The Mid-South Wrestling Association was as real as it gets. Ex-wrestler turned promoter "Cowboy" Bill Watts just started up the territory in two states: Louisiana and Mississippi. The territory later grew to include Oklahoma, as well as parts of Arkansas, Missouri and Texas. The promotion is known for its road schedule, with the wrestlers usually competing seven days a week (including two shows on Saturdays and Sundays) and the long distances between towns.

After mostly tag team competition, I was excited to work a singles program under Watts. He was seen at the time as one of the best wrestling promoters around, and his television show was just starting to take off. Mid-South was bringing its fans its own unique style. While Jerry Jarrett's Memphis wrestling was all larger-than-life, goofy cartoon-like characters, and storylines, Mid-South, was more real.

Their characters blurred the lines between good and evil. The matches felt more life-like and realistic. One way to get this feeling was Watts was known to give some shoot bonuses from time to time. This meant if two guys went out there and did some shoot fighting for the first few minutes, Watts might throw them a little something extra because he loved a fight. It also helped make his brand look different to the fans.

Watts understood great storytelling that people could relate to. Being a former wrestler himself, he helped create the week-to-week, storyline style of wrestling, in an episodic formula that you still see today on TV.

Watts protected the business by keeping its secrets from practically everyone. Everything was always on a "need to know" basis. For one, he led his own employees to all believe that everything going on was real. The people who set up the ring, the ticket seller, and even the hotdog vendors had no idea it was a work. He figured if the ignorant guy selling programs up in the stands believed and got into watching a match, so would the fans around him. The excitement would be contagious. Not smartening up those who didn't need to know secrets also meant less potential they would leak how something worked.

He even worked the hall owners when booking locations for his shows. Watts only booked venues that had the ability to provide for two separate locker rooms; one for the good guys and one for the bad. See, his wrestlers had to live the part and "live apart." Enemies wouldn't ride or eat together, and they also stayed in different hotels. If there weren't two different rooms at an arena, he would demand that some kind of wall or divider be erected. Fan favorites and heels couldn't go anywhere where they could cross paths publicly.

Speaking of going places, that was all we did in Mid-South; get in the car and go places. It was absolutely horrible. There were no major highways in Louisiana and we were totally brutalized by all the back-road traveling. We spent our whole life in the car.

Bill Watts put me with Buck Robley as a mentor behind the scenes. I rode around for hours upon hours with Buck. He was one of the bookers and creative guys in Mid-South. Every ride was a lesson with him and the car was his classroom.

Buck Robley was a semi successful wrestler in his own respect back in the 60's and 70's. After his in-ring career ended, he went on to managing and booking behind the scenes. He was your typical old school wrestler who always lived his gimmick 24/7. He was also someone who was known to stretch the truth, which was actually a plus in professional wrestling.

Buck was very heavy into drugs and alcohol, however. He was also always gambling away practically everything he made. Whether it was dog or horse racing, sports, or even who could shit the fastest, if you could bet on it – he was making a wager. Regardless of Robley's shortcomings, he had an intuitive mind for wrestling. He was the person behind Ted DiBiase, Jake Roberts and even the Junkyard Dog.

As a mentor to help show me the ropes, Cowboy Bill Watts put me with Buck Robley.

STALKER

We didn't fly much at all ever during my time with Mid-South, but we did get booked as a talent swap to go work a Harley Race show over in Kansas city. When I showed up to the airport, Bill was waiting for me and having a coffee at one of the little shops. He pointed out one of the fans and cautioned me.

"Now don't look right away. Be discrete, but do you see that lady over there?" he asked, motioning by the door. I looked and I nodded to Bill. She sort of looked like a shorter, smaller, fatter female version of Greg Valentine.

"She is bad news, man," he said. "A real stalker. We need to stay here as long as possible, until she goes away."

We waited and waited and waited. I must have put down six cups of coffee, but she was not having it. She was going to hit us up for something when we walked out of the Java Stop, whether we liked it or not. Just like clockwork, Bill Watts was right on the money.

"Hey guys!" Gregora the Hammer said, as we walked out of the shop. "Hey, hey. Aren't you the new guy, Dizzy Golden? I seen your matches on TV!"

Bill looked at me crazily, then forward. He refused to look at the stalker. "Thanks for watching," Bill said.

"Hey, can I ask you something," she asked. "Where are you going?"

We ignored her the best we could, answering in one or two-word answers.

"Dizzy, hang on a second," Watts said. "I'm going to grab a paper for the flight." At that, he disappeared into a newsstand/bookshop and left me alone.

"Hey, hey Dizzy!" she said, in a gross sexual nature. "Hey, if you give me an autograph, I'll suck your dick."

I looked down at the pathetic little creature. She reached over and ran her chubby fingers over my forearm. The stout little hobbit looked like something straight out of Middle-earth. There was no way I was letting her suck my dick.

"I'm sorry," I said looking at my invisible wristwatch. "I'm going to have to take a rain check." It was probably obvious that I was repulsed, but I didn't care. The moment Watts made it back with his paper, I started really picking up the steam. "Hey, Bill. We really got to go. Aren't we going to miss the flight or something?"

Bill knew she must have propositioned me, just as she had all of the other guys in the locker room. "You don't want to stay and talk to your new friend a little more."

I puked a little in my mouth.

"Ummm, yeah," I said.

We started moving quickly, with Gregora right behind us in tow.

"Hey guys," she said. "Do you think maybe you have time to…"

Bill cut her off, "Look miss, we are really busy. We have to get Dizzy on this flight, okay?

Just a little further and we would have been to the security line, but those six cups of coffee had really taken their toll. "Bill, I got take a piss," I said, stopping in front of the men's room sign.

"Okay, I'll be right here," he said, shaking his head knowing that he was going to still have to deal with the troll.

"I'm just going to leave this here, okay?" I asked, setting down my carry on by the wall.

Bill nodded.

I went in and did my business. When I came out, both Bill and Gregora "The Hammer" Valentine were gone. My bag was right where I left it against the wall. I grabbed it and started towards the security post, where I could vaguely see Bill by the x-ray machine.

By the time I made it to security, Bill had already gone through the line.

I rushed up. I put my bag on the conveyor to go through the x-rays. It went through. The guard looked puzzled. He sent the bag through again, and then again.

"Can I see your ticket and ID, please," the guard asked, pulling me off to the side. As I got my paperwork out, another guard unzipped my bag. He riffled through it for a moment and then pulled something out and opened his hand.

It was a pair of brass knuckles.

"What the hell?" I said, scratching my head. "Those aren't mine."

This predated 9/11. It was the late 70s. But just like switchblades, knucks were still a no-no, and I was obviously in trouble.

The first guard radioed someone. In less than two minutes, there were three policemen on the scene.

"Honest, officers. Those are not mine."

They were looking me over. They checked my pockets and were digging through my wallet. They called my driver's license information in.

Great, I've been set up by that hideous chick from Lord of The Rings, and now I am going to miss my flight.

Missing my flight also meant pissing off my boss, as well as a loss of a pretty decent payday from Harley. Just before they dragged me away for questioning, Bill Watts backtracked. He pulled my butt out of the fire.

I don't know if she planted the brass knuckles in my bag as a favor to help me in one of my future fights, or if she was trying to get me caught for not accepting her disgusting oral offer.

"Thanks, Bill," I said.

"Did you learn your lesson?"

"Yes. Next time," I said to Bill, "I think I'll just take the blowjob."

We made the flight.

It is rumored that my Louisiana run was cut a little short when someone deliberately tried to hurt me. Porkchop Cash, who many say was just jealous of me for one reason or another, dropped me on my shoulder. Now, I usually don't have a whole lot to say that is negative about people, but from what others say today, he took it upon himself to injure me and to try and take me out of the business.

To this very day, I have never had the downtime to get it fixed. I have had to deal with this injury all my years. I just never had a full year that I could afford to take off. If you take a year off from the business, it is always possible that and you are putting the kibosh on your career.

Working in pain, I eventually gave my two-week notice. They wanted me for one more TV appearance to job me out one more time. Feeling bitter, I refused.

Watts withheld my pay and I left the territory completely broke.

I went to Oregon and multiple territories to make some quick money to pay the bills. Then, I started to think creatively about what I could do to make some good money again.

CHAPTER 7 – EARLY WWF

Being in favor with the promoter, Hulk pulled some strings and called in a favor. Wanting me back on the road with him, the Hulkster asked Vince McMahon Sr. to bring me in to help give me some more experience in front of a bigger crowd.

Because Hulk was in favor now, hiring me was a done deal. Come June of 1980, or so, I was back over to New York ready to wrestle again, this time as Eddie Boulder. Now, they weren't giving me a big television push or anything of the sort, but they did put me right to work on house shows. They literally just threw me in the ring, wherever they could. I wasn't winning every night, but I wasn't totally just jobbing out, either. It was somewhere in the middle. They used me a bunch to get guys over, but would have me win here and there so a victory over me could still kind of mean something, rather than one over a no-name "Joe Blow."

In the old days, you would get paid right on spot every night. This was good because I needed to get up some money for my new place. I picked up some competitive matches, as enhancement talent. That meant I was there to make someone else look good, but they didn't just squash me out. I got some offense in and looked pretty good in the ring. I was working in Hartford, Springfield, Cape Cod, places like that, all getting some experience - and not hurting myself in the eyes of future promoters in regards to getting hired elsewhere and still looking strong.

One of the first nights, I remember seeing Arnold Skaaland come in the locker room at the end of the night. He was the money man. He would walk over to each guy and pay them off, right there in cash.

The way they paid guys never really seemed to make sense to anyone. It was supposed to be some kind of mathematical formula based on your spot on the show and also the gate (ticket revenue.) In reality, they hooked up the guys they liked and slighted the ones they didn't.

I watched Arnold pay his regular crew of enhancement guys. He paid Johnny Rodz, Jose Luis Rivera, and maybe another guy. Then he came over to me. He intentionally turned his body to position himself in such a way that nobody could really see what I got.

It looked like a pretty good amount of bills. I knew it was a lot more than the other guys who were actually their regular guys. I quickly pushed the money into my pocket without looking at it and thanked him.

As the locker room cleared out, I met up with Hulk so we could drive out together and go get something to eat. We had a big cooler in the back of his car with sandwiches and yogurt in it, but I wanted something hot, something good.

A few of the guys were still packing up, but the locker room was mostly empty. Hulk pulled me into the hallway and looked around to make sure the coast was clear.

"So, how did you do?"

"The match went just fine," I said, knowing he didn't mean that.

"Brother," he pushed me on the shoulder. "What did they give you?"

I reached into my pocket, unrolling the bills for the first time. At this point, I never really counted the money right in front of the promoter. I felt like that was rude for some reason. I don't know why. I would always put the money in my pocket and look at it later. After a few years in the business, however, that practice eventually changed.

I counted it. There was $500. My eyes lit up.

"Holy shit," I said. "Five hundred for that?"

"Shhh! Don't you tell anyone, brother!" he said smiling, looking around to make sure nobody heard. "Guys here with deals have been here for years and still only get $200."

Clearly, they were hooking me up as a favor to Hulk. Extra money? Who was I to argue?

I worked all over the place for Vince, Sr. at this point. I worked with a lot of the big names and tried my absolute hardest to make them look good. I worked with guys like Pedro Morales and Bruno Sammartino. Bruno didn't care for Hogan, but he was super nice to me. He knew I was trying to make guys look good. One time, he even put me over in his hometown in Pittsburgh. I have total respect for that guy. He never tried to belittle the competitive enhancement guys.

I was still more or less freelancing and not really officially in the territory. This was five years before I would be called Brutus Beefcake, or be part of the Dream Team with Greg Valentine. I continued to work for New York for several months as an extra here and there.

I drove a lot for Hogan to shows in like Massachusetts and Maine, knowing soon I would have to take a little break to rehab my shoulder. I wasn't in the best shape at this time because it was tough to work out. I was pretty beat up. Hulk's green Lincoln at this point was also starting to show some wear and tear, as well. It needed some work. We were driving like 2,000 miles a week and working like 28 days out of 30 in a month.

Finally, a little break came. I liked making the money, but I welcomed some days off when Terry got a call from Japan. I dropped him off at Kennedy Airport and decided to take a sabbatical from the ring to give my shoulder some rest. I gave the car a tune-up and got all set to drive back to Florida.

The Tampa River Raft Race was something I always looked forward to. It would also be nice to contact some old friends.

MOONS OVER MY HAMMY

It was always a big event when I came back home to Tampa. I loved the sights and the smells. It just looked like home. Terry was in Japan, so I was driving his Lincoln, which by now we called "The Big Green Placadyl," because it looked just like a pill.

I met up with some old friends, as planned. We went down to watch the annual raft races and had a great old time. We were drinking and eating sandwiches, you know, just catching up on things. They were telling me who was sleeping with who. I was telling them about life on the road.

I went over to one of the boat owners cooler to grab another beer, and there she was. She had a little-bit-of-nothing bikini top on that was practically see through. I could see the outline of her nippys and everything!

"Hey Eddie," she said.

I immediately recognized the voice. It was Sally, and she was more drop-dead gorgeous than even before. Sally was the older sister of my high school sweetheart's best friend.

"Hey, Sally. How are you? Last I heard of you, I thought you were having a baby?"

She bit her lip a little and turned away. "Oh yeah. I did."

"Wow! Well, you look great."

"Thanks," she said, kind of undressing me with her eyes. "You, too." Flirting 101.

Last she saw me, I was just a scrawny bastard still dating Jessie Borden. However, I went from 165 pounds soaking wet with a brick in my pocket to something much different. As Eddie Boulder, I was all jacked up at 250 pounds. I had long blonde hair and a handlebar mustache that looked like something out of a Harley shop.

"Oh, you noticed," I said in a put-on effeminate voice, pretending to blush.

"I'm not really the mom-type though, you know. Not very maternal."

"No?"

"Yeah, my sister, Sarah, raises the baby. It was too much for me. I'm just not cut out for it," she confessed. "You want to go out and get some drinks and catch up?"

I really didn't know Sally at all. Her sister was friends with my ex-girlfriend, but that was it. We had barely ever spoken before, so there was nothing really to catch up about. The obvious come-on was pretty forward, but I didn't care. This girl was smoking hot.

We went out on the town. We hit up a number of bars, dancing and drinking. We had a good time. We got more and more buzzed and more touchy-feely. We made out a little on the barstools. There was a little groping, perhaps. Who knew that not being on Terry's tour in Japan was actually going to turn out okay?

What I didn't know was that while we were enjoying ourselves all night, someone was following us. That's right. Each bar we went into, upon our exit, someone was showing up and just missing us, then going up to the bartender and asking questions.

After a few more watering-holes, we got pretty intoxicated. Whatever happened after that, I don't even know. The rest is all a little blurry.

SLAM!

I popped out of bed, ready to fight a burglar. I looked around. It was not my place. It was not my hotel room. I didn't know where I was. I read the numbers off the clock. It was almost three in the morning. My head was spinning. I had drunk enough beers to kill a horse and really had no idea what was going on.

"Hello?"

I looked down. I was buck-naked. I heard some arguing downstairs somewhere. I heard a door slam, again. Then it slammed another time and I heard some glass break.

"What in the hell?"

I postured by the door to see if I could get a better listen to hear what was going on. I could just barely make out a man's voice shouting over Sally's.

"Sally…" I said, regaining my bearings. It all came back to me.

I knew from experience that I needed to cover up my balls and get the hell out of there.

By this point, I'll be the first one to admit that I was not an amateur. I had become an equal opportunity lover. Whether she had sheets or not and was at a low tax-bracket made no real difference on whether or not I would sleep with a girl. It also meant this wasn't the first sheet-less bed I had slept in of what was, perhaps, the house of a married woman! Girls with significant others didn't make a difference to me either. I just wished she had warned me at first so I could have had an escape plan mapped out.

"Wait. Is he still in the house?!" A voice bellowed up from below the floor.

I immediately started looking for my clothing, but they were nowhere to be found. I believe the trail of my attire started off in the living room and dwindled into nothing but a sock or two long before we got to the bedroom.

"No, no! Stop! Put that down!" Sally cried. "Don't you hurt him!"

I went into survival mode. Finally, I said, "Screw it. Any clothing will do." Just as I was about to shimmy into a pair of Sally's sweatpants, she stopped me and motioned under the lip of the mattress. Following her lead, I stumbled onto a medium man's shirt marked "Tampa Fire" and a matching pair of gym shorts. They were folded nicely in a stack just under the corner of the bed. Knowing she lived alone, I didn't like the idea that there was an "Emergency Cheater's Getaway Kit" right there waiting for me.

This bitch has done this before!

I was way too big for the clothing. The camel-toe constriction in my crotch was almost unbearable. Before making a bee-line to the window for my escape, I caught a glimpse of my ridiculous pathetic reflection in the mirror.

"I'm getting too old for this," I said.

I tried for a moment to adjust my outfit and realized that nothing fit. I was already pulling down the back of the T-shirt to try and cover up the 75 percent of exposed ass that was showing from shorts I couldn't pull up all the way.

"Run!" I heard Sally scream, followed by footsteps coming up the stairs.

Run? There was nowhere to run. "Jump" would have been the better word. That or "drop," maybe.

I threw up the window. Just before I went for my dive, I noticed a red silk house jacket and grabbed it to complete my outfit. Still, with a bum shoulder, I dropped down to a patio below. One thing you can say about wrestlers, they have an incredible threshold for pain. I jarred my shoulder on impact, but figured that was nothing if her husband had a gun.

I ran out of the two-family apartment and down the little alley. To sidestep injury, I quickly put on some ugly flip flops that I found on the porch. It worked, but just barely. I jogged down to the parking lot as fast as my sandaled feet would carry me, over broken glass and beer bottles.

I pulled on that bathrobe. It barely cleared my shoulders. I sprinted to my ride in the parking lot. Just like Bo Duke, I slid over the hood of the big green pill, picked the self-inflicted wedgie, then dropped behind the wheel. I looked in the mirror. A shadow in the moonlight was still running my way, and he had something that looked like a pipe that he was swinging over his head.

"Shit!" I said, reaching for my keys in an invisible pocket.

You guessed it. My keys were in my pants back in Sally's living room. I had nothing to defend myself with, and I wasn't dressed properly for a street fight. I fumbled around Terry's car, frantically, looking for a spare key. I felt under the seat and no dice. I opened up the glove compartment, and no dice either.

"I'm going to kill you!"

BAM!

The passenger side window exploded. Glass shattered and went everywhere. Next, there was another crash as the back window also fell victim. Shards of glass flew everywhere and pinged me in the back of the neck.

It was Riley Williams. He was a martial artist, first-degree black belt. I knew him well. Back in the day, he was constantly in trouble because of fighting. He loved to drink. This guy and alcohol was a bad mix. He was always in trouble. The only reason they never threw the book at him was that his uncle was a big name for the Hillsborough County sheriffs and kept bailing him out.

I needed someone to bail me out right now, badly. I turned and looked through the missing window. A huge blade came zipping down through the hood and into the frame of the door. I saw my reflection in the stainless steel.

Riley wasn't hitting Terry's car with a pipe. He was chopping through it with a fucking *Samurai sword!*

While Riley was trying to dice up the big green pill mobile, Sally was crossing the Dale Mabry Highway, where the Raymond James Stadium now stands. It was a busy main artery that ran north to south. She was trying to make her way to Little General convenience store to call the cops.

I didn't have a second to spare. Instead of waiting around to see Riley's sword skills, I pushed open the door. I started running as fast as I could toward the trees at the end of the lot. Riley ran over to the driver door and chops into the steel, breaking even more glass.

Feet don't fail me now!

I put those bullshit flip-flops to the test. Behind me I heard Riley yelling, "Hulk, or no Hulk, I'm going to kill you, Terry!"

Then, I realized it. Terry's car was well-known in Tampa. I now had the hair and the mustache. *That son-of-a-bitch thinks I am Terry!*

The idea that I was Hulk probably made it even worse. A guy like Riley was probably also jealous of Terry's success, let alone the fact that someone was squeezing his main squeeze. That would make him even angrier, thinking that a big ole' rock-n-roll wrestler was the one coming along to take his woman.

I made it through the darkness of the trees. I took one step into the parking lot and could see safety. Next door to Sally's apartment building was everyone's favorite 24-hour breakfast restaurant, Denny's. I ran right into it, thinking that crazy bastard wouldn't follow me in swinging his Castle of Grayskull sword like He-man.

Yes. I was dressed in clothing way too small for me and wearing one of Sally's bathrobes, and I ran right in without any reservations. The whole place went silent. All the vagrant patrons looked at me like I was an asshole, which is pretty ironic since those who patron Denny's in the middle of the night are usually the dregs of society themselves, but I digress.

I was standing in the lobby looking for a weapon among Penny-Savers and business cards. The only thing in sight that I figured I could use for an equalizer was one of those bank rope dividers. I unhooked the rope, grabbed the silver post, and turned it around in my hands ready to light him up. I was ready to hit a home run the moment he walked in the door.

He never came in. His buddy Marty was waiting for him in a Corvette. He scooped him up just in the nick of time. It wasn't five minutes later before the lot was full of cops.

I put the post down gently and hooked the rope back into the socket. I looked in a mirror by the door. I looked ridiculous. I tried to regain my composure. I smoothed the ruffled frills down of my housecoat down the best I could and tied the belt. Then I adjusted my hair. I went in and found a seat.

I sat down all calm in the closest booth. I picked up the menu and held it up to my face. A waitress walked over. I no-sold the whole thing like nothing happened.

"I'll take the moons over my hammy," I said.

I knew damned-well I didn't have my wallet, but I didn't care. When the bill came, I could always just wash dishes, or pose with the cook for some Polaroids, waist up, of course.

I woke up the next morning at Sally's. It wasn't that I was looking for more trouble. The car was trashed, and I really had nowhere to go. Riley's buddy, Marty, eventually called me and begged me not to press charges.

"Come on, Eddie. He didn't know it was you. He thought you were Hulk, I swear. He has heat with him for something else too at the gym," he said. It made sense. I had been growing out my hair like him and everything for an upcoming wrestling gimmick.

"Okay," I said. "But listen, Hulk is in Japan. You need to fix his car. Everything."

Riley made good. They fixed Hulk's car. I wound up hanging out with Sally for another week. One afternoon while she was working at her car rental job, I got a call from the sword-slinger himself.

We met up and sat down for some breakfast at the very same Denny's I had taken sanctuary. We talked it out and became friends. I learned that Sally was evil. She was as heel as they come. She was one of those girls that loved to cause heat with you and break up, only to get back together again. She was all about head games with Riley and making him jealous. She would like call him to hang out, then not be there, and be over in the bar shooting pool with some other guy, just hoping to get caught – stuff like that.

Once I learned her game, I left that scene as soon as I could and never looked back.

I would like to say, "All's well that ends well," but that isn't the case for this story. Maybe six months later, after he thought he had patched everything up with Sally again, she started up with the head games, once again. She stood him up and made him lose his mind all over again, flirting with someone else. She was brutal. She screwed with his head so bad, that he just couldn't take it anymore.

One day, he sadly decided that he was going to make his final statement to her to make her see the evil of her ways. He went way up in a parking garage in front of her work and jumped off. He fell 100 feet down, and his body hit a cable that pretty much ripped his body in two. His calculation was perfect. His dead corpse dropped all gored, right in front of her desk window where she worked.

There was a huge pile of blood and intestines all over the sidewalk. The funny thing is, she never saw the results of her cruelty.

She had called in sick that day to hang out with some other guy.

This is many years before "The Barber," but I still had arguably the most stylish and best hair in the sport.

This picture was taken right around the time Terry first started using the name "Hulk" after an interview with Lou Ferrigno.

CHAPTER 8 - AWA

I did a little bouncing around in the territories at around this time in my career. I was driving around with whomever I could to learn whatever I could to get better. My idea was that the more I knew, the more money I could make in the business.

In the first part of 1981, I went down to Memphis and worked for Jerry Jarrett again for a few months. There, I tagged up some with Eddie Gilbert. I also had some matches opposite Jimmy Hart and his team, Ali Hassan & The Angel.

At the time, I was crashing with Hector Guerrero at his trailer park. Terry flew in to see me in Nashville and told me about his movie deal. He went and shot his scenes and then, Rocky 3 came out with Hulk Hogan in it. That changed everything. Hogan had become a household name and could get pretty much whatever he wanted. After that, Verne Gagne called Hulk and he started working in Minneapolis.

Then, they called me up and made me a really good offer as well. They told me to pack up my bags and come to work at the AWA, in Minneapolis. So I drove the car all the way from Tennessee down to Tampa, picked up some of my stuff, and then headed off to Minneapolis.

From August to November in 1981, I was set to work for Verne Gagne and the AWA. The difference was that this time I was going to play the bad guy.

After they split us up in Charlotte, Terry started wrestling some as Hulk Hogan and also some as Sterling Golden. Playing off of the split up, and mostly because people thought we really were brothers, my name went through some changes too. I was Eddie Boulder, Eddie Hogan, Eddie Golden, Dizzy Golden and even Dizzy Hogan, depending on what the particular promoter felt like. The name Dizzy, or Dizzy Head, really came from Terry Funk. He just started calling me that after a rough night of drinking once, and the name stuck.

For two or three months, I drove around with Jerry Blackwell and Baron Von Raschke, to learn the art of being the heel.

Nicknamed "The Mountain from Stone Mountain," Jerry Blackwell started his career in the 1970s. Despite being a super heavyweight at sometimes almost 500 pounds, Blackwell was a very nimble and gifted worker, able to throw a great standing dropkick! He was also given the name "The Rattlesnake," because of his quick speed and aggression in the ring. He had a very different style and was a legitimate bad ass.

Jerry Blackwell had seen it all. It was good for me to get some info from him on rides and learn about how to work heel. He had been there and done that and was the epitome of what you would consider a grizzled ring veteran. This is how we learned back then. You would ride with one of the old-timers in a territory and really pick his brain. You would get in that car and open shop. Class would start the moment you started the trip, and the bell wouldn't ring until you made it to your destination.

Blackwell, himself, was known for his ridiculous feats of strength. One of the most famous stunts that he did sometimes during live interviews was to hammer nails into 2x4s using nothing but his head. Blackwell pounded a lot of his opponents like a hammer. Blackwell became a main event star in the AWA. He feuded with guys like Mad Dog Vachon and was also working with Hulk Hogan, too. (He would eventually become Hulk's replacement, in the future, taking his top AWA spot when Hulk would leave to go work for Vince.)

Jerry Blackwell and I would take trips from Minneapolis, Minnesota to Wisconsin. I remember on one of our trips, we were talking about some methods of really getting the crowd to hate you, when out of nowhere, we came within inches from nailing a deer. We spun out. I just sat there for a moment, and we watched probably twenty deer hop our hood and run to the other side of the road. That wasn't it, either. The whole night was a whitetail obstacle course. We saw even more deer on the road on way back from the show. I started counting. 10, 15, 20 at a time. We counted over 100 deer that night. We asked Verne the next day and he said the reason was is that there was no deer hunting allowed in Wisconsin at that time. The deer were smart. They would hear the gunfire and new it was that time of the season again. Then they would migrate to Wisconsin where they wouldn't see any hunters like they did in Minnesota.

Hulk Hogan was already on this tour, so it was cool to catch up with him. Terry and I shared an apartment right by Minneapolis St Paul International Airport. This particular place catered to a lot of flight attendants who were in and out of town, and other airline people for Northwest. We were probably seven minutes or so from the airport grounds.

The gym we went to was on Lindale Avenue, right off the highway. It was an old, old gym. It smelled like body odor and vomit. Paint would chip off of the ceiling and fall into your hair while you were lifting. It was always like 20 below zero outside, and it was a rundown little place with a cold draft. But all the muscle heads called it home. The Road Warriors and Nord the Barbarian used to go there - a bunch of them did.

There was also a place called Burnsville Bowl. It was located just over one of those bridges that collapsed in more recent days, the I-35W that killed 13 people and injured 145. That was also one of our big hangouts. After TV tapings a bunch of us would head over there, get drunk and wreak havoc. I remember we would play with Crusher, Mad Dog, Bobo Brazil, and Buck Zumhofe. They had midnight bowling so it was perfect. All night, we would just shoot balls down the lanes, and also down some of the girls in the parking lot, upon request. (You have to cut us some slack on this one. It was friggin' cold in that town! We needed to keep warm, some way!)

Minneapolis really had cold winters though. I remember, one time, we had been practically snowed in for three days watching movies after movies after movies. It was like a whiteout. I told Terry I couldn't take it anymore so we decided to head out to the Caboose bar, down the road. It was like a blizzard. We didn't have a dog sled, so we put on our snowshoes and jumped in the Lincoln. There was a foot and half of snow and we just plowed right through it. We did donuts the whole way there. When we finally pulled up to the bar, the snow was so high, we saw people shoveling the sidewalk just to be able to open the door.

"We better just go back," I said. So we turned around and we didn't even go in.

That was what Minneapolis was like.

Greg Gagne, the promoter's son, hated me. Whether he will admit it or not, back then, he was a huge Hulk Hogan fan and Terry wouldn't hang out with him. Greg was annoying. He was always kissing Hulk's ass. He was always following him around a lot and just not really fun to be around. The way he looked at him was, he was a bit of a nerd. I mean, don't get me wrong, he was a good wrestler, but he was like 180 pounds. We just thought he was never going to be a Madison Square Garden-type wrestler, working at that caliber, so Hulk didn't waste his time with him.

With me in the territory, Hulk just didn't have time for Greg. He was more about catching up with me and all, like the old days. Because of that, Greg got jealous and got me fired.

One match I was in Milwaukee. I was hanging out with the boys in the locker room and Greg came over.

"Hey Dizzy," he said. "We want someone to come out and do a run-in to take a backdrop in the main event."

"Sure no problem," I said. "I'd love to do a spot in the main event, if I'm making some of that main event money!"

Now it was quite obvious that I was ribbing him when I said that to Greg Gagne. It was very clear that I was going to do the spot and I was not really asking for money. But after I said that, they shipped me right out.

Greg later told people that I wasn't kidding around and that I really wanted more money. But the real reason was that he was jealous of my friendship with Terry! He was acting like a bitch, like a jealous girlfriend who didn't want her man hanging out with an ex. Very lame. Very Jim Barnett.

AWA RETURN

After I left, I went to Japan. Terry stayed in the AWA for some time doing his "American Made" gimmick. He wore all red, white and blue. He carried the flag. He made some good money for AWA and Verne with that. (This was just before Hogan left for WWF, as the Real American. There he would transition over to the yellow and red.)

After some really great experiences in Japan, I came back to the AWA for a huge stadium card called AWA Super Sunday 83. The event was held on April 24, 1983, at the St. Paul Civic Center, St. Paul, Minnesota, with 20,000 plus people.

There had been a few AWA stadium shows before this one, but most were pretty average and never filled the place. This one was the first real big one, however, due to, in part, the main event; Hulk Hogan versus the long time AWA champion Nick Bockwinkel. It had a double main event of course, the other of which was a required Greg Gagne tag match to fulfill the tradition of nepotism in wrestling.

Super Sunday took place before the first real annual big event of sorts before pay-per-view even existed. NWA's Starrcade '83 by Jim Crockett Promotions would come later that year on November 24, 1983 and was available only on closed-circuit television. (WWF's WrestleMania, of course, was the first annual professional wrestling pay-per-view event. That would take place two years later on March 31, 1985, at Madison Square Garden in New York City.)

AWA's Super Sunday was certainly one of the biggest shows for me ever at the time and one of the biggest ones of that time.

It was dark. Wrestling shows back then didn't have the crazy lighting like they do today, although AWA had some. I walked out of the curtain. I looked around dazed for a moment. It was just like waves and waves of people. I looked directly into a light and then at the indistinct shadow of an Indian coming towards the ring, after me.

Gene Okerlund was the ring announcer. He announced our match for the card; *Wahoo McDaniel vs. Dizzy Ed Boulder.*

Wahoo was a guy who got over for his character and toughness. His in-ring work was not about scientific moves and all. He was a brawler. Amongst the boys in the back, Wahoo was known for one thing and that was being stiff. In short, he hit hard. He liked me though,

Wahoo McDaniel was my opponent for my first big marquee show, AWA's Super Sunday.

so everything was fine. I worked old-school with him, which he loved. But if you crossed Wahoo, he didn't care who you were, you were in for a mess.

One time when Wahoo was a heel in the Carolina's NWA Mid-Atlantic, a fan plucked and snatched one of the feathers out of his headdress. With the feather in hand, he tried to disappear into the crowd, but Wahoo wasn't having it. Wahoo had just purchased that piece to add to his costume and, boy, was he pissed. He jumped the rail and went after the fan. The stupid fan at least had enough common sense to run away from him and rightfully so. Wahoo was screaming bloody murder.

While running for his life, the fleeing feather bandit ran right into a corner. Wahoo backed him up, and continuously knife-edge chopped the fan over and over until he went down. After the fan hit the floor, Wahoo took his feather out of his grubby hand and poked it back into his headdress. The audience loved it. Then, he just went and had his match like nothing happened. When the match was over, the EMTs were putting the fan on a stretcher, when Wahoo was going back to the locker room. Wahoo saw red, and he went back over and chopped the fan again on the stretcher!

I was in great shape for this high-profile match. Jerry Lawler also jumped in for commentary which helped. This helped lead me to WWF days. I was jacked with a tan and the long blonde hair; exactly what Vince was looking at for the expansion of his New York territory.

There was a buzz around this show that Hulk Hogan might have been set to beat Nick Bockwinkel for the AWA title. It was the perfect kind of match to finally change the title and usher in new young talent. But that's not what they did. The AWA didn't take the risk and subsequently missed the boat on Hulkamania and its potential earnings.

The problem was that Verne Gagne didn't want to change the AWA's old school style. He didn't like the idea of rock-n-wrestling. Also, Verne didn't want to share merchandising with Hogan, who was hot off his Rocky appearance. Verne said no to splitting the merchandise profits, so Hulk went back to Vince. This was perhaps a bad business decision by Gagne. Any money they lost in the merchandise would have easily been made up by additional revenues from house shows or the additional merchandise they would sell overall because of Hogan.

The bad business decision by the AWA turned out good for Hogan, and also good for me.

A lot of the pieces of the puzzle were starting to fall together for me. I was taking off and getting in good with the bookers in New Japan. I was just accepting a tour in CWA over in Austria with Otto Wanz, a huge international name.

I also had friends working in New York, which was vastly expanding and soon to take off. In New York, Vince McMahon was about to break all of the territorial rules and try to run his promotion all across America, using his syndicated show as a national commercial for his product. This meant big money and guys like Terry Funk and Terry Bollea could easily pull for me to get a spot. That is how it worked back then. Your former partners and opponents who worked well with you would tell the promoters who to hire.

Things were looking good.

CHAPTER 9 - PNW

From December 1981 to August 1982, I would wrestle in Portland as Dizzy Hogan. Doing more on my own as a singles wrestler at the start of this run, I knew I needed my own ride. After getting the call from Don Owens, I also knew I was going to be driving cross-country soon, and wanted to have a ride I could depend on.

Driving from Florida to Portland was going to be hell, so I figure, why not do it in style?

My parents were awesome. The helped me finance my dream car in Tampa to help me on my big journey to the other side of the country. That's when I bought my custom 1975 Datsun 280-Z. It was my first dream car; a two-door hatchback, 4 speed 6 cylinder. I dumped a whole bunch of money in it and did a bunch of work on it to get it ready for the trip. First off, I totally redid the motor. It was finished off in yellow and black. It had tinted windows and a spoiler on the back, with custom wheels. The front had bucket seats, but there were no seats in the back to give me all the room I needed for long trips.

Driving coast to coast was something else. It really gives you a unique perspective of what our country is like and how big it really is. I stayed in some real dives in the middle of nowhere.

Once I made it there, I rented an apartment in Clackamas. Clackamas is a nice place in a new developing area, just outside of Portland. Portland had a cowboy kind of feel to it. Being a beach bum with the long blonde hair, it wasn't long before I had a girlfriend. And then another, and then another.

That's right. I had three girlfriends - one in the morning to cook me breakfast, one in the afternoon for lunch, and one to tuck me in at night before I went to bed.

Amazingly enough, all of the parties were totally fine with our arrangement, too; the girls were the ones who suggested it. Honestly, I don't exactly know how I even stumbled into that situation, which admittedly is any single guy's dream. I guess it was just being in the right place at the right time. The three blondes were from Seattle, Washington and very into the rock-n-roll scene. They looked at me as being a rockstar of sorts, I guess. They were right, but one with a lot of friction burn, perhaps.

One day, the phone rang. It was Hulk, checking up to see how I was doing. He said it was 10 below zero in Minnesota where he was. He explained that he couldn't even get out of the house, because there was so much snow.

"So, enough about me," he said. "How are things there with you?"

I handed the phone to the first of three girls. She said something foul, and then passed it off to the next. Each of the three girls mentioned something filthy they wanted to do to me, or had already done. Finally, the last handed the receiver back to me.

"Does that answer your question?"

Hulk cussed me out like a dog.

PACIFIC NORTHWEST WRESTLING

From December 1981 to August 1982, I was booked to work with PNW.

The first version of the company was founded by Herb Owen in 1925, as the most Northwestern territory in the country. It became an NWA. The area really took off after Herb's son, Don Owen, made his version of Pacific Northwest Wrestling featuring most of the current top names in the business on a regular basis rotation. Not afraid to bring in top talent, Don Owen helped to make Portland one of the top wrestling territories between the 1960s to the 1980s.

Don Owens' Portland territory was known for its short trips and working regular weekly towns. The weekly schedule worked out mostly like this: Monday was a spot show somewhere, Tuesday was Portland, Wednesday was Seattle, Thursday was Salem, Friday was Eugene, Saturday was their Portland Live Event TV taping, and Sunday was another spot show. The regularity really helped a guy grow. While I was there, I was wrestling as Dizzy Hogan. I got some good camera experience because of that weekly TV taping every Saturday night in Portland. Much like the Sportatorium in Florida, we wrestled to a very small crowd of maybe 100, but the place always looked totally packed.

The locker room consisted of Rocky Johnson, Brett Sawyer, Stan Stasiak, Buddy Rose, Steve Pardee, Chris Adams, Rip Oliver, Mike Miller, and David Schultz to name a few. As far as the locker room was concerned, I hit it off pretty well with just about everyone.

Using the word "brother," really meant something to the wrestlers. A lot of us guys would see each other even more than our own families, so it was like we were hanging with someone more than just a guy we had to work with. This is why we looked after each other so much.

Here is an early Dynamite Kid (right) hanging at a show with Rip Oliver (left).

Rip bought a small camper just to beat up and drive the boys around in. It could fit two in the front and 4 or 5 in the back. We would all throw in for gas and he would drive us to Medford, Oregon some 300 miles away, the Yakama, Washington about 250 miles away. Down to Olympia & Tacoma, and then over to Seattle for one real big show a month. We would also cross over the border to Vancouver in Canada.

Rip was a funny guy, for a while, he had a gimmick going on that he called "The Rip Oliver Carry-Out Service." He went and got a stretcher with those words airbrushed on it. Whenever he or one of his heel buddies injured someone, they'd bring the "Carry-Out Service" stretcher to the ring. They would carry out the wrestler and laugh.

One time, I heard Rip was talking about doing the stretcher thing with Stan Stasiak.

Stan was in the locker room and had a towel wrapped around his waist. He didn't often change in front of the boys, but some of the older guys just didn't. Nobody ever thought much of it, except for maybe a guy like Jim Barnett, or maybe Patterson.

"Not sure it would work with Stan," he said.

"Why is that?" I asked.

"Because I don't think we could fit his enormous balls on the stretcher?"

Stan looked up. He kept an emotionless, straight poker face and continued to dry off his feet and get his socks ready.

"Oh, Stan's got the big one?"

"Not penis," Rip said, winking at me. "HE IS ALL BALLS."

"Big, giant balls?" I asked.

"The biggest," Rip said. "One time when we were over in Africa, Stan was changing. When he took off his pants, all these naked pigmies came running out of nowhere. I think they could smell 'em, or something."

"Really?"

"Yeah. They tried poking his nuts with giant spears, probably thinking they were giant poisonous blowfish, or something."

"Phssshhh," Stan snorted. We could see he was getting really irritated by our conversation, but he didn't want to yell. He just did that huffing thing where you exhale sharply through your nose out of frustration, when you are beyond disgusted.

Rip and I laughed. I had never heard the big balls thing with Stan before, even though I had worked with him quite a bit. After this, all the guys started hitting him with giant balls jokes.

One day, Rip was driving his camper. We were jabbing Stan about his testicles again, and he just couldn't take it anymore.

"Come on, Stan," one of the boys said. "Take 'em out."

"Let's see those big ole' beach balls," laughed another.

"That's it. Stop the bus, Rip," he said, getting red in the face. "Pull over!"

Not knowing if he was going to challenge someone to fight over the ribbing, or just run off into the wilderness, we all tried to calm Stan down.

"Come on, Stan." I said. "It is just in good fun."

"No," he said. "Nooo! Pull over, now!"

Rip finally slowed down and pulled over. We were in the middle of nowhere. There weren't trees or anything, and it looked like an empty desert. Stan didn't care. He pushed open the door and got out.

Everyone shifted to an open window on the passenger side of the camper. We expected to see Stan storm off into the field in anger, but that isn't what happened. He took about ten steps away from the camper and stopped.

Then, before our very virgin eyes, Stan Stasiak undid his trousers and dropped trow.

With his pants to his ankles, we all looked at his bare ass. His knees held tight together and it just looked like a straight crack from the ground up to his waist. The whole busload started cheering and laughing, hysterically. Then, it quickly progressed to the moment of truth.

Stan spread his legs open.

We gasped.

His big ballsack unraveled. Two massive balls dropped below his knees, then coiled and uncoiled again like a bungee cord. Once they slowed, we were amazed to see them settle at knee-level. His right nut hung lower than the left. It was magnificent. It looked to me like something you would see under a prize bull.

It was a legendary moment. We all looked at each other in disbelief, and then there was silence.

…Then the crowd went nuts.

DON'S BROTHER, ELTON

Within the same territory, there was a sub-territory of sorts in a small town called Eugene, Oregon. Don Owen's older brother, Elton ran it. The Eugene shows ran out of this little shithole of a building. There was usually maybe 200 people, if we were lucky and the pay was always horrible.

Elton was older than Don. He was a crusty old bastard who always had a nasty cigar in his mouth. He looked like a shriveled up Porky Pig with rosy cheeks. Elton was a character. He was all about seeing a real fight, and was perhaps a little bloodthirsty. He also wanted his matches to feel like there was an element of realism, as part of the Portland style. Therefore, as a Eugene tradition, Elton would always ask the boys to attempt a "shoot" portion at the start of every match. This meant for the first 5 minutes or so, a segment of what the fans were watching was actually to be unrehearsed, real shooting.

If you won the shoot portion of your match, you would get an extra $5 -10 "shoot bonus." Now, this bonus probably sounded like a good idea in theory for whoever won the shoot, but that wasn't the case. In a real shoot fight, people get beat up real bad. This formula could equate to more black eyes, broken bones and, the possibility that you could possibly take time off to heal. Rather than to take that risk, the boys would work the shoot and just split all the bonus money. See, they would tell Elton the shoot was on, then fake the real portion of the match and just have one of the guys appear to win!

Elton would just eat it up.

Elton would often go back and forth between the heel and face locker rooms. He was also the ring announcer, so he was constantly running around and also liked to watch the shoots.

One time I remember, Elton had just taken out a brand new expensive cigar from its wrapper. He was just about to light it, when a match ended early.

"Those mother fuckers," he said, rushing to get his index cards together. That match was supposed to go at least another 6 or 7 minutes!"

Elton rushed out to ringside to announce the winner.

Playboy Buddy Rose came back into the dressing room. Someone stooged Elton out to Buddy, and told him that Elton said his match was over too quickly and that he was not happy.

"Fuck that little troll," Buddy said. As he said it, he noticed Elton's new cigar sitting on a table with paperwork. "Hey guys! Hey! Get over here!"

A handful of us gathered around to see Buddy pull his tights down and push the cigar into his sweaty asshole. Then, very carefully, he re-wrapped the new cigar and put it back into its capped cylinder container.

"Good as new!"

After the shoot spot, Elton returned. He headed back to his work table and wrote something on a piece of paper. Then, we all watched in horror as he unwrapped the stogie and stuck it in his mouth. As Elton continued to dart back and forth, he finally lit it up.

"Ug, you boys need to shower or something," he said. "It smells like shit in here."

The boys tried not to laugh.

NEW GUYS IN PORTLAND…

This was where a lot of young guys went to learn and get experience. There was a mix of veterans and rookies that afforded the young guy just starting out went to cut their teeth, get experience and get some good advice from some seasoned ring veterans.

I wrestled the great new-comer in one of his first matches ever while at my time in Portland. We were working in a little building in Eugene, which was a total dump that Don Owens never ever put money into. The ring really needed some work.

A normal ring has a ¾ inch thick padding with a tarp over it. On this particular night, I remember the padding had shifted and separated underneath the tarp leaving a bare pit that was about four inches wide - just wide enough so that your foot could get stuck in the crack between the pads. The new guy was working great for a new guy. His dad was watching from the curtain, and he was very pleased. I charged him. He hit me with two arm drags, and then he was ready to go for a scoop slam. So off of the ropes, he goes to scoop me, and his foot dropped down an inch into the canvas and caught in the trench.

He wrenched his knee hard, and we both collapsed.

I fell down from the air right on top of him. Now, he was supposed to be the new big guy coming in and was also supposed to win the match. I knew something happened.

We laid there a second on the mat and finally he said, "My knee is gone!"

"Give me a small package."

He did and we saved the match, but they had to help him to the back. They took him away to the hospital. Curt Hennig was out for like 6 months after that. His father, Larry the Axe stuck around for a few weeks to finish out his son's bookings for him, worked an angle with Stan and Buddy, before heading back to Minneapolis.

I also walked into a gym one day in Portland where Sivi Afi would go. I saw this really strong, big guy who was just lifting racks and racks of weights, and he was really impressive. I befriended him and we started working out some together. I brought him to the locker room with me before one of our shows to help him make some contacts. David Shultz got him booked for Stu Hart in Canada for training and eventually, they sent him back. Billy Jack Haynes made a pretty good name for himself and is now considered a legend in Portland.

DAVID SHULTZ

As a side note to the story above, "Dr. D." David Schultz was the guy who infamously hit that 20/20 reporter John Stossel who was questioning the validity of our livelihood. David may be one of the craziest, badass bastards I ever knew, but, man, he was always good to me.

I remember one time, I was tired as a dog. I was trying to get some sleep after a double-shot at a hotel in Nashville. Some fans had apparently followed us back from the show and knew exactly where we were staying. So I was just about to fall asleep and all of a sudden, they show up outside our door. They start carrying on, making all this noise, yelling at us through the walls. I tried to bury my head in a pillow to drown out the noise, but that didn't work.

David opened the door, went out into the hall with nothing but his shorts, a pair of flip-flops and a 357 magnum. Boy oh boy, did I sleep good after that.

ANDRE POOP STORY

One time, I was sitting at a card table planning the biggest game of cribbage ever. I was playing with the Eighth Wonder of The World, Andre the Giant.

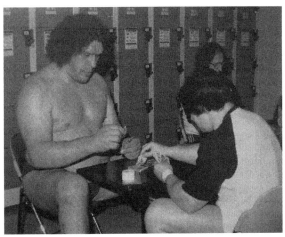

A bunch of the boys gathered around to watch the high-stakes card game. Quite often, Andre would play cards before matches, so this was not unlike any other time, except for the fact that we had a lot of money on the table.

Playing with Andre was ridiculous. His fingers were so big and thick that you could barely even see that there were cards in his hands. Take your hands and put both of your thumbs together. See how wide that is? Now that is how thick Andre's pinky was, alone.

While we were playing, we could hear one of the wrestlers over in the bathroom-side of the locker room just unloading.

"He is taking a nasty shit," Andre said, as I laughed.

We continued to play our game, when all of a sudden, a horrible series of farts where followed by a horrible series of splashes. A few seconds after that, the whole place smelled like the worst pot roast in the world.

All the boys started yelling at the person behind the booth walls making the offensive stench.

While I was still playing cards with Andre, we heard the flush. I looked up to see just who was the crapping culprit. The pooper was done and to nobody's surprise, we watched the door swing open for the big reveal.

It was Playboy Buddy Rose.

"It took two flushes for all the shit to go down!" he said. "I didn't want you to miss it, so I saved one."

It was then that the obese pig of a wrestler decided to come out and terrorize all of his critics. He came charging right at our card table. All the boys looked and saw that he had something that was not favorable in his grasp, and we made a break for it. They all parted ways as Playboy Buddy Rose came barreling at us, holding a thick brown turd in his hand.

Fortunately for most of us, we were able to get up and get out of harm's way. However, Andre was so big that he could not just get up at a moment's notice and make a run for it. Being he was the only person left in the room, Buddy bellied right up next to him and pushed the shit into Andre's face.

"No, boss, no," Andre turned his face and grimaced. "Please, get the shit out of here."

Andre couldn't move. He twisted his large frame against the wall as the tasteless turdburglar continued to torture him.

Playboy continued to push his giant poo mercilessly under the giant's nose.

Later on that night, there was a big battle royal scheduled. And as many of you know, Andre the Giant was the king of the battle royals. We were all in the ring, and the match had started. Then for dramatic effect, Andre came down a minute or so late to a huge pop from the crowd. At this point, we had all but forgotten about Andre getting poop under his nose, but the giant had not...

Andre stepped into the ring and went right after Playboy Buddy Rose. The giant shoved Buddy down, face first right in the middle of the ring. Then, he sat his 600 plus pound ass on Buddy's shoulder blades, facing the back of Buddy's feet.

He raised his sausage-sized thumb high in the air for all of the boys in the ring to see, and then crammed it down deep into Buddy's asshole. Yes. He checked Buddy's oil.

Gasping for air, Buddy screamed for help. All the boys, myself included, wanted no part of that. We tried our very best not to break character and continued to fight around the proctology examination that was happening before our very eyes. I'll admit it. I couldn't stop laughing, watching Andre jam a knockwurst-like thumb into another man's ass with a shit-eating grin spread across on his face.

"Andre?! What are you doing?" Buddy cried.

"Just looking to see if you got any more of those turds in there, boss."

The funny part about it was, *I think Buddy actually liked it.*

ANDRE THE GIANT

Andre the Giant often had a rough life, and due to that, sometimes he wasn't the friendly giant that he appeared to be on TV. We always got along just fine, however, when life shit on Andre, he sat back – literally. He could get easily annoyed and often had a very nasty attitude when things didn't work out for him. For example, if a hotel bathroom was a little too tight for the abnormally large Andre, he would just take a big dump on the bed and wipe with the sheets.

I don't necessarily believe he was mean when he left a mess. Maybe he just didn't think sometimes, or maybe it was just survival. But I just felt bad for whoever had to clean that shit. The architects were the ones who didn't design a cheap hotel bathroom big enough for a 7-foot giant poop machine, not the maids. However, it had to have been hotel staff that had to find a creative way to clean Andre's massive shit mountain without an industrial-sized pooper scooper.

If you were among the lucky percentage of staff members who got the "friendly giant" at your hotel, that version of Andre would take the time to actually tie up the sheets and throw his dumpling wonton out into the hall for housekeeping. However, 99% of most maids were not that lucky. Most of them found what looked like an open face burrito in the bed, with extra refried beans to top it off.

I remember one tour I did with Andre, over in Japan.

We were all staying in the Keio Plaza Hotel in Tokyo for a show with Antonio Inoki. The place was top notch. It really was an ideal place, located right near super nice shopping attractions and some of the best entertainment spots in Shinjuku. This luxury hotel had a stunning view over central Tokyo that really was spectacular.

The hotel itself was lavish. I have no clue what New Japan was paying for it, but it had to be a lot. Quite often, they would spare no expense when bringing in the Americans. They wanted us to experience the very best and wanted us to return. They also wanted everyone to see that the wrestlers from the States were top-talent and lived the lavish lifestyle of a superstar.

I remember we were way up in like the 90th floor. There were fancy chandeliers everywhere, and expensive paintings. It was really quite the experience.

Anyhow, Andre the Giant didn't fit in most of their bathrooms, just as he didn't fit in any of the bathrooms of the airplanes that would fly us to and from the country. What he would have to do is actually plan everything out very strategically, to try and not have to make a bathroom visit even once while on the flight home.

We had just finished the tour for Inoki and were ready to fly out. Andre knew he had to take his pre-flight shit.

After he did, he met me in the lobby. As we were waiting for another one of the wrestlers to make our exit to the airport, it seemed like the chandelier in front of the desk started swaying. We didn't know if it was from a tsunami or an earthquake perhaps, but all of a sudden, the lights blinked and a siren went off.

Andre and I ducked and went for cover.

A siren sounded. All of a sudden, a team of four Japanese guys dressed in hazmat suits ran by us and went up in the elevator.

I rushed over to the front desk.

"What happened?" I ask, thinking the worst. Maybe it was a big storm? Maybe it was a bomb? I had no idea.

It turned out that it was none of that. What had happened was that the little mama-san maid went into Andre's hotel room to make the bed and fainted.

Another maid went into the room with one of those surgical masks on and pulled her out. They were not used to what she had just seen. When she took a look to see what caused the distress from the first maid, much to her surprise, Andre had just taken a fresh shit.

The sirens were going off and the hazmat team went up into the room to disinfect it, and to remove the 40-pound steaming mound of crap out of the bathtub.

That was one of the most hilarious things I had ever seen!

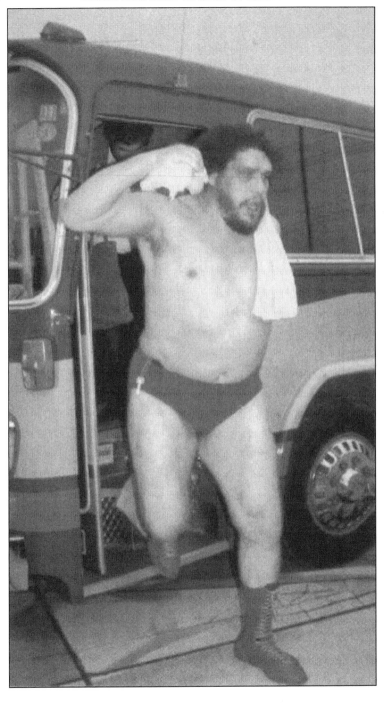

While Andre may not think twice about a maid having to clean up his cruelty-crap, he would go out to the ring and consciously destroy people he didn't care about, and if you pissed him off, you would get more than just a thumb up your ass. Andre would kill guys just about every night.

When green guys or jobbers were on the same card as Andre, they all would take a big breath before looking at the line up in the locker room before the show. If they saw their name next to his, many would often just leave and never come back.

You see, if you were enhancement talent and your name was next to Andre's on the card, it was like reading a death sentence. You knew he was going to destroy you. You would say a prayer and then make your last phone call ever, probably to a life insurance agent.

Nobody can fight the impulse to look at a train wreck. As an unwritten rule, the boys would always push and shove to get a glimpse through the curtain of what Andre was going to do to the new guy.

I don't know how many nights I saw Andre throw a guy down on the mat, stand on his hair, and pull him up by the arms.

LEAVING THE TERRITORY

I worked for Don and Elton for about year. We did really good business, but sometimes really good can actually be really bad.

Guys like Buddy Rose sometimes get a promoter's ear, and that can mean trouble. Buddy had Don Owens wrapped around his finger. A lot of the wrestlers get paranoid. That just goes with the business. Sometimes guys get nervous about losing a potential payday, or losing their spot. Being influential, if a guy felt threatened, he would just think of a way for the promoter to write the threat out of the picture, and that is exactly what happened to me.

That's when I headed to Japan.

CHAPTER 10 - NEW JAPAN

When I got cut in Portland because of the paranoid, turd-clutching Buddy Rose, it wasn't long before I found myself wandering around, looking to find my next meal.

When I first got booked for Antonio Inoki's wrestling promotion in Japan, I was in trouble. I had no idea what I was going to eat. I didn't like fish. I didn't eat sushi. I wasn't big on their soups.

Man. Am I going to lose a lot of weight on this trip, or what?

Fortunately for me, there was one dish. Looking to please American customers after WWII, the head chef of Hotel New Grand in Yokohama, Shigetada Irie, looked at some U.S. military rations and created a Japanese version of what they believed to be an American favorite. He called it "Spaghetti Napolitan." That dish was pretty much made up of spaghetti and ketchup with a little bit of chopped sausage for protein. Ketchup was regarded as a high-quality condiment in Japan well into the 1960s, and in that country, it never acquired the cheap down-market image that it has today in the West.

If it weren't for Spaghetti Napolitan, I probably would have died from hunger in my first trip to New Japan.

Hogan was on tour in Japan already by the time I had landed. It was nice to have someone there to help set me up with some accommodations to make the culture shock a little easier to endure. The first thing I was able to really enjoy was the luxury of having the perfect tour guide at my disposal.

Chaco was a beautiful Japanese girl. She was not as white-skinned as pretty much everyone else I would see in the country. She had a little color to her. She was darker like maybe she had some Korean blood in her, as well as Japanese. Anyhow, she was beautiful. She worked for an international modeling agency there and spoke perfect English. I mean, not even a trace of an accent!

My personal tour guide acted as a translator and helped get me around the city, during my downtime. First off, she took me around to find gyms, in a land that wasn't really big into bodybuilding and fitness. Gyms were very far and few between. She took me around to different restaurants and taught me how to order Spaghetti Napolitan. She really helped me tremendously.

I also had Masao "Tiger" Hattori. Tiger is a referee who has been involved in wrestling for over 35 years. He really knows wrestling. He was an amateur wrestler in college. He competed in All-Japan wrestling championships. He trained with Hiro Matsuda and Masa Saito, then made his referee debut in 1977 in the US. He joined Giant Baba's All-Japan in 1980 as an NWA-recognized referee, then moved over to New Japan in 1982. While I was there, Tiger acted as translator for the boys, and even a babysitter at times, to make sure that we didn't get ourselves into trouble.

The locker room wasn't all Japanese wrestlers. My tour also included some gaijin wrestlers like the Masked Superstar, Sgt. Slaughter, and Hulk, too. I got to wrestle Inoki and Fujinami, which was a real treat. But in a land where pro wrestling was a lot stiffer and hard-hitting, I really got lucky. Very early on working on my first Japanese tour, they put me in with the booker, Seiji Sakaguchi.

I remember Sgt. Slaughter coming up to me, when he saw my name across from "The Gooch" up on the wall.

"Hey, Dizzy," he said. "Don't hurt this guy. You can work him for like 5 or 6 minutes, very easy, and you are out. So easy you will love it."

Others concurred so that was the plan.

I wrestled Seiji Sakaguchi that night, and the boys were right. The Goochster didn't like to do much in the ring, at all. I had a decent old-school American-type match with him and put him over really big. Gooch was so excited!

I was instantly locked into a good spot for practically the rest of the entire tour. I was working with the booker all around the territory, in simple but solid 8-10 minute matches. All the boys were jealous that the new guy found a spot so quickly. Every night was a night off.

Japan was really exciting. For shows, we would all take the bullet trains to big cities, or ride in small busses to little cities. The bus rides were brutal. We would get up at seven in the morning, board the bus and usually not get there until about 2: PM or so in the afternoon. The way we survived all that driving was that we watched a lot of movies - a lot of the same movies, actually. I saw Rambo probably 18 times and can also quote all the lines from Young Frankenstein.

Everything in Japan was smaller. I felt like Godzilla when I decided to go for a jog. The mailboxes came up to my knees. The doorways came up to my neck. It was like I was living in midget-world for a while. Marty Jannetty, the king of midget hookers, would have loved it. One thing I really did like was that even in the smaller towns – there were beer machines. Even if there wasn't a place open to eat at night after a show, you could always get a big 25 ounce can of Sahi, or Sapporo beer.

Before I learned about yakitori houses on a later tour, I didn't have a whole lot of meat in my diet in Japan. Not being a big fish eater, it was a real treat when I could get a hold of a good piece of steak.

One night, I had a Yakuza sponsor at the Ribera Steakhouse in Tokyo. The Yakuza were a group of what some like to call the Japanese mafia. They were big fighting-sports fans and often had some good money to blow. A couple of guys asked if they could take me out to a steakhouse, and I couldn't accept the offer any faster.

When we entered the restaurant, I was in heaven. I could smell steak cooking and my stomach started to pop like it was a main event. They walked us back to a discrete little area in the back of the establishment and there were all kinds of the wrestlers' pictures on the wall. Let me tell you, that steak was one of the best I have ever had. I don't know if it was because I hadn't had very much more than a couple of crumbles of meat on my Spaghetti Napolitan since I got there, or if it was in fact that much quality or what. I was happy to have those guys treat me though, mafia-connections or not.

A Kobe beef steak could cost up to almost $300 in small towns, and I just wasn't making that much to warrant spending that much on one meal. I was making maybe more around $700 a week. $2500, a month. A $300 steak twice a week, and I wouldn't have anything left for beer. It was actually nice to have the Yakuza around to pick up a tab for me, from time to time.

MOB CONNECTIONS TO WRESTLING

Yakuza in Japanese loosely means, "Mafia."

Ever since pro wrestling began, you can trace back a relationship between organized crime and wrestlers. In America, there was a time when Bruno Sammartino was being "protected" by a couple of Italian brothers that he could not shake, and that he didn't want around. Rumor has it that he paid them a hefty sum for this protection. Do you think Bruno really wanted protection?

Another example worth mentioning was when Canadian wrestler Dino Bravo had his run-in with organized crime. Dino wanted to stay in the WWF, but at some point, Vince said that Dino just didn't fit into his plans anymore.

Dino was screwed. He was used to living the lifestyle. He had a crazy expensive sports car. He had a Mercedes. He had a huge home. The problem was, the WWF superstar paycheck came to an end. Dino wasn't an office employee kind of guy crunching numbers. Wrestling was the only thing he knew.

However, there was still a chance to have it all. Dino eventually got mixed up in some kind of cigarettes smuggling ring across the Canadian border that ended up leaving him with trouble. Dino was a nephew by marriage to a big Montreal crime boss named, Vic Cotroni.

Dino did a few jobs for his uncle and went to see the Indians to move some items. The Indians had the river so they could pass cigarettes, or drugs, or guns across it easily with nobody seeing. Here's the thing; the Indians were big wrestling fans. So when they saw Dino they recognized him and marked out. They wanted to deal strictly with him, direct. Because of this, Dino developed a monopoly with the Indians and he started making a lot of money for himself.

Because of Dino's notoriety from being a popular professional wrestler, he was able to attract even more customers to switch over to him. He became a super affordable supplier of illegal cigarettes. After a short time, his cigarette smuggling business did so well that the cocaine guys apparently went to see Dino and cut a deal.

Dino stored some massive $500,000 shipment in a warehouse somewhere. It apparently was only supposed to sit overnight, but ended up being there for longer than they had agreed on. After the third day or so just before the cocaine guys went to pick it up, the police found it and confiscated everything.

This, of course, pissed off the mafia. Dino and the mob members started blaming each other, pointing fingers about who was at fault. Dino's argument was that it was supposed to have been picked it up the very next day, and then it never would have happened.

According to various sources, Dino Bravo started giving away some personal belongings. It was clear that there was a lot of heat on Dino, and he didn't know what was going to happen to him. He also started trying to make peace with former rivals. When asked, Dino outright told a number of his close friends that he felt his days were numbered.

March 10, 1993, was a Wednesday. Dino's wife and his daughter went off to Ballet lessons. Dino was sitting in his favorite lounge chair at home in Vimont, Laval, Quebec. They say he was just there relaxing, watching a hockey game on his TV. Then, something unthinkable happened...

POP! POP! POP! POP! POP!

All of a sudden, 17 shots were fired. Many of them found their target. Seven bullets drilled into his head and another ten barreled into his chest and abdomen. It was horrible. Blood sprayed everywhere on the walls and on the ceiling.

Dino Bravo died instantly. He was 44 years old.

His wife found him later on that night when she returned. When she came into the house, she had their daughter in her arms, who was fast asleep. Fortunately for her, she didn't walk in and see her dead daddy.

The police reported that there was no forcible entry into his house. It was the winter, so they would have been able to see footprints in the snow outside leading up to a window or something. But there were not any, and apparently, whoever the killer was came through the front door.

Police believe the killer was likely someone who was watching hockey with him. The house guest must have got up, then shot him from behind when he least expected it. Reports show that "the remote control was loose in his hand." The thing is, forensic detectives say that when you get shot from the front and see the attack coming, you tense your muscles up. If it were a run-in situation, Dino would have gripped that remote very tightly at the moment of his death. This was just not the case.

Most believe that Dino's role in illegal cigarette smuggling in Canada directly led to his murder. Legend has it that his accomplice, Jos LeDuc, also learned a lesson about the mafia in Montreal the hard way. Some say that my former ring-mate from my Portland days also had a hand in that mess, and it too almost cost him his life.

Around this time, the mob found out LeDuc's partnership with Dino in his endeavors. They hunted him down, broke both of his legs, and also cut the top half of his ears off.

The Yakuza is an organized crime circle in Japan who has been found responsible for all kinds of violence and chaos in that country. They also have many accounts against them for smuggling, but that is not all. They deal in drugs, prostitution, the forced selling of stolen/shoddy goods, fixing fights, gambling rackets, and even forcing landowners to sell their land cheap so they can flip it for a profit.

I learned during my stay in Japan that the Yakuza is the real deal, and that you, by all means, want to stay on their good side.

GIVING YOU THE FINGER

In Japan, there is a symbol of apology after one makes a mistake, or acts in a way that is upsetting to his Yakuza leader. *Yubitsume* is a twisted form of Japanese mafia loyalty by means of dismemberment! Upon a first offense, the offender cuts off the tip of his left pinky and gives it to his boss as a peace offering.

The loyalty ritual continues at the cost of a new finger segment for each future shortcoming. Yubitsume starts with the tip of the pinky, then next moves next down to the knuckle, then finally down to the top of the palm. If there are more offenses, the cutting continues next on the ring finger, and so on and so forth, working backward all the way to the thumb.

This tradition stems back to the seventeenth century. The cutting origin stems from a subject's ability to hold a Japanese sword. The bottom three fingers of each hand are needed to grip the sword tightly, with the thumb and index fingers slightly loose. The removal of digits, starting with the little finger and moving up the hand, progressively weakens a person's grip on a sword. The idea was created so that a weak sword grip would force a Yakuza member to rely more on the group for protection—reducing misbehavior within the sect.

Many Yakuza members wish to appear tough to intimidate the weak. Some of the more important members have something known as "irezumi" in Japan. They are painfully hand-poked full-body tattoos created by inserting ink beneath the skin using hand-made tools with needles of sharpened bamboo or steel. And yes, from what I hear, these full body tattoos include genitalia. I can only imagine hand-poking your balls with a sharpened bamboo stick dipped in ink for hours; not my idea of a good time.

The Yakuza has been tied to shenanigans that often led to the forced success of wrestling promotions. Just like Bruno not being able to shake his unwanted bodyguards, sumo and wrestling promoters alike have often found new investors that they wanted no part in – but had no choice. One story that people often hear about is getting pulled over by bad police, who would actually force people to buy tickets to a wrestling show the Yakuza had some kind of investment stake in.

Many of the Yakuza would often take an American wrestler like myself out to eat to fancy restaurants. After all, most of them were wrestling fans - which was why they were connected to wrestling in the first place. In fact on a number of occasions, I let the Yakuza buy me dinners and answered their questions and posed in pictures with them simply because the dinners they offered were always top notch.

Buddy Landell once told a story about his dinner experience with Yakuza. Apparently, one evening, Buddy noticed a few of the employees at a fancy Yakuza-run restaurant had missing fingers. They placed a bowl of noodles in front of him and it was very clear that something was missing.

"How did that happen?" Buddy asked. "Was it a Ginzu accident chopping noodles back in the kitchen?"

One of the Yakuza then explained the Yubitsume finger offering ritual for serious offenses against the big boss. Later on that night, Buddy got out of the car and was greeted by one of the promoters for his big match. He ran up to Buddy, clearly excited, so Buddy grabbed his hand and shook it. While doing so, again, Buddy noticed that something was clearly missing.

The promoter was Yakuza. He only had three fingers on his hand.

"Goddamn!" he said, letting go of his grip. "Who the hell did you piss off?"

PRESS CONFERENCES & JAPANESE SHOPPING

Once you get off the plane for an NJPW tour, there isn't a lot of time for dining. Once you checked into your hotel, you didn't get to spend a lot of time there to shake off the jetlag. Inoki had your days planned out for you, on a rockstar-like schedule.

First off, you would have a big press conference right when you get there. Then, they would ship you right out on the road for more press. Now, don't get me wrong, they always flew me in first class and put me up in the best hotels. There was just a whole lot of running around, but after your obligations were up, you could find yourself a little downtime.

Shopping in Tokyo is an experience. Chaco helped me out tremendously. She took me into the subways and showed me exactly how to use public transportation. Unlike NYC which is auto-centric, Tokyo is rail-centric. This means that it was specifically designed and built for its population to move around by means of transportation via train. Learning this was huge because taking a cab around the city could quickly cost hundreds of dollars. I learned how to get from point A to point B on the subway for like 50 cents, or a dollar.

During one of my tours there, I remember that I wanted to get my mom a nice gift, because she was battling cancer. So Chako, the translator, took me to the Ginza International for shopping. She helped me get my mom a nice beautiful pair of pearl earrings.

After that, I told Chako that I wanted to buy some expensive stereo equipment for my Datsun, back home. I had done my homework and read that I could save hundreds, maybe thousands if I bought my stereo right in the country where it was made. So we left the touristy area and headed out to a real Japanese marketplace, Akihabara.

Akihabara is a district in central Tokyo that is famous for its electronics shops. In more recent years, it has gained even more recognition as being the center of Japan's otaku culture, devoted to anime and manga. It was an area in that time where only the Japanese did business.

Eventually, I found the right stereo for my Datsun car. Watching me negotiate had to be funny. I had this little calculator to translate money and I decided to let my language barrier work in my favor.

I would punch in some numbers, and then show the store clerks what I wanted to pay.

"Ohhh! No, no, no!" the salesman said.

I would beat them up on the prices so bad, that Chako was blushing. She would say a price to the man for me, then immediately laugh her ass off.

I was low-balling so bad, and I knew it.

"Oh! No, no, no!" the salesman would say. "Too low! Too Low!"

Finally, after wearing him down for so long, the man caved. I paid less than half for that stereo than I would have had to pay in the States.

ARM WRESTLING

One night, a bunch of the Yakuza took Dick Murdoch and me out to a bar, after a show. They told us they would buy us whatever we want, so who was I to say no?

The Yakuza-run place was very flashy. There were life-sized weird statues everywhere. The walls were red with gold trim. There were also a lot of colored dance lights coming out of the ceiling, and they were playing J-pop loud over the speakers.

It was difficult to make my way up to the bar because there were so many people, but I just walked behind Dick Murdoch who plowed through the people like Godzilla. A few people were really nice and went out of their way to help me through the swarm of people. They were all patting my shoulder and calling me, "champ."

On the hardwood dance floor, there were a lot of little 5'2 Japanese guys dancing, most of them poorly, like a scene out the movie *Revenge of The Nerds*. As I finally bellied up to the bar, I noticed that a lot of the customers looked like normal civilians, but there were Yakuza members here and there, identifiable by their full sleeve tattoos and missing fingers gripping their drinks.

Our main Yakuza sponsor spoke a little English. He asked us what we wanted.

"Whiskey," Murdoch said without missing a beat.

"I'll just have a beer," I said.

The Yakuza sponsor pushed a bunch of the paying customers aside, rudely and started pounding on the tabletop for attention. When the bartender saw him, he dropped everything and they quickly spoke in Japanese to each other.

The bartender got our drinks together and motioned for us to come over to the bar. We obliged.

"Oh, big, big wrestlers!" he said, pretending to flex his non-existent muscles. "We waiting for you!"

He yelled something to all the people sitting around the bar and everyone clapped. The bartender immediately pushed free drinks at me and called for someone in the back. A pretty girl came out of the back with two trays of appetizers for Dick and me. She set it down before us. Dick pushed two or three items into his mustached mouth immediately. Then, before you could blink, she was back with a huge tray of yakitori (meat on sticks) and more appetizers, all on the house.

"Wait, the Japanese eat meat?"

"Ya," Dick Murdoch said, stuffing his face. "Yakitore, it's called," he said, sticking two or three succulent finger foods down his gullet at the same time.

"I've been here three times and never seen these. How did I miss this?"

Yakitori was just what the doctor ordered. This getaway was perfect. As much as the Yakuza could be dickheads and even dangerous to some people, they did me a solid. I was tired of bullshit spaghetti. I was hungry and the food there was endless. Everything was just awesome.

Keeping consistent with my usual experiences with them, our members of the Yakuza had a little bit too much to drink and started to act crazy. Some of them kept pointing at me and saying, "Big arms! Big arms!" they would say, acting like they wanted to wrestle me.

Nobody fucked with Dick Murdoch. He was so big, they didn't dare. He seriously was as unapproachable as a toothless hooker with a mouth full of herpes.

Eventually, I got drunk too and was high-fiving them all. I was laughing at them and selling their drunken threats.

"Okay, let me get this straight. You want a piece of me?" I said laughing, half-drunk off my ass. "You boys want a piece of me?" I pointed at three of the sponsors. "You, and you, and you."

The Yakuza members turned and raised their hands to the crowd. We all walked across the bar, through the insanity of the dance floor and over to this big shiny, decorative table in a boxed off VIP section. A giant entourage of Yakuza hanger-ons followed us quickly in those tiny cute Japanese steps.

I sat down. I turned my baseball cap around and I extended my arm out, to accept their challenge in an arm wrestling match.

"Come on you bastards," I said.

The crowd roared. Dick Murdoch may have even cracked a smile. He folded his arms and shook his head. He stood in the corner at a high-top table, out of sight but close enough to make sure nothing could go too awry. He had my back, and I knew it.

One of the pretty waitresses wasn't sure exactly what was going on. She brought a fresh tray of sushi and little sauces over to me. She sat it down right where I was issuing the challenge. Dick Murdoch grabbed the tray and carted it over to his personal table, for himself.

"I'll take these, my lady," he said with his mouth full, sampling one on the way.

"You boys ready?" I asked.

They nodded. The crowd erupted and started cheering like the start of a horserace.

All three of them rushed the table and immediately locked up with me at one time. It was on. Simultaneously, they tried to push my arm down like a big lever. With all their might, all three of those scrawny bastards could not even do it, collectively.

I held them there in arm-wrestling limbo for a long time, until all of a sudden, one of them had enough. He fell off of the top of the mix. This unsettled the balance, and then the other two fell. After that, it was like a big rubber band. All of the energy that was stored up in my arm exploded. My arm snapped forward and I slammed my hand down hard right through the table.

Crrraaassshhh!!!

Here is the kicker. The table was made of a thick glass, but the fact that it was thick didn't matter. It exploded and shards went everywhere.

All blood.

"Holy shit!" I yelled.

When I pulled my arm back up from the wreckage, it looked like my arm was cut completely opened, filleted like a chicken breast. There was blood all over the table, my forearm and, the floor below.

"No no no!" Two of the guys ran and got me a towel from behind the bar to wrap my hand in.

Immediately, I was being pushed into a tiny car and rushed off to a strange Japanese hospital in the middle of the night. Dick Murdoch came with me and stayed by my side in a country that I did not know. That was pretty cool of him. The medics finally came in the room, and they sewed my arm up. They made me look like Frankenstein with big X-shaped stitches.

Fortunately for me, the injury was only just the skin. If it had cut an artery, I would've been in rough shape. They cleaned me up and I was good to go. I was hoping I could wrap up everything really well and continue on with the tour dates like nothing had happened.

When I got back to my room, I remember looking at my arm and trying to figure out if I could hide it with tape. I was hoping to just work injured and not tell them. A lot of guys will not report an injury and work while they are hurt. The reason many choose to wrestle injured is not only to avoid a missed payday, but also the possibility that someone could come along while they were healing up and take their spot.

Unfortunately for me, Dick Murdoch went back to the New Japan office and accidentally spilled the beans. After they heard the bad news, as a result, they decided to have me leave the tour early. They were just too worried that I might rip the stitches out in a match and further incur even more injury.

I had to make the best of it. Antonio Inoki himself told me that I would be back, so I wasn't all that worried.

The next morning, I was back on a plane ready to fly home. I had all of the shopping treasures that Chaco helped me find, and I brought them on as carry-on bags. The whole flight I made small talk and flirted with the airplane staff. I showed them my stitched up arm and talked wrestling with them. They ended up feeling sorry for me. When we finally got home to America, I barely even had to ask them to help me carry my bags off the plane for me.

I wasn't being lazy, however. I was actually being cheap!

Making it look like I was in severe pain, nobody questioned me walking right through the gate and by the guards. Nobody had the heart to stop me to see if I had anything to declare! That's right. My plan worked. I sold the arm and distracted the officials. The plane staff carried my bags right through for me, and I sidestepped customs. I didn't have to clear any of my international purchases. That meant no taxes on thousands of dollars in the jewelry and stereo equipment.

NEW JAPAN

After returning from doing some work back in the states, including the AWA Super Sunday 1983 in April, I was doing some shows in the Minneapolis territory. I drove around a bit and ended up bringing Mr. Saito around with me some. Saito enjoyed traveling and working with me and, in return, he got me and Paul Orndorff some more interest in Japan. So for another tour before working together in the WWF, Saito pitched Inoki a tag team combination of Paul Orndorff & Ed Leslie.

In April 1983, our plane landed. We met up with Saito, and he picked us up. The plane ride was hell and Paul Orndorff was already being cranky. Saito sensed it and he gave me a bottle of tuinals, aka "Reds" (an old slang term from the 60s,) hoping maybe they would help us sleep. We were right off the bat looking at a 6 or 7-hour bus ride just to get to the hotel.

I took one pill, and I was out like a light. As for Paul Orndorff taking a little napsy, I don't think that happened.

The hotel we rolled up on looked like something right out of a Kung Fu movie. In the past, I had stayed a lot more in the urban type jobbers in Tokyo, so this was a real change. Even before you could get in the place, you had to maneuver around a maze of their beautiful elaborate garden. Coming from a landscaping background, I was totally impressed.

Having an enormous, well-crafted garden is a huge status symbol for some establishments and businesses in Japan. Plants are carefully arranged to maintain their beauty. Trees, shrubs, and lawns are meticulously manicured. Since ancient times, large stones have also been strategically placed throughout these gardens to symbolize mountains and hills. Fancy smaller rocks and gravel are also used to line ponds and streams.

When you enter one of these old school, traditional hotels, you immediately take off your shoes as to not walk on the white bamboo matting. Paul Orndorff was pissed.

"Oh, come on," he said, cursing under his breath having to remove his tennis shoes.

Everything was very clean and sterile in the establishment, with the white paper walls and sliding doors. Once we made our way to our room, we found that there were not any beds. The host gave a quick explanation of the sleeping accommodations, and my tag team partner shook his head. Paul also didn't like this idea, as he looked at me with a contemptuous smirk and I could see that he was biting his tongue. What they do is have you pull out these long rolled up futons and sleep on the floor, kind of like a sleeping bag.

"I will see you for dinner at 6 pm," Mr. Saito said. He bowed a little and made his exit.

Paul looked around the room after he left. He opened up the door to the bathroom. "Dizzy," he said. "You gotta see this."

I came and looked over his shoulder. There was a squat toilet off the corner. It was basically like a hollowed out hole that was flush to the ground (pardon the pun.)

"It's just a little slit in the floor to shit in like monkeys!" Paul said laughing.

We tried to relax a little, but Paul was too wired up. I headed out and walked around the garden some more to take it all in.

Later that night, Mr. Saito brought us out to a "Korean BBQ." This idea was something that was so big in Korea that it caught on in Japan that I really wanted to try. The term in Korea, Gogigui, is the closest word to barbecue that we would have here in the States. It means "meat roast." These places are mostly all about having the customer roast their own slices of beef, pork, chicken, or other types of meat, right at their own table.

As we were being shown to our seats, we saw that the other customers were preparing their own dishes on some kind of gas grill that was actually built into the table itself. It was really cool. Afterwards, I would learn that some of the Korean BBQ restaurants don't have the built-in grills, but they rather would deliver a portable tabletop unit for diners to use for roasting. This place was the real thing, however, and it was awesome.

Paul Orndorff was with us and still stirring up a storm in this quiet little restaurant. It was very clear that he was jet-lagged, needed sleep, and that he didn't really want to be in Japan at this moment in time. It wasn't even the second day on tour.

A tiny little waitress in a robe came over. She tried to be as accommodating as she could be, but Paul didn't care. He only ended up yelling at her.

Emergency! Give this man a pill!

We had painkillers and a few uppers and downers, but Mr. Saito really came through. He threw a pill in Paul's mouth, and 10 minutes later Paul was all smiles. I don't know what he gave him but it must have been the ultimate Japanese Happy Pill.

Paul got out of his seat. He was a transformed man, laughing and hugging the wait staff.

"What the hell was that?" I asked Saito.

"Don't worry. I have plenty of them."

A few days later and we were back in Tokyo. Paul and I were working as a tag team, so I was traveling everywhere with him. Thank god for Saito. He left me his own special "prescription" for Paul, in case I ran into any more "emergencies." That bottle was a godsend. It really was personality in a bottle.

We beat the crap out of some young boys that night, and then a few familiar faces scooped us up after the show. The Yakuza brought us out for some more food, then promised to grab us for the big Sumo event tomorrow.

The next day a few fingerless Yakuza members pulled up to pick us up at our hotel. Now, normally, you wouldn't really want to get in a van with a member of organized crime. However, when you were a wrestler, you knew that they weren't going to be in any kind of danger or anything. They would treat you like royalty because they practically worshipped you for your role as a professional athlete.

Paul and I got into the van and one of the guys said that Tiger Hattori was already there waiting for us. One of the Yakuza guys spoke a little English, so it wouldn't have been all that bad without Tiger. But it was also nice to have our English-speaking babysitter there to answer any questions that we may have had, as well.

"Please," the one member with a red hat said to us, motioning to the seat behind us. We turned around. In the back of the van was a little cooler filled with two dozen small bottles of liquor.

"Now you are speaking our language," Paul said.

There was every kind of booze you could imagine in it, so we immediately did what pro wrestlers do best - drink. The Yakuza really knew how to treat their guests. Any sports in Japan are a significant part of Japanese culture and well-honored by all. Western imports, like baseball and football, are big with both participants and spectators. However, fighters were highly-revered as being macho and legendary and worthy of high-praise.

You could tell they were excited to attend the event. The driver and the front seat passenger were laughing it up and having a good old time. It is no wonder that sumo wrestling is considered Japan's number one national sport.

When we pulled up to Sumo Palace in Tokyo, we saw a big huge line at the gate. We parked and then were ushered in right by the line of people. We didn't need a ticket. All it took was a hand wave and a head nod from Red Hat, much like a Jedi mind-trick in Star Wars, and we were in.

In the arena, the first thing that we noticed was that there weren't any seats. People in the cheap seats sat on what looked like cushions on stairs to watch the event. Down in the center, we could see a platform with a dohyo, a ring made of clay covered in a layer of sand. A contest usually lasts only a few seconds, but in rare cases can take a minute or more.

We met up with Tiger Hattori and then the Yakuza took us right down to front and center. We walked passed all the sections toward the second and then the very first tier. We were ringside, right next to the ring. Yakuza went up to a few people who were already sitting. They said something to people in Japanese. I don't know what they said, but the fans immediately got up and ran off, freeing up their seats for us.

They were four or five of us. Paul Orndorff was there. We watched for a while. The rules of Sumo are quite simple: the wrestler who first touches the ground with any part of his body loses the contest. There are no weight restrictions in sumo, which seemed funny to me. That meant you could be watching one sumo wrestler in the ring with an opponent that was two or three times their size! As a result, it came to no surprise when Tiger told us that weight gaining was everything. "It really is the most important part of sumo training," he said.

The Yakuza disappeared. They probably killed the people who were in our seats before us, stole their wallets, and returned, bringing us some big beers. We watched a few more matches and polished off our drinks, then our hosts disappeared yet again and returned to get us.

"Follow us," they said.

We looked at Tiger and he nodded and got up first.

We followed them single file down the side of the entrance way and a guard lifted the barricade aside for us to allow passage. Then we found ourselves back in the dressing room. They introduced all the sumos to us. We hung out and discussed pro wrestling with them and vice versa through our interpreter, Tiger.

After the sumo matches, Red Hat took us to a disco right nearby that was jam-packed. He brought us to a private section and told everyone to "get the fuck out." Everyone bailed. We had some really good food, surprisingly enough at the club. I don't know what I was eating exactly, but I enjoyed it. I also enjoyed just watching the girls dance on the floor. Red Hat took notice.

For the most part, in the early-to-mid-eighties, the Yakuza wouldn't have liked the thought of an average white guy wanting to sleep with a Japanese girl. It was very similar to the taboo concept of a black man being with a white woman, here in the States around the same time. That is why angles like Farooq (Ron Simmons) with Sunny and Sensational Sherri with Harlem Heat got over with tremendous heat like they did with some racist wrestling fans. However, pro wrestlers were considered special and that is why Red Hat spoke up.

"You like the girls?" he asked me, watching my eyes on the dancing girls in the club.

"Well, who doesn't?"

Red Hat laughed.

Later on that night, the Yakuza brought Paul and me to a Turkish bath. We went in and this was one of the most lavish, expensive ones around. There is no way I could have ever afforded this on what Inoki was paying me, but that didn't matter. Like everything else, the Yakuza was footing the bill.

This place was crazy. They had both hot and cold pools. Whirlpool hot tubs. They had the massage rooms where the little mama-san would grab rails above you on the ceiling and walk on your back, barefoot. It was crazy.

I started out with the hot and cold pools. What you would do is start in the hot water, then go back and forth between the different temperatures. After I got out, a bunch of servants came running. They sat me on this little stool and all went to work, two or three girls per man. Then, these beautiful tiny little Japanese girls each had their own little buckets and they began to scrub us down from head to foot with sponges. It was seriously like the *You only live twice* James Bond movie, if you have seen that.

After I was fully lathered up with soap, they led me back over to the hot water and dunked me back in the water to rinse off. Then they brought me back up to the stool again, to repeat it all over again. Back and forth.

Now, I never got the massage treatment before and frankly wasn't interested in it. I always figured all that would be way too much money, but Red Hat insisted and they were paying. So on this particular night, I decided to go for the full-service treatment.

I sauntered slowly into this little wooden room. There was some kind of Zen music playing in the background and my little mama-san, started to oil up my entire back. She oiled it forever. Then, she flipped me over and put a hot towel over my face. She started giving me one of those deep muscle massages, which I have to admit, was great for a wrestler who constantly beats on his body.

I had almost fallen asleep when, all the sudden, I felt something like a feather duster on my leg. Before I even knew what hit me, she was on top of me. She dropped down and sat on me. I'm not sure if you have any clue what this service entails after that, but let me tell you. They ride you like crazy and jump up and down on you for a few a minutes - the whole deal. They do such a detailing job on you, that they clean you from the inside out!

After that, they scrubbed me down again. When I was good and clean everywhere, I was finally allowed to go get dressed and go to the bar. And boy, let me tell you, I needed a drink after that one. So I only did the full service one time, but I much would have rather just went to get something to eat and drink.

As far as women were concerned, I didn't need a full service like that. I was lucky. Whenever I was in Japan, I had contact with a Playboy Club Bunny in Osaka. If I called her, she would take the train all the way to Tokyo and provide me with any service that I wanted.

On a scale of 1-10, she was a 25.

PAUL ORNDORFF & ED LESLIE

So about that tag team… For those of you keeping score, they advertised Paul and me on a number of cards for New Japan with some of the younger guys in tag matches. The new generation of Japanese wrestlers was getting more fit than their predecessors. The "young boys" were into working out. They had their own weights on the bus, and it started to show. The Inoki boys were becoming known for being strong, very aggressive "shooters."

The term "shooter" is used in wrestling to describe a wrestler than can handle himself, in or outside the ring for real. One of their trainers worked a lot of the mid cards and he was just an awesome shooter. This guy was something else. He could just

Working with "Mr. Wonderful" Paul Orndorff in Japan was always a good time.

tie you up knots. Before a show, Paul and I would get some practice time in the ring so we would look good when it was time to debut our tag team. Paul and I were around 250-260 pounds apiece, but the young boy trainer would jump in and just toss us around the ring like garbage. The funny thing was, he was probably at least 50 pounds lighter than we were!

Paul didn't like that, so he decided all of that guy's students were going to pay on any show that we wrestled on. Paul was my senior, so I, of course, had to follow his lead.

Just to make sure we didn't get outshined, and to keep their shooting skills at bay, every night we would go out there and just pummel these fucking young boy guys. It really was ridiculous. No black eyes, or knocking teeth out or anything, but when they got out of the ring with us, they thought they had been in a fight with a rhinoceros. We never hurt them, but we banged them up pretty good.

The second week after we had debuted as a tag team, Tiger Hattori approached us after the match.

"So what did you think?" Paul asked, deadpan, as he was unlacing his boots.

"Ohhh you, you! You too stiff!"

I swallowed my laughter and hid my face in a towel, but Paul kept his cool and remained completely straight-faced. We were stiff, but we were not going to admit it.

"We are sorry," he said.

"Yes. Sorry," I said.

"We won't do it anymore," Paul said. "We promise."

A day went by and I realized that my hands actually hurt a little from beating on the young boys from the night before.

Then, it was the same thing the next night.

"Ohhh you, you! You promise, but still, too damn stiff!" Tiger said after the match.

Paul and I just about fell off of our chairs out of laughter. Man oh man, we were stiff, but we were not going to admit it.

"We are sorry," he said.

"Yes. Sorry," I said.

We may have let up on them a little bit, but we still wailed on them. You are supposed to get this a little in our business. It's like a food chain. Getting wailed on is a rite of passage.

Me and Hogan hanging out at Antonio Inoki's wedding.

CHAPTER 11 - MID-ATLANTIC, SECW & FIRST GOLD

From January to about April of 1983, I wrestled some for Jim Crockett in Mid-Atlantic Wrestling as Dizzy Hogan.

His company, Jim Crockett Promotions Inc., operated out of Charlotte, NC, and had been in his family since 1931. This promotion became the cornerstone of the National Wrestling Alliance. By the 1980s, Jim Crockett's Mid-Atlantic Wrestling and the World Wrestling Federation were the two largest promotions in the United States. (The Crockett family would eventually sell their promotion off to TBS - Turner Broadcasting System in 1988, resulting in what would become of WCW - World Championship Wrestling.)

Jim Crockett was seemingly a polite enough guy, but I think I only really talked to him maybe one time. I did work with a lot of great wrestlers there. For some reason, I rode around a lot with some of the midgets; Lord Littlebrook was practically always in my car. On shows, I teamed up with Sweet Brown Sugar (aka Butch Reed) a bunch and also worked with guys like Brian Blair, Mike Rotundo, and the One Man Gang.

I also had a bunch of title matches. They put me up against the NWA Tag Team Champions, Sgt. Slaughter & Don Kernodle. I faced my old friend Jack Brisco for the Mid-Atlantic Heavyweight Championship. I was even pitted against my future WWF Tag Team Champion partner, Greg Valentine, for his NWA United States title.

Though I didn't win any of those high-profile matches, it was all like baby steps. Little bits of exposure was setting me up for more and more opportunities. I was becoming recognized by promoters and also pro wrestling magazines.

There was one point worth noting here. On January 24, 1983 in Greenville, SC, I came to the arena and looked at the card that was scotch taped to the wall. It had all the matches and names written out in marker, I looked down to read this:

Dizzy Hogan vs. Porkchop Cash

Also, my name was circled, indicating that I was going over, clean. So, yes, I then had a dilemma. Do I go out and just work a regular match with Pork Chop Cash? Or do I get in there and let him know that I was not happy about our last match together?

Now, this was only a few years after he dumped me on my shoulder while working a match for Bill Watts, and then some of the boys came to me afterward and told me that he did it on purpose. Obviously, I didn't appreciate that and I still have him to thank for it being a nagging injury I still deal with to this very day.

This happened from time to time. Sometimes you would get booked with a guy that you might have a bit of a beef with, and you just haven't had time to sit them down and talk your differences through. You would have to then work them and do the best you could with the situation. A lot of guys will then step up and go the extra mile to make sure the match is the very best, leaving no room for critique in this instance. Power to them, but I don't think that is what I did on this particular evening.

When the match came, if I remember correctly, I was always on guard. I surely was not going to allow him to try that shit again. I made him do all the work. I didn't run the ropes. I didn't bump for him. I made him look like absolute garbage. I was still professional, don't get me wrong, but I did not go out of my way to make him look good at any point. (Also, it is possible that I made sure to lay in a couple of good shots as a receipt for my shoulder.)

I'm only human. I can't say that I would not have liked to see Pork Chop with a steak on his eye after our match.

GOLD & CAULIFLOWER EARS

When the Mid-Atlantic tour ended, I wound up going back to Pensacola and found a room to rent out on the beach in a big house. I shared the place with a guy and his girlfriend, plus a really cool reggae band player. I threw them a few hundred for a room a month and chipped in on groceries.

The Fullers always took me back with open arms. They really liked me there, and the door was always open. It was always a good experience for me, but on this particular tour, they put me with a guy who was a very well-known veteran at the time, a guy by the name of Ken Lucas.

After completing his run against Bob Armstrong, Ken Lucas teamed up with me for some tag matches. We made for some much-needed opposition to the Midnight Express. The Express was working under what we call "The Freebird Rules" where any two of the three members could wrestle in a tag team match at any given time. This meant I got to work with any combination of their comprising members including Dennis Condrey, Randy Rose, and Norvell Austin.

Ken Lucas exposed me to a lot of little tricks of the trade. We actually formed a decent team with good chemistry in the ring, becoming the only reputable team in the territory to go against The Express. This was booking that had been lacking for quite some time. After building us up as a team for a few months, we did what no team since the Mongolian Stomper and Stomper Jr. had been able to do in nearly a year. On June 6th, 1983, we defeated The Express for the Southeastern Tag Team titles.

This was the first time I ever won a championship belt! This meant the promoter had faith in us. We had a pretty good run with the titles, too.

One night we had a rematch against the Express. In this bout, it was the combination of Randy Rose and Norvell Austin. During this bout, there was another guy filling in for Dennis Condrey with them outside of the ring. His name was Black Bart. He was supposed to hit me with a cowboy boot and knock me out. Then, he was going to roll me into the ring and I would lose the match.

Bart initiated what we had planned. His partners drew the referee's attention, and the cowboy wrestler pulled off his boot and hit me with it on the side of the head. The problem was, he hit me for real.

Rather than holding it with your hand over the sole of the boot, he grabbed it by the leather on the top. It had a pretty good size lift on it. When he swung it, the heaviness of the wooden heel caught me just right and walloped me in my left ear.

My ear felt like it exploded. It immediately puffed up like a balloon. The pain was crazy. I spun around and didn't get right back in the ring for the finish of the match as quickly as I should have.

At this point in my career, nobody had smartened me up on what you were supposed to do after taking a stiff shot to the ear. There actually is an art form on how to not get a cauliflower ear, but I didn't know anything about that.

A cauliflower ear is an injury to the ear that causes internal bleeding and inflammation. The top part essentially puffs up and looks all deranged like cauliflower. You have probably seen it before on an older boxer, or MMA guy.

If you look, lots of the old school wrestlers later in age illustrate some pretty bad cases of Cauliflower ears. A lot of them get it way early on in their careers when they are younger guys, just starting out. What sometimes happened was that a lot of the older guys would put a headlock on you and jerk their arms back and forth real hard, leaving the new guy's left ear all roughed up. Some of them did this to weed out the rookies not tough enough for the sport. Others just did it to be mean. Either way, that kind of agitation would really mess your ear up, that is, if you didn't know what to do with it immediately afterward.

After Black Bart hit me, I eventually rolled back in the ring and lost the match. I walked back to the dressing room and it felt like the left side of my face was on fire. He really rang my bell. My ear was all swollen up with fluid, and I didn't know what to do with it.

I went back to the hotel room. My ear was a mess. I tried to lie down, but I just knew I was going to have a horrible time trying to sleep that night. That is when Ken Lucas came knocking at my door.

All I can say is Ken Lucas is the man. He went out and got a bag from the hotel ice machine and had me icing it for ten minutes every hour. His home remedy worked and he saved my pretty face.

THE MIDNIGHT EXPRESS
RAVISHING RANDY ROSE & LOVERBOY DENNIS CONDREY

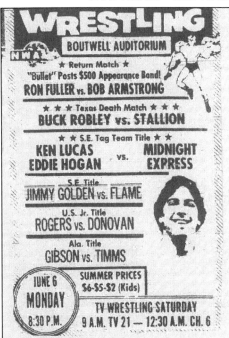

WRESTLING
BOUTWELL AUDITORIUM

★ Return Match ★
"Bullet" Posts $500 Appearance Bond!
RON FULLER vs. BOB ARMSTRONG

★ ★ ★ Texas Death Match ★ ★ ★
BUCK ROBLEY vs. STALLION

★ ★ S.E. Tag Team Title ★ ★
KEN LUCAS / EDDIE HOGAN vs. **MIDNIGHT EXPRESS**

S.E. Title
JIMMY GOLDEN vs. FLAME

U.S. Jr. Title
ROGERS vs. DONOVAN

Ala. Title
GIBSON vs. TIMMS

JUNE 6 MONDAY 8:30 P.M.
SUMMER PRICES $6-$5-$2 (Kids)
TV WRESTLING SATURDAY
9 A.M. TV 21 — 12:30 A.M. CH. 6

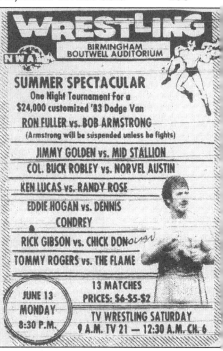

WRESTLING
BIRMINGHAM BOUTWELL AUDITORIUM

SUMMER SPECTACULAR
One Night Tournament For a
$24,000 customized '83 Dodge Van
RON FULLER vs. BOB ARMSTRONG
(Armstrong will be suspended unless he fights)

JIMMY GOLDEN vs. MID STALLION

COL. BUCK ROBLEY vs. NORVEL AUSTIN

KEN LUCAS vs. RANDY ROSE

EDDIE HOGAN vs. DENNIS CONDREY

RICK GIBSON vs. CHICK DONOVAN

TOMMY ROGERS vs. THE FLAME

JUNE 13 MONDAY 8:30 P.M.
13 MATCHES
PRICES: $6-$5-$2
TV WRESTLING SATURDAY
9 A.M. TV 21 — 12:30 A.M. CH. 6

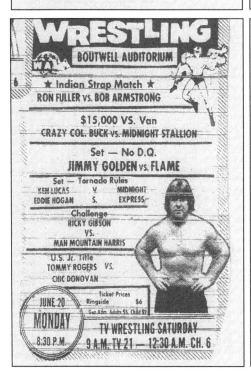

WRESTLING
BOUTWELL AUDITORIUM

★ Indian Strap Match ★
RON FULLER vs. BOB ARMSTRONG

$15,000 VS. Van
CRAZY COL. BUCK vs. MIDNIGHT STALLION

Set — No D.Q.
JIMMY GOLDEN vs. FLAME

Set — Tornado Rules
KEN LUCAS / EDDIE HOGAN vs. **MIDNIGHT EXPRESS**

Challenge
RICKY GIBSON vs. MAN MOUNTAIN HARRIS

U.S. Jr. Title
TOMMY ROGERS vs. CHIC DONOVAN

JUNE 20 MONDAY 8:30 P.M.
Ticket Prices
Ringside $6
Gen. Adm. Adults $5, Child $2
TV WRESTLING SATURDAY
9 A.M. TV 21 — 12:30 A.M. CH. 6

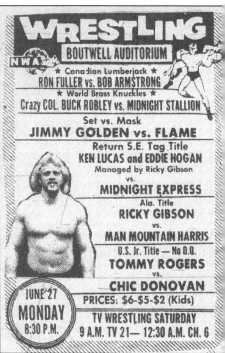

WRESTLING
BOUTWELL AUDITORIUM

★ Canadian Lumberjack ★
RON FULLER vs. BOB ARMSTRONG
★ World Brass Knuckles ★
Crazy COL. BUCK ROBLEY vs. MIDNIGHT STALLION

Set vs. Mask
JIMMY GOLDEN vs. FLAME

Return S.E. Tag Title
KEN LUCAS and EDDIE HOGAN
Managed by Ricky Gibson
vs.
MIDNIGHT EXPRESS

Ala. Title
RICKY GIBSON
vs.
MAN MOUNTAIN HARRIS

U.S. Jr. Title — No D.Q.
TOMMY ROGERS
vs.
CHIC DONOVAN

JUNE 27 MONDAY 8:30 P.M.
PRICES: $6-$5-$2 (Kids)
TV WRESTLING SATURDAY
9 A.M. TV 21— 12:30 A.M. CH. 6

STARSHIP OVER THE MOON

I remember icing my ear some the next day on the road on the way to another show with a guy by the name of Jos LeDuc.

Did I mention that Jos LeDuc was crazy? He was one of the first real early hardcore guys who would come out to the ring with garbage cans and weird items to use as weapons. He also had one of those "cheese grater" foreheads that you would see on some of the old guys, like Superfly Snuka, Dusty Rhodes, or even Abdullah the Butcher. Those hash marks were a badge of honor for some of the legends, worn with pride after years and years of chairshots, blading and headbutts.

Jos LeDuc had a custom van he called the Starship. I took many many, many trips with him in the Starship, along with his co-pilot a guy by the name of Jack Daniels, who sat right next to him in a brown paper bag. LeDuc always had a big bottle with every upper and downer you could imagine in it. Sometime, the Fullers would come along for the ride as well, though my guess is they weren't into pills, they were more into the booger sugar.

The Starship was insane. Between LeDuc and the Fullers, they had everything you could think of that wasn't good for you from A-Z in there. When you got into the starship, they made sure that you didn't say no. Jos would hand you everything, so much, you wouldn't know where to start.

You really had to keep the partying low-key on the way to a show so you could work the match. I mean, after all, the owners of the promotion were sitting right next to you in the Starship. However, after the show on the way back from Birmingham to Pensacola, it was a different story. We would hit warp speed, go through wormholes, dodge stars, fly through black holes and zip passed meteorites.

Riding in the Starship with LeDuc was always quite the trip. (Get it? Trip? Ok, that was bad.)

One particular time I remember related to driving along with him, but I was not in his van, I was in the in the passenger seat of Randy Rose's car driving behind him headed to a show for the Fullers. It appeared that Jos wanted to pass us, even though they were following us. That didn't make sense, however, because we were the only ones with the directions. Randy got into the right lane and they came up from behind us on the left.

This was before the advent of cell phones so we had no idea what was going on. Randy rolled down his window to see what the deal was, and to maybe make himself available for a question, if needed.

We looked out the window, ready to shout something over in the wind, and then to our surprise, we were looking at what I believe was one of the Fuller's asses in our face. We all flipped them the bird as they took off down the road.

A few minutes later, they slowed down again so we could catch up, Randy rolled the window down again to say something and then we got double mooned. We couldn't believe it! Joe got up on the seat while he was driving so he could moon us as well, as the car went by. Picture that; somebody driving, jumping up on the seat and mooning us at the same time. That was just Joe.

Moon us once, shame on you. Moon us twice, shame on us!

Randy was pissed, and we took off. We drove as fast as we could, probably like 100 miles per hour, to try and lose the Starship. We drove up a hill and out of sight. When we got to the bottom and then another straight-a-way, Randy pulled over into the breakdown lane. All five of us got out of the car and dropped our pants.

When Jos LeDuc finally came by, we were all in a line, mooning him away. The funny thing is, with our backs turned, we didn't notice that he was slowing down.

When we turned around, both of the Fullers had slid open the van door and immediately started spraying soda on our bare asses. We quickly turned around to pull up our pants. We looked to see all three of them mooning us, just as Jos hit the gas and took off again.

Jos DeLuc   **Robert Fuller**

CHAPTER 12 - CWA - AUSTRIA & OTTO WANZ

While working for AWA, I had the pleasure of working some with an Austrian man by the name of Big Otto Wanz.

Otto came from the strong man competition background. He held several tough man championships and even the world record for tearing telephone books in half. He was a really big name in the UK and really big around the world. Eventually, like another famous Austrian, Arnold Schwarzenegger, Otto jumped into politics and became the Mayor of Graz. Speaking of Arnold Schwarzenegger even today he says that Otto's determination and spirit was a big influence on his fitness and bodybuilding career.

Otto debuted as a professional wrestler right around my time, somewhere around 1978. Weighing in at 450 and some-odd pounds, it wasn't long before promoters were pitting him against some very famous international opponents including Antonio Inoki and André the Giant.

As a big man, he wrestled in that kind of slower style because of his size. On one AWA event, Otto was set to compete in a battle royal where they, unfortunately, didn't have any ring stairs. Otto was so big he couldn't easily climb into the ring, so he marched around and took some shots at a few of the boys. Then, he just turned around and made his way back to the locker room. He never even got in the ring! The boys either loved him so much, or they didn't notice, so nobody stooged his lack of performance to Verne.

Speaking of the AWA, Otto is a former American Wrestling Association champion. It is also important to note that Otto had something too; he had money. Verne and Otto did a little business together. Rumor has it that money exchanged hands. Otto literally bought the AWA championship for a time. They say Otto paid Verne about $40 grand to be the AWA champion so he could take the title back overseas with him and play it up.

Paying a lot of money to be the AWA champion wasn't a bad business move, however. It wasn't like a mark-thing for him to do at all; him just wanting to be able to say he held the AWA Championship. That strap meant a lot over in Europe that could equate ticket sales, so it was quite an investment for Otto. It is an understatement to say that Otto got a lot of mileage out of that AWA Championship title. People from all around came to see the local hometown hero, and to see the belt that he brought back to their land.

Many people behind the scenes thought it looked odd though, I must admit, at least on paper. Verne had all these big monstrous guys working for them like Hulk, Andre and John Studd, but then there was Otto. He was a little short fat Austrian guy, and he was the one holding the AWA Championship?

Anyhow, it was great when Otto gave me a call to wrestle in his big card of the year that they called, "The Big Finale." This annual big show in Graz, Austria always drew a ton of people, with a month-long build up of shows to put it over. It was even more of an honor to hear that I was the one Otto would be wrestling in the main event of the card.

That's right, it was no tour for me. It was just one big high-profile match. That was it. Otto flew me in however, five or six days ahead to make appearances to promote the Big Finale. They had a whole schedule of press conferences up and down Austria, as well as in Germany. The message was clear; I was a big bad wrestler from America and I was in the main event, facing their hometown hero, Otto Wanz.

I came over for the finale of the tour. Everything was done by the time I showed up to do press conferences for my big match. Before flying out, I ran into a few familiar faces there that I knew from the AWA, Mid-Atlantic, Pensacola and Mid-South locker rooms. There were some shows before our Big Finale main event with guys like Slaughter, Big John Studd, Bobby Duncum, but they were ready to leave as I was just showing up.

A few stragglers were left behind, however, due to flight issues. They too had no matches or anything scheduled, so it was going to just be party time for them until it was time to leave. This meant I was going to have about a week-long vacation with Baron Von Raschche and Maddog Vachon.

Otto was smart. Rather than pay for hotels all the time, he had like a little mobile home park set up for the wrestlers. Everything was more relaxed in Austria. You worked every couple of days, not every single night. You would only have to drive out about 150 kilometers to a show, which was like an hour and a half away. Otto didn't have you running all over the place.

One morning, I stepped out of my trailer and there was Baron and Mad Dog, all bright-eyed and bushy tailed.

"Hey, Dizzy," Mad Dog said. "You have to come with us!"

"For what? Get some breakfast?" I asked.

"Ok, that sounds good, but after," Baron said. "First, you have to see this."

I followed the boys, not knowing exactly what I was getting into. We walked through the beautiful old town, crossing the cobblestone street that was just starting to buzz with street life. Unlike America, everything in the city of Graz was clean and in surprisingly good shape.

"Okay," I said, chuckling. "Where are you taking me?"

"It's a surprise," Mad Dog laughed.

We carried on for a few blocks and then headed down a little hill. There it was; a nice big water park! As we approached from the slope, I could see that all kinds of people were starting to gather, to claim their real estate spaces for the day. In the summer, everyone was just out there camping. I was surprised that the two veterans were so excited for a swim. From the looks of both of their pale white wonder-bread asses, it didn't appear that they saw very much sunlight.

"Look Dizzy! Over there!"

In those days in Austria, topless was the norm. As we got closer, I could now clearly see that none of the women were wearing bikini tops.

I was in titty city.

There were big ones, small ones, old ones, young ones – everywhere the eye could see were boobs! The two older guys could hardly contain themselves. They were practically jumping up and down for joy. They were actually cheering.

"Yay for boobies," I said.

It was the first time I had been exposed to that, so it was a bit of a culture shock. The boys dragged me down to the pool to stand in the thick of it. The ladies of all ages were, in fact, topless. Some of the hottest girls in the world were standing right next to saggy grandma. It was amazing. We watched in awe as a couple of them were putting these kids into these gigantic buggy strollers, all with their boobs hanging and bouncing all about. It was tremendous.

Nobody cared. Billboards and magazines in Graz everywhere had breasts out all the time. Austria is cool.

Speaking of cool, Otto was actually the Mayor of Graz. He had a lot of higher up friends and he wanted me to check out a cool sight, while I was in town.

Baron Von Raschke knew the area, so he drove me for Otto out to a big track of land to Herberstein Castle in Styria, Austria. What a sight that place was! Sitting way up on top of a steep rocky cliff, Herberstein castle looked like something straight out of a fairytale.

This famous Austrian castle is hidden from plain view in St. Johann Bei Herberstein, about 30 minutes off the road from Graz. As we drove in on the winding road, we could better see all the gardens, vineyards and also the animal/nature park that surrounded it. The place was incredible.

Baron Von Raschke

Once we pulled up to the actual castle, this Duke guy came out to meet us, so we introduced ourselves to our host.

Because I was the top talent in the main event, the Duke was treating Baron kind of shitty. The Baron was older, and more towards the end of career. The Duke took an instant hating for the Baron and it was not a very nice way to treat fellow royalty.

If I asked a question, the Duke would give very interesting and detailed answers, going out of his way to explain everything. If the Baron asked something, he was very short to him, and answered in as few words as possible. He took every opportunity he could to shit on the Baron and was a real jerk for disrespecting him like that. Maybe he was threatened by his fake "Baron" title? I don't know.

The rest of the vibe around the castle was very tranquil. The land itself around the castle was a thousand acres wide. The Duke took us out in a golf cart to a big lake with what looked like a ski jump, with no snow. It was very much like a skateboarding half-pipe, but for skiers. We watched for some time, as different guys would go down the jump doing all these crazy flips into the water.

"They are practicing for what they would do for when it snowed," he said in broken English.

Even though I came from a skiing background, I thought it was just crazy. I elbowed Baron, "These people are nuts," I whispered.

After that, they brought us up to the Duke's residence, on one side of the 16th-century castle. We walked up to one of those huge egg-like wooden doors. It had the metal trim with the spikes and everything. When we walked in, it was funny to see the state-of-the-art alarm system with cameras and motion centers. The new technology was surrounded by ancient paintings and tapestries that were probably worth millions. The Duke's residential portion of the castle had 30-foot ceilings and crystal chandeliers, dripping with money.

"All the wood was recently restored," the duke said.

The floors were amazing. I never saw anything like it. It was fucking King Arthur shit. As I looked around, I noticed that behind a long, ten-foot door was a kid who was probably 6 or 7 years old. He was standing behind the door in the corner, with his nose against the wall.

"Duke, what is that all about," I asked.

"Tsssk," Duke said. "Punish. My son angers me, now he stand behind the door in the corner. Never mind him, now. It is dinner."

We went up to a ballroom that had, even more, tapestries and chandeliers. Apparently, Otto wanted to show off and have us to experience the most traditional Austrian meal, prepared by its best chefs in the area.

The Duke had quite an elaborate meal set up for us with all the trimmings. We had Wiener Schnitzel, the most traditional Austrian dish there is. It is made with boneless veal pounded down thin with a mallet and fried with a coating of flour, egg, and breadcrumbs.

After we had a meal that couldn't be beat, we thanked the Duke for his hospitality. As we prepared to leave, I noticed that his son hadn't moved. He was still standing behind the door with his face to the wall. He probably stood there for a couple of hours.

Later that night, I was off to the official grand finale press conference. The event took place as a "weigh in" at a gym in Graz. We first started by answering questions from the media, sitting at opposite ends of two long tables. I hammed it up a little to generate some interest. After the Q&A segment, we went over to get our official weights. Mine came in at about 255 versus Otto's, who tipped the scales at 440 pounds. Man, that's a lot of knockwursts.

After everyone left, I shook hands with Otto and chit-chatted for a few minutes about the castle, then the gym owners came by and asked if I would like to take a look at the gym. The owners were an in-shape couple with a nice little business. The gym was on the small end, but it had some great equipment, a tanning bed, and a little juice bar.

Before I left, the couple said, "If you want to work out tomorrow, or anytime, just come in. We open just for you."

So that is just what I did. I stopped in the next morning, had a good workout and a visit to their juicer. I tanned and then hung out with the couple for a while. It turns out that they were friends with Arnold Schwarzenegger, so I asked them to tell me stories about him. Then, during the day, I hooked back up with Baron and we went around for some more appearances and press conferences.

The next few days before the big fight were exactly the same. By the fifth day, I had had enough.

Tonight, I'm gonna hit the town. I have to find something to do. I am bored out of my head!

That night, I went out to the bar. It was the night before the big fight. I ran into a bunch of Americans from a marching band all the way out in Austria. They were staying over in Graz, and I didn't care what they did with their free time. I was just glad to finally be around some people who could actually speak English, again.

They recognized me from all the fight cards that they were seeing all over the city, so they let me join up with their group, and we went out to another bar. The bar was some kind of sports bar with memorabilia all over it. While I was looking around the place, I noticed that there was an older woman in the back by the cooler. I was about 26 or so. She was about 40 years old, but very striking. I went over and tried to talk with her. She didn't speak much English, but enough to know what I thought of her. Her name was Helga, or something close to that. Helga and I closed the bar down and then we went out to find yet another bar.

It was probably two in the morning. Helga and I were walking down the center of Graz on their Cobblestone streets. Deep in the town, the place was packed with all the locals. It was the night before my big fight and my picture was just plastered all over the place. Helga really liked that. She would point at the picture then pat me on the chest and laugh.

The next bar was a real dive. The people recognized me though, and all my drinks were free. Helga and I drank a lot. They literally would not let us leave. On more than two or three occasions, I tried to call it "a night," but someone would just pull me back in for "one more drink."

Come five in the morning, or so I ducked outside the bar. I could see that the sun was coming up, and knew it was about time to turn in. I noticed that various street vendors were just beginning to claim their turfs. I saw a flower cart. I had spending money in my pocket, as a bit of a draw (advance) out of my payday from Otto. As the vendors were setting up, I grabbed up a bunch of their roses and brought them to bring back to bar.

"This is a perfect way to thank all you people for buying me drinks," I said. I then opened the bouquets and start throwing the flowers all over the place. The people cheered. After that, they picked up all the roses and put them in vases. They spread them out all over the bar. Everyone was popping.

"All right, Helga," I said. "I really have to get out of here, now. The big fight is less than 24 hours away."

"Twenty four hours?" she repeated. "Wait, we have one more drink."

"Okay," I said, "But this is the last one."

We crossed arms and drank, trying to look cute. After that, everything went blurry.

Fade to black.

When I woke up, I didn't know where I was. I had no idea what time it was, or even what day it was. I was a dizzy, drunken mess with a hangover that felt like a hundred pounds of bricks on my head. I looked around. From what I could survey, I had awoken in a bed in what I believed was Helga's apartment, but she was nowhere to be found.

I scrambled to find my clothes. They were all over the place. I found everything but one sock and figured that was close enough.

It was two in the afternoon, and I didn't know where I was.

I rushed out on the street. I looked around and saw my face on wrestling poster and knew I was at least close.

"Sir," I asked a man on the sidewalk. "How do I get to the fights?"

He shook his head and shrugged.

I needed to get back to the arena to my hotel room, which Otto got just for the night before the fight. You know, the one I never used.

Eventually someone I apparently drank with the night before recognized me. He squeezed me into this little Mister Bean car and brought me to the hotel. As I ducked into the lobby, I saw that Otto was already there, and had been waiting. I looked up at a big clock above the reception check-in desk. I was only about 15 minutes late, so I decided to play it cool.

Otto had no idea that I had been out partying all night.

We went up to my room discretely, in separate trips up two different elevators. In the room, I met with Otto. We talked out what our match was going to look like, and paid me in US money. He explained that it would be around ten rounds.

"And in the end, I will do my finish," he said. "It is called the steamroller. It is basically me doing a summersault towards you, then I jump up and land on you."

"Sounds like a deal," I said, counting the money and then burying it away in my bag.

Otto left. I went back in. I admired the room that I hadn't slept in and then got showered. After lunch at the hotel, I headed out to the arena. I saw some guys from England that I met in Japan from a previous Japanese tour. The boys in the locker room were teasing me because Otto out-weighed me more than 200 pounds.

"He is going to just flatten you, you know, Dizzy," one said.

"Actually, Dizzy," another said. "He is very stiff in the ring, but if you don't hit him back for real, he will be even stiffer."

"Yes," another would chime in. "You should hit him as hard as you can. He wants you to. And he wants you to try and slam him, even though you will never get his fat ass up!"

The boys were brutal. I was still relatively new, but I hadn't been born yesterday. I knew their advice was just a bunch of bullshit. They were right about one thing, he was really big. He was usually considered in shape at 410 pounds, but tonight, he was closer to 460. Only wrestling like one match a year now because he was the mayor, also meant that it probably wasn't going to be his best match of all time.

The place was packed. Everyone came out to see Dizzy Hogan take on Otto Wanz. We went at it hard for the first three rounds or so, but of course, there was no evidence of anything that the boys in the back had been saying. Then, come the third round or so, I decided to play along in an attempt to get a rise out of the boys in the locker rooms who were all watching from the cracks in the curtain.

I picked up Otto Wanz and slammed him.

The whole place went quiet. They didn't even know how to process what they had just seen. The up-and-comer surprised everyone. Nobody had ever heard of anyone slamming him, before! It was quiet and then the crowd went crazy. They got behind Otto, their local hometown hero, like never before.

Everything after that went perfectly, except for the fact that he would end up cutting the match short. We probably only did half about what we had planned. It went about 5 or 6 rounds. He small packaged me. He rolled out of the ring and his back went out.

After the match, they had to bring him out on a stretcher and ambulance. But he left with a standing ovation.

I took a shower and got dressed. I didn't see Otto that night, but I knew he had to have been delighted. After the arena cleared out, I jumped in one of the local guy's car and headed out for some drinks. I may or may not have gone and also found Helga for one last round of cocktails.

The next morning, I met up with Otto at the hotel. They had already adjusted his back, and he was feeling a lot better. Despite a little pain, he was in great spirits and everything was all good.

"Dizzy!" he said, like an excited school girl. "Look at this!"

He handed me a newspaper. The newspapers that morning after the fight were all the same. They all said our match one of the best matches they ever saw Otto in. We shook hands. I had made a friend for life. Even though I was leaving Austria, he promised that he was going to give me very high praise and recommendations to all the promoters he worked with back in the States.

"Thank you, my friend," I said.

I grabbed my bags. His buddy volunteered to drive me to the airport in Frankfort, in his beautiful four-door Mercedes. I dropped into the back seat, waved at Otto, and he took off like a whip. In only a few short minutes, we were whizzing by cars on the world-famous Autobon, where there were no speed limits.

I tried to nap a little on the ride. I remember looking up at the speedometer. That bastard was going at least 120 miles an hour!

It was raining. Little did I know that sunny days were on the horizon for my budding career. At that very moment, Otto was calling Vince to give me a good recommendation.

CHAPTER 13 - WWF (JULY 1984-JULY 1990)

"Brutus was the best. A few people said it was Hogan got him into the WWF, but that's just not true. Don't get me wrong. Having a friend helps for recommendations, but if Brutus didn't have what it took to succeed, he wouldn't have gone anywhere. Vince didn't push him in the biggest promotion in the world for just nothing. Kids liked him and he really had a look. He was sexy... disco sexy to be exact. Disco sexy, brother! The fans loved him and the ladies loved him even more!" - "The Magnificent" Don Muraco

I had just come back from Otto's match in Austria. Things had turned out really well. What I had found out was that Otto had originally wanted John Studd, or even Hulk Hogan to work with him, but they couldn't get the dates off from WWF. They were doing so well in New York that Vince couldn't afford to let them go. That is why they asked me. Without Hulk available, they decided to go with his "younger brother, Dizzy."

Otto didn't expect me to do as well out there, as I did. But with the whole bodyslam spot and all, I exceeded his expectations. Otto was so happy that he decided to take the liberty of calling Vince McMahon up in my behalf. He only had good things to say about me.

With both Hulk pulling for me and Otto, Vince decided to give me a shot at a spot in New York on TV.

I was jazzed. We set up a meeting to figure out my new name.

When I showed up to Vince's office, Hulk and Vince were already there. I shook their hands and sat down. While we were sitting around throwing some ideas, Linda McMahon, his wife, came in with some ideas of her own.

"I think you should pattern him a little bit after Baron Mikel Scicluna," she said. He was an older Maltese professional wrestler who worked for Vince, who wore tuxedo shirts and had a whole ladies man thing going for him. "I also think he should have like a cane."

His wife had already been kicking around a character idea that she wanted to see on WWF television. She had a lot of ideas of how she wanted this new particular character to be portrayed, and they were now hoping that I would pan out to play this character.

The idea was that I would be the ultimate male, a Chippendale-type wrestler, almost like a stripper. As far as what I would actually be called, she only really had one idea, and that was the word "Beefcake."

Oh my God. Beefcake? Is that going to be my name or what?

"Would Beefcake be a first name, or will it be a last name?" Vince asked. The room started to throw around some other ideas of what could maybe go with the word/name.

We eventually started going with the idea of alliteration. Alliteration is a literary term that means both the first and last name would have the same letter or sounding letters. Some examples of this included Bob Backlund, Pat Patterson, or even Hulk Hogan. Using this formula made the name catchy and poetic in a sense.

"Maybe Barry, or Billy?" Linda asked.

Vince said, "How about Bobby?"

"No, it should be something really far out, and out there." Hulk Hogan said.

"Yes!" Vince said. "Because he is different, his name should be different."

We sat there for a few minutes riffing names. It was like skatting to a jazz song. We rattled off practically every B-name we could think of.

"Wait, you know Popeye the Sailor? How about Brutus, the bad guy from the cartoon?" Hulk asked.

"Oh, Christ," I said. "Brutus Beefcake?"

They all laughed.

This was supposed to be my big break. People from all over the world dreamed of coming to Madison Square Garden to perform, and I was about to fulfill a dream. However, I was going to do so with people calling me *Brutus Beefcake?* I wasn't prepared to be that outrageous. I couldn't even say the name to myself without laughing. It sounded totally ridiculous.

"That sounds perfect!" Vince said. He put out his hand and then did his best ring announcer voice, "…and in this corner, Brutus Beefcake!"

And that was it.

Since this was in a day and age when WWF didn't have their own seamstresses to create costumes, I was responsible for designing (and paying) for all my clothing myself. Back then, you had to live the gimmick as much as possible. This meant Vince expected me to travel around and be Brutus Beefcake twenty-four hours a day, seven days a week. That's just how it worked.

The Hulkster told me to fly back down to Florida and talk to this guy who used to make clothing for the local bands.

"I mean, this guy is amazing," he said. "He made all of our band costumes for Ruckas, and he makes all the rock 'n' roll band clothing for like everyone in that area. He has even done a ton of outfits for superstars including Aerosmith, Hendrix, The Temptations, Sly & The Family Stone, and even Cher."

"Oh, Cher?" I laughed. "That's good."

The Hulkster was right. I flew back to Tampa and the guy was waiting for me.

Michael Braun was Jimi Hendrix' personal fashion designer. If you have seen the iconic Hendrix outfit he wore at Woodstock, you may be familiar with Michael's work and just didn't know it. His label "Michael & Toni" has been a very big name for Rock-N-Roll bands as well as other entertainers since the 70s.

I pulled up to his monster home in South Tampa. It was a 6,000-square-foot place off of a really nice area, South Bayshore Boulevard. His clothing factory was actually located in the bays of his six-car garage.

When I drove into the driveway, I looked into his workspace `through the opening. It appeared that a giant S&M shop, a crayon factory, and a Salvation Army thrift store had exploded, and whatever was left was hanging or scattered about the garage. It wasn't exactly what I was expecting, to say the least, but it was cool.

"Michael?" I asked.

"Yes?"

Michael Braun, Jimi Hendrix's personal fashion designer, made all of the Brutus Beefcake ring gear, using the same craftsmanship he used for big name rockstars.

Michael was probably in his mid-thirties, with curly brown hair and a short beard. The hard rock designer was working away on a sewing machine, picking at some sparkly, golden material. He sat amidst stacks of drawings and rolls of crazy materials.

"Brutus Beefcake," I said, almost smirking at the sound of it coming from my mouth for one of the first few times outside of Vince's office.

We talked for a bit. Michael Braun and I had something in common; *he was a boat racer in the 60s.* We talked about racing some. I guess he hurt his arm and then switched over to designing. We talked a little about boats, and then I brought up his work with Jimi Hendrix.

"Very polite guy," he said. "He was shy. He would get uncomfortable about getting measured and eventually told me to just make everything with a size 28 waist. Price was never an object."

That was cool for him, but I remember thinking that I wasn't made of money. I was hoping maybe to get a good deal on some digs, like a friend discount, or fellow boatsmen.

Michael showed me around a little at some things he was working on. He showed me some pictures, as well. The area had racks and racks of clothing. He had a number of projects all in the works.

"I remember going to this old garment district in Manhattan and buying all this old-lady fabric," he said. "You know, really loud, like silk material with red roses, yellow daffodils on black backgrounds, and I'd make all of Jimi's shirts from this stuff," Michael said. "The louder the better. It's the best cloth you can buy, anywhere."

We discussed the thought of "Brutus" as a stripper, or a Chippendale. "We want the ultimate male," I said. I talked to him about our ideas. His face lit up. He brought me over to a rack for a glam rock band project that he was up to on the other side of the garage. There, he proceeded to show me some vests and spandex tights.

My eyes popped right out of my head. He had all of these lace-up leather vests and boots with tassel fringe - all kinds of just crazy stuff. I had never seen anything like it in my life. The bright colors. The zebra and leopard prints. It was perfect.

In the end, the rock-n-roll designer came up with the building blocks of what would become the Brutus Beefcake look; an open airy vest, bow tie, long gauntlet gloves, and spandex leggings – all with various bright colors and animal prints like cheetah, leopard, and zebra.

I gave it a few weeks and I got a bunch of the first outfits made. In the meantime, I had been dieting heavily to go for that leaner, dancer/model look. Since I am genetically a fairly thin guy, I dropped about 15 pounds easily. I went from probably 260 down to 240, and did look more slender. I cut off the blonde shoulder-length hair and went for a short, cleaner look. I also died it dark and slicked it back.

When I came back from Florida with all that Brutus Beefcake stuff, I went straight from the airport to Vince's office. I got changed in a bathroom off the lobby, then headed right up the elevator. I pushed open his door for the first time in full gimmick. Vince dropped his pen, along with his jaw.

"Oh. Oh yeah! That's it," he said, looking at me standing in the frame of the door. "Brutus Beefcake!"

Not knowing exactly where it came from, I did the Buddy Rogers strut as I walked through the door. It came out very naturally with the ridiculous clothing on. That was probably my very first strut.

"How could this not make money?" Vince was blown away. As you may or may not know, with Vince, it was all about presentation and judging the book by the cover. You didn't have to be the best wrestler in the world, but you had to have a look that he could sell. The designer did just that.

I immediately was written into the WWF fulltime schedule on the spot.

The next day, I was all set up to go to Poughkeepsie, New York. Nobody was privy to any of this. They put my name down on a list as Brutus Beefcake and I parked my car and headed into the locker room a few hours before a show.

Arnold Skaalund showed me in. He fumbled through some papers on his clipboard then took out his pen. "Who are you again?"

"Brutus Beefcake," I said in a soft tone.

"Got it, Brutus."

Ha ha! He doesn't even recognize me! I wonder if this new look will fool the other boys?

I walked down the familiar hall to one of the dressing rooms. I had been to Poughkeepsie before with my run in 1979, only a few years before. I got there early knowing that there would have to be some talk about what they were going to do with me, however, I probably had gotten there too early. There wasn't anybody really there yet. So I went about my business. I hung up my clothing, put on my vest and tights, and sat down to wait with a newspaper. Just like any other show, you are constantly rush, rush, rush… and then… wait, wait, wait.

While I was getting dressed, guys were just starting to pull up to the arena.

As a sign of respect, you always go up to the wrestlers in the locker room and shake their hand. I don't care who you are. Everybody shakes hands gratuitously. It may seem a little obsessive or even strange when people from the outside see it. If a guy comes into a crowded room, he goes out of his way to shake everyone's hand in sight. There have been cases in the locker room where if you did not shake somebody's hand, somebody would actually take it as a personal insult and may actually take it out on you in the ring for not exchanging pleasantries earlier on in the back.

The tradition could, perhaps, come from the fact that many wrestlers are paranoid because a big portion of the world around them is fake. Maybe, perhaps, the idea is to shake everyone's hands so that paranoia does not kick in and subsequently someone feels they have been left out because you are out to screw them.

And then there was also the old school wrester's secret handshake that eventually died (thank god) in the 90s. This began during wrestling's early roots in its carnival days. It was a way for you to identify someone who possibly wasn't smart to the secrets of wrestling. The shake looked firm, but it was in reality very loose, like you were holding a dead fish. This would show the boys you were one of them, but you just hadn't worked in their territory yet. Back in the day, you couldn't assume if a guy was good, or not. One test was really good wrestlers shook hands lightly, and crappy ones shook stiff. The firmness of the grip came to mean how stiff they would be in the ring with you. A girly, dead fish handshake was preferred. It meant you worked light.

I don't know how it got its start, but this tradition of going out of your way to shaking everyone's hands in sight was real. As I was lacing my boots up, each one of the wrestlers came over to shake my hand. When you work with a new wrestler that was when the shake was the most important, it was either an opportunity to introduce yourself, or out yourself as someone who didn't belong.

Morocco came over and reached out his hand.

"Don Morocco."

"Brutus Beefcake."

Morocco nodded. I shook his hand with the worker handshake. He looked at me funny for a second. He had never heard of me. He walked over to his locker and went about his business.

"Nikolai Volkoff," the big Russian said. I shook his hand with the deadness.

"Brutus Beefcake."

This is a riot! I've worked with those guys 100 times before and they do not recognize me. They all think I'm a new guy.

I went over to the mirror to wash my face in the sink. I could see why I was probably 20 pounds lighter, with dark hair, clean-shaven, and sexier than ever.

The same handshaking tradition continued as some of the boys came in. Then we sat around waiting for our turn with the New York State Athletic Commission.

It was pretty funny. I sat there and looked at some magazine and knew damn well that all of the guys were checking out the new guy. However, I do not think it was a territorial stare down. It seemed like they all recognize me, but they didn't know how. It's like they knew me, but couldn't remember from when or where.

Tony Garea was periodically sticking his head into our dressing room and calling guys to come out into the hall and get their blood pressure checked they could be cleared to wrestle. As we were waiting, George Steele really started to stare. It became very obvious that he didn't care I knew he was staring. Finally, he decided to speak up and say what everybody else was thinking. He chose his words and spoke, of course, in such a warm way that really would have made a newcomer feel welcome.

"Who the fuck are you?!"

I waited a few moments for dramatic effect before answering. The whole room dropped pretty much everything they were doing. A few guys in the corner who were playing cards put them down on the table. Other guys dropped down their newspapers, magazines, or whatever it is they were engrossed in to kill time. The silence was deafening it and all eyes were on me.

"Brutus Beefcake."

"We know. We know. You said that before. But we all know we have worked with you somewhere. However, nobody can seem to place it," George said, walking my way slowly. "Now again, I said, who the fuck are you?"

George Steele was a nice guy, and very smart. It was killing him that he didn't know how he knew me. It is also clear that he probably had asked everyone in the room and they too felt the same way. They knew that they knew me, but nobody knew how.

"It's me, George. Dizzy," I said smiling. "Dizzy Hogan."

It was almost like something out of a cartoon. Everyone leaned forward slowly. They all squinted their eyes and looked at me. Then, one by one, I saw a light bulb turn on over each one of their heads.

Everyone laughed. Everyone, that is, Except the one guy who himself was famous for playing jokes - *and that was Mr. Fuji.*

"You mother fucker!"

At that, Fuji grabbed his cane that was leaning against the wall next to his card table. He picked it up, held above his head, and charged straight at me.

I dropped everything. Fuji was crazy. I ran out of the locker room and down the hall with a short little Asian man running after me with a cane, who is swinging it right above my head. I could hear the roar of laughter behind me followed by applause from all the boys.

Welcome to the World Wrestling Federation.

MISTER FUJI – MASTER OF RIBS

Before I discuss my debut, I think I need to explain why Fuji did or did not appreciate my little joke, not telling the boys who I actually was. A lot of the boys loved Mister Fuji. Some of them even called him Uncle Harry. While he was beloved, he was the king of pranks. His jokes were both legendary and borderline evil. He would pull them in the locker room, in hotels, in airports, in restaurants – nobody was safe anywhere.

Fortunately, I never fell victim to any of them. However, he really was an instigator and an innovator when it came to practical jokes and pranks.

Nothing was sacred to Mister Fuji, the devious one.

In my first run with the WWF, there were very few people in the locker room who were more respected than Hulk's heel manager, "Classy" Freddie Blassie. Even though Blassie was a well-respected bonafide legend, that didn't mean that he was immune from Mister Fuji's evil ways.

Freddie Blassie spent a lot of money on his flashy wardrobe. It meant a lot to him to look a certain way, and he spent some serious money on his threads to accomplish that. One of Fuji's favorite ways to mess with a guy was to hit him where he was most passionate. In this case, that meant for Blassie he needed to mess with his clothing.

One time during a match, Fuji noticed that Blassie had his whole suitcase in with him in the locker room so he could go directly to the airport from the show. When Blassie went out to ringside, it was game on.

Fuji immediately took all of Blassie's regular street clothing and ring attire and laid it out on a table. Then he grabbed a ladder. Then, piece by piece, he stapled and superglued all of Blassie's clothing to the ceiling above his lockers. When Blassie returned, you can only imagine the priceless response; his face turning red and steam coming from his ears!

"Fuji!!!"

"The Red Rooster" Terry Taylor was another one who had some of his clothing customized by Fuji Tailors, INC. After showering, Terry went to put on a new expensive suit that he had just purchased and bragged about to the boys. When he put it on, he found out that Fuji had taken the liberty of re-hemming the pant-legs to somewhere, oh… above the knee. Knowing that if he caused a scene, he would get even more shit from Mister Fuji, Terry pulled the pants on and walked out of the arena like nothing happened.

Constantly traveling is one of the worst things about being a professional wrestler. When you don't see a wrestler in the ring, he is either probably driving, making hotel reservations, or setting up flights. As if figuring out your travel is not already bad enough, Mister Fuji always found a way to make it worse.

Life on the road with Fuji for some was Hell.

One example of this had to do with Mr. Fuji and an intentionally prolonged road trip. In a hotel lobby, Fuji heard a new guy didn't know the way to the show, so he offered to jump in with him and give directions. The star-struck rookie agreed, hoping to talk with the ring veteran and gain some wisdom. However, Fuji basically said nothing but directions for three hours.

After the show, Fuji said he would drive the same wrestler back to the same hotel from where they had come. Fuji, behind the wheel, made it back in 10 minutes. The rookie was confused as they pulled up to the destination so quickly, until he heard Fuji laugh. Then he realized that earlier he had been put on a three-hour wild-goose chase, just for the sake of a rib.

One of the worst things you could do was ever make your flight arrangements on the phone within an earshot of the devious one. If you did, he would nicely pick up the phone for you, call the airport, and have your tickets canceled on your behalf. You would then miss a booking, and even worse, lose money.

If you made it onto the plane, you were not safe, either. One time, Fuji pulled an evil prank after a Guam tour in the late 70s on an Armenian wrestler named Pampero Firpo. While Pampero was sleeping, Fuji took a six-foot chain and padlocked his carry-on bag under his seat. But, that wasn't all. Then he superglued the lock shut. Needless to say, it was a tough day at the office for Pampero. After finally freeing his luggage, airport officials took Pampero off to an office. You see, while trying to cut the chain, the next flight was delayed. He had to then try and explain to Customs why it was bolted like that in the first place.

Another time on the road, after arriving in a little Podunk town in the middle of nowhere, "Beautiful" Bobby Eaton went into the arena for a show. He wrestled his match. When he came back out at the end of the night, he tried to start his car and nothing happened. "What the hell?" Bobby said. Bobby got out of his rental. He went around and popped the hood, and then just stood there.

To his surprise, he found that the entire engine of his vehicle had been completely removed! Talk about dedication to your craft! Fuji paid close to $1000 of his own money just to pull off that prank.

Master Fuji was a master chef. Even your food and drink was not off limit with Mister Fuji. If you were say drinking a cup of coffee, Fuji would slip in some laxatives in it when you weren't looking. Then before your match, you would either walk to the ring crossing your legs and praying for the best, or skipping the match altogether, shitting your brains out like a demon.

Tor Kamata was good friends with Fuji, but that didn't make his food off limits. A bunch of guys after a show drove up to West Haven in Connecticut where one of them had an apartment with some extra rooms to crash in. On this particular night, the Samoans were there cooking Bar-BQ and everyone came to the party. The Iron Sheik, Bobby Duncan, Rick McGraw, Stan Hansen, Rick Martel, Mr. Fuji and Tor Kamata all came.

To go along with the grilling, Fuji decided to also prepare some type of stew. Kamata took a healthy portion Fuji's gruel, but none of the boys dared to. They all knew better.

"This is very good Fuji," he said, taking a heaping spoonful to his mouth.

Fuji nodded.

After dinner, Fuji came out with his big pot to offer one last helping to anyone who would eat it. When he made his way over to Kamata, he nodded as if to indicate he would like some more. Fuji dipped the ladle deep into it the pot and pulled out the head of the dead cat.

All hell broke loose and the boys had to hold Kamata back from killing Mister Fuji.

He pulled this same joke on Skandor Akbar, Billy White Wolfe and some other wrestlers, who were unsuspectingly dining on what was believed to be "marinated chicken." Fuji said he marinated and grilled it "teriyaki style," while Muraco was out buying them a bunch of beers. After they ate it, Muraco asked what they were eating, then revealed a bag of bones and all the guys began to puke. All was delicious until they pulled out a cat's head of a paper bag, revealing that the actual wrestlers' lunch was General Tso's Kitten.

The worst Fuji rib I ever heard, one could only hope is not true. It was allegedly done to his partner Tanaka, who was a villain in one of the James Bond movies – the one who threw his hat as a weapon. The way the story goes, Tanaka was going behind Fuji's back in the office trying to gain an office position that Fuji held. However, Mr. Fuji found out and swore revenge.

Time went on. Fuji lived right next door to Tanaka's family. Tanaka was about to leave for a new territory run so Fuji called him to have one meal.

"Tanaka. Come on over, let's have a get-together. You are moving soon, so one last time. Bring your family. You like spaghetti? We'll cook up some spaghetti and whatever you want."

Tanaka agreed.

His family came over for a wonderful spaghetti and meatballs dinner that he prepared. The kids and his wife all ate heartily and had a grand old time. Then, Fuji disappeared.

"I've got a special surprise for you!"

Mister Fuji returned with a covered silver platter. When he lifted the cover, the whole family went berserk. They were staring at their own family dog's head.

Legend has it, Tanaka left the territory the very next day.

I'm not sure if this is true, but if it is, that was very mafia.

After I first started coming back around from my accident, there was a new guy on the scene. When Lex Luger first came to the WWE, some of the boys thought he kind of had an attitude. There was no handshake. He would just kind of come into the room and wouldn't talk to anyone. He was just coming from Georgia, so either he was feeling like a black sheep, or actually thought that his shit didn't stink.

We were in the middle of nowhere after a show in Philadelphia and headed out for another show. It was almost midnight. A bunch of us stopped at a country-western themed diner that had a little bar. We all sat down at a bunch of tables, probably four of them, that were already pushed together. It was late at night, but we still tried to protect the business as best we could. The heels kind of gathered three or four tables over to the right, and the faces on the opposite end.

Now, I don't know if Luger was shy, or not, but when he came in a little bit after us, he went to sit off at a table by himself.

"He not good enough for us?" Fuji asked the Powers of Pain, who were sitting at our cluster of tables. Fuji had heard about Lex's attitude, or the way he had been acting since he showed up and he didn't like it. He did not like it one bit.

Fuji got up with his back to Lex and unzipped his fly. He reached into his zipper and pulled out some of the bulge in his underpants. All the boys knew what was going to happen next.

You see Fuji had a history of pissing on things. When he would get a reaction, he would just no-sell it all together. That was his joke. He had no qualms taking out his junk and just peeing where ever he damn well pleased. Earlier that week, Fuji was talking to the manager at some hotel in their bar. I go over to Fuji and look down… and there he is, just pissing away in a potted plant! He was just talking to the manager the whole time. The manager was so confused that he didn't know what to say.

So Fuji goes over and sits across from Lex at his high-top. There were no tablecloths. They were both sitting just right, sideways, so we could see the whole show.

We waited for a while. Fuji was just talking, drinking his drink, and filling his bladder. Once he was ready, he put his arm behind his back and gave us the thumbs up.

The boys gathered around to watch.

"What is he doing?" Warlord asked.

Master Fuji pushed his fingers into his trousers masterfully and fiddled around with his devious penis. Maybe he was trying to chub up so that he would have extra length and better aim, I don't know. Then all of a sudden, it was the moment of golden truth.

A nice stream of urine came jetting out of Fuji's crotch and landed directly on Lex's boot under the table.

Lex didn't move.

I don't know if it was because he had heard about the way Fuji is relentless with evil pranks if you "pissed" him off, or if Lex just didn't feel it.

Either way, it looked to us like he just let him piss all over his foot. But I digress...

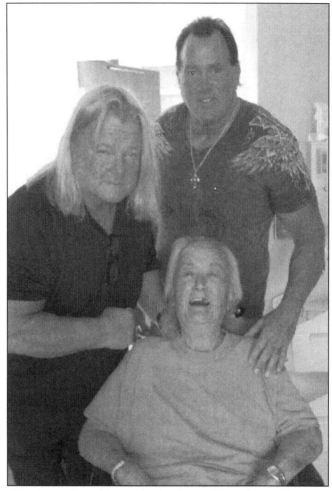

The Dream Team (Greg Valentine & myself) reuniting with our good friend Mister Fuji before he passed in August of 2016.

BRUTUS BEEFCAKE TELEVISION DEBUT

I would first appear as Brutus Beefcake on WWF television in the late summer of 1984 in teasers. What Vince had me do was walk out to the ring in full costume during squash matches by various babyface wrestlers and just watch. That's it. I would just stand there, put my hand up to my chin, observe and then leave. What would happen during my observation time on television is that the commentators would see me and put a mysterious spin on my presence to help create interest.

"Who is this strange man?!"

I continued to just walk around and watch matches. Occasionally, I would skip around the ring and maybe blow kisses, but that was it. It was a pretty easy payday for a few months. Vince McMahon, or Gorilla would just keep up the "Who is this mysterious guy?" shtick.

After a number of weeks of this, the commentators made it known that Brutus was looking for a manager, so then the pissing contests began. What they did was have all the managers begin to offer their services to me, courting me for my business. The angle was established that all the current WWF managers wanted to sign "the next hottest property." So when I would come out to ringside, a different manager each week would approach me and whisper in my ear. These including Captain Lou Albano, Freddie Blassie, and Bobby "The Brain" Heenan, to name a few.

In the end, however, Vince decided to push the idea that Brutus was very different and therefore should have a different and new manager, one that the current WWF audience didn't know.

LUSCIOUS JOHNNY VALIANT

Johnny Valiant competed in the WWWF for Vince McMahon's father. He held the WWWF World Tag Team Championship two times. Beating Tony Garea and Dean Ho on May 8, 1974, his first title run lasted over a year. His second title run was with his other storyline brother Jerry when they beat Tony Garea and Larry Zbyszko back on March 6, 1979.

After he retired from active competition, Johnny V. went on to a successful career as a manager. He managed a fan-favorite Hulk Hogan in the AWA in the early 1980s, and Vince hoped that he would be like a New York version of Bobby Heenan in the WWF, due to his quick wit and comical ways. Luscious Johnny V. wasn't doing all that much on the road, so when he got the call, he immediately accepted Vince's offer to take me on. You see, although both Hulk Hogan and Bruno Sammartino were not very friendly with each other, they both were friendly with Johnny Valiant and had been pulling for him to come and work for Vince, Jr.

Eventually, on WWF TV, I had a big reveal to show the world just who my manager was going to be. All the managers came out and lined up. Finally, that is when "Luscious" Johnny Valiant, someone nobody was thinking of, was chosen to guide me in my wrestling career.

MAIN EVENT STRIP CLUB

Johnny on the microphone helped get me over tremendously. Being the brains behind the brawn, he was also the initial voice behind the Brutus Beefcake gimmick. Johnny's deal was that he would mostly only appear on TV, not house shows, therefore he didn't travel with me much. However, if there was a need for a voice, Johnny was there.

After signing on with my official manager, they decided to reintroduce me on WWF programming with an actual vignette. Being originally portrayed as a male stripper, Vince decided to have Johnny and I go to an actual exotic male review strip club for women to put over my gimmick. He wanted to get actual footage of me dancing at a real Chippendale-like bar that he could air on television.

The only problem with this idea of stripping in front of women was it scared the shit out of me. Now don't get me wrong, I had no problem with a woman dancing for me, I just had no idea what it was like being on the other side of the stage.

The story behind shooting the scenes of this vignette is pretty funny. We went out to this place aptly called "The Main Event Night Club" in December of 1984. When we got there, we were brought to the back dressing along with two cameramen. You would think we wouldn't fit in, but we were right at home and nobody seemed to notice. All of the dancers were there putting on similar clothing. They all looked like members of the Village People and nobody seemed to care how I was dressed.

I got in gear – a nice shiny vest, some yellow striped zebra skin spandex pants, and two sets of gloves. The idea was I could pull off the outer longer glove and reveal the shorter gauntlets underneath as part of my strip act. Johnny Valiant couldn't have fit his role better. His look screamed the perfect blend of circus ringmaster and aging pornstar. As for me, I was afraid that I was going to vomit.

Now, I never really got cold feet, or stage fright on a wrestling show. I had done hundreds of them and it wasn't really a big deal anymore for me. But the idea of going out on a stage in an element that I was unfamiliar with, and also doing what Vince wanted me to do – that was scary. I didn't want to mess something up and lose my spot before I even started.

Vince had actually paid the club money to let me dance and to let his company film it in front of their customers. In return, he promised to leave the fans hot. This meant at the end of my dancing routine, I needed to commit fully.

Vince wanted me to undress down to my G-string to make the ladies pop. I didn't know where to begin. I watched a few of the dancers before our spot, to try and figure out what I was supposed to do. The male strippers were gyrating and pelvis-popping in ways that I couldn't even imagine. I just could not see myself doing that and feared being booed off the stage.

"What the fuck, Johnny?!" I said, watching a construction worker practically piledrive people's faces with his penis. I pulled the curtain closed.

Johnny laughed. "You will do just fine."

I started to worry, then I started cursing under my breath. Then, I reminded myself of Paul Orndorff, all stressed out in Japan. Then it was simple. Everything became very clear on what I had to do to make it through the performance.

The Ultimate Male needed the Ultimate Japanese Happy Pill.

Fortunately for me, I had three of them left in a little aspirin bottle in my gear bag. I popped all of those bad boys, drank a tall glass of water, and I was ready to hump the world.

It was finally our turn on stage. Johnny went out first to introduce me and stayed on stage to be my hype man. It didn't make a whole lot of sense to the women at the club, but they didn't seem to care. They had a pro wrestler positioning to become half-naked (or more) in front of them, and they were in heaven.

As Johnny started his promo, I looked around at the fans. In a couple of words about the women at this club, they were just like most any typical female fan at a wrestling show. Most of them were pretty rough, both in appearance and in personality.

"So I want you ladies to really give it up for my man," Johnny said in a bright yellow hat. "My main man… Brutus Beefcake!"

The music hit. Patty Smyth's "The Warrior" would not have been my first choice, but it was my dancing song. Fortunately for me, by the first few bars the Japanese Happy pills started to kick in. I was good to go. But then, they REALLY started to kick in. Taking three of those Japanese Happy pills may have been a little excessive, but seemed like a good idea at the time.

I was dizzy. In a daze, I started doing my best Carlton Dance. It was very, very, very white, but at least I didn't care. I went right up to the girls' faces to shake my junk. Then, I danced back over to Johnny Valiant to give him a little action, too.

I felt drunk. I tried to pull the long black and silver gloves off, to reveal the shorter ones underneath, but it wasn't happening. I had to have

Johnny actually help! After the shorter black gloves with yellow lightning bolts were revealed, I made my way over to the ladies to work the crowd.

Giving a lap-dance to Grandma Higgins was probably not something I would have done sober, but that too now seemed like a good idea. Grandma loved it. She cupped my balls, she checked my oil like Andre, she did everything short of giving me a whipped cream handjob right there in front of everyone.

Even high on chill pills, I had to get up off of Grandma. She was handling everything. I turned around and made a break for it, towards Johnny.

"Take it home," Johnny said, laughing, meaning, "Let's finish this and get out of here."

Johnny held up his jacket. I was supposed to take off my pants behind it, let them fall to the floor and then wrap myself in his coat. However, three Japanese Happy Pills made the dexterity needed for that finish nearly impossible. I ended up taking my pants off, then letting the jacket hit the floor.

Johnny almost died laughing. He started chanting along with the music, "Beefcake! Beefcake! Beefcake!" The women didn't care. They were just trying to catch a glimpse of me in my skivvies.

So who was I to disappoint? I pranced around in my underwear as the music finished up.

The women loved it and Vince got his footage.

CHAPTER 14 - WRESTLEMANIA

With Johnny Valiant in my corner, I was gearing up for some super card idea that Vince McMahon was calling, "WrestleMania." Vince was risking everything, banking on the awesome group of guys in his locker room to really bring in the bucks. Since that gamble, WrestleMania has become the Super Bowl of professional wrestling. It has the same international appeal as the NFL's big marquee show, airing in more than 160 countries in more than 30 languages.

I was around for the very first one.

THE HILLBILLY PLAN

I had been wrestling in a bunch of singles matches getting wins against anyone they could afford to me, all in an effort to build me up. They had me on this awesome strong winning streak over undercard talent like the aging Chief Jay Strongbow, Tony Garea, and a who's who of classic WWF jobbers. I was being well-protected before WrestleMania leading up to something that I hoped would be really good for me.

Around this time, Vince contacted Jim Morris, a wrestler who was working the wrestling scene in Memphis, under the ring name of "Harley Davison," with a biker gimmick. He wanted to pay him to sit in the audience and eventually get beat up by me.

They seated him prominently in the front row of all the WWF TV tapings, so that he would be in all the camera shots. The commentators eventually "noticed" that the big guy was at every show and then pointed him out to the fans watching at home. They would just have him clap and cheer and they would put the cameras on him and call him "WWF's #1 fan." Once he became recognizable to their audience, after plenty of exposure week in and week out, then the real plan kicked in. Jim was going to take a hit, then become the catalyst that would push me into a future program with Hulk Hogan.

The idea was genius. Wrestling fans liked him because he looked like a hillbilly-type wrestling fan himself that they could relate to. He was like a big cartoon. He was a shaggy-bearded, simple-minded, backwoods hillbilly that your average wrestling fan could easily relate to. Clad in blue jean overalls, he was very much like the stereotypical fan sitting in every audience across America.

How could anybody hate that?

After many weeks, Vince McMahon (as a TV commentator) went over to the audience to interview who they came to know as super-fan "Big Jim." After that, Jim was asked to be a guest on Piper's Pit. There, Roddy Piper offered his services to train him to become a wrestler. But as a wrestling fan, Jim revealed that if he were to become a wrestler, he would rather be trained by the very best, his favorite, WWF Heavyweight Champion Hulk Hogan.

A week or so later, Ken Patera and Big John Studd were victorious in a tag team match. They took things a little too far with the Hulkster, while his super fan was watching in the audience. Big Jim finally jumped the fence and Hulk Hogan prevented him from getting his hair cut by Bobby "The Brain" Heenan.

Hillbilly Jim was born.

After that, Vince produced a number of vignettes to be aired on WWF's TV in the early weeks of 1985. These videos showed Hulk Hogan's appreciation in training Jim how to wrestle, and even giving him his first set of wrestling boots. This footage was made to make Jim even more likable, so that when I finally beat him up, it would piss off the fans all the more. My actions, in turn, would also piss off Hillbilly Jim's new friend Hulk Hogan, who would seek vengeance and set up our big feud.

Hillbilly Jim appeared ringside for matches with his mentor Hulk Hogan to establish their friendship. He also had a singles match at an event created just to promote WrestleMania called "The War to Settle the Score" on February 18, 1985. Before Mania in April, I was supposed to beat him up, leading towards what many believed to be an inevitable "Hillbilly Jim versus Brutus Beefcake" match at WrestleMania. There was talk about me injuring Hillbilly Jim at Mania, so the Hulkster would want to get his vengeance on me for what I did to his friend. The problem was, Hillbilly's injury turned real and altogether too soon.

In San Diego, I was working against Hogan before any real feud. Hillbilly Jim was in Hulk's corner. During the match, Johnny Valiant tormented Hillbilly Jim and he started chasing Valiant around the ring. During this chase-spot, Hillbilly lost his footing and slipped on some fan's soda at ringside. He fell down hard and legitimately broke his leg.

In a case where fiction became reality, we got our injury, but the timing was all off now, and it was real. They had to take Hillbilly Jim out on a stretcher, and we soon learned that he was not going to be able to wrestle again for at least another six months!

We had all that build up, and then we had to go back to the drawing boards. To play it off well, the commentators decided to really make me look like a piece-of-shit dastardly wrestler, saying stuff like, "Brutus Beefcake injured Hillbilly Jim intentionally."

During the several months off for Hillbilly's recovery time, they created a few similarly-dressed "Hillbilly Jim family" members. These included Uncle Elmer, Cousin Luke, and Cousin Junior, to avenge Hillbilly Jim and continue the feud. However, the Hillbilly clan wouldn't have time to debut until after WrestleMania. So rather than to face Hillbilly Jim at WrestleMania (which would have been the obvious pairing for us,) I was going to be facing someone else.

"LIVING LEGEND" BRUNO SAMMARTINO

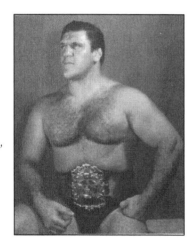

"I would love to give a quote for Beefcake's book. I thought that Brutus was always in good shape and a good wrestler. I was also impressed with how many different gimmicks he was given over his career, but always did everything he could to get the most out of what he was given to work with. In the ring, I personally got to wrestle him a number of times and always enjoyed it very much."
—Bruno Sammartino

Bruno Sammartino is a former world champion. In Bruno's 20-year run with the WWWF, he famously held the Heavyweight Championship for a total of over 11 years! He had a record-breaking 2803 day run with the gold, which is a record that will likely never be broken. He is a great man and has a lot of history, integrity, and honor. He is very passionate about wrestling and knew at the time that he was getting older. He started to become very concerned with what type of guy was going to replace him and take his spot, for the best interest of the business. It eventually came out that while he liked the Hulk Hogan character, he didn't like the man's activities outside of the ring.

"He just wasn't a very good representation of the business, or a model for young people to look up to. He didn't walk the walk," Bruno said.

Even though he didn't like Hogan, he didn't hold it against me. Even though I was considered Hogan's buddy to some people, Bruno and I were actually pretty cool. I was raised to always be respectful, and subsequently, I always showed Bruno the respect that he deserved. This attitude went a long way in the locker room.

Before WrestleMania, I had the opportunity of being able to work against Bruno several times, even including our first match together in his hometown of Pittsburgh, PA. I remember that match clearly. He pushed me hard that night, and I took big bumps for him. I made him look as good as possible in his hometown, and he really appreciated that. Because of that night, we always got along.

Enter David Sammartino, son of the Living Legend.

When Vince told me that I would be facing Bruno's son at WrestleMania, I didn't really care. I just knew it wasn't going to be quite as good as it could have been actually wrestling his father. David was a nice guy, but he probably only had his spot with Vince because of who his father was. Nice guy, but he didn't exactly have the showmanship, or the charisma that you really needed to be where we were at this point in the game.

Granted, I only had a few years of experience myself, but I was coming along nicely. My work was solid in the ring, and the fans absolutely hated me. David was even newer than I was, and I felt he was going to just go out there and go through the motions during the match. David probably should have been booked as a heel to get better confidence in his early days with WWF. As a heel, you would usually call most of the matches, meaning he would call all the shots.

WRESTLEMANIA'S TURN OUT

When Vince McMahon announced his idea for WrestleMania, most of the territory pro wrestling promoters around the country thought Vince was crazy. They figured he had finally signed his own bankruptcy papers and that they could also finally lure their talent back that Vince had pulled from them. His rival promoters were actually pulling for WrestleMania to fail and the ultimate demise of WWF, although that wasn't in the cards. Vince was no dummy.

"WrestleMania was the ultimate in calculated risks," Vince has often said. "If Mania had failed, the future of WWE would have been bleak."

WrestleMania was officially the first real professional wrestling pay-per-view event ever. It took place on March 31, 1985, at Madison Square Garden in New York City. While the setup wasn't much different than any other house show at MSG, Vince's gamble had paid off. Vince McMahon's main competition in the wrestling industry at this time was with Jim Crockett Promotions' NWA. Vince wanted to offer a mega-card, and he decided to piggyback off of the success of Jim Crockett's annual big show "Starrcade" (which began airing in 1983) by also making his show available in multiple locations on closed-circuit TV.

The attendance for the event was a hot crowd of 19,121 fans. You really could feel the "excitement in the air," as they say. When I pulled up to the garage that day, I knew the hype had paid off. The hall right below MSG held another 10,000 people who were there because there were not going to be any seats left in the arena. All of those people were fully willing to watch it live on a closed-circuit TV in the hall.

Such a demand! I can't believe it! Vince really pulled it off!

The almost 30,000 people in attendance were just a scratch on the surface. The event was also seen by another million viewers through closed-circuit television in many big halls across the country, making it the largest showing of any event on closed-circuit television in America at the time.

This had never been done before. Vince had all kinds of media reaching different people than your traditional wrestling fan who looked like Hillbilly Jim, with three teeth in their whole head and two of them rotten. The locker room really stepped up in loyalty. Nobody was holding Vince up for more money or anything. We knew the risk he was taking on us. We knew we needed to be there for each other; promoter and talent. He was betting on a lot of really good wrestlers, and nobody wanted to disappoint.

The turnout that day was spectacular. It didn't happen by mistake. Vince planned this and bet everything he had on this one single event. The strategic placement on the calendar of WrestleMania's date in itself was very important. Vince couched it on the Sunday between NCAA men's basketball Final Four on Saturday and the championship game on Monday. There was virtually no competition. There was no football, no baseball, no Olympics, and no college basketball. The date selection was perfect.

Everybody was psyched. There was a different feeling there. The audience really was a smattering of all walks of life. I saw rich people. I saw poor people. I saw attractive women. I saw ugly men. I saw people of all ages all gathered in the name of professional wrestling, like never before. So how did this happen?

Vince McMahon decided to cross-promote the WWF with pop culture, to bring in this new mainstream audience and create a "Rock-n-Wrestling Connection." His hopes were that if he used celebrities from pop culture, he could pull in a whole new demographic to his show. He wanted the first WrestleMania to have a larger than life feel to it, with a combination of special guests from both the entertainment world, as well as sports.

To help make this happen, he had signed a deal with MTV and aired two wrestling specials to drum up interest for *WrestleMania*. The first MTV wrestling special was the one where Hillbilly hurt his leg. On July 23, 1984, *The Brawl to End It All* aired live from MSG. There, Wendi Richter beat the Fabulous Moolah to win the WWF Women's title, with Cyndi Lauper in her corner. Six months later on February 18, 1985, *The War to Settle the Score* had Leilani Kai, beat Richter to avenge Moolah and capture the title, with Cyndi Lauper again at ringside. Cyndi Lauper, a pop star, brought WWF into the popular eye. (Many people argue inversely that Cyndi Lauper's singing career was pushed into the mainstream because of WrestleMania, and all the media she received for the participation in it. Who knows? Either way, it was a win-win situation for sure.)

Talking up WrestleMania for almost a year before the payoff, interest had time to marinate. Other celebrities were booked for the buildup for Mania including Muhammad Ali, Liberace, the Rockettes, and Major League Baseball's Billy Martin. Those names allowed WrestleMania to receive crazy publicity, which professional wrestling would never have accomplished before this. The awareness helped not only sell out MSG, but also helped secure multiple closed-circuit viewing locations around the country in the days before pay-per-view was available to all on cable TV. (WrestleMania was, in fact, the first to tap the few stations experimenting with PPV.)

MY MANIA MATCH

David and Bruno weren't getting along in these days all that well. Many people feel that David resented his father for not pulling more strings for him in the WWF. Others speculated that Bruno didn't like the fact that David might have experimented with steroids. I can't speak to either of those rumors. I don't know where the disconnect actually was, but you could tell backstage that they were acting more like they were just working together, and less like they were blood.

We had both Jay Strongbow and Rene Goulet there as agents for our match. An agent was someone who would sit in on the discussion of the match and offer ideas. They would also make sure that the match went in a direction that was good for what the office was trying to portray. They told us that Vince wanted us both to look good so that nothing major was really going to end up happening in the match.

The match was solid; nothing special but we did a good job. The action favored both of us at the time as it was pretty much 50/50 booking, as each of us alternated having the advantage. After I threw David out of the ring, Johnny Valiant slammed him down to the cement floor to begin the finish. He was then attacked by Bruno, and then all four of us ended up fighting in the ring. The match ended in a big schmoz, no-contest.

For the main event, Vince was rolling the dice once again, this time with a wrestling card formula. Rather than to feature his top drawing star (Hulk Hogan) in a major singles match, he did something else. Instead, he put Hulk Hogan with a TV star in a tag-team match as the main event, against Roddy Piper and Paul Orndorff.

That TV star was, of course, Mr. T from the hit show *The A Team*.

This main event also had Muhammad Ali as the special referee, with Billy Martin as the ring announcer and Liberace as the guest timekeeper.

From what I understand, Pat Patterson was the in-ring referee to make sure it came off as planned. Mr. T, was inexperienced and a little nervous because of that. He also was legitimately not well-liked by Piper, because he felt a celebrity in the ring had no place wrestling. Mr. T was street smart. He wasn't just a Hollywood actor. He had his guard up just in case to make sure that his opponents wouldn't try and legitimately injure him in an effort to make wrestling look even more real and even more respected in the public eye.

McMahon's big gamble worked. WrestleMania helped fund WWE's continued national expansion and even sparked the start of the company's global growth. Mr. T worked out, and he stole the show, in my opinion. He delivered. He did a super job considering that he was not a professional wrestler, and his participation also helped bring WWF into the mainstream spotlight around the world.

As a side note, there was really only one group that was not happy with the product. Being as this was in the early days of PPV, all the bugs had not been worked out as of yet. For one audience, there was a casualty in service. A technical glitch ended the WrestleMania closed-circuit broadcast early into the showing at the Civic Arena in Sammartino-country; Pittsburgh, Pennsylvania. While they got to see my match with the Living Legend's son, they lost reception long before the main event. They did not get to see Hulk Hogan teaming with Mr. T.

They were pissed. The feed broke a few matches in and they were never able to get it up and going again, online. The fans were so into the idea of missing the match that they practically started to riot. Just like Boston

Gardens, they took everything they had and launched it at the big screen. Sodas, beers, pizza, you name it.

To appease angry fans who missed the match and subsequently pelted the screen with garbage, Vince gave the footage to a local ABC affiliate WTAE-TV two weeks later. In a successful attempt to save face for his growing company, WrestleMania was broadcasted on network television in its entirety for everyone in the Pittsburgh area for free.

Smart move!

"PARTS UNKNOWN" MADE KNOWN

Just for the record, Brutus Beefcake resided from the world famous, "Parts unknown" for quite some time. However, one day, they came up to me at a TV taping and said they were going to have to give me an actual city name that they were going to announce me from.

"Where?" I asked.

"Simple," Pat Patterson said. "San Francisco."

I know he was throwing a gay jab at me again, but I don't know why. Maybe it was his way of flirting, or maybe just wishful thinking. Who knows? He wanted to get a rise out of me, for sure, but I wouldn't put him over. There was no way I was going to let him think he got one over on me, so I just went with it.

THE FIRST ACTION FIGURE

I was one of the first guys that had an action figure. The very first royalty check was somewhere in the area of $20,000, which was unheard of for merchandise residuals like that in the early 80s. On top of that, I actually got to do a commercial for mine. In order to shoot that, I had to join the Screen Actors Guild early on in 1985. That was the beginning of even more pretty cool stuff for me, as far as future opportunities were concerned.

THE WRESTLING ALBUM

1985 was quite a pivotal year for the WWF. After WrestleMania and the success Vince saw from his "Rock 'n' Wrestling Connection" crossover promotional movement, he knew it had to continue. Looking to continue to push the WWF Superstars into the mainstream, he asked Cyndi Lauper to help him put out an album!

Lauper agreed, but only to participate under a disguise and credited with the pseudo name "Mona Flambé." With the package deal, Vince also secured David Wolff as the executive producer of the project. He was Cyndi's boyfriend and manager, who was also incidentally a huge wrestling fan and the real reason why Cyndi agreed to promote WrestleMania in the first place.

Vince's ultimate goal was to keep the ball rolling. He wanted the WWF cemented within the spotlight of pop culture. He wanted to continue to grab the attention of the MTV audience, but this time in the medium that their network was familiar with, *a hit music video.*

In order to make a music video, however, we first needed to have the music. David Wolff contacted his friend, rockstar legend Rick Derringer, to be the producer. He had been doing some cool multi-platform stuff with Weird Al Yankovic that he thought would make for a good match.

We hit the studio. The album was basically David Wolff's concept.

Jimmy Hart was also very heavily involved in the song making process. What many people don't know is that before he stepped foot into a wrestling ring in Memphis, he was in a fairly successful band called the Gentrys. David, Rick, and Jimmy had to first figure out where the real "Rock and Wrestling" connections were, as far as talent was concerned. Some of the wrestlers coming from a performance background really were actually good singers. David, Rick, and Jimmy unearthed the fact that a few of the WWF Superstars had real talent, and what they did was kind of channel those people into the project.

The general idea was to use some of the songs on the album as wrestler entrance theme music. Before this, I think The Fabulous Freebirds were among the first to play rock music for an entrance. When they saw the atmosphere music helped to create for their walk to the ring, they soon recorded their own track, "Badstreet USA." After that, others followed their lead to some degree. However, after the Wrestling Album, more attention was being placed on what your theme song would be, and how it reflected who you were as a character. This project really changed the way the business looked at entrances.

In the end, the songs came out to be very catchy. Being produced by Rick Derringer, they had a rock and pop appeal and turned out okay, for a bunch of wrestlers. To really add to the whole wrestling feel, David had all of the album's tracks interlaced with commentary from the WWF's announce team, Vince McMahon, "Mean Gene" Okerlund, and Jesse "The Body" Ventura.

So in October 1985, "The Wrestling Album" was released with 10 awesome tracks worth of WWE wrestlers trying our best to sing. The first single was a remake of Wilson Pickett's "Land of 1,000 Dances." You know the song. It is famous for its "Na, Na Na Na Na" hook.

Jimmy Hart took the creative license to change the lyrics, here and there, so that individual wrestlers could sing personalized solo lines in the song with a wrestling twist. My line, of course, was amazing:

"I'm gonna do the strut, up and down your spine!"

Thank you… Thank you… (Bow.)

The music video for "Land of 1,000 Dances" was a who's who of the 1985 WWE roster on a recording studio soundstage. We were all wearing our full ring gear, singing in unison, and dancing – yes dancing!

That little few seconds you saw of all of us on screen took nearly all day long to shoot. It was all laid out to look really chaotic, but in reality, it took a lot of work to get that look of insanity. Then, later on that night, we were all rushing off to wrestle on a show.

Rick Derringer was also there on stage with Cyndi Lauper. Cyndi Lauper was in her disguise, probably because she didn't want to be associated with such a pool of bad talent! For my spot in the video, they had me standing on the stage right next to Meatloaf. I thought that was just awesome. He was there, all positioned up on a drum set, but he was not really playing the drums. He was just there to look the part. I had already been around Derringer and Cyndi and got to know them, but I remember seeing Meatloaf was really cool. I was kind of a fan.

We had a long day on that stage, over and over and over, singing that thing.

Tito Santana thought the whole thing was ridiculous. I would look over at him while the group was singing, "Na, na-na-na-na, na-na-na-na, na-na-na, na-na-na…" I remember, I could see him laughing over and over again under his breath and shaking his head.

"Why are you laughing, Tito?" I asked him, between takes.

"I think I have just a horrible voice to have in song on an album," he said laughing.

Every wrestler had to film their individual parts separately, and then we had to film the group parts, as well. Then, get this, in the evening at the show, we had to perform the bit for the live crowd for even more footage.

For the next two weeks, all I had in my head was that stupid riff. "Na, na-na-na-na," Those bastards must have played that song a hundred times that day. The music video played everywhere, as well. It was on MTV, NBC's Friday Night Videos, Saturday Night's Main Event and all the WWF Programming. Its reach was surprising and pretty amazing.

None of the singles received any real heavy radio airplay, but The WWF Wrestling Album as a whole reached #84 on the album sales charts! Kids everywhere owned it.

The fold-out cover of the record is pretty iconic. It features McMahon, Okerlund, and Ventura in the front, with all the wrestlers going crazy behind them on the performing stage in the recording studio.

As far as other singles were concerned, there were a bunch. The Junkyard Dog, Mean Gene, Nikolai Volkoff, Hillbilly Jim, Jimmy Hart, Captain Lou and even Roddy Piper sang their own songs.

Piper's song, "For Everybody" is a cover of "Fuck Everybody," by Mike Angelo & The Idols. The Piper version includes Rick Derringer on guitar, Cyndi Lauper on backing vocals, and the Tower of Power horn selection. However, the WWF could not allow any profanity on a product targeting children, in part, which called for the chorus change and the words "kiss my ass," being changed to "kiss my trash."

Hulk Hogan had an anthem that sounded like the Rocky theme recorded for his ring entrance, however, the use of this song was only short-lived. They ended up using this track for maybe a few months, and then it became the exclusive theme for his cartoon, "Hulk Hogan's Rock 'N Wrestling."

The real winner of the album was "Real American," a song made famous after Hulk Hogan decided to adopt it as his entrance theme. It wasn't really made for him though, however.

Before any of the songs for the album had been recorded, Rick Derringer had already recorded a rough demo of the tune. Written by Derringer and a guy named Bernard Kenny, they set out to just create a great, patriotic song that Vince would maybe like. When the WWF first started working on the project, they were all trying to figure out what songs would be on it, and if they would all be original tunes, or not. When Derringer played the track for Vince McMahon, he fell in love with it right away.

"Oh, wow," McMahon said. "We can really use this!"

Vince originally decided to assign "Real American" to The US Express, so that Barry Windham and Mike Rotundo would have a good theme song. If you listen to the commentary between the songs on the album,

Vince McMahon actually says the song is, "dedicated to Windham and Rotundo." However, shortly after the album's release, Windham left to go to the NWA, National Wrestling Alliance.

Rather than to let the great track go to waste, Hulk Hogan decided to abandon the use of his Rocky-sounding, piano-heavy "Hulk Theme" for ring entrances.

"Even though it's never been a single," Derringer says, "it's turned into maybe my most successful song, ever." Hulk Hogan walking out to "Real American" for so many years has kept the song recognizable, but Derringer's guitar work is great, and the message continues to resonate with people beyond the wrestling. You hear it randomly played at sports events, political gatherings and just about anywhere.

The WWF Wrestling Album marked the first big initiative by the WWF to create their own original entrance themes for their wrestlers. In years following that project, WWE's original entrance themes have often become cult classics, and they have since released dozens of sequels.

Though my "strut" line was limited, I did enjoy it, and it was fun. I am thankful that I was thought of and was included.

JYD versus Brutus Beefcake on a house show from Sidney, Australia in 1985.

CHAPTER 15 - DREAM TEAM (1984 - 1987)

My mentors in the ring were veterans like Baron Von Raschke, Verne Gagne, Bobby Duncum, Mr. Wrestling II, Ivan Koloff, and Bobo Brazil. These guys had done it all, and I could listen to their stories for hours. The wrestlers from the 60s and 70s made a big difference in my career and helped me tremendously. I had learned that whenever a vet was around, there was always the potential to learn.

Luscious Johnny Valiant also shared some knowledge and stories with me. We didn't really travel together much, because he was really only being brought in for TV. However, he was a great storyteller and I loved talking to him when I could.

One story I remember him telling me was when he found himself sharing a hotel room with Andre the Giant. As I mentioned before, the Giant was huge. He was billed at 7 feet 4 inches, 520 pounds, and things are proportionate, if you know what I mean.

On one particular evening, Johnny was trying to watch the Yankees game on television, but Andre kept getting in the way of the screen. To make matters worse, for whatever reason, Andre didn't feel like covering up. You see, he had chosen to parade around the room in the nude. Yes, his baseball bat was swinging harder than anyone on the field.

After they had both retired to their beds. Then, the seven-foot man uttered the sweet words that Johnny Valiant least wanted to hear at the time, "I'm lonely."

"Go to sleep Andre," Johnny said, thinking about putting a wine cork in his asshole.

Later that evening, Johnny said he awoke to a loud rustling sound.

"Andre was having a wrestling match with himself," he says, "…and he was winning."

After WrestleMania, the WWF really took off. Hulk Hogan became an even bigger star and the company was making money hand over fist.

After the David Sammartino match at WrestleMania, they finally put me up against WWF World Heavyweight Champion Hulk Hogan. The idea was to put someone with him he was familiar with so we could have some good matches and to help continue the ball rolling.

Historically up to this point, anyone they plugged into the Hulk Hogan program did well, so I was excited to be working with him on both a friendly level and a professional one. The WWF started running sometimes two or three different shows in different areas a night. Guys lobbied their hardest to try and get booked onto the card that Hulk was on because he was selling out everywhere. If you were on the Hogan show, you would be looking at a much bigger gate. It was that simple. It was the difference of say seven or eight thousand on the "B card," versus a sold-out arena of 18,000 on the "A Show."

Putting me with Hulk Hogan made sense. The fans hated me for what I did to Hillbilly Jim and they wanted to see me go down. Once the dates were announced with me in the main event, we started selling out places, but way in advance.

If we were in say Oakland, they had already sold out 2 weeks before our arrival and then we would see 2000 angry unsuspecting fans outside the arenas wanting to get in, looking for tickets on the day of tickets. People couldn't get in, so the arenas started getting creative with their seating and even sold extra seats and standing room only admissions. It didn't matter. They still turned people away and people were pissed that they couldn't get in.

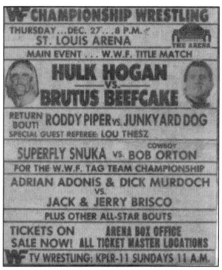

I remember on one of my very few nights off trying to explain how big everything had gotten to my father.

"Take a look at the map," I said. "Now, pick a state, any state, and I will tell you if I wrestled there with the WWF."

"Got it," he said. "How about Ohio?"

"Yep. Of course. Ok, now you will see the bigger dots all over, right? The biggest dots are the biggest towns, and the next smallest big dots are the secondary towns. What do you see?"

"Columbus?"

"Yep."

"Toledo?"

"Yep."

"Cleveland? Akron? Dayton? Cincinnati?"

"Yep, yep, yep, and yep. Oh, and Youngstown, too. Yep."

We literally hit every one of the dots – *all of them all*. That is how big the WWF had become. I worked Hulk Hogan through the rest of the year and made more money than I had ever seen in my life. In some of the bigger cities, if I was on the main event, I was making $10,000 - $20,000 for one match maybe!

Now, certain guys wouldn't get that kind of pay, but sometimes, it was their own fault. They were afraid to speak up, was all. If I didn't like the payout, I would just say something and right away, Arnold would leave the room for a bit, then eventually return and make good. It is true; the squeaky wheel got the grease. Think about it this way… If you were like happy, they wouldn't pay more. Why would they? Who is going to give up money and pay more for something when they do not have to? The promoters took advantage of guys for sure, and maybe only paid them $600, $700, or $800 a week, when they should have really been making more than double of that. Everyone would back up the fact they thought they should have made more money, at least from time to time. But if you were too afraid of losing your spot and didn't say anything, it was likely your own fault.

When Hogan was booked with someone else, they just put me with anyone I could beat to get more wins. They took good care of me.

The WWF money was changing my life. By the end of 1985, I was banking a lot of money.

I bought my first house on Madeira Beach, St Petersburg, right near "Treasure Island." I paid $90,000 in cash and never even lived there myself. I bought it, and the very next day I put it up as a rental property.

Then, of course, it came time to buy some toys. Finally, I was able to buy my dream boat. Just like you would see on Miami vice, I picked up a Limited Edition Miami Vice Scarab, a real world championship speedboat. It was identical to the Miami Vice boat you always saw Crocket and Tubbs in, but only a little shorter. This particular 21 footer was built for pleasure boating in the Gulf and Intracoastal. It was blue, white and teal, and all decked out in chrome underneath. There were two buckets in front and a bench in the back. It could easily go 65 miles per hour and turn on a dime.

Incidentally, I would have this boat a long time and I really loved it. After my accident (which we will talk about shortly,) I left this boat with some friends who really didn't know how to take care of a boat and it got messed up. I was sad to see it all in disarray, so I called this guy I knew from Minneapolis. He was half owner of the Vikings football team and he fixed the boat up again for me. I eventually put a new motor in it, a racecar motor with a 454 big-block, giving the Scarab something ridiculous like 700 horsepower.

That thing could dance! It sounded like a freakin' drag strip out on the water when I lit it up.

You could hear us coming a half of a mile away!

THE DREAM TEAM

"It was always a pleasure working with great workers like Greg and Brutus Beefcake. They really were great workers, and every match was always perfect."   *- Dan Spivey*

After my Hulk Hogan run was up, instead of just burying me and sending me out to pasture, they decided to reinvent me a little. If you look at some of Hulk Hogan's biggest feuds throughout history, after the big program was over and Hulk had beat him at a PPV, a guy would lose some stock.

This was a normal phenomenon in professional wrestling. When the audience finally saw the villain defeated by the hero, they lost interest in him. Revenge had been sought, and the villain would then lose credibility with the crowd as being a potential threat. In the territory days, this is when you would send that heel off to a different territory and just bring in some new blood for your main babyface to face. However, we were approaching a time in the business when Vince was laying out his cards so that the WWF was the only game in town.

Rather than to send me stepping, they decided to move me over to the tag team division and reinvent myself. The WWF had a number of neat tag teams and decided that a good heel faction was needed. The plan was to try me out with a few guys and see what worked. That is when they put me with Greg "The Hammer" Valentine.

George Scott at the time was the booker. He was a Carolina guy. Greg knew George really well. He was the one that decided to put us together for a few matches to fill holes in the cards and see what happened. The shows were selling out and they liked what they saw. George realized that it was a good pairing, right away. That is when George decided that maybe we should be something a little bit more long-term.

Just before the creation of the Dream Team, Greg was in an awesome storyline. He had just won the Intercontinental Championship from Tito Santana. Greg "put him out with a bad leg injury" from his dreaded figure four leg lock. As some of you may remember, when Tito returned after healing up his bad wheel, he mastered the very move that put him out to use against Greg, himself. The brutal feud with Santana had quite a story and I was happy to have been paired with a guy as on fire in the spotlight as Greg was.

On WWF television in May of 1985, there was a meeting of manager minds with Johnny Valiant and Jimmy Hart, to make this union happen. An alliance was proposed, created to destroy competition and also capture the WWF Tag Team titles. Jimmy Hart offered up his man Greg "The Hammer" Valentine in an alliance with Valiant's guy, Brutus Beefcake.

Greg Valentine was the WWF Intercontinental Champion, and I had just been a major threat to the WWF Heavyweight Champion, Hulk Hogan. With two such top talent names combining forces, it only made sense that we would be known as "The Dream Team."

The Dream Team was managed by both Jimmy Hart and Johnny V for a very short time. The idea didn't make sense for long-term, but it was a nice idea to get over the transition of putting us together for a few weeks. After this, Jimmy was kind of in and out of the mix, according to the storyline. He managed other names, but I guess acted like a silent partner, at times, with The Dream Team.

The idea in itself of co-managers made for too much nonsense outside of the ring. It made things hard to work around when calling a match, as well. Co-managers were also not very cost-effective to Vince McMahon, so of course, Jimmy Hart was dropped from the group very early on. However, Jimmy Hart wasn't left out in the cold. They really had other plans for him. He went on to manage his own team, *Bret "Hitman" Hart and Jim "The Anvil" Neidhart - the Hart Foundation.*

Greg and I just clicked. It was kind of a neat idea. We had the pretty boy/nature boy gimmick paired with the Chippendale-type gimmick. Greg went in there and did the heavy-lifting, I was the faster, more flashy guy pushing for the heel heat. Once they had teamed us up, they could see they had something. He was the bully. I was the arrogant, cocky jerk. We had all the hate-able bases covered, and we gelled really well together.

Early on into our newly formed tag team, we had our initial focus on Tito Santana, who Greg was still in a feud with. So what they would do is, they would just add another mid-card babyface to the mix on shows to team with Tito, and that would be our match. For instance, it would be Tito and the Junkyard Dog one night, who the commentators would say were "both highly ranked contenders for Valentine's Intercontinental title." Having the babyfaces chase a belt instead of actually holding it was always a good way to keep the fans interested. The thought was, if Tito could maybe, just maybe, pin Greg in the tag team match, he would earn himself another title match and a chance at revenge.

We worked with Tito for a good run. Tito was a great guy and a very underrated worked. He was the best. On April 21, 1985 in the Maple Leaf Gardens in Toronto, we had a phenomenal match with Tito and Ricky Steamboat. Many people today look back at it and consider it to be one of the best tag team matches of the 80s. The match was used to sell WWF's Coliseum Home Video release "Best of the WWF Vol. 4" and you can probably see it on the WWE Network now. Steamboat and Santana was almost as great an alliance as the Dream Team. (Almost!)

After really working had to make the team work, our efforts did not go unnoticed. Rene Goulet, I think it was, came up to us one day before a show.

"I have some good news, and some bad news," he said, putting his hand on Valentine's shoulder.

"Okay," Greg said.

"Vince finally wants you to drop the title to Tito," he said.

We looked at each other. Losing the gold would knock us down a notch in the eyes of the fans. Even though a championship title wasn't real, it did translate to money. If you had the belt, you worked more on cards and you were higher up. Even though the cash was political, in theory, you still saw more of the money when you were higher up on the card, always. However, before we could say anything, Rene laughed.

"I know what you are going to say," he said. "But the reason for this is… what I am trying to say is…"

"Just what are you trying to say?" Greg snapped, who didn't like being messed with.

Are they breaking us up? One of us is being let go?

"We are going to build you up to put the tag belts on you."

So just as promised, Santana beat Valentine in a steel cage match for the Intercontinental Title. Then right after that, they put the Dream Team in a program with the reigning WWF World Tag Team champions, the U.S. Express, Barry Windham and Mike Rotundo.

At the first WrestleMania, the Express dropped the titles to the Iron Sheik and Nikolai Volkoff. They then beat Sheik and Volkoff for their second WWF Tag Team Championship run, on July 13, 1985. It was aired on the WWF Championship Wrestling program for everyone to see, so the fans loved them. They were the clean-cut American boys, fighting for the love of our country. They came to the ring to Bruce Springsteen's, "Born in the USA," as their theme music.

This feud was great because they were so beloved, and we were so hated. The audience was always hot when we were on the card against each other. Add the fact that Barry and Mike were among the best technical workers in the WWF, and our matches were always a night off at the office.

TAG TEAM GOLD

Again, the idea of the babyfaces chasing the heels is the ideal situation for booking. It really gives people something to look forward to – them winning. They want to see the bad guys get their asses kicked, so badly that they want to buy tickets to the show. To throw gas on the fire, we wanted to add the injured babyface angle into the mix, much like Greg did with Tito, to make the storyline even hotter.

On August 24, 1985, the night came where we were set to win the titles. We were working a show at The Spectrum in Philadelphia, which was a very big wrestling town. We had a great match with Barry Windham and Mike Rotundo. In traditional "good guy versus bad guy" fashion, we decided to work our manager in on the finish, which always helped get heat. In this case, we decided to go with the classic foreign object use gimmick, by using Johnny V's lit cigar to blind Barry. Utilizing both the cheating and injury angle, plus hurting the heartthrob's pretty face we all agreed was perfect.

So, when the ref was distracted, Johnny took a few puffs on his trademark cigar so you could see the smoke, then he handed it over to me. What I did was put the flame out with my finger the best I could. I quickly pushed and poked my finger up into the cigar. I'll have to admit. It was pretty hot, hotter than I thought it was going to be. I had put matches out before with my finger, but that was certainly different. I burned my finger a little, but it was worth it.

Then, I grabbed Barry Windham. Protecting him the best I could, I rubbed Johnny V's lit cigar into Barry's eye. I mostly rubbed my dirty finger all over his eye entire socket, palming the cigar and mashing it the best I could. The soot looked great. Barry sold it like a champ and it looked like I killed him. Immediately after that, Greg pinned Barry at around the 19-minute mark.

"And the neeeewww... WWF Tag Team Champions…"

The house was pissed to say the very least.

We worked The USA Express a few matches after this. Barry continued to sell the eye by wearing a pirate-like eye patch which actually was pretty bad ass. However, before we could really draw big money off a major rematch for the titles, Barry Windham's contract expired, and he took off to work for Georgia.

THIS ONE IS ON US

Once they gave us the belts, we were still hated, but the fans respected us. Wherever we would go to eat, we never once had to worry about money. The tab was always picked up by someone who recognized us. Now, I can't explain why that was, because at shows we were super hated. However, it was always the same story.

If it were late at night in, say, some nice little New England diner, we would show up and they would bring us to the best seat in the house. People would recognize us, and rather to be in full character, we would in turn just be nice to them.

Now, I know there is something to really be said for staying in full character at all times. However, at a food establishment, this is probably not the best idea. You never want to piss off the guys in the back who are handling your food. You never know what nasty things they could be doing to your sandwich.

So it was always just our rule of thumb, be a dick on the show, but be pretty cool when you went somewhere to eat. This rule paid off.

Every night it was free meals. Everywhere we went, "It is on the house."

It became almost a guaranteed deal. We learned that if we signed an autograph here, or there, or took a picture with some of the wait staff before the check, they would always, always, always refuse our money.

That whole year, we ate free every single day. It got so bad, we didn't even bother to bring our wallets in with us from the car.

DANGEROUS DAN, THE LEFTHAND MAN

For the most part, locker room fights almost never happen in professional wrestling. They especially didn't happen in the WWF while I was there. The wrestlers were all pretty much family, for the most part.

We rode together, ate together, and spent time with the other wrestlers more than we did our own actual families at home. The few of us that did not agree with each other were almost always professional and almost always left their problems outside of what would happen in the ring.

When a real fight in the dressing room did occur, it was always brutal but fast. There is an unwritten rule regarding these types of fights; *you break it up right away, but only after until someone wins.*

The reason for this is, if the dispute is not settled and there is no closure, it always ends up meaning more ill will and another fight is going to happen anyway. The other reason for this is, when a guy is out on injury, it messes up storylines and hurts all of us.

There was one pretty good fight in the WWF locker room early on in my tenure with the company. While I didn't see it happen, the worst backstage brawl started in the ring and continued after the match. According to the witnesses that saw this violence bleed into the space behind the curtain, they say it was one of the bloodiest displays they ever saw.

I heard about the juicy details immediately after it happened from my good buddy, Tito Santana who was right there.

The backstory started up at a TV Taping in Toronto on May 4th, 1986 for Primetime Wrestling. Danny Spivey was told he had to wrestle with Adrian Adonis, and wanted no part of it, due to his reputation. He had also worked two matches with Adrian back in January in Waterloo, Iowa, and Denver Colorado. Adrian Adonis stiffed him pretty hard in the match, but Spivey never said anything because he was still relatively new in the federation.

Adrian was pretty tough. In Amarillo, he legitimately offered any of the wrestlers on the roster $1000 if they could last 5 minutes with him shooting in the ring. Nobody could do it.

Adrian was a little bit of a bully. He figured that he was a top talent and was being primed to run with Hulk Hogan soon, so he could do whatever he wanted to look strong. They were booking him in a lot of enhancement matches at this time, and the problem was, Adrian liked to beat up the jobbers. For the past few months, he was beating up guys like Lanny Poffo and Scotty McGee. Spivey wanted no part of him taking liberties with him in the ring.

Spivey worked his match reluctantly with Adrian. Just as he thought, Adrian figured he was just a new guy that he could also take advantage of, so that's just what he did. He kicked him hard, hit him hard, and cussed him out like a dog for real. After the match, Spivey was waiting for Adrian in the locker room. He was charged up and cursing up a storm.

"I'm going to fucking kill him," he said.

Seeing the heat exuding from the 6'8 monster, Scotty McGee and the Dynamite Kid of all people, recognized the fact that they needed to help cool him down. They scooped up Dan Spivey, got his shit together, and rushed him out of the arena

The next night, Spivey was on another show with Adrian at The Civic Center in Brantford, Ontario, Canada. When Spivey showed up, a few of the boys tailed him as he went right to Adrian's dressing room.

Backstage, the boys all knew Adrian was a tough guy, but nobody knew anything much of anything about Dan Spivey. We all thought he was just a polite new kid in his 20s that Dusty Rhodes had discovered in WCW. Nobody knew he had lied about his age and was really in his 30s. They had no idea that he was a bouncer and an ex-bookie that collected money for the mob, had served time in jail. He was a legitimate bad ass himself.

"You are lucky the boys got me out of their last night," he said to Adrian who was applying makeup in a mirror. "I'm warning you, you ever pull anything like that with me again, and I am going to let you have it."

Adrian didn't say anything back. He just kept on with the makeup and ignored the threat. Spivey left. After that, however, Adrian had a few words for the stragglers.

"The next time I get the pleasure of working with Dan Spivey," he said, rolling on some lipstick, "I am going to light him up and teach him a lesson."

The very next night in Flint, MI, Adrian Adonis was going to get that chance. George "The Animal" Steele was scheduled to face Adrian that night, but he ended up calling in sick. Apparently, he was in the hospital with a bad case of food poisoning.

Everyone already knew what was said and what had happened the night before between the two. Like they say, telegram or tell-a-wrestler. The way it worked was when you showed up to a venue, you would look for a list of matches taped up to the wall by the booker. The wrestlers would look it over and that was about it. When everyone showed up to this show, however, everyone popped the moment they saw the card. Pat Patterson decided to book Dan Spivey as George's replacement, versus Adrian.

Irony? Seems kind of coincidental, doesn't it?

Apparently, Spivey told Pat outright that he didn't want to work with Adrian. Pat left to see if anything could be switched around. When he returned, Pat told Spivey that Adrian said the sentiments were likewise, so Pat went to call Vince. When Pat returned again, he shook his head.

"Vince said we have no choice," Pat said. "You have to work with him tonight. But he did say it would be the last time you ever have to work together."

Who knows if Pat really called Vince, however? He was a sadistic bastard and likely set this up just to watch a show.

Spivey hunted down Adrian and said, "I'll work you again tonight, but I'm warning you, if you try any more shit with me – I'm going to let you have it."

When the match finally came, a few of the boys (including Tito and Jim Brunzell) gathered by the curtain for some "front row seats."

Spivey was introduced and went to his corner. Then, Adrian Adonis was announced. He came to the ring with his manager Jimmy Hart. Then, he put his arm up in the air and blew an air-hanky snot-rocket all over his arm.

Adrian Adonis always tried to be as gross as possible.

"You are fucking disgusting," Spivey said. He wasn't lying, either. Adrian was disgusting - it's just that plain and simple. "Jimmy! You tell him to get that snot off of his arm, right now, or I'm not working with him!"

The bell rang.

Adrian immediately started in, shooting on Dan Spivey again. He was being arrogant, talking trash, and trying to rub his juicy, throat-load snot all over him. It was clear that he was pissing Spivey off even more than the night before. He was punching him pretty stiff, and he was kicking him stiff, too.

Finally, Spivey had enough. Rather than to lead on that he was about to fight back, he took a few more stiff shots to let Adrian believe he was going to get away with whatever he wanted. Then, he just waited for the finish.

In the end, Adrian went to put the sleeper on Spivey, which was the plan all along. However, when Adrian went for the hold, Spivey put his hand up to block his arm from going under his chin. Spivey then broke the hold, broke kayfabe, and got ready to break whatever else he needed to break.

"I've had enough of your shit!" Spivey said, shoving Adrian's heavy frame into the corner.

Then, Spivey beat the dogshit shit right out of him. Spivey was strong as hell. He hit Adonis with a number of hard right hands. Before Adrian could get his guard up to block more from the right, Spivey then hit him with a ridiculous left uppercut that knocked him right out.

Adrian Adonis' bulbous body went limp and dropped. Adonis hit the mat hard.

"Wait a minute. Ref that's not right!" Jimmy Hart shouted up from ringside in amazement. Jimmy was laughing a little, knowing that finally, someone had the nerve to stand up for themselves.

Spivey covered him, for the pin.

The ref yelled, "No, no! This is not the finish!" He refused to count, tapping Spivey on the shoulder to argue with him in character, to try and figure things out.

"I changed the finish. He's not going over tonight," Spivey said, dropping down on the mat to cover Adrian once again. "Now are you going to count, or not?"

Spivey covered the pear-shaped corpse again. The referee tapped Spivey again and continued to argue. Spivey stood back up.

"Okay, guess not," he said. "Then, you are going to have to D.Q. me."

Spivey turned around. He kicked Adrian as hard as he could in the face.

There was already blood everywhere. Then, there was even more. The ref called for the bell and Spivey walked back to the locker room. The audience was going nuts! Spivey went back to his dressing room and he was pissed.

In the back, Jimmy Brunzell was running around yelling, "Danny killed Adrian!"

Everyone wanted to know what happened.

Adrian came back from the ring a bloody mess. He came looking for Spivey and all the boys gathered around.

Adrian rushed into Dan Spivey's locker room.

Spivey grabbed a chair to hit him with, but the boys grabbed him to keep a weapon out of the equation. Looking for an opening, Adrian went for a leg dive.

Dan Spivey broke loose and got out of the way. Adrian charged him again, and Spivey hit him again with another left uppercut that split him open even more.

Thinking it was all over, The Junkyard Dog grabbed a hold of him so he didn't kill him. Adrian got up. His face looked like a zombie and you could actually see the whiteness of his cheekbone poking through the wound.

"Shit! Here he comes again Danny, here he comes!" the Dog said. He let Spivey loose again, right as Adrian reached him.

Another ridiculous left uppercut!

Then, Spivey jumped on top of Adrian, pounding down into his face. That was it. Dan Spivey was the clear winner. Everyone jumped in and separated them.

Adrian was bleeding everywhere.

Randy Savage grabbed Dan Spivey. He dragged him away to his dressing room, to end the assault. After that, Randy took Spivey off to see the medic. His hands were swollen from punching on Adrian's noggin so much that he had to ice his fingers.

I can't say the same for Adrian. A little ice wasn't going to cut it. He ended up with something like 200 stitches in his face. His run with Hogan had to be delayed until he healed.

Chief Jay Strongbow coined his new name in the locker room, "Dangerous Dan, The Left Hand Man."

The next show that Spivey and Adrian were on together, Adrian was still all bandaged up. When he walked into the arena, there was Dan Spivey. Adrian was about to say something to him, but Don Muraco stopped him.

"It's over, Adrian. If I were you, I would just keep my mouth shut," Muraco said.

Adrian Adonis walked by Dan Spivey, and that was it. They never had a match together, again.

REPLACEMENTS

We defended the belts for eight months, primarily from a reformed US Express. With the unsuspected absence of Barry Windham, Vince quickly replaced him with a virtual look-a-like in Dan Spivey. Dan was really good and a nice guy, but the fans knew the difference. Replacement members of an established team never really seem to do well, because the audience is always seemingly smarter than the promoter thinks they are. Danny and Mike didn't really take off, and subsequently the team lost momentum. This was fine for us, because it probably lengthened our reign.

Hillbilly Jim who was out on injury was brought back to try and replace the USA Express' void in the tag team scene. After "ripping his kneecap out of its socket" during our match in San Diego (or slipping on a wet floor, however you want to look at it), he was coming back seeking revenge with reinforcements from his "family."

We started working with Hillbilly Jim and Uncle Elmer aka Plowboy Frazier from Memphis, at first. He really was a character. Vince brought this behemoth of a man from Memphis wrestling, home of Jerry "The King" Lawler fame. He was a perfect fit to be from the Hillbilly Jim family. Plowboy Frazier was huge. He was over 500 pounds of redneck. He stood about 6 foot 10. He drank raw eggs in the locker room. Many of the boys thought he was funny as hell, while others just thought he was a gross scumbag.

It was fun to work with the Hillbillies. They were our exact opposites and the contrast was something we could really play off. Jim was in decent shape, but he didn't at all look like the flashy Dream Team in his thrift shop overalls. And Uncle Elmer… he never saw the inside of the gym. He was the real deal. He was a big fat redneck with jittery hands, big greasy double-chin jowls, and a body riddled with moles and skin tags. He legit didn't use deodorant. Occasionally, if he was feeling overly hygienic, he took out a big mason jar with something that looked like piss to slather under his arms after a match in the locker room.

In his Memphis days, Uncle Elmer, then known as Plowboy Frazier, was a walking flea market vendor. You always got extra fleas along with whatever it was he was selling. He was known for always trying to unload cheap knock-off stuff that he would try to sell the boys in the locker room. He was like that shady kind of guy who would open shop in a back alley with watches hanging inside his coat. One time, he would try and pedal bootleg wristwatches and swore they were real. They would look real enough, but after closer inspection, the brand names were all one letter off. If you weren't interested in buying a "name brand" watch, he would pull out a designer engagement ring with a 10-carat diamond for $15.

For a time, we worked with Jim & Elmer for the WWF World Tag Team straps at MSG. This eventually turned into a long series of 6-man matches with the Dream Team adding Jesse Ventura, or Jimmy Valiant, against the Hillbillies adding their new family member, Hillbilly Cousin Luke.

Our program became a six-man act to get over the new member of the Hillbilly stable. As Cousin Junior, Lanny Kean wrestled barefoot and carried a horseshoe inside a ratty bag. He was quite the character, but he only lasted a short time and fans often wonder what happened to him.

"Everybody loved him." Hillbilly Jim says. "He looked like a super little hillbilly. He wrestled barefoot and kicked people like a mule. He was perfect for the job. He did all the things that we needed. Then, he went crazy!"

One of the urban legends that the boys tell is that Lanny really was a Hillbilly. When he got his first taste of a WWF paycheck, he didn't know what to do with himself. Some say he showed up in a fancy limo to a show all dressed up in designer clothing one time. He had a bit of an attitude and said he was going to take the weekend off. Then, he never came back!

George Scott, who was the booker then, had worked with another hillbilly-like wrestler, Gene Lewis, on two different occasions in Charlotte. Gene was then brought in as Cousin Luke for Cousin Junior who was MIA. Though nobody ever knew for sure, it is believed that Luke replaced Junior, because of a possible drug problem that made him an unreliable performer.

DOG FIGHTS

Everybody kept gunning for the Dream Team. The WWF had an excellent tag team division at this time. After the US Express dissembled, we were challenged by the Killer Bees and the Islanders. But the real threat was the British Bulldogs.

Davey Boy Smith and the Dynamite Kid were excellent in the ring, but as far as speaking was concerned, they weren't really up to speed; they weren't ready promo-wise to be thrown right in as champions, in my opinion. As a babyface, you usually did all your fighting. You didn't need a guy to do your speaking for you, you let your actions speak louder than words in the ring.

Either way, they decided to use Captain Lou to do the mic work for the Dogs to try and help get them over as characters on television. I'm not sure Lou was the best pick for that team to develop them, however. Most of the time, he was in outer space, himself.

On television, they were good. But behind the scenes, Davy boy was bad, and Dynamite was even worse.

The British Bulldogs engaged in the regular bad ribs. Davey Boy would shave your eyebrows on a flight if you fell asleep. Dynamite would put twenty locks on your bag so you couldn't even get in it. If you partied too hard and passed out in a hotel room, they would take off all your clothes and draw all over every inch of your body with permanent marker. However, they would take pranks to such a level that you could barely consider it a prank anymore.

Davey Boy would do stuff like grab my scissors and cut people's pants up when they were out in the ring. When they would return, it would be 5 degrees out, but they would be rushing off in the snow in Bermuda cut-off short shorts. Dynamite would take it a step further, he would wait for a guy to get in the shower and cut up their boots. Now, a pair of pants is one thing. They would cost like $25 maybe. But a guy's boots could be $250 on the low end. Some guys had one pair of boots their whole time wrestling in the business, but Dynamite would come by and cut it all to shreds.

The Bulldogs were also known for sticking together. This really meant they put Superglue on the worst possible places. They Superglued guys' zippers on bags, then Superglued the zippers on their pants, inside. They Superglued some of the guys' car door locks shut.

They were horrible.

I remember one time we were working at a high school gym somewhere. Somehow, they convinced a custodian to break out all of these locks and give them the master keys. Then they would take every single belonging they could out of a guy's bag and individually lock each item up separately into a school locker. You could see your stuff in the locker and knew where it was because of the lock - you just couldn't get to it. The problem was, they would then take the keys with them and leave town.

In Pennsylvania, there was a guy who would rent his ring for all the towns in that area. He was a super nice guy, who had a slow son. He used to let his son help put up the ring to make him feel special. When the WWF was using the Pennsylvania ring rentals, the Bulldogs would always get to the show early to actually help put the rings up, but really it was just to mess with that one kid. They would make fun of his voice with real bad Popeye impersonations. They would give him wedgies so bad they would rip his underwear. And, because some say they were allegedly steroid freaks, some say they would poke the kid in the ass through his clothes with a needle. I never saw it, but I heard these accusations more than once.

Dynamite was so bad that he would even rib his own partner when there was nobody else around to rib. They say Davey Boy Smith developed an obsession with "injectable vitamins." Davey was kind of muscle-bound and couldn't inject himself. For those of you that are unfamiliar with steroid use, sometimes they are injected into one of your ass cheeks at the bottom. Davey Boy, clearly being such a big guy, couldn't bend around properly and reach that area on his own so he would ask Dynamite to do it. Dynamite pretended like had no problem, but I think that wasn't the case. Dynamite would switch the steroids with milk. That's right. Davey Boy Smith got a daily dosage of milk shot into his rear end. Needless to say, once Dynamite admitted his rib, The British Bulldog found a way to inject himself.

Probably the worst rib that they did was to the rats. Late at night after a show, they would pick through the groupies and find one to bring back to their hotel room. They would all typically party pretty hard until she would pass out.

You wouldn't even believe what they did, if you saw it yourself.

KNOCK! KNOCK!

"I'm coming!" I said. I looked at the clock. It said something like, 4:00 AM. It was admittedly blurry from a couple of stiff drinks. I got out of the bed. There may, or may not have been a girl in it with me.

KNOCK! KNOCK! KNOCK

"Who is it?" Greg asked, rolling over in his bed.

I wrapped a towel around me from the bathroom. I looked through the little security fish-eye in the hotel room door and saw Dynamite.

"Brother! Open up!"

I pulled the chain across and let him in. He looked frantic.

"What's wrong, brother?" I asked.

He shook his head. He looked really upset. "I don't know what to do!"

"Is it Davey Boy?" I asked, thinking the worst. Immediately, I thought maybe they partied too hard or something, and we were going to have a mess on our hands.

"Come on," he said, rushing out into the hall.

I followed him down the hall. When we got to his room, he stepped aside to catch his breath. I could hear the television on in the background. I went in first.

The door was already open a crack, but that is not the only crack that was open. I looked in the bathroom. Davey Boy was nowhere to found. Then, I stepped into the bedroom area.

No Davey Boy, but there was a gorgeous girl, however. She was passed out, completely buck naked on top of the covers. And she was not alone.

Matilda, the team's English bulldog mascot, was standing on the bed with her. Then, I couldn't believe my eyes. The dog was going to town, licking away at the unconscious girl, on some strategically-placed peanut butter.

"Oh my God!" I said, disgusted.

I turned around and Davey Boy jumped out of the closet with a Polaroid camera, laughing his ass off. He was trying to get a shot of me and the girl going doggy-style.

Before he could snap a picture of my face in utter denial, I grabbed the empty jar of Skippy off the table. I hurled it at him as hard as I could in the face. He dropped the camera, and hopefully, it broke. I pushed by Dynamite in the doorway, who was practically dying from laughter.

Wanting no part of that situation in the event that the girl was to wake up, I ran in terror back to my room and shut the door.

I climbed into bed. From the other side of the room, I could hear the Hammer stirring.

"What was it?"

"Oh nothing," I said, trying to get comfortable. "Just Matilda going down on some rat."

"Oh," he said deadpan, rolling over to go back to sleep. "Good."

Nothing surprised us from the Bulldogs.

THE LEGEND OF HAKU

As I mentioned before, the Dream Team also worked with The Islanders, Haku and Tama. I would be remised if I did not tell about how much of a badass Haku really was. Some people claim that Haku is probably the toughest bastard that has ever stepped foot in a wrestling ring. Those people would be right. However, saying Haku was "tough" is not strong enough of a word. He is a legendary tough man and his legend comes with an endless amount of unbelievable stories.

Haku came from the Isle of Tonga, and people eventually came to call him "Tonga," as a nickname. He trained with some of the top name sumos in Japan and really learned that sport, long before he learned wrestling. Now, he is pretty much the Chuck Norris of wrestling.

I have a great Haku story to tell, but first, here is a little collection of stories that other wrestlers have told about him so that you can get an idea about the true level of his "bad-assery."

All the wrestlers learned early on to never mess with Haku. A number of the boys were there when there was a disagreement between Jesse Barr, aka Jimmy Jack Funk and Haku. In the end, Haku gouged one of Barr's eyeballs right out of the socket, causing him to have to wear a glass eye, later on in life.

Jake "The Snake" Roberts had a few words to say about Haku. "If I had a gun and was sitting inside a tank with one shell left and Haku is 300 yards away, you would think he is mine, right?" Roberts asked. "Well, the first thing I'm going to do is jump out of the tank and shoot myself because I wouldn't want to only wound him and have that bastard pissed off at me."

My friend "The Million Dollar" Ted DiBiase also told me about a time that the WWF was in a rough part of St. Louis for a show. He said that everyone had been drinking and having a good old time when a very big fight broke out. The police showed up. Haku saw the fight and was trying to help break it up. In the process, police thought he was part of the fight, so they maced him and handcuffed his hands behind his back. DiBiase swears that Haku looked at the police, tilted his head and snapped the chain of the cuffs in half.

Bobby Heenan has many times gone on the record to say that Haku is, in fact, the toughest man he ever met in his life. The Brain remembers a bar fight where Haku, "reached into the guy's mouth and he broke off the entire bottom row of the guy's teeth." Heenan said that is no exaggeration, either. "If I hadn't been there and seen it myself, I wouldn't believe it!"

Another legendary wrestling manager in the golden years of the WWF was Frenchy Martin. He also said he once saw an incident break out in a bar where Haku defeated six men in a matter of seconds. After seeing that, Frenchy said, "If you are ever given a choice of going to Hell or facing Haku, you would be well advised to choose Hell."

Rick Steiner talked about the time Haku fought eight police officers at a hotel. He said, "The police shot Haku with mace. Haku didn't sell it at all. He just closed his eyes and sucked it all in. He just opened his mouth up wide and drank it.

Ric Flair recalled once being on a tour with Haku over in Japan. He said how he was sharing a locker room where two events were going on at the same time with a bunch of basketball players. One of them moved his luggage, and he ended up throwing a basketball player out of a second-floor window.

One time, Chris Jericho and Haku were also in Japan. Jericho had his headphones on and was jamming out to some rock music. He was walking to the baggage check area. Some mark had been following him for like 10 minutes, and he was getting really annoyed. As he was about to pass through, he felt a tug on his shoulder. He turned around and shoved the mark away – however, it wasn't a mark! It was a female security guard who was trying to get him to stop, who he couldn't hear. Seeing their cohort laying on the floor, five security guards got pissed and attacked him. Haku saw this and came running. He took out the guards with ease. Bodies were flying everywhere when the real police showed up. They locked Jericho and Haku in a room for two hours, when someone finally came in and suggested that they "tip" the guards to make the problem go away. Chris gave everything he had, which was like $7, but Haku came through with a good amount, and they let them free.

Bill Goldberg praises Haku for helping him early on in his career. He appreciates Haku for his wisdom and his guidance, but also admits "Tonga" could flip on that baddass-switch like nobody else. "He taught me more than 90% of the people in the business... He was so smart. But there is a whole other side of him. He could get in a bar fight, get pepper sprayed in the eyes and just laugh at the cops and break their handcuffs. He could turn into a totally different human being!"

Kevin Sullivan and his fellow Dungeon of Doom member, Meng (aka Haku), went to a pub once after a show in some backwoods hick-town. It must have been quite obvious that Meng wasn't from their parts. Right when they walked in, a guy playing pool called Meng the n-word. Meng went right over to the guy, nodded, and gave him the throat pinch just like Mr. Spock on Star Trek. Another guy jumped in, and Meng knocked him right out. The final guy jumped on Meng's back. Meng flipped him over and he bit through his shirt like a wolf. The white material instantly turned red as he took a chunk out of the guy's back. "It's time to go," Kevin Sullivan said. Meng nodded, then spit a piece of shoulder blade out on the floor. As they drove away, police cars rushed the parking lot, but no charges were ever filed.

BAR FIGHT WITH HAKU

All the boys above have some crazy stories that they tell about Haku. I have one, too.

One time, the WWF was in town. A bunch of us were staying on a commercial strip right by the Baltimore Airport. There were two hotels there. We all had our rooms reserved at the Marriot I think, but before checking in for the night, we went to hang out at the other one across the way.

The other hotel had an awesome bar, and it was always packed. On this particular night, they had a DJ there playing music. It was crawling with some of the hottest women I had ever seen. We didn't know at the time that it was also crawling with trouble.

So Haku and this pretty cool fire-juggling Samoan wrestler named Siva Afi walked in. They met up with me and a few other wrestlers at the bar. We decided to move and all sit down in a darker corner to have something to eat.

While we were eating, my fan radar was going off. We were being watched. As a wrestler, it seems there are always some eyes on you, surveying your every move. They watch you in the gym. They watch you in the grocery store. Nowhere was really sacred. You get used to it, though, and mostly people are cool. Usually, even though it can be a little annoying, it is a good thing. It means you are over enough that people recognize you. That means money. Sometimes, however, it could be bad news. Every so often, those eyes were not watching you from a distance in fandom admiration, they were sizing you up.

We all had a few drinks. Most of the boys had left, when Haku, Siva Afi and I decided to leave. On our way out, one of the guys who was staring at us the whole night made his move. He rushed over to get in front of us, with four of his friends in tow.

"Hey, aren't you guys fake wrestlers? The ones on TV?"

I shook my head and started to walk by them, but Haku reached his hand up and held me back like a mother stepping on the brakes fast in a car.

Now, Haku took it personally when someone called wrestling "fake." He hated that. If someone uttered those words, Haku always felt the need to display the realness of his ability by any and every means possible. Fighting dirty was by no means off limits.

The guys were clearly blocking our way from leaving, and it looked as if they were trying to pick a fight with us, just to see how we would react. If they wanted a reaction, I knew they were about to get it. Haku was having none of that.

"Fake wrestling. Yes," he said. "The fake stuff, yes. I'll show you."

Without even thinking, he reached over and grabbed the bully by the scruff of his neck and pulled him in close to him. Now, mind you, there were four other guys there, but that didn't matter. Haku grabbed his skull, centered his face in from of him, and leaned forward.

I honestly thought it looked like he was kissing him at the time, but that was no kiss.

Haku opened his mouth and bit his nose off.

He bit his fucking nose off!

Blood immediately spurted out of his head like a socket. The bully cupped his face and screamed, feeling the missing flesh from his nose. It looked as if Haku bit off the entire tip and maybe his whole right nostril.

"ARGGG!" he shrieked in terror. "MY NOSE!"

Haku would have said, "What, do you want it back?" – but it's not polite to talk with your mouth full, so he spit the red blob right back at him, boogers and all.

Immediately a huge bar fight broke out, like in the old West. Haku and Siva were totally killing people. Bodies were flying left and right. By the time everyone in the whole place was throwing fists, I grabbed Haku and pulled him out a side door. We ran up a little hill with grass on it, laughing the entire way. We went up to our hotel, the Marriott, and Haku came into my room. We looked at each other and started laughing.

Haku cleaned the blood filth off of his chin in the mirror.

Before he left, there was a phone call. The police were in the lobby and looking for Haku. He took his medicine like a man, and they took him away.

I jumped in my rental and found my way to the police station. I posted bail for him because I wanted to help, but I later found that that was the best money I ever spent. As we drove back to the hotel to try and get like three hours of sleep before the flight, I looked over at Haku. I guess there was some worry about legal repercussions that maybe bothered him some. He was watching the raindrops in the headlights. We didn't talk. It was quiet at first, then I nudged him a little with my elbow.

He shook out of it and smiled a little.

"You okay?"

"Yes, I'm okay. Thank you, my brother," he said. "You have a problem ever, I'll protect you. I have your back."

After that, he always did have my back. Incidentally, no legal recourse was ever taken. Haku called me one day and told me that everything turned out fine. The bartender was a big wrestling fan and told the cops that they started it all! So, nothing ever happened after that fight, except that the jackass who started it probably ended up looking like a jack-o-lantern.

Bunkhouse Battle Royals in Boston were the absolute WORST.

BUNKHOUSE HEAT

Even though I was in the Dream Team, I still did pretty well for myself in singles competition. In early 1987 in Boston, MA, I remember being booked to work with Blackjack Mulligan, and then again later in one of his bunkhouse battle royal matches. I had worked him some around my debut and they put me again with him, off and on, when I was tagging with Greg.

The Bunkhouse Battle Royal matches became a part of Blackjack's gimmick at this point, in the twilight of his career. What we did was have a quick match early in the evening, then meet again at the end of the night in an early form of what would later become known as a "hardcore match," except in a ring full of people wearing whatever they wanted. We would all walk down the aisle and come out in cowboy boots and jeans and all.

The audience at the Boston Garden had a reputation. They were bad for throwing cups of ice and garbage into the ring when they got angry. They were known for doing this so much that Vince knew never to use newer ring mats whenever they were in this town. They were so bad that Freddie Blassie even lost his vision from getting directly hit in the eye with an egg.

I was a heel and had already pulled some shenanigans on Blackjack earlier in the evening, and dodged one beverage on the way out. Little did I know that was only a foreshadowing of things to come.

Later on that night, I finally came out for the bunkhouse, the signature match of Blackjack Mulligan. Guys like King Kong Bundy, Don Muraco, Dan Spivey & Mike Rotundo, the Islanders, "Duke of Dorchester" Pete Doherty (a Boston legend,) Scott McGee, and my partner Greg Valentine all came down to the ring in street clothes. There were also probably guys like Corporal Kirschner, Jimmy Jack Funk, Hillbilly Jim and Dick Slater in there with me as well.

I remember Leapin' Lanny Poffo (Macho Man Randy Savage's brother) in one of these matches. He came down to one of these bouts decked out in a full suit of armor. It was ridiculous, but awesome.

At the end of the battle royal, it was just Blackjack and me. I hit him with a low-blow nut shot, and that was it. Boston was beyond pissed and they erupted. All of a sudden I got pummeled. Full cups of soda and full cups of beer came flying into the ring from all corners. They came zipping so hard and at such a rate that, in no time at all, I was standing six inches deep in garbage.

I'm glad I was not in Mexico, where this is the norm. In Mexico, they would look for the biggest, baddest, hombre wrestler they could find, and pummel him with cups of piss and diapers full of shit. Despite my good looks and my boyish charm, I was pegged the clear target that night at the Garden. I couldn't understand it though; I wasn't scary looking at all. I was 6'4 and about 250 pounds. Mulligan was probably about 6'6 and 340. He looked like a beast, but they didn't care. They looked at me like I was the monster. Maybe I would have been better off in Mexico!

They hated me. They wanted me dead and kept throwing more. It started getting so bad with the garbage that Blackjack just said "screw the finish" and stayed down to cover his face. He was laughing on the mat, and I could tell it. All the while, I was ducking cups and dodging sandwiches, waiting for him to get up so we could get on with the finish of the match.

It wasn't happening.

What the hell? There is so much shit in the ring, it is unbelievable! Beer, soda, hot dogs, half-eaten hamburgers, French fries, cups, batteries… Wait a minute. Darts? People are throwing darts?! What the Hell?! That is bullshit!

Then, all of a sudden, some lady holding an infant whirled something that looked like one of Lanny Poffo's Frisbees. That's right, a yellowish blur came roaring right at me, spinning like a saw blade. That mother-chucker hurt.

Before I could move, it nailed me right in the face. There was pepperoni in my hair and mozzarella in my nostrils.

That's it. I have to get out of here… and NOW!

I sold the pizza.

Instead of pretending it didn't bother me, I held my face. I cried about my hair. I made it seem like getting a puss full of pizza was the worst thing that could ever have happened to me.

Now, normally selling garbage to the audience was the worst thing you could do. If you showed that getting hit with trash bothered you, they would only do it more. If you exposed a weakness to a blood-thirsty audience, they were going to jump on it and go for the ill. The evil Beantown bastards did exactly what I thought they would. When they saw my (intentional) unwanted reaction to the pizza, they started throwing even more and more crap.

Because Mulligan was not going for the finish, I finally had a reason to eliminate myself. I hopped out of the ring, as they pelted me with everything they could find that was not bolted down, running back to the locker room.

"Feets don't fail me now!"

DROPPING THE BELTS AND THE BALL

The British Bulldogs continued to be an on-again, off-again threat to us on TV. We eventually learned that the Dogs were scheduled to get one last final tag team title shot against us at WrestleMania 2. We were soon informed that we would be dropping the titles to them. We were not happy.

Whether it was hubris or not, Greg and I honestly felt we were the hottest team. We believed that it was too early to be handing the straps over, as there was still money to be made with the babyfaces chasing the titles. However, nobody would listen to our plight. Their minds were made up.

The championship Dream Team run was done.

A year after the first WrestleMania, Vince wanted the WWF to really appear to the public that it was, in fact, a huge, ever-expanding national promotion. Image is everything. Therefore, Vince decided to have WrestleMania 2 broadcast live from three different locations, simultaneously. The PPV was the first national one. It took place on Monday, April 7, 1986, which makes it the only WrestleMania to date that was not held on the customary Sunday evening. WrestleMania 2 took place at three venues: the Nassau Veterans Memorial Coliseum in Uniondale, New York; the Los Angeles Memorial Sports Arena, and the Rosemont Horizon in Illinois.

With our match set to go from the Rosemont, I remember Greg and I being a little bit down before the show about the planned finish before the event. Greg was pretty upset. Even though I didn't like the idea of dropping the belts, there was one cool thing about this match. Ozzy Osbourne was in the corner of The British Bulldogs.

Ozzy was a bad ass. It was a good thing WrestleMania 2 was in Rosemont, IL, instead of San Antonio, TX, the site of WrestleMania thirty years later. The reason for this is that Ozzy was so bad, he wasn't even allowed in that city.

Ozzy told us a story that night about how he got so drunk that he woke up, walked down the street to the Alamo, and urinated on it in front of a bunch of people. One of those people was a cop. Though the fine he received for public urination was something like only $50, that wasn't the real problem from this territorial pissing. The fine didn't even amount to a slap on the wrist, but Ozzy was also banned from ever playing San Antonio again.

I guess later on in 1992, he got booked to work there and needed to make good with the city. What he ended up doing was made a public apology to the city and also donated $10,000 to the Daughters of the Republic of Texas, the same organization that maintains the Alamo grounds. The city finally forgave him and allowed Ozzy Osbourne to play two nights at the Freeman.

After we lost the titles, Vince had us, the heels chasing the Bulldogs. You could tell from the sound of the fans that they became less interested in our program, after that. Following WrestleMania 2, we had a series of steel cage matches with the Bulldogs during the summer of 1986, but it didn't really matter. The Bulldogs had the belts, and the people lost faith in us for being a credible threat to the titles.

On the WWF programming, Gorilla Monsoon was apologetic for us losing the belts in his commentary. His theory was that the Dream Team never mentally got over our WrestleMania 2 loss. Gorilla actually told me in confidence that he, and many of the other WWF officials believed that we were the best match on the card that night.

The Dingo Warrior made his move from WCCW to the WWF in 1987.

ULTIMATE WARRIOR

In 1987, a new guy graced the presence of the WWF locker room, much to the eventual chagrin of some of the boys. A lot of guys in the locker room didn't like Jim Hellwig, aka, The Ultimate Warrior.

I didn't have a problem with him, and neither did Greg, really. We all hung out a little bit. We worked out some together. I think the real reason that some of the boys didn't like him was that they didn't get to even know him. He was pretty much in his own world. He didn't hang out in the locker rooms. He wasn't a drinker so that meant he wasn't drinking in the boys' hotels, or hanging out in the bar with anyone after the shows. Maybe they perceived that as antisocial, or stuck up. I'm not sure that was the case.

He was married at that time and not up for any shenanigans whatsoever. He didn't fall into the regular category of the wrestler of that time who was out partying, or drinking, or pill-popping. Jim just didn't do that. He was into his training. He was into his diet. He took all that serious. You could tell just by looking at him how serious he was about his health and staying in shape.

One of the reasons why a lot of the guys didn't click with him at that time was because they never saw the inside of a gym at that time, and that was what Jim was all about. Guys like George Steele, Kamala, there were a number of guys who just didn't work out at all and had nothing in common with him. I mean, let's face it. It was easier to not have to look around between shows to find a gym and find time in our busy schedules to find time to work out.

Greg "The Hammer" and I liked to work out. There was many a morning where we would go down to a hotel gym somewhere, and pump iron with him before heading out of town. We were among the few that got along with the Ultimate Warrior, at that time.

A lot of his matches were probably two minutes long at most, with a minute and a half of that being his entrance. Jim Hellwig was pretty persistent in what he wanted his matches to look like. However, his persistence and his success didn't at all make him a bad a person. He made diplomatic moves from time to time. For instance, He knew Andre didn't really enjoy getting jobbed out. So what Warrior did was, he would bring the gift of a nice bottle of wine for Andre every night they worked together. With Andre, I think this kind of worked. He loved his wine, brother. He could sit on a bus and drink a whole box of it like it was Kool-Aid.

I remember seeing the Ultimate Warrior walking into the dressing room every single night with a brown paper bag. He would go and find Andre, who would probably be sitting at a table set up in the dressing room, playing cribbage with someone like Tim White the referee, or an old timer like Arnold Skaaland. Warrior was making good money then so he would drop big bucks on his drinkable thank you card. It was always like a hundred dollar bottle of some super tasty, sweet bottle of French wine.

"Thank you, boss," Andre would say. Andre would pull the bottle towards himself and take the cork off with a pocket knife, then drink the whole thing while he played.

While this was, in fact, a nice gesture, Rick Rude saw this and didn't like it. Maybe Rick was jealous, or maybe he was offended because he felt he worked hard to get Warrior over and never got any kind of token of gratitude.

One night, I was by my locker. Rick Rude was changing next to me, and we both saw Warrior come in with the bag and present it to Andre the Giant.

"Beefer look. I've worked with this son of a bitch probably a hundred times, dealt with all of his bullshit and busted my ass to help get him over," he said, nudging me to look at the gift-giving ceremony before us. "That's not him being nice, you know."

"How so," I laughed, waiting for a good one.

"That's because he's afraid," he replied. "I work him, right? But I don't get to drink fucking French wine, I don't even get a cheap bottle of Gatorade from that motherfucker."

I laughed. There was a little resentment there, but I understood why.

"Andre doesn't even bump for the Warrior and he gets the good stuff? It's bullshit, I tell you," he said. "I'm out there getting his ass over, working my ass off to try and help him and he doesn't do shit for me. He does it for Andre because he is afraid of getting the shit beat out of him."

After that, I heard Rick Rude stiffed the hell out of Warrior whenever he could in the ring.

As Brutus "The Barber" Beefcake, I became a featured headline attraction. I was no longer just in the tag-team ranks, but I was elevated to the top of the cards. I am super thankful and lucky to have experienced this.

CHAPTER 16 – THE BARBER (1987 - 1990)

"You want a quote for Brutus "The Barber" Beefcake? Well here's your quote... The first time I ever saw Brutus, as far as I was concerned, he was over! Then they gave him the scissors. In all my years of wrestling, I never saw a "wrestling barber." I had also never seen someone who could take a strange gimmick like that and turn it around into something really great until he did. ...There's your quote!" - Bobby "The Brain" Heenan

"Ed's life is one that started out as being just an average kid from the Port Tampa area, to one who grew up and became an international superstar. The way he did this was through a lot of hard work and staying grounded all the way. His career tells the true American success story that proves the inspirational idea that if I can do it - so can you. ...When I first saw Ed, I was really impressed with his size, look, and passion for wrestling. I knew he had what it took to become a star. I've stayed friends with him ever since then, and I am very proud to have helped him along as he became an international star. All this time, he has remained a humble person." - Gerald Brisco

Come the start of 1986, Roddy Piper had taken five or six months off from the WWF. Around May, Adrian Adonis and Jimmy Hart replaced his famous talk show with a new interview segment called, "The Flower Shop with Adorable Adrian." With no Piper's Pit, Vince decided to use Adrian as a foil to establish Paul Orndorff's slow-burn heel turn against his friend Hulk Hogan. Adonis, incidentally, was a great talker. He developed this story arch by making "Mister #1 Wonderful" question being number two and having to live in Hogan's shadow. Little did I know at the time, but while "The Flower Shop" was making Orndorff turn to the dark side, it would also indirectly make me see the light.

Turning into a fan favorite and running with a silly, afterthought gimmick was soon going to make me a household name among wrestling fans around the world. At the time, I had no idea of the magnitude.

In August, Vince contacted Piper and confirmed his return. Vince decided that Piper working with Adrian could mean big money, if they were feuding over who had the best talk show. So on WWF programming, Adonis aligned himself with Piper's bodyguard, Cowboy Bob Orton to add fuel to the fire. To better fit his new bodyguard role, Vince had Orton do everything he did with Piper, but with one thing different, a pink cowboy hat.

Piper came in asking the flower people for his timeslot back and was rejected. It was established that Orton was a sellout and Adrian had stolen everything Piper had in his absence. This turned the once-hated Piper into an instant favorite in the fans' eyes. They appeared on each other's shows for a few months. This culminated in a battle between the two talk segments that ultimately lead to the destruction of both of sets. Eventually, the two agreed to a hair vs. hair match at WrestleMania III.

Okay, so where do I come in, you may ask? Besides the fact that I would eventfully host the Barber Shop, a segment better than any of them, how do I fit into the story?

To promote this match, Adrian started to bring scissors around with him to matches, to show the audience what he was planning on doing to Piper at the big PPV. During this time, Jimmy Hart reestablished his working agreement storyline with Johnny Valiant and we began pairing members of his stable with Johnny's. On the February 28, 1987 episode of WWF Superstars, Adrian Adonis teamed with the Dream Team against The Can-Am Connection (Rick Martel & Tom Zenk) and their partner, Leaping Lanny Poffo.

Although I didn't exactly know it at the time, this match would play a huge role in the upcoming Piper vs. Adonis match and forever alter the course of my career. We had a good match, and then came the miscue finish. Adonis pulled me into his oblong body. He played it off like he thought he was cutting Rick Martel's hair, but actually cut mine off, by mistake.

Having a pretty boy gimmick of sorts, I sold it like I couldn't handle the fact that my perfect hair had been cut. I "lost it," and then lost the match, too. Dino Bravo, Johnny Valiant's new acquisition, came in the ring to try and console me, but Adrian left with Jimmy.

The miscue in the match planted the seed for what they told me was to be a possible "Brutus Beefcake face turn" they were thinking about at WrestleMania III.

Piper's return to the WWF was limited. He was soon to film the 1988 sci-fi film "They Live," directed by John Carpenter, where he would develop his famous catchphrase, "I came here to chew bubble gum and kick ass - and I'm all out of bubble gum." He was exploring his career options as an actor in Hollywood and was leaving again right after the pay-per-view. The WWF had turned him into a huge babyface with the whole Adrian Adonis program, and they knew they had to fill his void once he was gone.

The idea was that they would have Piper pass the torch to me. I was honored, but man, those were some big shoes to fill.

WRESTLEMANIA III

WrestleMania III was in front of 90,000 plus fans on March 29, 1987, at the Silverdome in Pontiac, Michigan. For those of you who may or may not remember, the main event was Hogan versus Andre the Giant. Once again, Vince was out-doing himself. This PPV announced a record attendance of 93,173, which was the largest recorded attendance ever of a live indoor event in North America at the time!

Vince had to pay us pretty well for this one. I had, not one, but two pretty good spots for the evening, myself; one in my final tag match with Greg Valentine, and the other in the finish of the Piper/Adonis hair-versus-hair match. It was a good day at the office, to say the least.

Fresh off teasing friction within the Valiant Camp on WWF television, it was the Dream Team with Johnny V & Dino Bravo in our corner taking on the Fabulous Rougeau Brothers; Jacques and Raymond. To continue with the infighting angle, the match was loaded with arguing and miscues between Greg and myself. (One example I can remember was when I jumped off the ropes to hit Raymond and accidentally hit Greg, instead.)

The match ended with Dino Bravo jumping off the top rope and hitting Raymond, then rolling Valentine over on him for the pin. The idea was this was something I should have done for the team but did not. This further secured Dino Bravo's spot in the Dream Team and signaled my exit. In the end, Valentine, Bravo, and Valiant left the ring together, without me.

Soon after, the "Hair vs. Hair" match came. It was anxiously awaited by the audience as it was also billed as Piper's retirement match from professional wrestling before becoming a full-time actor in Hollywood. Roddy Piper cut a pre-match promo backstage and left for the ring. Then, Adrian followed suit. Fresh off of the idea of the Flower Shop, Adrian had a pair of hedge clippers with him and a mirror for his promo. He said he was going to cut Piper's hair and show him the results. The props for that promo would be a future piece of the puzzle for me.

Roddy Piper fought a great match with Adrian Adonis. In the end, Jimmy Hart popped up and sprayed some perfume in Piper's face. Adrian saw the opening for the sleeper and put his opponent down on the mat. "The Adorable One" then prematurely let go of the hold and raised his hand in the middle of the ring. The ref turned his back to the "unconscious" Piper, and I jumped into the ring behind him.

The audience went wild. I have to take my hat off to the writers, the payoff was even bigger than I had imagined.

I sat Piper up. I slapped his face a bit and rubbed his shoulders to make it like I was getting the blood flowing again – which would be yet another puzzle piece. When Pipes awoke, I ducked out. He put the sleeper on Adrian and won.

The crowd went even crazier. I looked around and couldn't believe my eyes at the sheer amount of humanity caught up in one moment. They were cheering for Piper, and they were also cheering for me.

I jumped back in the ring. I grabbed Adrian's hedge clippers and handed them to Piper.

Now, Piper was supposed to cut Adonis's hair, but he didn't. I was supposed to ward off Jimmy Hart and let Piper get his revenge, but it ended up working the other way around. Piper passed the torch. Instead of taking the payoff for the almost year-long feud for himself, he let me have the spotlight – the new guy. I had just turned face from a miscue, but that was it. I didn't have the history with Adrian like he did. This was a very unselfish move that would push my career like never before. It was a very class act.

The way Piper tells the story is that he had done a number of hair-versus-hair matches in his day with guys like Chavo Guerrero. He said the payoff haircutting part at the end was always difficult for him, because his opponent's hair would get sweaty and wet during the bout. This would, in turn, make it nearly impossible to cut. Because of that perceived problem, Piper says he was not trying to be a nice guy, he was just being lazy. I don't think that was the case though. I think Piper was trying to hook me up.

When I went to hand him the shaver, Piper laughed.

"No, you do it," he said.

Piper knew what he was doing. He pushed the shaver back into my hand and told me to do it, and then went over to take care of Jimmy Hart like I was supposed to do. He put his foot on Jimmy's back and held him in place just as we had planned for me to do, while he watched me get the rewards of humiliating Adrian.

I didn't argue. I started cutting.

We had a little battery-powered hair trimmer at ringside. Rather than to use actual scissors to do the job, the plan was to buzz Adrian's hair off in no time, for an instant gratification pop from the audience. But as much as the producers wanted him bald by the end of the segment, it just wasn't happening.

I was cursing up a storm.

"Why is it was taking so long?" Adrian asked under his breath.

"I don't know!" I whispered to Adrian. "Cut, damn it!" No matter how hard I tried, those damn clippers were not cutting. I couldn't get the hair trimmer through his hair because it was too wet. It seemed like an eternity.

I looked over at Piper who was laughing at the whole scene.

Shit! These clippers are not doing anything, and I know the shears are not going to do much better. What am I going to do?! I need something else and the locker room is like a mile away!

Now, as you may or may not recall seeing, the locker room for WrestleMania III was a hike. They had special ring entrance carts built just to transport the wrestlers to and from the ring. They were built to look like mini-rings with ropes and turnbuckles, and they seemed to add an extra degree of specialness to the event, but they served two purposes. One was to keep the wrestlers' entrance time down, because it really was a long trip from the locker room to the actual ring. And the other was so that Andre the Giant didn't have to endure an extremely long walk to and from the ring, due to his health. (He was pretty worn down. Walking was even a chore for Andre at this point in his career.)

While I was freaking out in the ring, trying to garner more than a pinch or so of hair that we could throw in the air for everyone to see, someone jumped in the ring and pushed real barber scissors into my hands. It was a godsend.

I immediately switched tools, and it worked. They were nice and sharp, and they chopped big clumps off of Adrian's head in no time. Now, I know those scissors were not brought there by anyone from the WWF. They were not scissors from under the ring, perhaps, used to cut the tape for the ring ropes, either. Though it cannot be confirmed, it would make for a great story if they were, in fact, taken from a fan – which is what many people said after the match. The scissors supposedly came from a quick-thinking security guard who did not work for the federation, who spotted them in the audience. That is pretty cool, if that's what actually happened.

Both Adrian Adonis and Roddy Piper helped tremendously to create the building blocks of what would be the next chapter of my career.

ADONIS RUNS

Adonis was supposed to then start a feud with me, continuing where Piper had left off. He appeared on one or two WWF shows with a completely shaved head, swearing revenge for me damaging his pretty look. This run would have drawn some good money, however, this run didn't happen.

Adonis was fired in May 1987 for what the WWF officials called, "violations against dress codes after repeated warnings." Around this time, the company encouraged some nice slacks, a button up shirt, and maybe a suit jacket when you arrived to the arena, at the very least decent looking jeans and a collared shirt. Adrian, however, had put on a lot of weight, and I guess was more comfortable in Kmart sweatpants, rather than what the company wanted him to wear to best represent them.

Because of this, Adrian left the WWF shortly after WrestleMania III, and never really started his program with me. He filmed one little spot that they played during some squash matches where it was revealed that he had completely shaved his head bald, after the pay-per-view. The idea was we would have played off of his anger and embarrassment of being bald, with him perhaps, wearing a wig. This would have opened endless possibilities up of me pulling off his wig during matches, for a huge pop, but that pop would never be.

Adrian was let go, and he returned to go work for Verne Gagne once again in the AWA. (Incidentally, he continued to go with the Adorable gimmick there without Jimmy Hart, but was rather managed by Paul E. Dangerously.)

I'm not sure why WWF officials felt that Adrian wasn't classy, and didn't display carrying himself with the dignity that a WWF Superstar should. It is just puzzling to me. One time, I remember in Japan I worked with Adrian Adonis when he seemingly had everyone's best interest at heart.

We were way out in one of the smaller towns where everything was always a little dated, but the buildings were still always nice. The small town halls didn't usually have separate locker rooms or wrestler toilets, but this one did. So after the matches, everyone was showering, when all of a sudden, Adrian came running in where the boys were.

"Hey, guys! You gotta see this!" he said, acting very excited.

At first, we didn't move. The water felt good and nobody felt like going anywhere, but Adrian was persistent.

"Guys, I'm telling you, you will not be disappointed!"

Adrian had a way with words. I don't remember how he worded it exactly, but we instantly thought there was a naked woman waiting for us in a bathroom stall.

Believing that this excellent geisha girl was waiting for us in our very own locker room was plausible. We were often lonely on the road, and it was like dangling a carrot under the horse's nose at this point in the tour. With that being said, four or five of us quickly dried off and went running. We pulled on our towels and followed Adrian down the hallway, excited at the idea of whatever debauchery could be at hand.

When we finally made it to the bathroom, Adrian opened the door of the stall.

There was no girl to be found, only a toilet with no back on it – just a handle. But the miracle of a western toilet in the land of the rising sun was not the spectacle that the adorable one was pointing out to us.

There was projectile poo all over the place. It just hung there. It wasn't just on the back wall above the toilet, either. Adrian's crap completely covered all three tiled walls in one nasty long brown stripe!

Man, it looked like a horse had just given birth.

It was all brown and clear and yellow nonsense. It looked like he had emptied a super soaker full of brown gravy all over the place - *full fecal jacket.*

All of us practically puked at the sight. We ran away down the hall, faster than we ran in. In the distance, I looked back to watch in horror as Adrian pulled the very polite referee, Tiger Hattori, into the stall to see the mess. Ten seconds later, the ref was running behind me. He was screaming, gagging, and barfing his lungs up just like the rest of us. He couldn't believe it at all.

Adrian was so proud of it. The rest of the night, he tried to get everyone who was left in the building to go and look at his poop spray, for fear they would miss it.

In the end, I just don't understand why the WWF didn't think he was fit to represent them and let him go.

PARTYING WITH PIPER

While I was still working heel in the WWF before The Barber run came along, we all had a double shot over in New Jersey. I was working a program with a really funny guy, the Junkyard Dog.

We both had set it up to ride along with Roddy Piper over to the second show. At this time, we still protected the business. Two wrestlers couldn't be seen together getting in or out of the car together when one was a heel and the other was a babyface. They were never supposed to mix, hence the use of separate locker rooms by most promoters. So we just did that thing where we would drive down the block, and grab up the wrestler where nobody would see us.

"Thanks, Beefer," JYD said, sneaking into my rental.

"Thanks for what?"

"You know," he said. "For letting me come along with you and Pipes."

"Why is that?"

"You know why I wanted to come along, right?" the dog asked laughing, knowing that we both knew.

"Because Piper always has the very best, Oregon green bud pot?" I asked rhetorically. "No, no, I have no idea."

"Yep," the Dog said. "That's it!"

"Ha ha ha!" I said. "Why do you think I asked to hitch a ride with Piper in the first place? I got this rental."

We laughed.

I don't know what the deal was exactly. I think Piper said that his neighbors grew it, or something, but he always, always had an unlimited supply. And just like Piper was generous with me at WrestleMania, Piper had the reputation for being generous with his pot. He always shared and was never once called Rowdy Roddy Bogart by the boys.

We were in Woodbridge somewhere, about 25 minutes from Newark, off of Route 9. The road over there was pretty easy to deal with and it paralleled the Jersey Turnpike. So we drove a little bit and caught up with Piper at a park and ride.

When we got there, we both jumped into Piper's Cadillac, and we were off. The Dog went in back, and I was the designated navigator in the passenger seat, navigating with a roadmap. We drove about ten minutes or so. I kept looking in the mirror and turning around back at the Dog.

Both of us were waiting for the other one to speak. Neither of us had the nerve to see if Piper had any of the good stuff.

"Okay, boys," he said. "It was very polite of you not to nag, but you know what you guys are thinking."

We all laughed.

"Not me," Brutus said. "It is all Dog. He is jonesing in the back seat!"

"Well," he said. "I hate to disappoint you, but I don't have the regular supply today."

The Junkyard Dog slumped down. He put his tail between his legs.

"Awe shucks," Piper said. "You didn't think I would let you down, old boy, do you?"

Piper took out a folded piece of paper and tossed the bundle back to the Dog. He quickly opened it and took out this huge chunk of hash.

"What the hell?!" I said, with my eyes bugging out of my head.

"I knew you would like that," Piper chuckled. He looked back at the Dog in his mirror, again. "Now careful there, big fella, you are going to drool all over it!"

Junkyard Dog was staring at all the hash in his lap. He was in heaven, but he didn't know where to start.

"How are we going to smoke this?"

Piper always had pot and rolling a joint was never an issue. Sure, he also got good hash from his people in Oregon, too, and also other shit from out of there. But usually, we would be in a room or something. The sheer size of the hash brick was overwhelming.

"Easy," Piper said. "Just put it in your lip like chewing tobacco."

JYD and I looked at each other. We shrugged, and we broke the boulder into three pieces. We all pouched up our lips like cowboys. Piper and I, were somewhat conservative in portion-size, however. But the Dog, on the other hand, was not a dog, after all. He was a big pig. He put a giant wad in his jaw that looked like a tennis ball.

A half an hour later, the Dog was snoring.

The music was on. We were laughing so hard, we were in tears. I don't remember the show that night, or anything else. All I remember was trying to wake up the Dog in the backseat, and he wasn't having it.

I ended up working someone in a mask, instead. The Junkyard Dog stayed in the car asleep all that night and well into the next morning. He finally woke up on our way out of town the next afternoon. When he came too, he just leaned forward between the two seats in Piper's Cadillac.

"Are we almost there yet?" he asked.

"Dog! Show's over," I said. "You slept through the whole thing!"

JYD looked into Piper's mirror puzzled.

"He's right," Piper said. "We had the show, went to bed, and it's the next day now," he confirmed.

There was a long pause. We watched that marinate in the Dog's brain for a moment. He sat back and looked out the windows to see which way we were driving. When he realized that we were leaving the area and knew we weren't ribbing him, he leaned forward again.

"Really? Good then," he said. "Do you have any more of that hash?"

BIRTH OF A BARBER

When I walked into the next venue after WrestleMania III, it was just business as usual. I strolled into the War Memorial Arena in Rochester, NY, found my dressing room, and started to lay out my gear. I was going about my business when Rene Goulet and some of the other producers came over to me in my area. Rene was holding a white jacket. He stretched out his arm and handed it to me.

"Here it is," they said, reaching in the pocket.

"Here is what?" I asked taking the jacket, somewhat reluctantly.

"Your new gimmick," he said. "You are the Barber now."

"THE BARBER?!"

Nobody told me I was taking on a new persona. I had spent so much time and money in "Brutus Beefcake" that I couldn't believe it. My jaw hit the floor.

"That's right," he said. "You are a wrestling barber now, *The Barber*"

I didn't like it. I didn't like it one bit. I had worked for a long, long time on getting the look just right for Brutus Beefcake. I had put my own money, blood, sweat, and tears into creating the character, and how they now wanted to reduce me to being a hair stylist, just because of a stupid one-off angle we did at the PPV? It didn't make any sense.

"I am not The Barber," I chuckled, sarcastically.

"Oh, yes – yes you are," he laughed. "Says Pat."

I should have known.

Pat Patterson was gay. He "gayfabed" for a long time, but all the boys knew he liked men. Take nothing away from him, he was and is still probably one of the best storytellers in the game, but if I was trying to be a lady killer in the ring, cutting hair wasn't my idea of getting chicks. A barber was just about the furthest thing that I could think of from being masculine.

A barber, however, was right up Pat Patterson's alley.

You see, Pat Patterson's life-long partner, Louis was some kind of stylist or something. Having me be a "barber" just felt like it was a way for Pat to get his jollies. You know, seeing a decent-looking wrestler in barber attire was probably a way to get his rocks off at my expense.

I immediately pictured Pat sitting in a barbershop chair with one of those black smocks on. When the barber started running his fingers through Pat's hair, you would just see the black material of the smock rise and pitch a tent in his lap. I got cold chills.

Disgusting!

I grimaced. The idea that sex sells was true. I knew this. But I didn't like the idea that my new character was perhaps created to appeal to an old fat white guy in his 50s. Pat Patterson was not my ideal target demographic. I was more of a Chippendale for chicks, not for dicks. I was down with the hoes, not the bros, you know what I'm saying?

It felt like Pat was projecting some kind of weird fetish onto me and would live vicariously through watching my matches or something. I don't know. All I knew was I didn't like any of it.

"Come with me," Rene said.

Rene walked me out of the War Memorial in Rochester and down the street with a photographer at my side. We ended up at the doorstep of an old barber shop, with one of those red, white and blue spinning barber poles, but it was broken and had seen better days. The place was really run down. The room had that sterile smell of what would be like your grandfather's haircutting place of choice.

Everything had apparently been already set up, in advance with the shop owner, meaning he knew about the shoot before they even told me about my new gimmick. Rene handed this old Italian guy an envelope and shook his hand. Then, the impromptu photo shoot began.

I'm not sure how many of those pictures ever saw the light of day. From the one or two I did see, you could tell by the look on my face that I was not happy at all about the situation. I couldn't smile. I couldn't even contain myself. To say "I was angry" would be putting it mildly.

When we went back to the arena, Rene was trying to make small talk, but I wasn't buying it.

This is bullshit. This is bullshit! I don't deserve this bullshit. Why change something we worked on so hard for two years. I did everything they wanted!

I went back into the building and headed for my locker room. Word had already gotten around. A few of the boys were there and already knew. They were snickering.

"Brutus the Barber!" one yelled.

I refused to sell it.

I was set up in an old dressing room with a bunch of shelves with baskets instead of lockers. I slammed the door behind me. Then I started kicking and smashing everything in sight. I was pulling the baskets off of the shelves and punting them across the room.

I tried to calm myself down. The way that Pat Patterson worked was, if he knew you didn't like something, he would enforce it even more.

I put the jacket on slowly and went over to look in the mirror. I adjusted the comb and the little scissors in the pocket then pulled it off and stomped on it. I picked up the jacket and threw it against the wall behind me, right into the trash.

I think a producer cracked open the door and saw me, then turned around. I knew that he must have seen my frustration and went off to stooge what he had seen. I didn't care.

I'm not fucking doing it.

I got dressed for the show in my regular Beefcake gimmick. In my mind, it looked so much better than a stupid white lab jacket with a couple items in the pocket that the audience was barely going to be able to see. I was doing some pushups to get a little pump on when Hulk came in.

"Hey Brutus," he said. "What the hell is up?" Hulk asked, looking around at the ruins of my dressing room.

"I don't know. I think they want me to quit," I said, "and I am thinking about it. This is not right."

"Look, I heard about what they want to do," he said. "You know what though, brother? You should just keep being Brutus Beefcake. Wear all the other shit, plus their jacket. Just make it an extra accessory, you know?"

"But how am I going to get over that I am a barber," I asked.

"Look, brother, they want a barber, give them a barber. But tell them the only way it is going to work is that you actually cut other wrestlers' hair, like almost all of the time," he said.

He had a point. The hair versus hair thing had been going on in countless arenas in countless territories long before me, and it always got a big response.

"So essentially, all of my matches would be like hair matches? That would be my specialty match, like Blackjack has the bunkhouse matches."

"Everyone one of them," Hulk said, laughing, trying to make lemonade out of lemons. "Yes. If you are fighting Brutus the Barber, then you are going to get your hair cut. That's what they want, right?"

I scratched my chin.

It could work. But the threat of losing your hair had to be every single time to catch on, to make sense. The commentators would have to really put over that threat whenever they called one of my matches. I would have to threaten every one of my opponents with getting their hair cut, just like Adrian Adonis was doing to Roddy Piper in his promos leading up to the PPV. The difference was, the threat would be to every single person I wrestled against, always.

"You actually might have something there. So like Jake Roberts has his snake at the end every single match, I will knock an opponent out, then attempt to cut their hair?!"

"Go with it brother!" Hulk said. "Embrace it. It could be big money."

I reached for the jacket. It was half in and half out of the can. I dusted it off a little and put it on and looked in the mirror. I picked up the comb and scissors and popped them into the lapel pocket. Hulk patted me on the shoulder and walked out.

The sleeper hold was a move that Piper used occasionally, as well as Adonis. Piper was leaving the federation anyhow to pursue some acting opportunities and I knew it would be no big deal for me to add that to the extension of my new character. Ken Lucas my old tag partner also used the sleeper. He actually taught me some cool spots and timing for it. When that light bulb went off in my head, I came up with the winning formula.

Sleeper hold. Sit them up, and cut their hair. Rub their shoulders, hit their neck. Wake them up like I did at Mania. Then, when they wake up, show them the results, and they are pissed!

Despite the fact that Pat Patterson was turning me into a barber for stroke material, and despite the fact that I actually hated the idea at first, I decided to give it a go.

Once I had the full idea fleshed out, I went right to Vince McMahon to get it approved. Vince likes that. Though a lot of guys are intimidated by him, he wants people to approach him with ideas. Even though he does get off on having power, at the end of the day, he respects a person more when they have the guts to stand up to him, or approach him with something that they think is right.

I gave him my whole concept of how I thought it should work. I explained how a jobber match would go. I explained my ideas for everything at the end of my matches. I also explained my twist on how I wanted the look.

I wasn't just going to be a barber. I was going to take on the barber gimmick mixed with the Brutus Beefcake gimmick. So, it wasn't going to be a generic wrestler wearing a barber jacket - it was everything Beefcake; the boots, the pants, and the gloves, also with a beefcake-style barber jacket.

I was also going to carry a bag with scissors, clippers, shaving foam, hair color – whatever I needed. On top of that, I was going to also adopt the garden shears and a mirror like they used at WrestleMania.

Vince loved over-the-top. He loved my twist on the idea and how I was going to work all of that stuff together. He gave me the okay on the spot. Once he did, everyone knew the hair gimmick. They knew that from now on if you wrestled with the Barber, it was likely that your hair was going to get cut by the end of the match. After I received the approval, he left it up to me to be creative. …And that is how Brutus "The Barber" Beefcake was born.

THE LOOK

Despite what some may think, I did not just chop my old wardrobe. What I did was go back to the drawing board for similar, yet different all new clothing. I went back to my designer Michael in Tampa, and I told him my ideas. I had seen some of his cut-up work and also some of his fishnet pieces that he had made for his rockstar clients before. I knew that was more the direction that I wanted to go in for the Barber.

The idea was I would be the sexy, Chippendale-like, male exotic dancer barber. You know, sort of like the pizza delivery guy stripper at a bachelorette party, but only a barber. We wanted the clothing to look like rockstar stripper gear, but also like a madman with scissors went total ape-shit on all of his clothing. So he went right to work on similar tights like he made for me before, but cut huge holes in the legs, added tassels, and put fishnet underneath it.

Randy Savage was also wearing Michael's stuff too by now. I had already introduced him to my guy in Tampa. As much as Randy was an asshole, I still wanted to help him when he wanted the help. Liz was his deal. When they took her away, he decided to depend more on his clothes for heat. The clothes ended up helping, too. In the end, however, we made an intentional effort to keep our looks separate. Michael worked hard to make sure that "Macho was Macho, and the new Beefcake was Beefcake."

Michael really delivered, once again.

CLASSIC BARBER JOB MATCHES

On April 23, 1987, I debuted as Brutus "The Barber" Beefcake on a TV taping in Worcester, MA at the Centrum. I defeated Johnny Valiant, my former manager with the new character and everyone loved it! I ended with my new submission, the sleeper and after the bout, I shaved off part of Johnny V's head while he was unconscious. He pretty much jobbed out to me and helped make me what I am today.

Struttin' and cuttin' baby!

There used to be a real art form to what people would call a "squash match." The traditional classic squash match does not really exist today, and it is a shame too because it was a great vehicle to get someone over. A "jobber," or "talent enhancement" as they were sometimes called, were brought in on an as-needed basis. The booker would call a regional guy and pay them on a per-night basis. The jobbers would then go out there and bump and sell moves for one of the regular guys under contract to make them look strong.

I had jobbed a little early on for events in my first run with the WWF, but not for an extended period of time. The thing about it is, if you jobbed too long, then you could get type-casted. There are a lot of guys out there who were okay with "jobbing out," and liked to come in just for the exposure. I was not one of them.

For my initial jobber matches to get over the new gimmick, I carried a bag with me to the ring. Inside the bag, I had scissors, an electric razor, hairspray, glitter and a mirror. I also carried a pair of garden shears with the handles taped to look like barber poles down to the ring with me, as well.

It no longer mattered what I did in the ring during the bout, it was all about what happened after the bout was over! At the end of the match, I would use a sleeper hold as my finishing move to set up a haircutting session after the bell. After my hand was raised, that is when the really important stuff for my character would actually happen.

After being victorious, I would do my "Beefcake Strut" around the ring, while "snipping" my fingers like scissors. This would indicate to the crowd that I was about to give my unconscious, defeated opponent a free haircut. Then, using scissors, my shears, or an electric razor, I would cut off some hair and throw handfuls of it into the air to pop the crowd. Sometimes I would cut a little hair. If they pissed me off, I would cut a lot of hair. Sometimes I would even spray a big "B" on their chest with hairspray spray-paint and douse them with glitter. My bag of tricks had everything I needed to get the job done.

It was much like The Million Dollar man sticking money in his defeated opponent's mouth, just to add insult to injury. I was able to take even more liberties with talent enhancement, because the jobbers all came to know the deal when you were booked against Brutus "The Barber" Beefcake.

A classic WWF jobber named Dusty Wolfe was one of these guys. We contacted him for an interview for the writing of this book so you could get a better idea of how the rules changed behind the scenes when you were booked against me.

For a long time, Dusty would go out there and give it his all just to make the others look good. Usually, he would maybe make $50, or $75 for a match. However, Dusty and any other jobber were expected to go even further above and beyond the regular expectations of a squash match when Brutus The Barber was opposite their name on the card.

If you were booked to face me as enhancement talent, you quickly learned that part of the deal was different than working anyone else in the Federation. You would go in the ring and give it your all, but you would leave a part of you in that ring. This meant that you were getting a haircut at the end of the match and a clump of your locks was not going to make it home with you.

A lot of the guys liked this booking because they would actually be compensated for the bad haircut, as well. A bunch of the guys would line up and request a spot with me on a TV taping rather than someone else because they would go home with a $200 barber bonus, which was a lot more than what you would normally get paid for a job match.

On one particular taping, I called a few spots with Dusty Wolfe. The finish was going to include a leapfrog, and then an unexpected sleeper hold right out of a universal spot.

A "universal spot" in wrestling is often used to get the babyface over. I know you have seen it before. This formulaic sequence can have slightly different moves added to it, but usually looked like the following, especially in the late 80's and early 90's:

The heel has a side headlock on the babyface, who pushes him to the ropes to escape. The heel then comes off the ropes and shoulder tackles him. Now, the heel runs to the ropes, and the face gets up from laying on his back but drops back down. As the heel comes running, he jumps over the babyface's body and continues to the other side. As the heel runs back, the babyface leapfrogs up in the air and the heel ducks under, still running the ropes. Finally, when the heel comes back, the babyface gives him a hip toss, a bodyslam, and a then a dropkick.

At the point of the leapfrog, I was going to actually have Dusty jump over me, then immediately slap on the sleeper for the finish. However, there was some confusion on just who was jumping over whom. Dusty thought that I was going to jump over him. However, I thought he was going to jump over me. Because of this miscommunication, we both ran at each other and put our heads down, to allow room for the anticipated leapfrog.

We both ducked and bent over. It looked like two goats charging each other, and we banged heads, right in the middle of the ring. We both fell back very hard. After that, I don't even remember how we finished the match, but I do remember that when we got back to the locker room, Vince was waiting. He saw the whole debacle and yelled at us.

"What the hell was that?" said the angry Irishman. Before I could even explain, Vince told us that we were going to go back out there and do the match, all over again. "We need that footage for the TV taping, and by damn, we are going to get it," he said.

The second match turned out fine. Dusty had a few words to say specifically about this night:

"It is funny when I look back at it now," he said, reminiscing. "A lot about that night is still a big blur. Because we banged our heads together so hard, I don't really remember how the first match ended, but I do know this. I got two haircuts that night, and it wasn't just a little trim above the ears. The Barber really went to town! He cut so much of my hair off. I figured it was okay though back then because my hair would always grow back. I can't really say the same thing, today."

The amount of hair that I ended up cutting always had to do with how the guy was in the ring. There was no set haircutting rule from the office; it was completely up to me. Every wrestler was at my complete mercy. If somebody tried to hurt me, or if they went off script, or if they were the shits, I would cut a whole lot more of their hair than someone who was decent. In this case, if I shaved a whole bunch of his hair off, I am sure there was a legitimate reason in my mind. I probably either thought the headbutt was entirely his fault, or I was still just angry about the whole situation.

Either way, Dusty Wolfe walked away with a patented reverse Mohawk on that particular evening.

1987–1990 CLASSIC BRUTUS STORYLINES

In the storyline, Greg and I broke up at WrestleMania III, after we defeated The Fabulous Rougeau Brothers. Greg and I argued the whole time, and Valentine and Valiant left with Dino Bravo without me when we were done. In the very next match on the PPV, I helped Piper beat Adonis, and earned my new nickname, "The Barber."

After this, I then feuded some with my former partner Valentine and also my ex-manager Valiant. By the end of our feud, I had Valiant's head completely shaved bald.

HONKY TONK MAN

Next, I started my first build up towards what was supposed to be an eventual run with the Intercontinental Heavyweight Championship, held by the Honky Tonk Man at the time. He had recently turned heel, after turning on Hulk Hogan.

This was a fun program. Honky was managed by Jimmy Hart, but also had a "mysterious valet" named, Peggy Sue. She wore a blonde wig with pigtails and sunglasses in an attempt to obviously conceal her real identity. For the most part, Sensational Sherri usually played this role for all television appearances and PPVs, but at house shows, it was actually Jimmy Hart in drag.

We had a lot of run with this run on house shows. I would often get disqualified and lose my chance at the title, but then chase Jimmy around after Honky had left for the locker room with the title belt. Eventually, I would catch "Peggy Sue" and strip her down to her underwear. I would then reveal it was Jimmy Hart to the audience and pull his falseys out of his bra. The audience ate it up. Jimmy was always a bit of a Hulk Hogan stooge, but fun to work with. He didn't mind being the butt of the joke.

The final level of the program on the house shows leading up to WrestleMania IV was great. I would surprise the Honky Tonk Man with my own valet to counter Peggy Sue's presence at ringside. I debuted a valet of my own, "Georgina," on some shows to help me catch and strip down Jimmy Hart at the end of matches.

Georgina was a much more disgusting and hideous depiction of a woman than Jimmy Hart, being played by the hairy-backed George "The Animal" Steele in drag. Georgina would undress Jimmy Hart then take his own shirt off. The funny part was the green-tongued Animal always looked like he was wearing a Velcro sweater when he had his shirt off.

This Mania took place on March 27, 1988. It was at the Atlantic City Convention Hall in Atlantic City, New Jersey with about 20,000 people in attendance.

For this match "Colonel" Jimmy Hart and Peggy Sue were in the WWF Intercontinental Champion's corner. Honky Tonk and I had a pretty entertaining match that we had fine-tuned at all of our house matches with Mania in mind. In the end, he went to the top rope, but I pulled him off, clotheslined him, then slapped on the sleeper hold. Jimmy Hart popped up on the apron. He nailed the referee from behind with his megaphone.

I ended up winning by disqualification, which meant that Honky kept the belt because a title does not change hands via DQ. With Honky "asleep" in the ring, I chased Jimmy Hart, held him down, and gave him a haircut. He sold it pretty well, kicking and screaming like a bitch the whole time. But before I could then cut Honky's hair, Peggy Sue rolled in and woke her "boyfriend" up by pouring a pitcher of water on him. It was all very cartoony, but the fans loved it.

Our feud ended at WrestleMania IV. In the end, I did not get the belt, as Patterson had promised me, but they say that I would get a run with the belt after Honky lost it to someone else in the near future. He was disqualified at the PPV to keep me looking strong without a pinfall so that I would look like a viable contender in the near future.

GUEST PASSAGE - OUTLAW RON BASS

"Probably one of my favorites I ever worked with is Brutus Beefcake. He is also still the one who people ask me about the most, among the people I worked with while I was up in New York. We did that spot where I wound up juicing him on TV, and he was a real sport about it, making me look good.

That was the first time that deal had happened up there in years up there and it really left quite an impact, because of how he sold it.
– Outlaw Ron Bass"

Switching me out of my program with Honky, they decided that they wanted to move me over to a series of matches with my old friend "Outlaw" Ron Bass.

To start off this program, Bass attacked me after a match on the WWF Superstars of Wrestling show. Once again, we decided to go with a massive blood angle, having him bust me open this time with a spur. This was like a shout out to our past, only this time, I didn't have Ron cut me open like when I was a scared rookie. I handled the dirty work myself.

We made the match extra violent. Ron Bass had a whip he called "Miss Betsy" which came into play. He really laid in on me. As a result of the "injury," on August 29, 1988, I was unable to face Honky Tonk Man at the first ever SummerSlam for the IC Heavyweight Championship.

To finish this program, I defeated Ron Bass at The Sun Dome at the University South Florida, on one of the highest rated Saturday Night's Main Events of the time. At the end of the match, they wanted to drive home the finish that we didn't quite get with Adrian Adonis. They didn't want me to just snip some of his hair off and throw it into the air. In the end, they wanted me to get full revenge on what the cowboy had done to me, costing me my final shot at the Intercontinental title. They wanted Ron Bass totally bald at the end of the match.

What we decided to do was have me cut some of the hair with scissors, then head over to ringside for the electric trimmers to quickly do the job. Now, I had learned since the Piper/Adonis Hair vs Hair match at WrestleMania III. Rather than to use a portable battery powered trimmer, this time we had a military grade electric razor plugged into an extension cord handed off to me from ringside. That did the trick. I was finally able to remove all of Ron's hair in moments and they got the pop they were looking for from the crowd for TV.

That particular "Hair vs. Hair Match" was one of the highest rated Saturday Night's Main Event of the 1980s. Ron told me that it was, perhaps, one of the highest paid deals Ron ever had because we both got paid royalties through the WWF and also from *Saturday Night* by NBC. It really was a pretty lucrative deal for us.

Wrestling today is a little different. What we did back in my day was focus on the personalities and the stories. We kept it simple. That match with Ron was classic "Good Guy vs. Bad Guy." Back then, there were not all these side stories and variables. I think a lot of the new crazy stuff gets lost in translation. That was the beauty of our era. We kept it simple. We made it believable. We worked our butts off out there, night after night, and we gave the amount of professionalism our business demanded!

Bass really was the perfect foil, but he really was a good guy, behind the scenes, too. He had a really good sense of humor. Here he is telling a rib story that he played on Hulk and me, back in the day:

"Back in the Memphis days when we were in the Tennessee territory, Terry and Eddie Boulder used to travel together. Now, we were working in Jonesboro, Arkansas that night, and Hogan had just bought his new Lincoln Continental. At the end of the show, Hogan and Beefcake were in the new car and headed over to a McDonalds and went through the drive-thru.

I followed them over in my car, and they didn't realize that I was right behind them.

"Nice new flashy car," I said to Big Pete Austin who was sitting in the passenger seat next to me. "Not for long."

Pete looked at me puzzled.

I waited until the cashier at the window handed them their bags, and then I hit the gas.

BAMMM!

"Holy shit!" Pete said, laughing.

I tried to just bump them, but I ended up getting them pretty good. I don't think I actually left a mark, but that didn't matter. Hulk and Brutus threw open their doors. They jumped out of the Continental and ran straight for me.

I already had the window open. I reached under the seat and grabbed my .357 Magnum and pointed it out the window right at them. They froze. They stopped dead in their tracks like a deer in headlights. They did a total turnabout face, ducked down, and rushed back to their doors. As they were running back, Brutus turned around and saw Big Pete. Then he looked back over and saw it was me on the other side of the gun. He started laughing.

"Wait, Terry!" Brutus said.

Hulk didn't wait, however. He jumped right into the driver's seat and sat right on top of his hamburgers.

"It's just Ron," Brutus continued.

"When Hulk turned and realized it was us just messing with him, he reached under his ass for his spoiled dinner. He got out of the car and started throwing flattened burgers at us that looked like pancakes." – Outlaw Ron Bass

SURVIVOR SERIES 88

The first match of this Survivor Series five-on-five match was on the Intercontinental level. I was teamed up with IC champ The Ultimate Warrior, The Blue Blazer (Owen Hart), and Jim Brunzell who subbed for Don Muraco who had unexpectedly left. We took on the team of the Honky Tonk Man, Ron Bass, Danny Davis, Greg Valentine, and Bad News Brown. Our team won with Warrior as the last man standing.

This event was mostly uneventful. The real thing that stands out in my mind was a feud that was leading up to this PPV – but I don't mean a feud that was going on in the ring.

Before a television taping leading up to Survivor Series 88, a lot of us went to catering to have some lunch. I was sitting there having something to eat with some of the boys, and the British Bulldogs were there, as well. Little did I know that when Dynamite Kid walked out of the room after having his meal, he was about to get a receipt for a bunch of his earlier actions – *one that would stay with him forever.*

ROUGEAU VS DYNAMITE

I think the real heat started somewhere, maybe a year before where Jacques and Raymond were booked in a 20 minute Broadway match with the Bulldogs. The Dogs had finished their run with the Dream Team. At this point, they hadn't been beaten by The Harts yet for the belts and were still the Tag Team Champions. They didn't like the idea that the Rougeau Brothers were starting to go the limit with them and considered the brothers a threat to their title run.

"Fuck those guys," I remember Dynamite saying to Bulldog after the match as they were getting ready to leave the arena. It was very clear they were not happy about the strong booking of the Rougeaus. "A Broadway is not happening again, I'll tell you that."

It was on. The Rougeau Brothers then fell victim to some brutal British Bulldog bullying pranks over the next six months. The Bulldogs cut Raymond's clothing up into ribbons once during a match and put the shreds all back into his luggage nicely. They also stole Jacques' bag at an airport and threw it in the garbage. To say the brothers were probably sick and tired of getting ribbed in this manner would be an understatement.

Fast Forward to an Upstate, NY house show in Syracuse at the Onondaga War Memorial on September 25, 1988.

Syracuse was not very far from the Rougeaus' hometown. There was a 45-minute flight to Montreal, and the brothers wanted to make it. Now, they figured a plane ride from Syracuse to Montreal was very short, but they would need to change their position on the card, in order to make it to the airport on time. When you are on the road 21 nights a month, an extra day would have been great to go home and see their families.

The Rougeaus saw the card on the wall. There were 8 matches, with two of them being tag-teams; one as the third match, and the other as the eighth match. They were working with the Harts late on the show, and the Bulldogs had Demolition early. There were no flights possible for the Bulldogs to get home. The Rougeaus didn't think it would be a big deal if they switched the order, so they went to Chief Jay Strongbow to see.

"We would like to know if we could wrestle our match with the Hart Foundation third tonight instead of towards the end? We want to fly to Montreal after our match to have one more day with our families - that is, if you and the Bulldogs are cool with it," they asked.

Strongbow figured it was fine and went and told the Bulldogs. Now, I don't know if it was because they were mean, or what, but they got pissed. The Bulldogs, in fact, would not have been able to go home themselves. They lived way over in Calgary. The Bulldogs did, however, tell Strongbow that the switch was ok.

The boys packed their bags and got everything ready to catch their plane, right after their matches. Jacques was playing cards with Curt Hennig waiting for his match, and asked him to watch his bags so that the Bulldogs didn't pull one of their trademark clothing destruction pranks out of revenge.

"You never know with the Bulldogs," he said to Mister Perfect. "They said the switch was okay, but who knows."

"No problem," Curt said. "I'll watch your stuff." The Rougeaus wrestled their match and then came back. After they showered up, Perfect looked at down at Jacques bag, then back up at him. He looked down, then back up again. Jacques realized it was a sign and shook his head.

"No, no!" Jacques said. "We don't have time for this right now. Did they?"

Curt looked down and then back into Jacques' eyes, again. Jacques quickly unzipped his bag open and checked. Everything seemed in order. He couldn't find anything wrong fast, and Curt just shrugged.

"Well, if they did anything, I'm just going to stooge it out," he said. "Come on, Raymond, we have to go," he shouted across the dressing room. They rushed out and quickly got to their plane, on time. While they were gone, however, Curt decided to play one of his own trademark pranks. You see, he was an instigator, too. He told the Bulldogs they were going to tell on them. He got them all riled up and exaggerated the threat.

When Jacques got home, he was better able to see if any damage had really been done. I guess his work-out gear was missing, just some cheap shorts or something, but that was it.

When the brothers returned back to work on September 29, 1988, they flew to Miami, Florida. Now, I didn't see anything at this show, because I was at MSG working Ron Bass for a TV taping in New York. But the B card was set to happen at The Miami Arena. Despite the distance, it wouldn't take long for me to hear about what transpired.

Their father, Jacques, Sr., lived in town. He brought them to the show, then went up into the stands to wait for the show.

From what I gather, Jacques was playing cards at a table with Curt again, with his back to the locker room entrance. He couldn't see people coming in. The Harts came in, Cowboy Orton came in, and then the Bulldogs. Dynamite didn't say a word, but just blindsided Jacques with a roundhouse to the face. He knocked him off the chair and jumped on top of him, punching him over and over again in the mouth. The poker cards flew everywhere, and the table toppled.

"Hey, leave him alone!" Raymond his brother was already injured. He hobbled over on a crutch to break things up. Dynamite punched him too and knocked him off his crutches. Dynamite had caught Jacques good. His mouth had immediately started swelling up. Nonetheless, Jacques pushed through to save his brother.

"Oh, you're going to beat up a guy on crutches now, too?!" Jacques said, spitting blood.

"No. You're right," Dynamite replied. "I'll wait for him to heal, and then I'll beat him up!"

Dynamite left. Jacques looked at Curt. He was pissed for not giving him any warning. He got up and went off to a bathroom to assess the damage. Soon after that, the boys say that Tony Garea went to see the Rougeaus in their dressing room. Jacques was nursing wounds in the mirror, looking at the swollen face in front of him.

"Take your things and go home," Tony Garea said.

"Nope," I said. "I'm here to work. I'm going to wrestle the Harts, still."

Jacques was smart. He knew that the Harts were tight with the Bulldogs. If he left early without working his match, he would look weak and

it would certainly be the talk of that group. The Rougeaus had their match
with the Hart Foundation. Jacques had to take all of the bumps with his
messed up face too, because his brother still had the leg injury.

When they got in the car, nobody talked. Their father had already
been smartened up and Jacques told me later that it was a long quiet ride
home. And after that, Jacques didn't talk to anyone for three days.

Their next show was on October 2, 1988 in Rockford, IL at the
Metro Centre. On the flight there, as they were landing, either Dynamite or
Curt ribbed Jacques again. When they flew into Chicago, just before we
landed, the flight attendant made an announcement.

"Ladies and gentlemen, we're thrilled to have wrestlers from the
WWF on board this flight, and we welcome them to Chicago. We also want
to congratulate Jacques Rougeau on his recent boxing match!"

The boys all popped.

Finally, Jacques broke his silence with Raymond. "I need to make my
comeback."

When the brothers got to their hotel room, Raymond immediately
started showing Jacques some boxing moves on the pillow. Raymond was
more the tough guy out of the brothers, and Jacques wasn't much of a fighter.
However, he knew that he needed to toughen up quick, or else the nonsense
was going to keep going on.

The Rougeau Brothers worked another show in Battle Creek, MI
against the Harts. Later that night, Jacques finally called his dad, the first time
after Dynamite beat him up in Miami.

"I'm okay, now," he said, fumbling his words over a fat lip. "I
wanted you to know that I am planning my comeback for tomorrow, or the
day after."

"I knew you would. You are smart," his father said. "You have to do
it, son. I know it might be hard, but it is something you have to do to keep
respect."

"I know."

"Now, before you go for your comeback, go to the bank first and get
a roll of quarters. When it comes time, you hold those in your fist and hit him
in the mouth as hard as you can," he said. "Hit him like you want to kill him."

His father was no slouch. Jacques Rougeau, Sr. was a tough guy
himself, working with guys like the Sheik and Abdullah the Butcher in his
days. He had also been a bouncer when he was growing up in Montreal. He
knew.

On Monday, we all flew out to FT Wayne, Indiana for a TV taping. At this point, the Rougeau Brothers were working the Harts and the Bulldogs were working the Tag Champs Demolition every night on mostly all of the B cards. I was working Honky in Intercontinental matches in the A cards. However, at the shows for television, the A, B, and C shows all intermingled, and this is when new pairings would often occur.

Jacques and Raymond went over to a bank around 10 and had to wait for it to open at 10:30 am. At around this time, some calls went over to the hotel rooms. What the brothers didn't know at the time, Vince was requesting everyone he could reach to come in a little early for an impromptu meeting at 11:00 am.

Usually, I was never at a taping that early, but Hulk Hogan and I were actually both already there.

Our regular TV taping day schedules were almost always the same. Most often, when Hulk and I were on the same shows, we would both get up pretty early and I would head over to his place for breakfast. Very seldom was breakfast ever provided by catering at the venue for the shows, and when it was, it was always garbage. Bagels, toast, donuts, muffins, you know - carb shit that none of the boys except the Big Bossman would want to eat.

The good thing was, because Hogan had a special meals deal in his contract, I would wake up and go to his room and we would always order this massive breakfast, every morning. None of the boys had room service worked into their contracts, but Hogan did. The WWF always picked up his entire bill, including our breakfasts and all expenses.

At this point, this was not at all like back in the days where we had to accept whatever the buffet had to offer on the menu. We would get all specialty items cooked up for us. We would get egg whites, fancy omelets with hamburger patties in them, sausage, bacon, and even steak - all that, and maybe a spoonful or two of cereal when we were just really being pigs.

We would eat as much as we could because, once we got to the arena, we didn't know when there would be time to eat. See, you were expected to be at the arena between noon and 1:00 pm. Guys would come in and have lunch with the crew at catering before things would get a little hectic.

So Hulk would order all this stuff and me and him would just eat it all, like pigs, before heading over to one of the better gyms in the city where the show was. There was a lot of burping going on during our workouts on TV days, let me tell you. We would work out for a good amount of time.

Then we would always head over to the venue super late when we were good and ready.

Technically, I was supposed to be there the same time as everyone else, but because I was Hulk's friend and he needed someone to work out with, I would often show up late with him, and we would miss lunch altogether. Nobody was going to question the Hulkster on why he was late, and because I was with him, I always got a pass. Since we planned our lateness arriving after lunch had been served, this is why we would always have to load up on a really good breakfast.

On this particular morning in Ft. Wayne, Hulk wanted to talk with Vince about some storyline ideas he had for his program with Big Bossman, so we grabbed something quick, worked out and went straight to the venue.

It was pretty impressive. At around 11:00 am, there were actually quite a bit of the boys wandering around. Vince managed to get together mostly everyone there an hour earlier than usual. The Rougeaus, however, were absent.

"I heard what happened," he said in a conference room at the arena, referring to the Bulldogs without looking at them directly. "I just want you to know that if there are any more fights like this in my locker room, I am going to have to fire anyone who is involved," said Vince. "Consider this your warning."

The ironic thing is, Jacques was probably buying his roll of quarters the very moment Vince was speaking to us.

I was sitting in the locker room looking at a newspaper while Hogan was walking around somewhere in the arena talking to Vince. The locker room was actually a big open area with three dividers. The Bulldogs and Dino Bravo were in my section of the locker room. They were talking small-talk when Jacques and Raymond walked in. Then, everything went quiet.

This is going to be interesting, I thought. I knew exactly what was going on. A number of us were taking bets on when we thought things were going to break out. I knew it was only a matter of time.

Raymond looked around and said something like, "Let's go in the other room, over there. There's more room." But Jacques was still trying to save face.

"No, this is as good a place as any. Let's just set up in here," he said.

The Rougeaus put their stuff away in the cubby lockers. Jacques sat down and pulled out a book and started to read. The Bulldogs and Dino Bravo were somewhat surprised that Jacques was not unsettled by their presence. The Bulldogs were actually quiet. Knowing Vince had laid down the law, eventually, they just got up and left.

Jacques remembered something his dad said. "When you go to make your comeback, make sure it is after 1:00 pm because it is hard to fight back on a full stomach."

I talked to Jacques for a few minutes, then followed them out as they went to sit at ringside. A lot of times, the boys would gather around the ring a little before the show to try out a few sequences, or practice a few spots. Ringside was a social place before a show. It also provided an opportunity to go polish up a little before the big event.

Because I had very little going on at the taping, I was basically a nomad for this taping. It was the typical "hurry up and wait" scenario for me. You hurry to get to the venue, then wait for what seemed like an eternity. My spot on the card was just a jobber match to keep me strong on TV for my matches with Ron Bass. I was working against enhancement talent Gene Ligon that night, beating him with the sleeper.

Vince was walking around ringside, talking to Hulk about the show. Jacques and Raymond walked by them on their way over to the ring. I think Vince was waiting for him to complain about Dynamite, but he didn't. He was fixing on fixing the problem, himself. He never said a word.

The brothers got in the ring for a few minutes. After the brothers got out of the ring, Vince walked by them again and saw that Jacques didn't say anything. He was puzzled. He knew that they should have had a gripe, but they still were not talking to him about it. I think that is when he got worried that they were going to take the matter into their own hands.

"Guys, you missed my talk earlier," he said, approaching them, himself. "I need to talk to you for a minute, later. Maybe an hour or so?" Vince said.

They nodded. Jacques took Raymond off to the side.

"We have to do it now. If we don't and I wait until after Vince warns me, then we will be out of a job. So we have to do it before he tells us we can't," he explained. "Are you sure you want to help me?"

Raymond was tough. He was in for sure.

The Rougeaus were up against the Bulldogs, but they also had to worry about the rest of the boys. The Dogs were in with The Harts, and Bad News Brown who was another real badass, as well. The brothers knew that they never had a bad relationship with any of the others, but things could turn sour after attacking their buddy, Dynamite.

Jacques was smart. He decided to wait until the Bulldogs came out of catering with full stomachs before making his hit. Now, there was a hall wrapping around to the cafeteria in the backstage section of the arena. What he did was position himself just outside the doorway with his brother across from him on the opposite wall. This strategic positioning made the hallway more narrow, so Dynamite would have to walk in between both of them in the corridor and give them the advantage.

Jacques stood up against the wall right outside the door with his roll of quarters in hand. I had no idea what was going on when I wandered to the cafeteria looking for something to eat. I walked right by the two brothers in standing in tandem and went in, looking for something meaty. I had no idea of what they were planning.

I went through the line and grabbed me a plate. The Bulldogs had come in already, just a little bit before I did. They were over at another table eating with the Harts. I sat down for a while, eating my meal slowly, talking to some of the boys at the table. Don Muraco was finishing up. He got up and left, and Cowboy Bob Orton followed him out.

Meanwhile out in the hall, Pat Patterson ran into Raymond and started up a conversation. This probably made things look even more natural and innocent out in the hallway, on their part. Eventually, I think Bret and Anvil left by themselves, and then soon after Davey Boy.

It was the perfect storm. Dynamite just happened to be last in leaving, and he had none of his buddies around to even the odds. The timing was just ideal for what Jacques had planned. Dynamite had nobody to watch his back.

When Dynamite finally left, he stepped out into the hall and there was Jacques. Jacques said he intentionally put his head down, falsely avoiding eye contact to throw Dynamite off his guard and make it seem like he was still intimidated.

Dynamite liked that. He walked over towards Jacques holding a cup of coffee and just stood there. He said nothing, trying to make things more awkward between the both of them. He puffed out his chest a little.

Jacques waited until he was about four feet away from him, and for the first time in a while, he spoke.

"Hey, how we doing?"

Dynamite pushed out his chest more and started to get in his face. He smiled a really cocky grin to intimidate him. That was the straw that broke the camel's back, and also few of the camel's teeth.

BANG! Jacques swung his iron fist, loaded with the roll of quarters. It connected hard. He let him have it with everything he had.

Raymond was on the other side of the hall. He had been a great distraction only to Pat Patterson, who was still talking to him at the time of the shot. Raymond watched, but then saw that Dynamite was not going down. He pushed Pat out of the way to charge the scene, while offering more instructions.

"Jab, Jacques!" Raymond yelled. Dynamite was down to one knee, but he was not out. He was grabbing Jacques tights and pulling himself up.

"Jab!!!"

Jacques drilled Dynamite Kid two more times. Dynamite finally dropped down on both knees, then Jacques hit him a few more times for good measure. Blood was pouring out of his nose like a waterfall.

"Help! Help!" Pat Patterson looked at the bloodshed and started screaming like a little girl. "Help! Somebody get help!"

At this, I jumped out of my seat and ran out to the hallway to see what the commotion was all about. Patterson was running down the hall as fast as his chubby ass could carry him. Bad News Brown had just come out of nowhere and grabbed Jacques to stop the punches. Jacques didn't resist at all to being pulled away.

I looked down at Dynamite who was already a mess. He was shaking, holding his jaw. Four teeth came out; two on the top, two on the bottom. Blood was spurting everywhere.

With one hand pointed at Jacques, and one holding his crimson jaw, Dynamite snapped.

"I am going to fuck you up! I am going to fuck you up!"

"Yeah?" Jacques said, pointing back. "Well, the next time you fuck with me, I'm going to put you in a wheelchair," he said, before walking away. Raymond gave his brother a slap on the ass like a football player. He was very proud of him.

The Harts came running up to the scene. As a few of us were attending to the bleeding Dynamite, the Rougeaus were off to find Vince and tell him what had happened.

The brothers looped around the hallway until they got to where Vince's office was stationed for the event. Raymond knocked on Vince's door. Jacques was standing behind him covered in blood, but none of it was his own.

At this same instant, Randy Savage opened his door across the hall. He saw Jacques in all his bloody glory, who nodded. Savage made a gross-out face and retreated back to his room. He wanted no part of whatever was going on. Vince's door teetered open.

"I told you I do want to talk, but just not now," Vince said through the crack. "I'm in a meeting with Hulk."

Jacques pushed Raymond out of the way and pushed the door open. "No, Vince, we really have to talk now."

Behind them, Macho opened his door again. He poked his head out and got another look at Jacques blood-soaked t-shirt again.

The overly cautious Jacques turned back and made eye contact with Savage. He smiled, knowing something crazy just happened, and shook his head. "Oh yeah!" Macho said in character, as he shut the door again.

"We can talk later," Hulk said, seeing that something pressing was up. "I'm out of here, brother." At that, Hulk got up and walked by the brothers, slapping Jacques sympathetically on the cleanest part of Jacques shoulder he could find.

"Good lord," Vince looked over the blood and knew that his official warning was too late. He ushered the brothers into his makeshift office and locked the door behind them. "Listen, I'm going to walk you to your bags, and let this cool off. Then, we will see you at the next town."

Vince walked them to their dressing room. Everybody there already knew what happened. Nobody said a word. They got their stuff, and Vince walked them out to their car.

Vince knew there was time to let things die down. With multiple shows happening on the same dates, it wasn't actually that difficult to keep the two tag teams away from each other, by booking them all on separate events. The Bulldogs were already off to the hospital, but then they would be flying out to a WWF UK tour.

After the attack, there was a rumor that Dynamite was planning revenge against Jacques. I heard it everywhere. It was the talk of the locker room. Vince was worried that Dynamite was going to try something at Survivor Series 1988, during the big 20-man elimination tag match. The match had almost everyone in arguably the hottest tag team roster that WWF ever had. The match featured two big teams; the Rougeaus, Demolition, Brain Busters, Bolsheviks, and Los Conquistadores going against the team of The Bulldogs, the Rockers, the Hart Foundation, the Young Stallions, and the Powers of Pain.

There was some talk that Dino Bravo mended his issues with Jacques during this time and approached him at a show. "I have good news and bad news. The good news is the Bulldogs gave their notice," Dino said. "The bad news is …the Bulldogs gave their notice."

Jacques then realized that if the British Bulldogs were leaving, they had nothing to lose. They could do whatever they wanted on the way out with no need to worry about any repercussions. Jacques, in fear of his life, made some calls to some people he knew in Montreal. He also pulled Dino Bravo back aside and said, "I know you have connections. I call my family every night by midnight. If ever I don't call them and it gets back to you…" he pulled a piece of paper out of his pocket and showed Dino the Dynamite Kid's home address.

Dino nodded, understanding exactly what he meant.

Vince met both teams at an airport before the PPV. He told them he needed them to both stay professional for his show. After the Rougeaus left the room, he told Dynamite that the company would pay for his teeth and that all heat should be squashed. He also warned Dynamite that Jacques knew a lot of important people in Canada, and it was probably in his best professional interest to not continue on with the rivalry.

Survivor Series 1988 came. It also marked the final night for the British Bulldogs in the WWF. The Rougeau Brothers didn't know what was going to happen until about an hour and a half before the show, when Vince called both teams into his office.

Dynamite proposed a gorilla press on Jacques, where he would toss Jacques onto Raymond. Jacques immediately agreed to show there was no heat, and also that he was not afraid. After the meeting, Vince told the Rougeaus this time to stick around. He then told them that he wanted them to leave as soon as they were eliminated, and to not even to take a shower. He didn't want to take any chance of foul play being it was the Bulldogs' final match with the company.

In the end, Dynamite worked with Jacques without incident. The Rougeau Brothers were the first team eliminated, with Bret Hart over Raymond in a small package. The Bulldogs were kept in the match much longer, booked that way obviously by design. By the time the Dogs were finally eliminated, the Rougeaus were already out of the building.

Years later, Jacques returned to the WWF as The Mountie. Davey Boy called him into a shower in a locker room to have a few words. Davey told him that he no longer talked with Dynamite and wanted to let bygones be bygones. There, they shook hands and squashed their heat.

Jacques Rougeau, aka The Mountie, with Brutus at Big Event 13, Nov 2017.

WRESTLEMANIA V

WrestleMania V was at the Boardwalk Hall in Atlantic City, New Jersey on April 2, 1989. The third match on the card was a non-title match against the self-proclaimed "Million Dollar Champion" Ted DiBiase.

Though this match was nothing special, DiBiase was a great worker. We had a hell of a match. In the end, I put the sleeper on Virgil who hoped up on the apron, to distract me. I released DiBiase from the hold and went after his bodyguard. DiBiase followed and we just brawled outside of the ring. We were both counted out. Before the match, however, I shook hands with the event sponsor, Donald Trump, who was sitting in the front row. Who knew years later I could say that the President of The United States watched one of my matches at ringside?

MACHO, ZEUS & NO HOLDS BARRED

After WrestleMania, Vince McMahon decided to dabble even more in the entertainment industry. He decided to try and make his own movies. "No Holds Barred" was produced by the World Wrestling Federation under a

"Shane Distribution Company" (referring to Shane McMahon) set to be released by New Line Cinema on June 2, 1989. (This was the first endeavor of the WWF making movies, which later would create WWE Films.) The initial goal of the film was to continue to push the idea that Hulk Hogan was also a successful actor, several years after Rocky III.

Tiny Lister was represented by Peter Young, the same agent that I had for my television commercials and all. He represented Hulk Hogan, George Foreman, and Mr. T, as well. Hulk thought it would be good to have him audition for a character named Zeus.

Back then, wrestling angles seemed to always go better when it was a black man versus a white man, more so than just two white guys against each other, or two black guys. Using the racial tendencies of some fans against them to take their money was something that really worked. The old adage, "A fool and his money are soon parted," was certainly true in this aspect.

Tiny was 6'5, and 300 pounds. He was about the same size as Hogan, if not an inch or two taller in his boots. When he came into to interview for Vince, we had him walk into his office in full gimmick. He drew the Z's on the side of his head, taped up his arms with black tape, and oiled up his whole body. He did a hundred pushups and smashed open Vince's door with no shirt on. Vince hired him on the spot.

When the No Holds Barred guys finished the script, Vince and Hogan hated it. They actually went and re-wrote like the whole thing in like three days. With many saying how cheesy the final product was, I can only imagine how bad that original script must have been!

When the filming for the actual movie "No Holds Barred" came along, I was kicking around some in the locker room, but I really didn't take part. They filmed some wrestling segments at house shows with guys like Ax of Demolition, Stan Hansen, Jesse Ventura, and Gene Okerlund.

At this point, I was not very into the idea of getting my acting chops on. I knew Hulk was making some good money, and that was great. But the way I looked at it was, if I wasn't getting paid well, I wasn't interested in a bit part. This early in the game, I considered myself more of a wrestler than an actor. I'll admit. I was just feeling lazy with the wear and tear effects from the road.

This is my day off. I don't want to go out there. I have no lines, so I'm not going out there to be filmed.

Even though I had a SAG card, rather than to put my name in the hat with the others for screen time, I just sat in the locker room. I was more content to just smoke some cigars and drink, while watching everyone else go out and work for only a little bit of money. If I had known it was going to turn into a pretty good money angle for me after the film came out, I probably would have participated.

During the filming, Hulk told me there were some issues. When two 300 pound guys start throwing haymakers at each other something has to give, right? In this case, that something was Zeus' nose. Hulk Hogan accidentally broke Zeus's nose and Tiny went off into a corner and cried! Hulk Hogan also cut up his hand very badly on glass shards from the broken mirrors, requiring stitches. So, as fake as the acting may have seemed, at least they were really trying to make it look legit.

Tiny traveled around with us a number of months at house shows, filming his parts. Him and Hogan both had separate dressing rooms from the other guys. This may not have been a good idea for Tiny. Because of this, he had a lot of heat from the boys, seeing how he was an outsider. He was from Hollywood. He wasn't a wrestler. He had never even been trained how to wrestle a lick. A couple of guys like the Samoans, helped him out a little, but that was it.

One night in San Diego, Tiny was taking a shower after his appearance. He was minding his own business and was soaped up pretty good. Jake "The Snake" Roberts called a few of us over to the side of the showers.

Jake didn't say anything. He just held his fingers up over his mouth, as to indicate not to make a sound. He didn't need to say anything. We all knew exactly what he was going to do.

So Tiny was showering, and singing some kind of song under his breath. It was relatively quiet, except for his voice and the sound of the water splashing. Jake bent over and picked up something next to him. I shook my head and bit my lip. I watched as Jake reached into his old army bag and pulled out Damian.

Then, all of a sudden, the huge eight-foot python went sliding in across the tiles on the shower room floor, right at Tiny.

We all looked at each other covering our mouths. Jake didn't smile. The cold bastard had done things like this so many times before, he just folded his arms and leaned against the wall for the payoff.

We waited. Tiny didn't notice it at first, which made it even funnier. He continued singing a few seconds, until the huge boa constrictor slithered up to him and brushed against his foot.

The singing stopped and turned into screaming.

Now, Tiny had a real deep voice, but in this case, he started cursing like Michael Jackson and Prince both, in falsetto.

When the filming was over, the film actually debuted at #2, with $4,957,052 in sales the weekend of its release. It was right behind *Indiana Jones and the Last Crusade*. We thought that this was good, but it really dropped off after that. Vince McMahon, who produced the movie pretty much broke even after distribution fees. The final tally was something like $16,093,651 in ticket sales.

Around the time of the film's release in 1989, they started me in a program with Randy "Macho Man" Savage. On "The Brother Love Show" they pitted me against Savage. Also in attendance was my good friend and Savage's new manager, Sensational Sherri. What we did to get her over as a hated heel with Savage was to have me suggest to the fans that they call her a name that she would come to absolutely hate, "Scary Sherri."

It worked. The fans bought it and an angered Savage attacked me.

At the same time, Hulk Hogan was also engaged in a feud with Randy Savage over the WWF World Heavyweight Title. Therefore, our feud became intertwined so that it would lead up to SummerSlam, where I could once again team up with Hulk Hogan, but this time in a WWF ring. For this match, Vince had planned all along to borrow again from Hollywood to drum up mainstream interest, by using "Tiny" Tom Lister, the villain from the film No Holds Barred, in the main event.

While Tiny had shot a bunch of footage at WWF house shows, none of that tape ever made it onto WWF television programming. The idea was after the movie, he would actually be introduced to the WWF fans on TV as a wrestler and work some shows to both promote the film, and generate ticket sales.

There was even a rumor that if the movie did extremely well, we would probably have had Hulk Hogan versus Zeus at the next WrestleMania. Beyond that, they talked about having Zeus actually taking the belt from Hogan and having Hogan chase the belt thereafter, in a massive rematch.

Lister's movie role was an awesome, larger-than-life, brutal monster heel named Zeus. This character he brought to life translated perfectly from the screen into the wrestling ring. With a few basic lessons and some coaching from Hogan and myself, Vince brought Tiny on the road to wrestle as that character.

The *No Holds Barred* project then produced even more television material for the rest of the year, on 1989 WWF programs.

Even though he was playing the same character as in the movie, WWF commentators put a spin on Zeus. They put the movie character over huge as a "very real threat" to the wrestlers of the WWF. They said he was a real fighter that movie producers booked to bring the film more legitimacy. The bookers then had Zeus do some promos and run-ins to make him look invincible by no-selling any moves tried on him. The no-selling was also good, because Zeus' wrestling ability was limited.

Vince was smart. To build up for our feud, he wanted Zeus to appear to be a horrible and deadly person outside of the ring. He leaked to the Enquirer and other magazines that Tiny Lister was a former gang member who had murdered three people, and had beat his wife. That element of question resulted in more people thinking Zeus was the real deal, which also generated more ticket sales. Tiny actually started receiving death threats on his home answering machine!

On the road, Vince made Tiny stay in his hotel room and never leave - no unnecessary flying back and forth to home, either. That would only expose him to more people. At the time, Tiny was dating the hot model from the MC Hammer music video, "Have You Seen Her." They ran up a phone bill of like $15,000, one month and Vince paid it like it was nothing to protect the evil villain image he was trying to depict.

Eventually, Zeus called out Hulk Hogan in an interview. The storyline revealed that Zeus was jealous for being billed under Hulk Hogan on the movie posters. He felt he was the real talent in the film, and he also didn't appreciate having to lose to him in the film, either, as he was the better fighter.

Following the idea that "the enemy of my enemy is my friend," Zeus aligned himself with Randy Savage. During a match I had with Randy Savage, I was then attacked by Zeus, setting up our main event tag team bout at SummerSlam.

We actually rehearsed the SummerSlam 89's main event of Hogan/Brutus vs Savage/Zeus the night before in an empty ring in the arena. That is something we like NEVER did in the WWF. Somehow, Vince managed to have the whole place free of employees, so we were able to walk Zeus through everything he needed to do, in order to help get Zeus ready for the PPV.

When the big match finally came, Zeus was a little nervous during the match. Now, Tiny was a huge music fan. This would later contribute to his success in acting in various hip-hop related roles with guys like Ice Cube. Around this time, James Brown kept getting arrested. During 1987-1988, the

Godfather of Soul got arrested four separate times for charges including domestic violence, assault, drug and weapons charges, and for a high-speed car chase on a highway. To calm Zeus down, we kept screaming, "Free James Brown!" to make Zeus laugh and get him focused again. It worked!

In the end, the match turned out fine and we were victorious. We sent the crowd home happy. However, that was not the last we would see of Tiny. The crowd response was so good that they kept him around for more.

Following SummerSlam, Ted DiBiase "paid for Zeus' services" to lead into Survivor Series. For that show, "The Hulkamaniacs" (Hulk Hogan, Jake Roberts, & Demolition) were set to take on "The Million Dollar Team (Ted DiBiase, Zeus, & the Powers of Pain). Zeus was eliminated from the match via disqualification after refusing to break a lethal chokehold on Hogan and the Hulkamaniacs ultimately went on for the win.

My Zeus feud continued on right after Christmas to build up for a really weird PPV. The numbers didn't lie. Ticket sales didn't dominate the box office, so Vince decided to repackage the movie and try to make some more money off of it in another way. For this holiday special pay-per-view, Vince decided to put together a show that was half matches, and half move. He called it, "No Holds Barred: The Movie-The Match." The model for this PPV was a rematch from SummerSlam in a steel cage, along with an encore presentation of the actual movie.

The wrestling match part of that PPV was not live. We actually filmed it at a Wrestling Challenge taping two weeks earlier in Nashville, Tennessee on December 12th. Once again, however, we left the people smiling, with an early form of the Mega Maniacs defeating Savage and Zeus.

As a side note, Tiny was really fun to work with. He was a natural performer, and what he may have lacked in wrestling knowledge, he certainly made up for on the performance side of things. Boy, could he act. He was a natural. You really believed that he was a big huge freak of nature that was out there, ready to kill someone. In reality, that just showed how talented he really was.

Tiny was really a big loveable guy. He was a real professional and a pleasure to work with. (I wouldn't want to be on his bad side, however. The guy was as strong as hell. He benched something like 550 pounds!)

I would later work again with him in WCW, too. Great guy.

WRESTLEMANIA 6

In the middle of 1988, Curt Hennig returned to the WWF. Come the beginning of October, promotional vignettes started airing on WWF television, debuting his new character. This is when he took on being an arrogant villain who claimed to be "absolutely perfect" in everything that he did, earning him the nickname of "Mr. Perfect." The promos illustrated his superiority in other sporting endeavors, like hitting impossible basketball shots, hitting home runs, bowling a 300 point game, running the table in billiards, throwing and then actually catching his own "Hail Mary" football pass.

Hennig wrestled for almost a full year with an absolutely perfect record of no pinfalls. Come October of 1989, he joined forces with Leaping Lanny Poffo.

Before this new union, Lanny was a competitive wrestler who most of the boys gave a lot of offense to because they knew him. They offered Lanny more offense in squash matches, in part, out of respect for him, his brother Randy "Macho Man" Savage, and also because many of them had worked for his legendary father, wrestler/promoter Angelo Poffo. So for the longest time, Lanny still was only enhancement talent, but one that the fans came to know.

Eventually, however, Vince took favor to his hard work and offered him a scholarly poet-like gimmick and spot with Hennig. Lanny was not really a jobber anymore. At this point, he was working in a manager spot for "Mister Perfect" Curt Hennig, as "The Genius."

At the 1990 Royal Rumble, after my match with my opponent, The Genius, Mister Perfect attacked me to begin a feud between us and set up our

match at WrestleMania. So on April 1, 1990, we were at the SkyDome in Toronto, Ontario, Canada for the biggest pay-per-view matches of the year. WrestleMania VI on this particular year had an announced attendance of 67,678, which was also a record for the SkyDome.

For my match, it was the culmination of revenge on Curt Hennig. I was set up to be the first person to pin "Mr. Perfect" Curt Hennig, thus ending Perfect's lengthy undefeated streak on television. Now, before the match, under orders from Pat Patterson, the agent for our spot, Chief Jay Strongbow told me that I needed to cut hair to leave the fans happy. He said that I would not do it to Hennig, however. He told me I was to cut Lanny's hair, the next person down the line.

It would have been nice if he had told Lanny, however. At the end of the match, Lanny was in the ring, but saw me coming with the scissors and made a break for it! He jumped right up and ran down the aisle.

What the hell? Where is he going?! Get back here! This is WrestleMania, man!

When Lanny saw the scissors, he panicked. But I also panicked because he was running away from me. On a house show in the middle of East Lugnut, Missouri, it wouldn't matter if the after-match festivities didn't pan out as they had planned, but this was our biggest event of the year. WrestleMania was our Super Bowl, and I was worried that the powers-that-be were not going to get the finish that they wanted.

I legitimately had to run after Lanny down the aisle and drag him all the ways back into the ring to give him a haircut, so they would have the proper footage.

Come to find out, nobody had told him that he was supposed to get his haircut at the end of the match. In fact, it is quite possible that the agent, Jay Strongbow, led him to believe he was free in the clear to get out of there. Either that, or Patterson himself was ribbing Lanny. I don't know.

When I got back to the locker room, it was a shit show. You see, after posing for the fans some in the ring, there was just enough time for the shit to already hit the fan backstage. When I headed for my dressing room, out of nowhere, I was blindsided by Randy "The Macho Man" Savage.

Now mind you, Randy was nuts. If he was mad at Elizabeth, or worried that the boys were looking at her in the locker room, he would lock her in a basement somewhere with nothing but like four Lean Cuisines. Randy intentionally huffed his chest up and banging into me.

"What the fuck was that?!" Randy said, looking ready to fight to defend his brother.

"Whoa, whoa, whoa Randy," I said. "It wasn't my fault. He was running from the finish!"

Lanny was off in a corner. He was clearly upset, but I don't think it was because he was now minus some hair. I think he probably more felt like he was being bullied or something and that I went into business for myself.

"What are you talking about?" Randy said.

"Ask your boy, Patterson. He was the one that called this finish. Strongbow told me, but it's obvious he didn't tell your brother. He was running out of there, right after the finish, before it was done."

Randy tensed up. You could tell he wanted to smash something.

"Now, you can fight if you want to, but make no mistake about it," I said trying to diffuse the argument, "I didn't make a mistake, or just do that on the fly to mess with him. That is what they told me to do!"

GUEST PASSAGE – THE GENIUS LANNY POFFO

We contacted Lanny Poffo for the purpose of this story, to give you some additional insight on his take on this topic:

"So you want to know about taking a haircut from Brutus after WrestleMania VI? Well, in order to do so, I have to first give you some of my history with him, to better understand.

When I was still in Memphis, Bill Dundee came up to me and told me with the way that I cut my promo, I should probably be wearing a suit of armor. At first, I didn't like his statement, but then I started thinking about it. Because he was such a little midget of a wrestler but still successful, he may have actually known what he was talking about. I figured it is actually tough for a little guy to get over in a sport of big men like professional wrestling. So, I decided to go ahead and take his advice.

I went out and actually bought a legitimate Sir Lancelot suit of armor from the Broadway play Camelot. It cost me about $1800. It wasn't a real suit of armor, it was a high-end stage costume, but it really did the job. I wore that for about a year and a half in Memphis, and it did help get me noticed. I did well with the suit for the first couple of times, but soon after everyone in the territory had seen it, it was no longer really all that funny. The gag got old real quick, so I retired the gimmick. It is sort of like going back to the strip beach on the third day. Once you've seen both sets of what people had, they are no longer all that interesting to look at, after so many times.

Fast forward to my WWF days…

Howard Finkel came up with the idea for Blackjack Mulligan to do these bunkhouse battle royals and the whole point was to wear something odd. Before the first one, they also booked me to go on Tuesday Night Titans, the WWF talk show, to promote it.

I did not want my appearance to be just an enhancement guy who would end up being boring. If I did that they would never ask me to come back on the show again. So, I wore the suit of armor and I also read a poem that I wrote for the upcoming match. It worked.

When I got in the ring for the Bunkhouse Battle Royal, I was wearing my suit of armor. The audience loved it, but I am not so sure the other boys in the ring wanted to put it over. But then there was Brutus. Brutus was the best. He came over and would punch the suit of armor and sell his hand like it hurt. He's a great performer and really helped me finally get a little bit of my money's worth out of that costume. After those matches and taking that risk of looking different, they started using me more and more. I wasn't just an enhancement guy anymore, I was something else. I had to thank Brutus for that, in part.

Later at the 1990 Royal Rumble, I would get to work Brutus again, but much later, after his Dream Team days. This time, I was tag teaming with Mr. Perfect against Brutus "The Barber" Beefcake and his partner Hulk Hogan, in the main event! Whenever I worked with those guys, I was always very excited. Getting to headline MSG was a big deal. I had worked at the Garden 23 times before, but I can only remember the two times that I was a headliner. By this point, I knew the deal. I had probably gotten a haircut from him on a dozen occasions before, and I was always happy to do so. He put over my suit of armor, so I was glad to return the favor.

So to answer your question - there was one time that I bailed on Brutus, but it wasn't my fault. I would have happily sacrificed some locks to get him over, if I had known that is what they wanted me to do. Chief Jay Strongbow did not tell me that I was supposed to get my haircut at the end of the match with Brutus, early on that night. He also told Brutus quite the opposite. Because of that, I did run out of the ring and Beefcake had to come after me to bring me back in for the haircut. Strongbow wasn't a great agent. He didn't always tell you everything you were supposed to know. He also wasn't a big fan of my brother, Randy Savage, and it is possible he mislead me to leave quickly and cower away only as a means to get back at him.

After that miscommunication, however, everything was always good between us. Brutus would offer to only cut a small sniping of my hair, but I would refuse. I would always ask Brutus to cut big chunks out of my hair. After a pretty good run with him, I ended up looking like a chemo patient.

Working with Hulk Hogan and Brutus Beefcake was a dream for me at MSG. I was like a fat girl on prom night. It is one of my favorite highlights in my career, and I was happy to have to wear a wig because of the Barber. Thank you."   – Lanny Poffo

After our WrestleMania VI match, the Ultimate Warrior beat Hulk Hogan in the main event on the same show for the Heavyweight Championship. Hulk and I both knew this was coming. For some time, Vince was trying to find someone to replace Hulk Hogan to be the new face of the company. Soon after, the Warrior holding two championships gave up his Intercontinental title. Then, they created a tournament to re-crown the IC Champion, airing over a few episodes of WWF programming. Curt Hennig dropped The Genius as his manager without incident for the tournament. In the storyline, they had him defeat Jimmy Snuka in the quarter-finals on May 5th, and then finally beat Tito Santana in the finals on May 19th. After winning the belt, they wanted Curt Hennig to be taken even more seriously, so he took on "The Perfect Manager" Bobby Heenan as his new advisor.

A serious Curt Hennig was a funny idea, however. As many people know, Curt Hennig's practical jokes also were legendary.

One story I can think of was when Rick Rude was having a hard time getting it up, due to some pain pills he was taking. He confided his problem with Curt, who also had taken the same pills before. Curt told him that his doctor had him inject some steroids directly into his dick.

Rick Rude must have been desperate. He did just that and his hotdog swelled up like a German knockwurst. If you ever heard the medical warning for Viagra about the four-hour boner emergency, this is exactly what happened. Rick Rude had such a giant hard on, that it got all blown out.

Rick went to the hospital with a bulge in his sweatpants that looked like a cantaloupe. When he got to the emergency room, he disrobed and it looked like he was hung like a cereal bowl. The medics tried to drain some of his blood from his penis. I guess it got infected and caused him some issues for quite a bit of time after that.

Curt Hennig thought that was just great.

Come the SummerSlam PPV of 1990, I was supposed to have a rematch with Mister Perfect and actually win the title. It would have made for a great storyline arch, but that is not what ended up happening.

"The Texas Tornado" Kerri Von Erich had to sub for me on the night that I was supposed to win my first WWF singles title. Missing my opportunity to hold the WWF Intercontinental title wasn't the worst thing to happen to me then, however. *It was the reason why I couldn't make it that was horrible.*

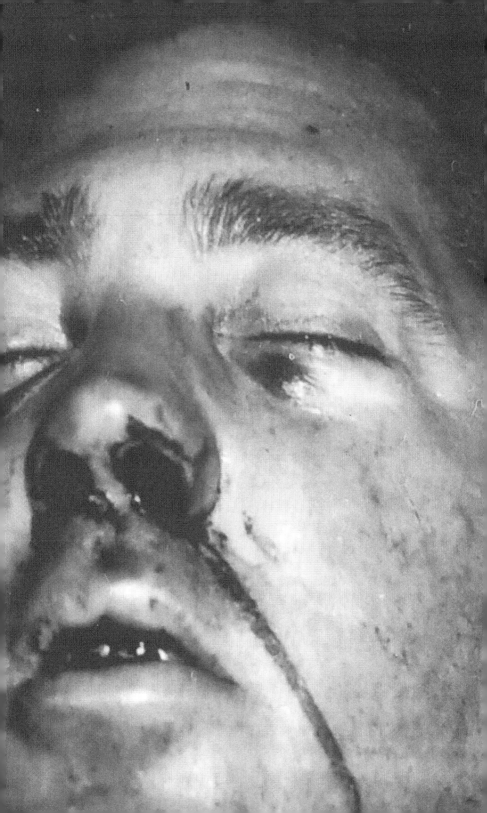

CHAPTER 17 - THE ACCIDENT

Silence.

There was a light, peaceful breeze drifting over Brown Lake. It was 90 degrees in Lutz, Florida, or as some call it, "Redneckville," about ten minutes away from Land of lakes. I was standing in about two feet of water, only about 5 miles away from where they were shooting Edward Sissorhands.

I heard a few lame firecrackers go off and looked up to see some frightened geese fly by over one of the most beautiful houses you have ever seen. A few people pointed upwards and then continued scurrying about, setting up some red, white and blue streamers.

I needed this party. I had just been served my divorce papers. My business was gone. My two homes in California were gone, and now my both my parents were gone, too. I had just buried them both with my mom a year ago, and then recently, my father.

I took a sip. Relaxation was just what the doctor ordered.

One partner of one of the biggest boat manufacturer's in the world, Mastercraft, was about to go all out and throw one hell of a shindig. I was fixing on having one hell of a day and drinking far more than most people could in a year.

Mike was a good guy. Every Fourth of July, he would have a number of his employees come by and some of his best customers to what looked like a mansion. He would spare no expense on the best barbecue, booze, and bottle rockets that money could buy.

We got along great, so of course, I was one of the first people he invited and got there early to help out before the festivities began. See, before I was a wrestler, I was practically a champion water-skier. After training some at Cypress Garden, by 16, I was behind the wheel of a competition-level ski boat, pulling lines of legendary water skiers doing crazy acrobatics and stunts in front of audiences. By high school, I was behind the actual boat showing off my own skills. One of my best tricks was water-skiing barefoot on one foot; a stunt that most people couldn't pull off as a seasoned adult. Years later, add some WWF money to the mix, and you can probably guess why I had become pretty good friends with my boat dealer.

Mike's boat selling success was evident. I looked over at his Miami Vice-looking pearl white house overlooking the lake. It had the big spiral stairwells. It had the sliding glass doors. I wrinkled my nose a little bit. I missed my one fancy place.

"Come on, silly," a cute, tanned girl said, pulling me by the hand. Nancy Rude was the perfect complement for the beautiful beachfront backdrop on a beautiful day. She was a showgirl in the Las Vegas strip production of "Abracadabra." Some of you may even remember her time in the ring as a valet named "Raven" in World Class Championship Wrestling alongside her famous wrestling brother, Rick Rude. She was in her mid-20s when I met her in Georgia, working with Sunshine that night. I was about 21.

Nancy yanked me out of the water. I jogged up toward the patio as the sand got stuck between my toes. With Mike, I helped Nancy pour a few bags of ice into a few lines of coolers with pretty much every adult beverage imaginable. Mike and two other bikini-clad girls dragged out a long table from the shed to begin the set up for what would be a huge spread of food to feed a huge party of people.

Mike disappeared for a minute, then returned with a really cool boom-box, like you would see on the shoulder of a break-dancer in Brooklyn. He kind of shuck and jived my way, then put his stereo down on a stone retainer wall by the porch. He flipped a few switches and started playing some hair band.

I nodded along sympathetically with his attempt at short-haired head-banging.

"Hey Beefer," he said. "This is just temporary. I got a real band coming over to play later."

"Awesome," I said, thinking about how I could maybe weasel in on the jam session.

Nancy finished filling the last cooler and adjusted the drink, nicely. She came straight to me and handed me a found treasure; some kind of strawberry wine cooler. I looked down at my hand a little bit in contempt.

"Well, it's all we had on ice so far," she laughed.

I shrugged, but I drank it anyhow.

We trotted back out towards the lake and stepped up onto the long platform dock. A few of Mike's guys buzzed away on jet skis. Good thing Nancy wasn't on one of those. She came by the night before and chipped her teeth. As I approached, I saw that one of his employees was finally hooked up to a line.

The boat pulled away. The cord went tight and the boy flew up about 6 or 8 feet in the air, but then the rope went dead. He dropped right back down onto the platform, slid onto his side and flopped into the water like a dead fish.

"Shit! Is he okay?" I asked, looking over at Nancy. "He didn't connect it right!"

We both ran to the scene.

"Hey, kid. Kid!" I yelled. I bent off the side of the dock. I looked down at the shattered reflection of my face rippling in the water. I cupped my hands together and shouted again, "KID!" Just before jumping in, I heard faint splashes come from the other side of the dock. I switched sides and saw his head come bobbing up.

"Hahaha!" The kid laughed at his own ridiculous performance and then realized it hurt. He rubbed his ass and then the back of his skull. "Owww."

Once I knew he was okay, I grabbed the Kevlar rope dangling from the side of the dock. It was the same sturdy kind I liked to use. It was specially designed not to give any play at all, where regular ropes would probably stretch up to 20 feet with a person being pulled.

The kid pulled himself up on the dock.

"That was a close one." Nancy messed up his hair and laughed.

"You wanna see how it's done?" I asked. I was already wearing my repelling harness and was ready to go. After I collected his gear, I secured myself in and then latched the wench to the reel out on the boat. I tugged it a few times, then I walked back out towards the beach. "This is how you do it," I said, giving a thumbs up to the boat driver. The driver nodded back. The boat pulled forward and the rope began to uncoil. Finally, once there was no more slack, the rope went taut. I ran a number of yards along the shore and then up towards the dock.

PFFFT!

The parachute opened up behind me and easily filled with air. I went from zero altitude to like 350 feet in seconds. I went way up into the air in a directional parachute that allowed me to move from side-to-side. I could veer way over to either the left or right by the way I pulled the strings.

If you have never parasailed before, you have never lived. A floating euphoria comes over you. It is overwhelming, and it even helped me forget my divorce for a moment. That feeling is something that I still, to this day, cannot even put into words. Once you reach peak height, it is so unexpectedly peaceful that it feels like an out-of-body experience. You feel like a bird, or an angel even, in every positive sense of the feeling. Soaking it all in, I tried my hardest not to close my eyes and just feel the air on my face, because the view below was amazing. Looking down, the waters under the Florida sun were so transparent I could see any little stone beneath them.

I jerked the line to the right. I was no longer behind the boat, but rather off to its side over the land. I was actually flying over the palm trees and the rooftops. We looped back around, and then I saw Nancy and the kid waving up at me by the dock.

"Watch this!"

I repositioned my chute so I could fly right above them, then I pulled really hard and made my whole body flip upside down. I hung there for a moment and felt all the blood rush to my head. That was just me. I lived to perform. I lived for the excitement of being on edge. Whether it was motorcycles, boats, or parachutes - that was just how I chose to live my life.

When we came back around again, more people had collected. I did one final flip to end the show and then dropped down into the water to a round of applause.

A few others went up after me and everybody had a great time. After they were done, Mike had us lay out the parachute to dry. Then, we bundled it all away in the utility shed for lunch.

An hour or so later, everything was ready. A number of early bird party-goers were starting to make their entrances. Dancing started early and people started drinking. I was eating a cheeseburger when I heard a familiar voice call me out from behind.

"Hey, Beefer!"

I turned around and saw Brian Blair, yes, that Brian Blair - the very one that the Iron Sheik wanted to make humble. Brian was with another guy who looked familiar, but he was also with some girl I had never seen before. I imagined she was some kind of ring rat, so I smirked and laughed.

After we said our hellos, Brian said, "Okay, now listen, guys. We have to get my friend here up on the parasail!" He gestured to the girl, and I shook my head.

"Well, I don't know," I said, coming to the host's defense. "Mike doesn't really want it out for the party. He doesn't mind people using the ski jets, but the parasail is too much hassle and mess, he said."

But in typical Brian Blair fashion, he just wouldn't let it go. "Awe, come on man!" Brian started to throw a fit, he was really pushing to get the girl up on a line and wouldn't take no for an answer. He kept it up until Mike came over.

Mike is just generally a good guy, so he eventually gave in. Still holding his spatula from grill duty, he ran out to the storage shed and started to drag the whole damned thing out again, by himself. I could see he was annoyed by the way he was rushing. He knew in about an hour, his whole compound was going to be crawling with people, and he wanted Brian's parasail spin to be over with by then. That way it would not become an activity option for the general public.

I put down my grub and ran over to help his cause. I jumped in the water and helped set up the 400 feet of rope. I untwisted some of the tangles, as Brian got his girl suited up.

There was no wind and it was hot. During the morning there was a little breeze, a little wind resistance that helped fluff out the chute, but at this point, there was just nothing. I helped him smooth it out the best I could, as Mike rushed out to the boat. Then, I sifted out in knee high water to unflip a few loops in the rope.

Mike started the motor, and the rope began to straighten. She didn't move or anything. She just stood there like an idiot and let the Kevlar pull her.

FIZZZ!

The boat face-planted her directly into the sand.

Basically, what you are supposed to do is run like 10 or 15 steps and then you go right up like Superman. She didn't know shit, so she dropped like one in the bowl. We all laughed.

Mike spun back around so she could get another go at it. I yelled a few directions to her from off to the side in the water, and she seemed to understand. Once she brushed the dirt off of her face, she gave Mike the thumbs up.

Mike nodded and took off.

Mike's boat was badass. It could pull 21 skiers easy at 400 horsepower. I watched him dart straight out and the big motor was roaring away. I turned to make sure she was free in the clear and that I wasn't in her runway. In that split instant, Mike turned. This time, instead of driving straight out, he made a quick turn left to follow the edge of the shore. Before I realized there was a change in course, the cord pulled taut.

Right as I turned to see where she was, there she was.

I never saw it coming.

FUMPPP!!!

She got about six feet off the ground, but panicked. She flailed her legs, then crouched a bit, almost like a cannonball diving formation. Both of her knees nailed me square in the face. The impact was like a fucking battering ram.

Her knees ripped me right out of the water. Nancy said I did a full gainer; an entire backflip with my heels straight above my head, before landing back on my feet. I dropped to my knees.

Time stopped. There were flashes of light, but I couldn't see anything. My body broke out into a cold sweat.

Optic nerve damage.

Palate broken.

Sinus cavity crushed.

Entire facial structure shattered.

The people around the beach had no idea. There were no lacerations, at all. There was no huge crack, or bleeding. My skin held it all in, but most of the bones in my face were just pulverized into hundreds of pieces. I tried to scream for help, but nothing would come out.

I can't open my mouth! My teeth are stuck together! I can't see!

I tried to look around, but I couldn't see anyone. I couldn't see anything. All I could hear was water splashing and the sound of the motor dying off in the distance. I started to choke.

I can't breathe! Help!!! Oh my God, what am I going to do? It's over. It's really over. I am a dead man.

My face felt like it was melting. It felt like there was a sweat sock in the back of my throat. Something was choking me out so I couldn't inhale. I had no idea at the time that it was actually the complete collapsing of the upper inside of my mouth. The area that separates the oral cavity from the nasal cavity was broken, forcing bone shards and tissue down my windpipe.

My jaw was smashed shut. I had to take my thumb and pry it passed my lips. I forced it in between my teeth and jammed it upwards so I could push up the roof of my mouth to allow enough space for me to breathe.

Nobody knew how bad it was.

Finally, my body couldn't take it anymore. I toppled over into the water, writhing in pain.

Brian came running. He thought I just got hit in the mouth.

In writing this book, we called up Brian Blair. When we asked him about the accident, he said he still has nightmares about it, to this very day. He had some interesting words for us:

GUEST PASSAGE – BRIAN BLAIR

"Everything was cool at first. We were all just hanging out and having a good time. I was up near the house getting something to eat with our friend, Ed Barbera. Some of the guys were down on the beach swimming and drinking.

I remember looking down at one point and seeing that Beefcake was up to his waste or so helping out with a parasailing ride. He was out there in the water quite a distance away from the boat straightening the line. It was really long and tangled and needed to be uncoiled so when the boat would pull away, this one girl on the shore who was harnessed in, Tracy, would have an easy ride up into the air.

It was then that something happened that nobody expected.

Mike took off with the boat thinking all was clear, but Beefer was looking the wrong way. He didn't realize it. When the boat headed away from the beach, it turned and pulled Tracy right at the unsuspected Beefer in the water like a sitting duck.

Realizing that she was being pulled right at him, I think Tracy tried to clear him as she began to elevate in the air. That's why she pulled and lifted her legs up, like a cannonball dive, to get herself out of his way. She yelled. Beefer turned around last second. He took her knees right to his face and flipped over.

I said, 'Holy shit!' I dropped whatever it was that I was doing and started my way down the beach to see if he was ok. He stood there for a second, so I thought maybe he was, but then I watched him go down and back under the water.

I ran to where Beefer was as quickly as I could and dragged him to the shore. I sat him on the beach. He was sluggish and mumbling. I asked if he was alright. He couldn't really talk and was putting his hand in his mouth and all, so I started hitting him in the back with my palm to try and get water out of him. He coughed a little.

This one red-headed kid who owned a hardware store came running over. I said, 'Go call an ambulance!' as I helped Beefer back up to the patio. He wasn't supporting much of his weight very well. It was like leading a main event boxer away from the ring who ended up losing the match, badly."
– B. Brian Blair

WAITING

Man… After about that time, Brian led me over to a chair. One of the girls ran to the house to also call an ambulance for me. They should have called the life helicopter, but they both made the mistake of calling the local ambulance from the University of South Florida. While the University was a legit hospital, they were more of a community hospital with no facilities for trauma. They just weren't prepared for what we were about to bring.

I hid my face in a towel full of ice. My head was throbbing. I could feel my pulse in my neck, and I could hear it in the back of my skull. I waited for what felt like an eternity. I knew that everyone in the place had surrounded me in that chair. I couldn't see them, but I heard the hysteria around me. I must have looked really bad.

Because we were really out in the middle of nowhere, it took about a half hour before I heard the distant cry of sirens. When the emergency team got there, they took the towel of ice off my face and everyone could see the swelling had gotten worse. My head was like a blowfish.

They put me on a gurney and up into the ambulance. Rick Rude's sister rode with me. Rather than to try and keep me calm for the whole ride, she was freaking out herself. She was yelling for everyone to help me. An idiot in ambulance said, "Awe, honey, he is ok. He just has a broken jaw." I knew it was far worse than that but I couldn't speak to tell him. I was trying to tell people with my hand in my mouth, how really bad I was hurt, but still, nothing would really come out.

The genius ambulance workers dropped me off in the waiting room and left. Nancy started raising Holy Hell. I didn't know where I was because I couldn't see. I just continued to hold the roof of my mouth up and hoped for the best. A little blood was coming out of my nose and finally, that was enough to get someone out for me.

They brought me into a little room and checked my blood pressure. It was way, way up there. *They thought I was having a heart attack.*

Once they got me into the ICU, the doctor started taking a bunch of x-rays. That was when he realized that much of the bone around the center of my face was concaved bone shards.

My facial bone matter was practically powder.

At this point, they were too afraid to put me in another ambulance. Nancy told me later that people were practically running around in circles. They knew they didn't have the proper equipment to take care of me.

Since I couldn't see, the rest of the story is kind of blurry here. I know that someone called my attorney who immediately started making calls. He learned that an Armenian doctor was in the area and he was considered to be, perhaps, one of the best palate doctors in the world - *Doctor Matuz Habal.* The problem was, nobody could seem to locate him on his day off, in a day when cell phones were not prevalent. The fact that it was a holiday made it even more difficult.

Eventually, his son was located and then reached at a medical school in Boston. Lucky for me, the son was a wrestling fan. The son finally reached his father. "Dad, you've got to help Brutus!" After that, everything moved more quickly, all within a few hours of time.

The pain was becoming unbearable and I couldn't even take an aspirin, because it was life-threatening head trauma. Fortunately, Doctor Matuz Habal showed up in less than an hour. He was a very famous doctor for the Shriners that has been a great help for birth defects and all kinds of palate issues. In more recent times, he is the guy who helped a baby born with its brain in backward. He saw the stack of x-rays that the practitioner had taken to try and figure something out and began to flip through it. Then he just started throwing them – looking and throwing, looking and throwing.

In no time, they started bringing in all of this special imaging equipment on 18-wheelers. These were like mobile units in trailers, specially made for when they can't bring a patient to the proper facility. The trucks rolled into the parking lot and the rides began. They wheeled me out to the lot over and over again on the gurney to try and figure out a 3D map of what my skull should look like, which would have been impossible to do with just a photograph.

"I don't understand how you are still alive," he said. "Hang in there, my friend. I will do my best for you."

Must be strong. A will to live. I just won't die.

Lying on the table, I was in and out of consciousness. From what I understand, nobody could seem to find a picture of me without me making a goofy face. Having a picture for the doctor to work off of was crucial when having him try to create what I really looked like. If they went by the ones that my sisters and Nancy had, I would be rebuilt with eyes bugging out of my head and my tongue hanging out of my mouth. Eventually, the 3D scanner recreated a digital image of what it thought my skull should have looked like. They finally got everything in place.

Take me in, or kill me. I'm done. I'M DEAD!

The pain was unbearable without meds, but help was on its way. The doctor didn't just bring in a few helpers. He brought in three different teams; a sinus team, an oral surgeon team, and a brain trauma team. A dozen people came in to help me. He had just the clout I needed, and just in the nick of time.

"Brutus," the doctor said. "The first thing we are going to do is try to save your eyes. It will maybe take 5 or 6 hours, but we need to save your optic nerve. Then we will repair the sinus, and finally the facial structure."

They cut me ear to ear, like a Walkman sits, across the whole top of my head. They pealed my face down like a latex mask beyond my nose, lower and lower.

They showed me pictures. Without the skin, I just looked like a bowl of spaghetti. You can't even tell what you are looking at. It was a hollowed out mess. Everything from my cheekbones to my eye sockets was gone. All of the bone matter was shattered to splitters. The doctors needed to totally reconstruct my face with titanium, a highly-risky surgical procedure that had never once been done before. But to keep me alive, it needed to be done.

They had only ever done what they were planning on dead bodies before. In testing, they dropped big metal balls on the face of cadavers to see what kind of weight the titanium plates could handle, and in the end, it worked. However, again, it had never ever been done on someone alive before. I would be the first. This was like some real deep, deep Discovery Channel type shit.

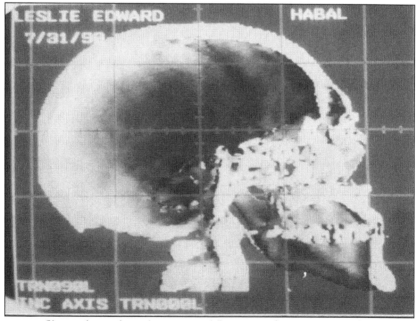

Sixteen hours later, it was over. They created an entire new frame to hold my face together. It was like Papier-mâché and little strips of steel. Inside the maze of metal, they wired everything together with bone graphing. They harnessed bone from the back of my skull to repair my face, then patched over the hole in my head with some drywall Bondo-type shit.

There were 8 strips of titanium zigzagging all across the internal surface of my face. They used 32 screws, 100 feet of wire and more than 100 hundred staples. My jaws were wired shut. There were also dozens of prickly sutures in the roof of my mouth to hold everything up where it had been torn.

My eyelids were sewn together, so I couldn't see the horror show. That was probably a good thing.

The neurosurgeons didn't know what the outcome was going to be. They didn't know if I was going to be able to walk again, or if any kind of movement was going to be affected. In fact, I learned that a few people in the team didn't even expect me to make it through the surgery. They thought all the hard work was going to be done in vain, as the crazy operation was going to be a fatal failure.

My head had swollen up like a basketball. My lips were like tomatoes.

After the operation, I had a tracheotomy. I was on a breathing machine and on life support. I was in a drug-induced coma in the ICU for over 12 hours. The doctor knew he couldn't just let me wake to my own devices. He needed to gradually bring me back slowly, once I was stable.

With my eyes sewed shut, I couldn't see. With a tube down my throat, I couldn't speak. He also knew that I wasn't going to know where I was. If I had struggled even a little bit, it would be all done. The bone grafts would shift and I would undo everything they had worked on for hours. I couldn't panic or the molding on my face was mush.

Therefore, I was tied down to the bed and called the one person they thought could help.

Hulk Hogan.

The Hulkster and his wife, Linda, were actually in another hospital about to have their son, Nick. When they realized that she was not ready to give birth, they decided to send her home. Just before she was released, they got the call at their hospital.

"It's Brutus! I got to go," he said, rushing from his wife's bedside.

"What do you mean?" she asked.

"He's been in a terrible accident," he said and off he went. The Hulkster immediately flew into Tampa and waited. Once I woke up, he was there talking to me so I wouldn't panic.

"Mmmph," I groaned.

"Shhh. Just sit tight. You did it, brother. You're not going to die," he said. "You are going to be alright."

My wife was gone. My business and two homes were gone. I lost both of my parents. My wrestling career was likely gone. My health was uncertain. The only thing I had left was a few close friends. That's when I realized I had been looking at life all wrong.

It was then I knew I was going to be able to fight and win this.

Mike was there and Brian Blair. Hulk flew in and a few others. They were all right there by my side, in my corner.

The doctors suspected I had no chance of recovery. They told me not to get my hopes up at a chance at wrestling, or even life as I knew it. They weren't even sure if I could speak, or walk, or even do really anything. I heard what they were saying, but I wasn't going to listening.

The next day, the doctors started unwrapping. I had 148 staples from one ear to the other. For the most part, everything was numb, except after they took off the bandages, I realized that one of the staples had caught the tip of my left ear and it stung like a fucking hornet.

I couldn't talk or see, but I immediately motioned for a pen by pantomiming drawing on an invisible sketchpad.

"He's trying to communicate!" someone explained in excitement.

Everyone scrambled to get Frankenstein something to write with. Finally, I had a mouthpiece after such a long time. Everyone gathered around, captivated by my every word. I took the pen and printed out slowly and deliberately:

Would someone please un-stable my fucking ear!

The whole place started laughing.

Then, I wrote out "thank you."

For the monster's next trick, they decided they were going to test my eyes. My buddies watched in horror as they attempted to cut the stitches and un-stitch my eyelids. Because they had pealed my whole face back for the operation, I had extremely loose skin on my face. They actually had to have one person pull back all of my loose skin so they could get at my eyes. It was like a fucking Shar-Pei droopy dog. After the stitches were gone, they had me point in which direction each letter was pointing to see how well the optical nerve surgery had worked for me.

They couldn't believe it. They had restored my vision to a perfect 20/20!

Once my trache was out, Hogan decided to take me out of the room for a walk. He helped me up to my feet and led me out to the hallway.

"You're doing it, brother," he said. Just as he spoke, my right eyeball fell out of the socket and hung out on my cheek like an old man's dangling testicle. "Oh shit, brother," he said, obviously not trying to alarm me.

"Whahhh?" I asked, not knowing I looked like a freak show wearing a pair of those slinky eyeglasses.

"I think that's enough. We better get you back." Once I was back in my bed, sitting upright, the doctor came in and really gently pushed my eyeball back in the socket.

Aside from the Vader-versus-Hansen-like moment, I don't remember the next few days. Anything I might do could have made my bone repair to shift, and I would have been screwed. If I sneezed, it could have torn my whole face apart. If I got sick, I could have drowned in my own fluids. I was between life and death and needed to watch my every move.

Knowing this, Doctor Habal had me heavily sedated. While the bone grafts solidified, quite often, I was just sitting in this big hospital room by myself. My head was swollen. My mouth felt like sandpaper. I wanted guests, but at the same time I didn't have enough energy to entertain them, and I also didn't really want them to see the condition that I was in.

A number of the boys came were concerned. They came in and hung out in the hospital room with me, from time to time. Eventually, Sensational Sherri Martel came by during visitor's hours.

We had some history. I met her long before WWF, when I first broke into the business. The boys knew this and tried to prepare Sherri before she came in to see me at the reception desk. It was obvious that Sherri had been crying on the way over. They didn't want her getting me upset, too. Sobbing would probably have melted off my face.

"Sherri, you are not helping him by coming in the room and losing it, you know," they told her. "He's pretty banged up, and we need to be careful about setting him off." You need to be careful not to show you are upset. It could be contagious."

Sherri manned up. She smoothed her skirt down all lady-like and gained her composure. "Everything will be just fine. I'm totally okay. I just want to tell him that I am here for his support."

The front desk sent her in. She took one step into my room. She saw me, screamed bloody murder, and ran out as fast as her two feet could carry her.

We all had a good laugh again.

BACK TO THE SCENE OF THE CRIME

Somehow, word got out that my Screen Actors Guild membership had expired a few days before the accident. When the people at SAG saw this, they decided to revoke my insurance retroactively before the accident, even though the check was in the mail and only held up for the holiday. Nice right?

When the hospital found out, they decided they had to throw me out early before I was really cleared. It didn't matter that I was still so fragile that any slight movement in the wrong way would have started a domino effect of titanium inside my face. Ten days after surgery, they were releasing me from the ICU, under strict conditions from Doctor Habal.

The plan was to go get me out of the hospital in one piece and move me to Mike's house for rehab, which was a super clean, sterile place. However, that trip needed to be a smooth one. I had to take everything very easy. The doctor said I was okay to move, but any kind of fender-bender accident in the car on the way to Mike's house would kill me.

The nurse wheeled me out to my sister's car. She helped me into the backseat and wished me good luck. My sister's car pulled away slowly down the road. We only made it a block or so away, before I was asking her to stop.

"Hey, Karen," I said. "We need to make a pit stop at the grocery store. Please. Pull over here."

We drove into the parking lot.

"Are you okay, Eddie?" She asked.

I got out of her car. My head still felt like it weighed a hundred pounds, but that is not why I had her stop. One of my buddies had a nice, brand new black Corvette that I was just dying to see.

I took a few steps away from the car slowly, and Ginger saw my boys. She immediately knew what was up.

"No, no, no!" She said as I crawled into the back of the Corvette. "EDDIE!"

"Hit it!"

That is just how we rolled.

Anyhow, everything was fine. I got settled in for my stay at Mike's house. Karen showed up, pissed of course. Then, my other sister, Ginger came as well. The doctor wanted two people on hand at all times so that I would have 24-hour surveillance.

A few rough nights passed, and Terry's attorney, Henry, gave me a call.

"Hey, Beefer," he said. "I have some good and bad news. What would you like first?"

"Good first," I said, sitting up in the bed with piles of cushions to my either side.

"Okay. I made some calls to the Screen Actors Guild and the hospital. You did have some grace period coverage, after all, and that covered the hospital time. The bad news is they want you to sit tight here, as not to keep moving you around, so we can't send you back to the hospital."

I didn't care. They did say I had coverage, and that was all that mattered. The 18-wheelers brought mobile units at $50,000 a pop for the 3D scanner equipment. Luckily, SAG took care of 85% of the hospital bill.

After that, the money stress was gone. I made a deal with Doctor Habal. All I had to do was go to the Shriners to speak to the sick kids and their parents, and tell them my situation, like 4 to 5 months later. Then he brought the bill from around $1,000,000 down to something like $100,000. The Shriners paid for most everything.

Happily hanging at the Shriners Hospital after my operation with the kids and Doctor Habal - the man who literally saved my life.

Speaking of Doctor Habal, during one of his early visits, he came with some printouts to show.

"You had suffered a stage 3 concussion. Here I want you to look at this," he said. He held up a picture. "This is the brain scan of a 10-year vet

boxer. See that layer? That is a protective membrane. It is like a cushion."
The brain was all messed up. "Now I will show you yours."

I expected to see that the accident had done something that rattled
my head so badly that my cushion was going to be worse than the boxer's.
Then he showed me mine. There was practically no damage to the membrane.

"Well, how do you explain that?"

"That's just it. I can't," he said. "The amount of damage doesn't
make sense to even me," the doctor said.

"That's good, right?"

"Good? Actually, it is impossible. The only way I can explain it, is it's
a miracle."

THE RULES OF REHAB

For about nine months, it was really touch and go. I had all these
rules I had to follow that seemed pointless. I had to sleep sitting upwards. I
couldn't lie down, because they were afraid that it could cause internal
bleeding. I had to have the two people at Mike's house watching me at all
times, so one could watch me sleep while the other slept. You see, I had to
have someone next to me so I wouldn't topple over from left to right as I sat,
sleeping. I also was not allowed to bend over, forwards, due to pressure
concerns in my head.

I thought all of it was a bit ridiculous. It was like a big lazy vacation
where I watched tons and tons of garbage television on Mike's big screen.
However, I was pretty restricted in moving about or doing anything except
watching Judge Wapner and bad 80s flicks. I was pretty much in disbelief that
all of the stupid rules were important, until one day I rushed to see the Wheel
of Fortune.

I dropped the remote control off the bed, and I didn't want to wait
for help getting it. I got up and bent over to reach the clicker, and then it
happened. It looked like someone took a tall glass of blood and dumped it
out on the floor through my nose.

Mike's house was lavish, decked out in a plush light grey carpet.
Now, it looked like a crime scene. My sister Ginger got on the phone and
called the doctor who told me to immediately put ice on my face.

"As long as blood stops, we are okay, but if it keeps coming, will
have to bring you back here."

Fortunately for me, it stopped. Things looked good, that is, except
for Mike's rug. It looked like freaking Hellraiser.

The doctor put me on morphine and painkillers. I was prescribed to one garbage can full of pills a day and not a milligram more. The painkillers barely helped, though. My whole skull was broken. The only thing that really helped was holding ice on my face until it melted. I packed my head in ice for most of the day, every day. And then, I packed my head in ice at night and slept with my head in an igloo cooler. I mainly used the painkillers to knock me out so I could get some sleep. Then, I would wake up and start the whole thing over again.

I mostly ate and watched any movie I could get my hands on. With my jaws shut, I could only say a few words, and they all sounded like a bad Humphry Bogart impersonation. If I wanted pork chops and applesauce, I could ask for it, but it was going to have to come out of a blender, first.

That's right, everything I ate was liquefied. I had Spaghettios in the blender. I had hamburger and ice smoothies. Really, I drank the liquid form of anything you could think of… anything, that is, except for dairy. Not being able to drink milk really sucked because you can't really have a milkshake with no milk in it. At the time, I was totally craving some protein powder with milk in it for protein shakes. However, that was against the rules.

"No dairy. No milk. Nothing that can make you sick."

I drank lots of fluids. About two weeks later, I went from 250 to 230 pounds. Over the next few months, I started to look more and more like a stickman. By the end of my stay at Mike's place, I was a whopping 195 pounds. I couldn't take it anymore. I was so weak that I couldn't even walk upstairs without help. It was even worse on my muscle loss that I wasn't allowed to do anything for fear that my liver might fall out of my nose. I couldn't do any exercise. I had to just sit there and let them bone grafts heal.

Finally, Doctor Habal did a check up on me and gave me the "Ok" to move out of Mike's and go live with Hogan. He said, "I want to see you in 6 months," and I agreed.

TIME TO HULK UP

I flew to Northridge, California and Hulkster welcomed me with open arms. I was more than 50 pounds lighter when we met up. He knew I was weak as a cat, but we looked at it like this; it was a brand new starting point.

Things were going to be different under Doctor Hogan's rules. At Mike's place, I lost 55 pounds of muscle in 3 months. Living with Hulk Hogan, however, losing weight was not an option. You don't lose weight hanging out with the Hulkster.

For one, I became more active. We went to the gym every day and, once I could eat protein, I was all over it. I pounded as much "Hulk Hogan Python Powder" that my stomach could handle. I started to become alive again. That was not all, however. Hogan helped me locate some extra good vitamins to help me heal up from the accident. Hogan knew everybody, so when he decided to look for a miracle drug that could really help me, it wasn't long before he had an answer.

What happened was Hulk put me in touch with someone who knew this doctor in the Bahamas who ran some weird "anti-aging" clinic. The doctor was legit, though. He was also at the same time doing all of this groundbreaking stuff to help cancer patients. The doctor was also experimenting with brand new Human Growth Hormone HGH steroid medications that we obviously couldn't get yet here in the United States.

This HGH drug was supposed to help heal cancer and other diseases, and also be extremely instrumental in the healing process after major surgeries to build muscle. Once I got the information from the doctor, I learned it was going to cost about $14,000 for this new miracle drug that nobody knew anything about. I was skeptical about spending so much, but Hulk didn't care what it was going to cost. He grabbed the phone from me, took out his credit card, and immediately ordered this weird stuff that nobody really knew all that much about in the states yet.

This was 1990. While steroid use was already popping up in the 80s, HGH wouldn't be seen at all in the States until 1991. Nobody really knew what to expect, so I felt like a lab rat, but I didn't care. I was such a mess at this point that I was willing to try anything.

When the wonder drug came, I started taking the doses and rehabbing hard. We made sure we got to the gym every day. We worked very hard to get me well. The mindset was to work out to get my body healthy and also take the growth steroid to heel up my face, but my face is not all that it helped.

That drug was insane.

While at Mike's place, my body had shrunk. I was out of the gym on injury for such a long time that I had gotten really small. But the moment after I started taking that medication, the growth hormone was building muscles in my face and was also building muscle all over my body.

I could see right away. The combination of my Hulk Hogan work out and that wonder drug was ridiculous. My atrophy was reversing before my very eyes. I gained over 30 pounds in 6 weeks. You do the math. That's a half pound each day!

One day, I was jet skiing at Hogan's place near the Gulf of Mexico. After we were done, we both hit the showers on separate sides of the house. When I had finished, I stepped up and hit my head right on the track that held the big shower door in place. The flange caught me right on the scar from the operation on the top of my head. It tore it right open.

The blood didn't really bother me. After working with Ron Bass, it was more like a paper cut in comparison. I grabbed a towel. I pressed it on my head and went to the kitchen to get a bag of frozen peas. Then, I just sat in the den with a makeshift ice pack on my head.

By the time Hogan had finished his shower, it looked as if I had taken a bloodbath. I didn't realize it, however, as I was used to so much worse pain than that. I was just sitting there watching The People's Court and blood was trickling all down my neck and back. I didn't realize it, but it looked pretty bad. There was so much blood that it looked like I killed someone on his white couch.

"What the hell?!" Hulkster said when he saw me. "Holy shit!"

"So I guess it is worse than I thought?" I changed the towel and applied more pressure. The bleeding wasn't stopping.

We quickly rushed off to Doctor Habal's office. When we got there, I actually walked right by the doctor in the hallway. It had been probably four months or so. He hadn't seen me at all since all the training and the "anti-aging medication" that Hulk put me on.

He didn't even recognize me.

It was just such a drastic change. In not even two months, I gained back almost 40 pounds of muscle. My skin was tan. My hair was blonde. I was all pumped up. The doctor couldn't even believe it was me until I told him.

"This is tremendous!" he said. "I don't know what to say. I don't know what you are doing, but whatever you are doing, keep doing it!"

He gave me a cheesy high-five, and I went with it. I loved this man. He saved my life and I still owe everything I have to him, today. To say I was elated would be to put it mildly. I was psyched that he felt I was on my road to recovery.

"By the way Doc," I said. "Do you think you could put a couple of staples in my head?"

He gave me twelve staples. I could barely even feel it. I was on Cloud Nine.

CHAPTER 18 - RUN-INS & BARBER SHOP

Early 1991, I was thinking it was time to get back into the ring, but I had to know for sure. I was a little nervous. The doctor at one point told me I would never wrestle again. He said I would never be able to ride a motorcycle again, and never get on a Jet Ski, again. Those were all the things that I loved, and I wasn't going to let an injury hold me back. I had already been back on the road, and back in the water. That accident was not going to stop me.

I wasn't going to let what some doctor said hold me back from doing the one thing I wanted to do most.

THE RUN-IN MAN

On the other hand, I am not going to lie to you. I was scared. I didn't want to get into the ring and have something happen in a match that was going to mess me up for the rest of my life. I knew I was walking around with a completely rebuilt face. I didn't want to like take a dropkick, or something, and have to pick my left cheekbone up off of the mat.

As much as people may want to think that Vince was all business, he is not. He knew I had been through an awful lot and it became obvious to me that he had a heart.

"Vince," I said on the phone with the owner of the WWF. "I'd like to get in the ring again, maybe just a little bit at a time, to see."

"Well, what if we had you do some run-ins or something to see what you think?" he said. "Something off the storyline, in case you aren't ready yet?"

… And that is just what we did.

So for a short time in early 1991, I decided to get my feet wet, again. I decided to start my possible comeback slowly, by becoming a mysterious masked character that only did run-ins.

For the most part, I just threw together whatever weird costume I could. For most of my ensembles, the mask I wore was Hulk Hogan's. It was left over from some angle he did with an American-Made gimmick back in AWA. I also often wore a deep sea diver bag around my neck, like the ones they used to collect shells and items up off of the ocean floor.

Then during random matches, I would run to the ring when people would least expect it and attack various heels. I would interrupt a victim's match, punch them a few times, throw a headbutt, and then immediately retreat like I had just committed a crime. A few of my victims included Rick Martel, Dino Bravo, Earthquake, and the Mountie.

Now remember, this was just a means to test out my nerves, my face and possibly to ward off ring rust. The point of this was to see how I felt in the ring after the accident. I was never officially booked to wrestle in a match and was never given an official name.

For a quick period of time during this run-in run, I thought that there was a chance that I was feeling up for a return. Vince said that if this were to end up being the case, maybe they would eventually have me come back and unmask for a reveal. Because of this possibility, I decided to spend a little bit of money on the costume as an investment. I had Michael sew me up some white fur over my gloves, and also make matching kick pads and a mask. I bought a nice pair of black executioner gimmick tights, with white skulls on one leg, and a huge ax on the other. This gimmick looked like a big evil skunk. Informally, under this regalia, I was called "Fur Face."

I never officially had a name. I really was the "Man With No Name" at this point, long before they would call me that years later in WCW. Some of the other unofficial names I was called by the commentators besides Fur Face included Mariner, the Run-in Man, and Mystery Man.

Vince was totally cool. He was very sympathetic about my situation. Though he had a reputation for rushing people off the injury list before they were often ready, he did not do that with me. He knew I had gone through some very serious shit. To his credit, there was absolutely no pressure. He let me decide if I was up to a full-time return, or not.

One of my last run-ins was in a match featuring Dino Bravo versus my former tag team partner, Greg "The Hammer" Valentine. He had just finished the pretty familiar "Hammer Jammer" run with Ronnie Garvin. This was the one where he wore a shin guard that he would spin around before his trademark figure four, and use it as a weapon. Deciding to do something different with him, Vince decided to turn him babyface.

In the event that I was going to return, some now say Vince McMahon already knew what he was going to do with me. His plan was that I would make a WrestleMania VII appearance, unmask, and possibly start up a Dream Team reunion with a fan favorite Greg Valentine. This actually would have been pretty cool.

In one of my last few "run-ins," I came to the ring and saved Greg from the hands of his former "New Dream Team" partner, Dino Bravo and his new acquaintance, Earthquake. I hoped in the ring and took the bad guys out with a headbutt. Then, I stood Valentine up, and dusted him off to make sure he was all good before my exit.

I guess we went with the idea of a headbutt because, in the event that I was to return, it would be a neat idea to use the headbutt. The headbutt would be more effective because of the metal plates in my skull. This idea was nothing new, but always very effective. A wrestler being able to capitalize off of an injury was something that fans saw quite often, and it always had a strong response. It would be very similar to Greg using his shin guard to enhance his figure four. Iron Mike Sharpe did it for years with his arm brace. Cowboy Bob Orton also used a cast for a long time as well. Even Lex Luger had a brief storyline where he supposedly had a "bionic arm," and would club people with a forearm for his finish.

Though everything went fine in my test run as the Run-In Man, I was still unsure about getting right back in the ring on a full-time schedule, so I met with my doctor to see what he thought. The idea of a headbutt also was a little scary, though I knew there was money in it. The doctor said that nature healed my face even stronger than it was before, and that it was now practically "indestructible," seeing that it was reinforced with flexible titanium.

"Seriously, a headbutt really isn't going to do much to your face," he said. "All the screws and plates would probably hold everything together this time, if you were to, say, have another horrible accident like the last one."

I smiled.

"I can't say on record that it is actually stronger," he said in a typical doctor fashion. "But between you and me, you are superman. You could probably put your head through a steel wall and everything would stay together."

Because of the head trauma also associated with my accident, he did say he wouldn't recommend ever taking any chairshots to the top of the skull, however. That was easy enough to plan against.

The idea that my face was strong was super encouraging, but something still told me to err on the side of caution. Therefore, in the end, I still didn't jump right back in the ring for a return, just yet.

At this time, another opportunity presented itself. There was a guy who owned a goofy golf place on St. Pete Beach that looked like Jurassic Park with dinosaurs. He was an older friend of Terry's back from his old high school day, growing up. Vince had hired him to be Hulk Hogan's assistant, but he was leaving under some weird circumstances.

When you are a super big name like Hulk Hogan was on the road, you often need someone to do legwork for you. It's not just carrying bags and all. Before a big name like Hulk Hogan just shows up somewhere, sometimes certain things have to happen. Like, if a very famous celebrity wanted to go to the mall, he probably was going to get swarmed. So the assistant would call ahead to give a heads up, maybe get a bit of extra security if needed, that type of thing. The assistant had to also act as security oftentimes himself to potentially keep talent out of harm's way.

Anyhow, the guy before did something really bad, and he went away. That is all I know. After that, I stepped in.

Vince told me to just travel with Hulk and help him, for a while, until I was ready to get back into the ring. I have to give it to Vince. He didn't have to, but he gave me a job when I wasn't exactly ready to get back in the ring. He gave me money to live on, too. I can't put him over enough for helping me out.

I went on the road with Hulk and did all the behind-the-scenes stuff. Around this time, Hulk Hogan signed a movie deal to film Suburban Commando. This meant not only was I handling his needs for appearances, but also on a movie set.

Since I had my SAG card, it was a very easy transition to pick up some work, actually handling scenes for Hogan in his absence! I picked up a gig as Hulk's body double and also as a stuntman role in this film. It was quite a learning experience, to say the least. My time on the Suburban Commando set was something that helped me get even more work in other films, as well in the future.

"If you want me to answer the question on whether or not Brutus was there to help Hogan, well yeah, he carried Hogan's bag. But just don't ask me what was in that bag…" – Greg "The Hammer" Valentine

THE BARBER SHOP

By the time Vince called me with the Barber Shop offer, I was ready. I had my fill of the movie scene for a bit, and I was ready to get back on TV. When Vince came up with Barber Shop idea, I may have been physically and mentally ready for a return to wrestling, but I was not entirely ready in every aspect, however.

I couldn't fit in my pants!

Now, this wasn't because of too much fast food, or too much just being a slob. I was actually in the best shape of my life. The thing about it was, my muscles had gotten so big from the training and the HGH that I didn't fit into any of my gear anymore. I was 265 pounds!

I dug into my closet to find the best gear I could to make a great impression for my return. I found one pair of tights that I really liked. When I went to put them on, I felt like a cougar trying to pull on her old prom dress. It just wasn't happening. I threw them onto the bed and tried another. The next one I could actually pull up over my ass, but the damn thing was a nut-hugger. Talk about camel toe… It squeezed my balls so tight, you could see what religion I was through the spandex.

Just like the diva that I was, I literally didn't have a thing to wear. No really, nothing fit!

I called up my designer Michael and asked him for some new outfits. He was a little swamped, but promised he would get something to me soon. The problem was that, with such little notice, the shipment of new clothing wasn't going to make it soon enough.

I am going to have to improvise.

Luckily because of the nature of my gimmick, there was hope. In the spirit of a true barber, I got my scissors out and started hacking away at the seams.

I sliced my pants right down at the sides of the legs, not to enhance the barber gimmick, but more so I could actually fit into them! Needing the extra space so badly, I ended up showing so much skin that I was wearing practically nothing.

I was booked to return as Brutus "The Barber" Beefcake in what was to initially just be a one-shot special appearance on April 23, 1991. I was scheduled as the in-studio guest for an episode of WWF Prime Time Wrestling, with my own interview segment. It was ironic, in a way. It was like I had kind of come full circle in that I was now following the Piper's Pit and Flower Shop act that had actually created my barber gimmick, in the first place.

The Barbershop with Brutus Beefcake featured Earthquake as its first guest at the Primetime Wrestling studio set. I figured that if I could knock that interview out of the park, it could mean bigger and better things for me back in the WWF. I figured right.

Bigger was an understatement. For me, 265 pounds was ridiculously huge. If you go back and see me in the early Barber Shop segments, my arms, my thighs, even my face looks twice as big as they did before the accident.

Some of the boys in the back were saying that I was giving the Ultimate Warrior a run for his money!

GUEST PASSAGE – MARTY JANNETTY ON THE BARBER SHOP

Rather than to tell you about the most remembered Barber Shop by the fans, and perhaps one of the most famous moments in wrestling history, I thought we would do something different. I thought you might like to hear about it from the person it impacted the most. That's right, why not hear the story from the horse's mouth (or jackass) my good friend, Marty Jannetty, himself! Here is a guest passage that Marty Jannetty wrote just for me and my book about the night that Shawn Michaels turned on him during The Barber Shop:

…One of my early experiences with Brutus Beefcake was in Boston. It was the night of his birthday, or maybe the night after. Either way, "Mister Perfect" Curt Hennig, Rick Rude and I decided to get a little something for the Beefer to help him celebrate his special day.

We went out and had some drinks, but Curt and Rick left a little early to set up the big surprise. It was my duty to keep Brutus downstairs in the hotel's bar for an extra hour or so to help make everything happen. This task really was a night off at the office.

Brutus Beefcake was the kind of guy you liked to bring to a bar with you after a show. He was a super funny and generous guy. He would buy you drinks, then buy ten girls drinks. Then he would pick up the ten girls, and you could have whatever fell off of him. There were so many girls throwing themselves at him that it really was a beautiful arrangement.

We were there for his birthday, so we had been drinking more than a little bit. I looked at my watch and figured that was plenty of time. Brutus continued to schmooze some with the ladies, and it seemed that he was never going to leave. That is when I decided to make my move.

"Hey, Beefer," I said, interrupting his small talk with a beautiful girl. "I got you a little birthday present. It's back in your room, waiting for you."

Brutus was buzzed. He didn't much think about how me, or anyone else getting into his room to leave a present was even possible. He just smiled.

"Oh, thank you so much, brother," he said. "You didn't have to do that!"

I nodded. I left a little bit before the Beefer. I found out that he left about ten minutes later, of course, with a lovely blonde on his arm. When I got back to my room, I brushed my teeth and got ready for bed. Just before turning in, I heard a commotion in the hall and cracked the door open.

A half-naked lady was running down the hall, and Brutus Beefcake was standing in the hall with puppy dog eyes. Without warning, right after that, a little person came skipping out of his room in lingerie. She jumped at his waist and grabbed his leg, humping it like a dog. She was dressed up like a total hooker.

I closed the door quietly, as to not make a sound, and laughed my ass off. Not even five minutes later, my phone was ringing. I got a call from Brutus.

"Marty!" Brutus said, on the other end of the receiver. "You better come get this fucking midget out of my room, and now!"

Believe it or not, that was tame. We did a lot of partying together. We went all over the world together, but we were always so busy back then that almost all of that is a blur, today. Now that we do some independent shows together, we get to see a whole lot more of each other, and it really is great.

I think the moment I really got to bond with Brutus, was right after a segment on his WWF talk show segment, The Barber Shop.

WWF had a tendency to split tags up at the most inopportune times. Before we signed on with them, Shawn and I decided we were not going to allow them to just break us up, if we didn't want them to. The way we looked at it was, they called us, and we were already a team. If that time came, we would quit and stay together if they try to split us up. We knew we were making money all over the place and figured at that time it just would be counterproductive to split us. We both stood by that hard.

We did pretty well as a tag team in the WWF. At some point, Shawn confided in me that eventually, he thought he may like to go into singles competition. At this point, we had been wrestling for a while in a good run, so I said, "Just let me know." I thought at that point I didn't know how long I was going to even still be in the business.

But then Shawn started getting a little arrogant. People didn't like his selfish attitude, but he didn't see it. He would say stuff like, "they are just jealous of my talent," and some of the guys in the locker room didn't like his conceit. I warned him. I told him on a number of occasions that he was going to start making some enemies if he kept it up – and he did.

One night, a few of us were in a hotel room drinking. Roddy Piper was there and Shawn started showing some of his attitude then. Now, I loved Piper man, but looking back, he did stir the pot a little. Before you know it, Shawn and I got into an actual fight right there in that hotel room. Now, Shawn is one of the very best wrestlers in the world, but that doesn't mean he is the best fighter, not by far. Things didn't go well for Shawn that night, and that was the turning point of our friendship.

Before that fight, we were like a couple together. We drove together. We had meals together. We trained together. We slept in the same rooms. We even had girls in the same room together and did our thing. And we even switched the girls out. But after that fight, he started talking poorly to me and I would have to ask him not to disrespect me. We never fully recovered.

Vince caught wind of our scuffle. Soon after our fight, Vince brought us into our office and made us shake hands. A few weeks went by, and then it was back to Vince's office.

"I thought you shook hands," he said. "But it is clear you are not the team you once were. I have decided that I want to break you up."

"Well," I looked over at Shawn, "I would have to talk this over with Shawn, first."

"I'm okay with it," he said quickly, cutting me right off with a smug look on his face. He didn't even bother to look over at me.

"It's settled then," Vince said. "Now. I want to make Shawn a superstar. Don't see you as a superstar, but I am sure you can help us make him go up there to that level."

"Well, what about me?" I asked. "I want to be a superstar. I'll train hard and do whatever I need to do."

"That's what I like to hear," Vince said.

A few days later, I got word of the plan. The split was to happen on Brutus Beefcake's interview segment, The Barber Shop. Brutus had gone through some hard times with his parasailing accident and all. To Vince's credit, they made a spot for him.

Shawn had a lot of heat with Hulk, so my guess is he probably was not a big fan of Beefer. I do know, however, that the Beefer didn't have any beef with Shawn, even though he was Hulk's friend. That was just how he rolled. He was friendly with everyone. Everyone liked him.

There was not much to go over in the back for the interview. We discussed the bullet points and we knew what to say. Then, Shawn was supposed to superkick me through the window on the set and then Brutus chasing Shawn offset to shield me.

They brought three windows in case it didn't look good. The idea was if the window break looked bad, we were just going to go ahead and do it again.

Once we got out to the stage, we did our thing. Shawn hit me pretty hard with that superkick. He laid it in. I mean, he really laid it in. I could feel the joy Michaels had when he hit me with that kick - right under the chin and really plowed it.

After he threw me through the window, I couldn't see behind me what was going on. I never felt that much from the window, I was still seeing stars from the kick. Shawn was supposed to run off like a coward and then tear a picture of us up. But he didn't. He stayed right on the set only a few feet away from Brutus, posing for the camera.

A normal person may not really pick up why Shawn's position change was extremely bad, but Shawn knew exactly what he was doing. By Shawn just standing there only a few feet away from me, it made both of us look too weak to fight him off. Shawn's positioning and body language was saying, "And if I need to, I will do the same to you, Brutus." Brutus as the babyface was supposed to chase him off, but couldn't. This made Brutus Beefcake look bad. Because Brutus wasn't supposed to get any shots in or do anything to ward off Shawn, he had to just shield me and do nothing. Shawn took his sweet time. He ripped up our Rockers picture and threw it right at Brutus and me.

I was sitting there bleeding for what seemed like forever. I remember trying to look over Brutus' shoulder thinking, "What the fuck is he doing? Why doesn't he get off the damn stage?"

Brutus just had to sit there and take it.

A real man would have turned around and gone after Shawn in the real world. He wouldn't have sat there. He wouldn't have ignored someone posing for the cameras after destroying his set. Shawn made Brutus look like something a little bit less than that.

After the spot, Brutus met up with me in the hallway going to the locker room.

"Marty, I'm sorry Shawn did it the way he did. It made us both look bad," he said. "At one point, I thought he was going to attack me to make me look even worse."

I was pissed.

"He really got me with that superkick. He did that on damn purpose," I said. "I wonder if I should go in the back and give him a superkick myself."

"No no no!" Brutus said. "You can't do that!" If you do, you will be done for sure."

I was seriously ready for a rematch from Shawn's last ass-beating in that hotel room. I argued with Brutus for a moment, but then realized he was right. He was the man. He had no real stake in the game, but wanted to see me be ok. He put in the time and helped me see right, again. He brought me down and helped me get my head leveled. We created a new bond after that.

If Shawn could sweep both pieces of shit off the stage that night, he would have and the stage would have been just his. Beefer could have also kicked Shawn. He could have also smacked the shit out of Shawn, but didn't. Keep in mind that he was high up in the company at this time, far before Shawn had much pull. He had his own talk segment and had been pretty much disrespected. But he stayed professional.

Once the smoke settled, he came and congratulated me for keeping my cool.

"Marty, good job, brother. You could have done all kinds of things to retaliate. But you didn't do this, and you didn't do that," he said backstage. "Good job."

"Thanks, man," he said.

"And if you are thinking about Shawn, he will get his. People aren't blind. If you do your friend like that, what are you going to do to the other guys? People know now what they are dealing with."

From that point, we had a great bond, thereafter.

Two years later, I was scheduled to face Shawn at the Royal Rumble. A few days before, Shawn and I were practicing our practice match at a house show in Denver. We had the fans on their feet for 20 minutes straight with all cruiserweight-type spots. It was very exciting. We were both blowing up at the 15-minute mark, but the fans cheers got us through it.

At the end, I remember thinking, "I have to get through that curtain." I walked back to the locker room and the agent, Jack Lanza, said that it was the greatest match he had ever seen. I thanked him but rushed to get away so I could go lay down in a side room under a table.

Lanza called Vince on a payphone to tell him the same thing right outside of the room. I could hear him saying that our match needed to be the main event at the PPV.

The next day, we were still the opening match at the Royal Rumble. They trusted us to get people into the show, but they added something last minute that just screwed everything up. They had Sensational Sherri come out around the 8-minute mark for a spot, and then we had to adjust everything we had already planned. In the end, the flow was altered and the match wasn't as good. Vince even stopped us in the hallway and said he was disappointed, because he had heard so much about how great the match was supposed to be and that we didn't deliver.

The next day, Vince called me and said he was letting me go. He said the decision has been made, because he heard I was intoxicated during the match, and that was what messed everything up.

I wanted to kill Shawn. It was clear that he got to McMahon. But then I heard Brutus' voice again in my head and didn't. Instead of going off to kick Shawn's ass, I went home and cried my ass off.

Three months later, Mister Perfect called me and said, "Marty I got your job back!"

"Not funny," I said to the well-known prankster.

"No, no. I was riding with Vince in a limo. Vince told me he felt bad that he had to let you go, because Shawn had to lead you around by the nose for the match because you were so drunk. That is when I told him that Shawn was lying. I said it was actually Shawn who had passed out from somas the night before in his plate at the diner. If anyone was screwed up it was Shawn!" he said.

"Are you serious?"

"Vince told me, I guess I will have Marty come back and beat him for the Intercontinental Belt," he said. "You just wait and see."

Pat Patterson called me later that day, and that's just what they did. At the TV taping, everyone was glad to see me again. Scott Steiner told me he wanted to beat Shawn's ass for me for lying. Koko B Ware actually went up to Michaels and said, "We all know who the real rocker is now."

That night just before I won the Intercontinental Championship title, I saw Shawn Michaels in the hallway on a payphone. Michaels, in a humbling moment, had to call his mom to tell her what she was about to see on TV.

Brutus was right. The level-head was the way to go, and it worked out for me in the end.

Thanks, Beefer. I guess I owe you a drink… and maybe another midget.   – Marty Jannetty

END OF THE BARBER SHOP

After returning to full-time status with the WWF in the spring of 1991, the Barber Shop was in full effect. The Rockers split up on the segment when Shawn Michaels superkicked his partner Marty Jannetty and launched him through a plate glass window. At the same time, he launched his own solo career. Regardless of how he did, my interview segment turned Shawn Michaels heel and led him to stardom.

Other stars were to follow; Jake The Snake, Andre The Giant, Randy Savage, Ric Flair, Ted DiBiase, the Legion of Doom – the list goes on and on. For about a year, my segment was used to further storylines and add to the character development needed to really make for good TV.

In one segment, Piper came back to continue to pass the torch to me, so to speak. He came on the set of The Barber Shop and really put me over big. There was no script here. The whole segment was kind of a nod to the fact that I helped him back in the day with Adrian Adonis, without really saying. Piper told the audience about my courage in fighting for my comeback after my accident, and turned the segment into a spotlight on me, instead of himself. It was a really nice gesture.

The final Barber Shop segment took place in February 1992. The newly-turned heel Sid Justice attacked me and destroyed the set, building heat for his feud with Hulk Hogan. Sid was horribly embarrassing on that last barber shop. I was supposed to cower away from him when he went nuts. The producers said, "Don't challenge him. We want him to look like a monster." The thing about it was, he was looking like a monster *at my expense*. In this case, I wasn't just helping to get him over for his upcoming match with Hulkster, I was pretty much just jobbing out.

Believe me, if I could have changed something, I would have. If I tried to look good, I would have lost my job. Maybe I should have. My contract was up anyhow, and the whole point to destroying the set was because they knew I was off to do a movie soon. This is how they wrote me off of television.

I don't hold anything really against Sid, of course. He was just doing his job. I just think it was a little bigger than it needed to be.

After this, I took about a year off or so. That is when we went to film *Mr. Nanny*.

Me on the set of Mr. Nanny in 1993.

CHAPTER 19 - THE MASK & DEPARTURE

Before WrestleMania IX, there were a bunch of allegations that led to a very public steroid case. The charges were that a doctor for the Pennsylvania State Athletic Commission, Dr. George Zahorian, was selling steroids illegally to WWF wrestlers in general, and the news was pointing quite specifically at Hulk Hogan. The other charge was that Vince McMahon was allowing it all to happen. Due to all the bad press, Hogan took a temporary leave of absence from the company in hopes to allow things to blow over outside the spotlight. This was probably a good idea.

When the steroid case finally went to trial, it very much threatened the WWE a year later in 1994. Vince was facing something like eight years in prison, if found guilty, which I thought was crazy. The prosecuting team actually subpoenaed me to appear and felt that I was going to be a key witness. However, when my lawyers provided my medical records, citing an accident that resulted in steel plates, screws, and wires in my head – plus the documented issues I had with memory, the lawyers immediately dropped me from their potential witness list.

Honestly, there were boys in the locker room who were right there to line up for any and all drugs the infamous Dr. Zahorian had to offer. Even though Rick McGraw's death was due in part to the easier availability of certain drugs from the doctor, he probably would have just found the stuff somewhere else because he wanted it so bad. It really is still on Rick himself for not watching his own intake.

In early 1993, Vince wanted me back on TV after a little time off from the Barber Shop. I was called up to make my return to the ring on Monday Night Raw. To really connect with the fans, they decided to use my injury from the accident in a storyline with Ted DiBiase and Mike Rotunda (aka Irwin R. Schyster,) Money Inc. I had an interview on RAW announcing my open contract and promoted an upcoming return to the ring. Knowing I was a catalyst for Hulk Hogan's also long-awaited return, I made sure to say his name over and over in the interview to make people think of him. This would also help anticipation for his comeback to the ring as well.

I had trained pretty hard and was pretty confident that there was to be no issue in hurting my face during my comeback match. But in an effort just to make sure, and also to further monetize off of the accident in the storyline, they decided to fit me for a protective mask.

Hulk and I had just filmed *Mr. Nanny*. During the making of that film, the special effects team built this really cool Iron Man-type suit, and I thought it would be neat to give me some kind of facial look like that for the upcoming wrestling angle. So, I gave them a call.

I told them I wanted something somewhat protective looking, but also something terminator-like, like a cyborg's face, to play off the idea of the metal plates in my skull. The Hollywood team came and casted my face. They had to plaster and form-cast my whole head. Then, they did the same thing just to my face.

We had just finished filming Mr. Nanny. The Nanny guys then went to work to custom create two different super high-quality masks. One of the masks was somewhat flexible, made from a hard rubber-like substance, the other was a more rigid, light-weight metal alloy and hard fiberglass. Both fit my face absolutely perfectly. They were painted red and yellow to compliment who I would be tag teaming with at Mania.

The mask was money. Then, all we needed to do was introduce a reason to wear the mask.

At this point, they did what good writers always did; with an end game in mind, they worked backward to fill in the blanks. They knew that Hulk Hogan was returning, and they knew that they wanted us to face Money Inc. at WrestleMania. They also knew that Jimmy Hart was, at this point, actually acting as Hulk's agent behind the scenes. So rather than to have to hide the fact that Jimmy would be seen with Hulk from time to time by the fans, they also decided that Jimmy Hart should be our manager at the big pay-per-view.

Then, the rest was like a big puzzle. How do we turn Jimmy Hart, a hated, wormy annoying leach in the eyes of wrestling fans, into a fan favorite?

In my return match with Ted DiBiase on RAW, "IRS" Irwin R. Schyster interfered. They rang the bell, as Money Inc. continued to double-team me. While this was happening, their manager, Jimmy Hart, did not join in. You could see the look of concern and conflict on his face when Ted DiBiase held me up to take a hit from his partner. IRS positioned himself and teased that he was going to hit me in the face with his trademark steel briefcase.

Finally, longtime heel manager Jimmy Hart saw the light and the unnecessary attempt to injure a man who had already been through such a tragedy. He did all he could to stop his team from hurting me, but alas, it was to no avail.

IRS slammed me with his briefcase.

It was my first RAW match and I was already being attacked, getting hit in the head with a metal Halliburton briefcase. I didn't have my protective mask on, or anything yet. They hit me in the forehead. I was by no means a victim, however, before the match, I talked to Rotundo. I looked over the briefcase and it had a lot of give.

"This should be fine," I said, after a little inspection of what actually was a cheap imitation Halliburton. "Now, you don't worry. You go ahead and hit me hard with that case,"

"Are you sure?"

I knew that once I got back into the ring that some of the boys were going to be hesitant around certain things with me. They all knew about the accident. Vince even had a clause put into my contract that nobody was supposed to hit me in the face unless it was first cleared. I didn't, however, want that to ever translate to looking weak on the television screen.

"Totally, we are going to Mania with this, so hit me hard. It will be fine. Just make sure you hit me with the center of the case."

When the spot came, Rotundo delivered. I covered my face and went down.

He caved the briefcase in.

Everything was fine. Jimmy came in to console me and passed me a blade. I got some color and looked a mess. The medics came out to the ring and took me out on a stretcher. I left the ring with a concerned Jimmy Hart, right by my side.

I felt it was a perfect set up for WrestleMania. When I got back to the locker room, it was evident that the boys felt the same way. It was nice to see the support. They were happy I was back in the ring where I belonged.

My return was a little before Hulk's. When Hulk Hogan came back, we were not set to work with Money Inc. individually as a promotional means much at all. The whole revenge grudge match was saved for Mania. We did, however, do a number of promos to help hype the match.

We officially renamed ourselves The Mega-Maniacs and did some interview segments to get over the idea that Money Inc. could have killed me with their irresponsible, selfish actions on RAW. During these promos is when I debuted the new mask, which got over big with the fans. We also debuted our new third member of the team, taking on Money Inc.'s former manager, "The Mouth of the South" Jimmy Hart. This was the first time WWF audiences (or almost any wrestling fans for that matter) had ever seen Jimmy as a fan favorite.

To get our tag team act down again for Mania, Hogan and I did start working some matches together leading up to the big match, however on house shows. Once we figured some spots out in the ring that we figured we could use, I have to say we looked pretty good.

HOGAN JET SKI BLACK EYE

Right before the big event, Hulk came down to Tampa to do some Jet Skiing with me. He was trying to showboat a little, and I had to warn him.

"Be careful standing up. If a really big guy like you stands up, the front end works like a seesaw and you could flip right over!" I said.

"Got it, brother," Hogan scowled.

So we are riding around, raising hell on these Polaris 750 Triple Wave Riders with directionals. On these toys, you would use a switch on throttle to get more power, by thrusting up or down. They were small but you could almost stop on a dime, they were so strong. You could make a real sharp right or left turn, then you could just take off at like 55 miles an hour.

I did a loop, and then out of nowhere, I see Hogan fall backward in the water, as his Jet Ski darted upwards. It flipped around in the air and came down front first, hitting him in the head.

WHAPPP!

I thought he was dead.

I zipped over and couldn't see him. He had gone under the water. Flashbacks of my own accident started to hit me. I started to worry and circled around the area, when all of a sudden, he resurfaced with his hand over his eye.

Hogan shook his head, but signaled to me that he was okay. The problem was, he wasn't.

Though it could have been a lot worse than it was, his eye was pretty messed up. We threw him in the car and rushed him over to the emergency room.

In the end, it was much more than just a black eye. He had fractured his eye orbital.

Come WrestleMania, we went in for our physicals. Hogan had a big bandage on his eye and the plan was we were just going to take it off, touch it up with a little makeup, and then we would make sure he didn't take any shots to the face from Rotundo, or DiBiase.

When we showed up to the arena, we were walking around saying our hellos, and when we came around the corner, we walked right into the Athletic Commissioner for the state. The Las Vegas Athletic commission took one look at Hogan and shook their head. Before they said anything, they wanted to shut us down. They weren't going to let us work!

We had to think quickly. An eye injury at this time was something that was not allowed by the athletic commission. With Las Vegas holding some of the biggest fights in the world, they just didn't allow things like that to slip.

"Ha ha ha!" I said. "We got you."

Now, many will tell you that I am old school and have the gift of gab. I have worked many fans in my lifetime to protect the business, and make wrestling seem real. In this case, however, I had to go the other way and work the athletic commission, by telling them that the injury was actually fake!

On the spot, we had to make up a story that DiBiase and Rotundo jumped Hogan as a storyline at a casino. We explained that the angle was eventually going to be aired on TV, and that it would be revealed that Money Inc. tried to take Hogan out before the match with some thugs.

"When he comes out to the ring, you will see. The makeup will look just like a black eye," I said. "Trust me, this is just a fake deal for TV."

Once we convinced them it wasn't real, we both took pictures with the officials and everything was good again. If we hadn't worked them, not only would there have been no tag match, but there also would have been no impromptu Hogan finish at the end. It would have turned out to be a pretty shitty, and uneventful pay-per-view all around.

So, at WrestleMania IX, it was very clear that Hogan was going into the match with a cut above a black eye for the WWF Tag Team Championship. We told Vince what happened with the commission, and he subsequently went along with our story. To account for the marks on his face, Vince had the commentators say that Ted DiBiase paid a group of filthy street thugs to take Hogan out the night before in a casino. In the end, we got revenge, but we lost by disqualification.

Hogan had worked another Heavyweight title reign into the terms of his return contract and Vince made good with that, right away. Later on that same night, Hogan won the strap by pinning Yokozuna, immediately after Yokozuna had defeated Bret Hart. It was pretty exciting for the fans to say the least.

WRESTLING DONTAKU - MORE WITH NEW JAPAN

Immediately after my WrestleMania IX appearance, I got booked to work one more show for New Japan. This booking was for the first "Wrestling Dontaku" on May 3, 1993, at the Fukuoka Dome in Fukuoka.

As part of working relationships between NJPW, WCW, and WWF, New Japan was paying big bucks to put on a crossover super card like never before.

WCW's Sting, WWF's Hulk Hogan, Jimmy Hart, and I all took part in this event. Top names from both of the big two in America on the same card never happened, so this was something very special. The main event boasted a dream match between the reigning WWF Champion Hulk Hogan, and their reigning IWGP Heavyweight Champion the Great Muta.

My match was quite a feather in my hat, with a pinfall over Massa Saito, clean in the middle. I'll tell you, this is perhaps one of the biggest paydays I have ever received for just one match. I made something like $10,000 cash for working him that night in Fukuoka, Japan.

WWF DEPARTURE

Although it felt like I was on a roll, WrestleMania IX was actually my final wrestling appearance on WWF television. I wasn't done with the company though for a few months, as I remained active on their house shows.

After Mania and the match in Japan, I teamed with Hogan in a number of matches against Money Inc. in June 1993 across the country. For most of those, we The Mega Maniacs usually won by disqualification.

My final tour for the WWF actually took place over in Europe for the whole month of July. At first, I think they figured I was just going to sign on again, as my 6-month contract was about to expire. Maybe to keep me happy and also to keep me looking strong, they had me defeat Terry Taylor. They actually had me beat him something like eight times in a row, then that was it.

Red Rooster had to pretty much kiss ass to keep his job. He was with the office for years and years after that. He was never ever a feature, or main event. He was always mid-card at best. Terry Taylor was a good enough guy, but he just never main-evented, or even came close. Why Vince brought a non-WWF guy in like this in to mentor his younger guys (who was never really successful mind you), I'll never know. I just never understood it.

WHY I LEFT WWF...

There were a number of factors involving my departure from the federation.

For one, Hogan promised me a job with his production company in the event of his departure, so he would have someone around he could trust. You see, Vince had been trying to replace Hogan for years, unsuccessfully like he did with the Ultimate Warrior. Vince has always had a weird love/hate relationship with Hulk Hogan. Some promises were made both on the cash and creative sides of things, and some promises were also broken.

Another factor was that there was also some weird friction looming over the upcoming steroid trial that Vince was soon going to have to endure. I am not sure both Hulk Hogan's testimony and Vince McMahon's testimony were going to match all that well. This is something that probably didn't bode well with Vince McMahon.

A final factor was that Hollywood was continuing to knock on Hulk's door. A new movie and television deal was on the table for some proposed show called, *Thunder In Paradise*. Producers Michael Berk, Douglas Schwartz, & Greg Bonann all had a hand in it. This option seemed like it could be really big and also mean a lot of money, calling for a lot less abuse to our bodies like we did in the ring. Hogan wanted me to be involved and have me do all his stunt work, because we all know Terry didn't like to take a bump.

Coming from the creators of Baywatch, I figured that it had legs and could have been the next chapter of my life. Come that summer we were in negotiations, talking to big Hollywood producers.

Shortly after this, I picked up a few more dates with New Japan. In August of 1993, I won in a singles match with Black Cat in Yokohama, Kanagawa. A few days later in Osaka, I teamed with Jake Roberts in a fun match with Hercules Hernandez & Scott Norton. However, it wasn't long before I was on the set of Baywatch, hanging out with David Hasselhoff, and also rubbing suntan lotion on Pamela Anderson.

CHAPTER 20 - BRUTUS THE STUDD

"I would love to say that Brutus was generous with the women, but he really never was. When he was around, they all went to him, and we never got any!" – King Kong Bundy

"Well, well, well. Brutus. What Can I say? I would love to offer a little story for your book, but I can't. There really is no story I can talk about of any kind, due to the adult-nature in content that would have to be described. I really can't say anything!"
– Fred Ottman (Tugboat, Typhoon, Shockmaster)

"Brutus would turn down some of the most beautiful women you ever would see. You see he had so much action he could be selective. He could do it because he could get any woman he wanted!" – Nikolai Volkoff

"I would take Brutus's leftovers any day of the week because the girls who were looking at me weren't half as good as what was falling off him... The only problem was, not many ever fell off." – Greg "The Hammer" Valentine

RATS

For anyone reading my story who doesn't know what a ring rat is, they were basically rockstar groupies but instead of following around a band, they followed professional wrestling superstars. To clarify something; they were not prostitutes. Some of the guys would look for escorts and actually pay for companionship and sex when they were on the road. Being on the road over 300 days in a year, I could understand that. But I never looked to pay for services, and frankly, I never needed to.

As a former WWF wrestler who traveled the world, I understand how it felt to be lonely on the road. It's funny, because wrestling is a business where you are all about seeing people. I would perform in front of thousands and thousands of faces every night and traveling to a new town the next day to see thousands and thousands of new faces once again. However, none of those thousand faces would be good enough to share your thoughts with. None of those thousand faces could you pour your heart out to with real problems. None of them really wanted to know the real you. They just wanted an autograph or a picture, or to see what you were going to do in a pretend fight. That was it.

The road really was a lonely place at times.

The term "Ring Rat" itself was pretty horrible. To me, it sounds like they were all low class and nasty, which they really were not. Some of them were very well-off, attractive and had a lot of money. However, on the flipside of things, some of them did, in fact, look like they could be Hillbilly Jim's sister or rather his pet Billy goat, but I would never hang with any of those foul ones. For me, if I wanted to be with a woman, she had to have all of her teeth and could not be able to successfully floss with rope. Also, if she weighed more than I did, or had more facial hair, it was probably not going to happen either, *most of the time.*

There were some really weird sexually deviant ones out there that helped keep antibiotic companies in business, man. Some rats would stalk a wrestler's hotel room, or stood outside the arena doing absolutely anything they could, hoping to get noticed by a particular guy. They would flash their tits, throw condoms at them, grab your penis when you walked by.

Most of the guys liked to go out after their shows. The rats knew this so they would fester and herd up. Then the rats would predict which local bars, nightclubs, or restaurant the wrestlers would go to. Then droves of them would infest an establishment, waiting to strike. Believe it or not, the venue didn't matter. I've seen rats willing to attack a guy in the most unromantic places you can think of, like porta-potties in the back alley of a bowling alley.

The really interesting ring rats were the regulars. There was a small group of these groupies that could kind of be trusted to, more or less, give a guy the girlfriend treatment and take care of them. When I say this, I mean, they would really go out of their way to make you feel like you were pretty much loved. They would drive 200 miles, pick you up, bring you to a show, bring you out to dinner after, and then have sex with you. They would pay for every little expense. It was almost like they were female sugar-daddies. They would give you gifts. They would have new clothing for you, they would give you gifts like gold chains, or watches. At the end of the night, they would bang you like they owed you money, then pay for the hotel room.

I mean, yeah, there was always a girl in a part of Texas who would road trip it 200 miles just to suck your dick, but the professional ring rat was more than just about sex.

There were a group of the boys who really took advantage of the rats, and it was pretty bad. The things they would do to a girl were just crude. Beyond crude! I was never in that company. They believed that you had to do filthy disgusting things to a ring rat so they would "know their role," and not risk affecting your personal life beyond wrestling. This mentality said you had to treat a rat a certain way, or else they would start to think they were something else. These guys said you had to be mean, but that wasn't me. I was always nice.

Some of the guys were just crude!

Jake "The Snake" Roberts in his bad days would run the rats pretty hard. The British Bulldogs would bring a rat in their room, allegedly commit unmentionable acts, and then throw them out.

The Rockers were famous for playing nasty pranks on the rats. They would always party all night (hence the name *Midnight Rockers*,) no matter what time they had to wake up in the morning. Sometimes if a rat fell asleep in their hotel room, then they would draw fake mustaches on their faces in permanent marker, or maybe drag them out into the hallway half-naked. They would sometimes steal my gimmick too, and cut their hair very oddly.

I was always nice to women, however. I was a lover, though, not a hater.

If the WWF wasn't in a particular town for 6 months, when I showed up, they would be waiting. I mean, I would literally get off an airplane, come down the escalator and see three, or four girls that I knew I could have, if I wanted to. I don't know if it was because I treated them nicely, or if it was my boyish charm, or what.

My mentality was I was not a fence builder. I would think, here is a pretty good looking broad, let her buy you food. Let her drive you around or pay for lodging. Let her buy you a diamond ring. It happened a whole lot, and I looked at it as fringe benefits, almost as being part of your job.

The professional rats had their own territories and almost made it like they were contracted to services guys in certain areas. There were a few regulars in different areas that you knew if you looked for them, you would find them every time wrestling came to that town.

Say you were going to Michigan. There would be Sally, who was always there because she was from that state. However, you might also see Christine from Ohio, or Shirley from Indiana, too, if they were willing to make the drive. I guess it depended on who was on the card, and who they liked seeing.

In upstate New York, like Syracuse, Albany, and some PA towns like Hershey, there was this one girl who was a little bit on the "butt" side. She was not the greatest quality, but she was willing to drive and put in the hours.

We called her "Ass-Eaten' Annie."

Ass-Eaten' Annie really loved Greg. We don't know what it was, but Annie would tote him around in her car, anywhere he wanted to go. She would go and get him anything his little heart desired. She was all about Greg Valentine, no matter who else was on the show. I mean, she would seek him out and drive 12 hours, if she knew Greg Valentine was on the show, hoping, in the end, to get hammered by "The Hammer."

We would all finish up a show and drive to a nearby restaurant. We would all be drinking, shooting some pool, and having a good old time, and then we would look over.

Off in a far away, dimly lit corner, there would be Annie holding Greg's hand and Greg would be romancing her. Man, we would see that and just laugh. Watching him feed her spaghetti and whisper in her ear. Gentle soft kisses on the lips.

Everything was so loving, but we all laughed because we knew better, because we knew how she got her name. We all knew it was only a matter of time before she would be shoving her tainted tongue up the Hammer's asshole later on that very night.

A lot of the rats kept their lives secret from their friends and family. They didn't want their mothers and fathers knowing that they would shack up with ring crew, just in an attempt to meet a wrestler who they could also shack up with.

This group today though is a dying breed.

The late 80s to 90s was the end of the rat era. I think stuff like AIDS, and the rise and downfall of the Attitude Era of Wrestling and Rock-n-Roll killed the possibility of any new generation of ring rats.

Alas, we sadly don't really have rats anymore.

Today, we don't have obsessed fans who are girls, willing to do anything for us. Today, we have obsessed guys with iPhones who want us to take selfies with us and sign their action figures. The funky-but-chunky comic book fanboy wearing a "Bullet Club" T-shirt, they are our new rats. And now, I have to politely decline. (Because if any of them want to flash me, or hook up, it just ain't happenin'!)

FIRST WIFE

So for those of you who are keeping record, I have been married three times. The first wife was a mess. She was one of those fixer-upper deals. You know, the kind that you fell for, only because of what she could potentially become – not for what she was at the time. I really thought I could fix her up, but I guess, in hindsight that was wishful thinking.

When I first met her, she was working at as a stripper. I worked on motorcycles with her stepfather, and that is how we met. My friends who knew her said it was probably not a good move getting in a relationship, but I just didn't listen. Hulk had her pegged from day one. He knew she was evil. He spotted her right away for what she was.

I can help this lost soul. I want to help make her something.

Around 1989 or so, I bought a place in California. I met her there through a guy who owned a company named Winks cycles. Wink was a little short bald guy. He had been in a really bad accident once, and he walked around with a limp. However, he was a killer mechanic. Wink used to come and work on my Harleys. He did exceptional work with my Softail Springer, and we really hit it off. Because of that, I used to get some of his employees booked to help out and work security when wrestling was in town.

An opportunity came up for me to run my own business, "Chick-a-mania," a flame-broiled chicken and burger place. We were lucky. I knew some people and pulled some strings so that Chick-a-mania was able to get a Liquor license for beer and wine. There were no bars in Yorba Linda, California because it was a high-end very strict place. There really were only a few pizza places in town, so our company had a great buzz on it.

The Hulkster came and helped me launch the business. He signed pictures, kissed babies, the whole nine yards. It was a great start.

I was gone a lot on the road with the WWF. I was away on tour probably 28 out of 30 days a month. My wife was supposed to help with it, but I since heard she probably had her hands full with something else; *penis.*

In December of 1989, I found out she was cheating on me, and had been fooling around with people every time I was away.

When word got out that she screwed me over, her own family disowned her. Her own family wouldn't speak to her. They all thought that she was a douche bag. When I first started seeing her, I met her parents. They all said, "Oh my god! She must have changed. She's with a star now and he will make her good again. Because of this, I was beloved by them all, and they all sided with me over their own blood.

The problem was, I didn't know her evil plan until it was too late; *take everything and bail.*

After WrestleMania 3 it was a whole different ballgame. Before that, I was on top of the world. After that, I lost my wife, and I lost my restaurant, Chick-a-mania, in one shot.

Not only did she cheat, but she was stealing out of the restaurant. When I thought she was finally done with me, she didn't have the decency to tell me. She just started taking and selling and hiding everything in sight. She robbed my safe deposit box. She robbed my gold and jewelry. She sold somewhere in the area of $50,000 worth of equipment for pennies on the dollars, somewhere around like $5000. In the end, she even ended up with my beautiful townhouse, my rental property, and my other place in Tampa, even though that was by construct.

While we were married, I made the mistake of purchasing another house on the lake. It was an awesome 3 bedroom, one story home. I bought it with one simple phone call for $110,000, and just rented it out.

Come July of 91, a year and a half later, we went to court. As part of the divorce, I promised to give her the properties, but only under the condition that she had to take the mortgage payments right along with them. I went to court in Orange County. The judge had my back from the start. His kids were wrestling fans! Before the case, he had his wife take their kids out to meet me in his private chambers.

When it finally came time to start, we realized that she had blown all her cash and could no longer afford an attorney. I pulled my lawyer aside and asked if he could act as her attorney also to finalize everything. The judge allowed it. The deal we made was I kept my money, and she got all the properties.

So in the end, two years after the accident, it was finally over. She assumed all of the properties, but also got stuck with all the bills that went along with them. I waited for her to come out of the courthouse that day with a huge smile on my face. When she finally did, I drove right up on her in my new Corvette and flipped her the bird.

I basically had nothing at this point, but a clean slate to start over with. No job. No income. If I gave the properties, I would never have to deal with her again, or even go back to that same corner of the world.

GREG VALENTINE BEACH WEDDING

Greg "The Hammer" Valentine in the mid-90s dated a woman named Julie, who eventually would become his wife. Before they got married, however, they had some kind of falling out, and Greg started seeing Madusa Miceli. He had been working some with her on the independents, so he called Vince McMahon and got her a job with the WWF. Madusa didn't want to sell her name to Vince, so she came in and started wrestling in New York under a new name, Alundra Blaze.

While she was on the road with the WWF, Madusa started sending all these postcards to Greg's house, where Julie had not moved out, yet. The postcards were possessive and written to drive Julie insane. The cards said things like "He is my man now!" and "Your loss, my gain!" and "Would you hurry up and leave the house already!?"

Eventually, however, Greg patched things back up with Julie, and they have been together ever since. After getting back together with Julie, they finally got engaged to get married. Greg and Julie decided to get married on the North Redington shore in Tampa Bay, down by the Hilton. To make things even more fun, everyone was instructed to attend in their bathing suits. It was a good thing too. It was 85 degrees on the beach that day.

Johnny Green was there from the midget wrestling federation. Brian Knobbs was there, too. Everyone there was wearing either swim trunks or a bikini, except one guy in a black leather jacket. That was Dickie Moran who is

**At Greg Valentine's beach-themed wedding, all guests were
encouraged to wear their own swimsuits.**

Julie's father; Greg's father-in-law, and Knobb's father-in-law, as well. Dickie was the most generous, gentlemanly, coolest guy on the planet. He was the kind of guy who always insisted on paying when you went out to eat, no matter how many people were there. In fact, he paid for their whole wedding. (We recently lost him, and he is sadly missed.)

Even though pretty much everyone was wearing swim attire, being the Hammer's "Best Man" was an exceptional honor, so I wanted to really look the part. To do my tag team partner justice, I wore the best (and smallest) tiger stripe thong money could buy.

Nobody knew it was going to happen, either. When the ceremony started, I walked down the aisle, perhaps turning more heads than the bride, but for a different reason. When I made it to the front, I was standing there next to Greg and the wedding officiant wearing basically an eye patch that barely covered my cock and balls.

"Hey, Beefer," Valentine whispered. "What the hell?"

"You don't like it?" I asked.

"No, it's not that," he replied, looking down at the white Speedo he had on for his beach-themed wedding. "Why do you get the cool thong, and I have to wear this big old diaper?!"

I got a great tan that day, too, with virtually no tan lines.

Time off from the road didn't happen much, so a bunch of us would vacation together whenever we could. At Greg's big wedding, a bunch of the boys planned to go to Hawaii to take advantage of some very rare downtime from the WWF. "Did somebody say beach?" I was in. It was me, Hulk, Macho, Knobbs, me and our respective women.

When the Hawaii trip had finally come, I had to take a different flight due to an appearance that made me about a day later than the others. When I finally got to my beachfront cabin, the boys were already set up out there on the shore. They had a boom-box going. There was a cooler with plenty of drinks. I was ready to party. I quickly tore open my luggage to get ready.

Now, I didn't give it much thought that Macho Man Randy Savage was going to be down there, when I was getting dressed to head over to the beach. Maybe, in hindsight, I should have.

"Hey, Beefer," Knobbs said, as I walked by.

The Hulkster didn't speak but put his hand behind his head for a low high five.

The whole gang was there. Some were lying out. Others were sitting on the resort's lawn chairs catching rays in the sand. I was ready. I pulled down my Adidas track pants. I bent over to spread out my towel and get my spot together. I may or may not have popped out my booty, spinning my whole backside around directly into everyone's face, hoping they would get a look. The gag worked again.

Miss Elizabeth's eyes almost popped out of her head.

Nothing but ass.

I, of course, was wearing the same sweet thong from Hammer's wedding.

I "no sold" the reaction of what must have looked like a naked guy walk out onto the beach to everyone. Again, that thing barely covered my beefy package, and that was it. I hopped on a chair and pulled a hat over my eyes. I didn't see it happen, but apparently, Randy got up and just started packing their shit. Without saying anything, he grabbed Liz by the hand, and they were out of there. He didn't even say a word.

When we got back to the cabins, we thought we would find a pissed off Randy Savage on his porch, but that was not the case. He was actually so pissed off that he checked out, paid for an early flight, and left the island altogether.

MISS ELIZABETH

In WWF, Randy Savage's jealousy over Miss Elizabeth was ridiculous. She was his wife at the time, but that didn't matter. That did not equate any kind of respect or trust, whatsoever. His jealousy surrounding Elizabeth would get out of hand so much so, that if another wrestler even glanced at her, Savage would chase them around the arena.

He was so protective that he would sometimes lock Miss Elizabeth in their dressing room and take the key with him to the ring in his boot. He figured, that way, the other wrestlers had no choice but to keep away until he came back from the ring.

One time at a show somewhere, a fan made the unfortunate mistake of throwing an egg towards the ring and hitting the turn post. A big wad of the egg ended up in Liz's hair and Savage about lost it. He jumped out of the ring and started pointing in the audience, demanding to know who threw the egg. Fans were scared and were pointing in the direction of one particular fan that was clearly guilty. The guy looked like he had seen a ghost. Savage hopped the fence and went right after the fan, screaming obscenities. The fan ran way up into the cheap seats in the stands, with Macho right on his heels, practically the whole way. If it weren't for security, I don't know what he would have done to that fan, if he had caught him.

Another time, Jerry Saggs farted a few feet away from Miss Elizabeth on their way to a WWF London tour in a plane. The moment they got off the plane, Savage bought another ticket and sent Elizabeth home. Vince was apparently pissed, because that meant Liz was going to miss an important TV taping. Somehow, they got word to Elizabeth at a layover in Concord to wait, and they had to book these crazy last-minute plane tickets from Concord to bring her back for TV at something like $7,500 a ticket.

I remember that there were occasions in 1989 where I was asked to fill in for Hulk Hogan in the main event at some house shows.

I was super-psyched. I mean, that meant a real lot to me that they felt I could be a suitable replacement for Hulk Hogan on a card. I mean, who could replace the Hulkster and really keep the audience happy? The first time they asked me to step in for him, I was a little skeptical. I didn't want to not live up to the expectation, fall short, and then have Vince think less of me. However, in the end, everything turned out fine. Nobody asked for their money back, and I got a great response back from the crowd. There was one thing I didn't like, however.

Savage didn't trust me anywhere at all near his girl.

For the end the match, the agents said that they wanted me to place Miss Elizabeth up on my shoulders. This was leading up to a jealousy angle on TV that was going to happen soon between Hulk and Macho, ultimately breaking up their tag team, The Mega-Powers.

However, that celebratory spot idea didn't go over all that well with Savage.

He wanted absolutely no part of what he called, "Love 'em and Leave 'em Leslie," touching his girl. He complained and they scrapped the spot.

MISSY HYATT

The first time that I met Missy Hyatt was on an airplane. We were coincidentally sitting next to each other and we talked quite a bit, and she seemed like a really nice person. I learned that Vince was bringing her out for a tryout for the WWF. She was being proposed to do a new shitty interview segment for the WWF that ultimately would fail.

All the boys on the flight were interested in her, as they would also be later in the locker room because she was so beautiful. But that one airplane ride that we had together pretty much cemented things together for us.

When things were all over with the WWF, that wasn't the end. We had talked together a lot about her love of the ocean and my love of boating.

When she was set to go back home, she made it a point to see if I wanted to go boating sometime on the water.

Doing my very best to keep eye contact with her, and not to be a caveman and just stare at her beautiful body, I agreed.

Some time passed, and eventually she called. She wanted me to make good on a promise I made to her about a Jet Ski date. I had just started seeing my second wife, a girl from Massachusetts, and barely even knew her yet. Nothing was finalized yet when Missy called me up, so I was free and in the clear.

"Of course," I said.

Come to find out, Missy was staying temporarily in Sarasota, Florida with her stepmother. This made things even easier. She decided that it would be fun to go jet skiing with me while she was out in Florida.

"Any idea where we should go?" She asked.

"I know this nice little bar called Beach Nuts. At Beach Nuts, you can spin out on the water, then drive your Jet Ski right up to the beach to the bar," I suggested.

"Sounds great," she said.

So that's just what we did.

For those of you who may remember, Beach Nuts was actually out on Treasure Island. It was on West Gulf Blvd., just past the intersection with Blind Pass Road that led to Saint Pete's Beach. It was just a bit north of Caddy's and the VFW. (It's not there anymore. Now, it is sadly all condos.)

The place was really great. The whole place was decked out in bamboo. It was a bar with excellent live music and was as I had described, strangely enough, right there on the beach. It had a real tropical feel to it, with everyone holding frozen drinks with fruit in their hands. Beach Nuts had those big colorful Tiki masks everywhere, torches out on the beach, and little coconut shells used as candle holders on all of the tables.

I met up with Missy there. She gave me a big hug and then we almost immediately took to the water like two little kids anxious to get on the rides at an amusement park.

We went way out and Jet Skied all around the water. She loved it. As the sun began to set, we decided to come back in to shore for drinks.

I remember looking at her back at the bar and thinking how beautiful she was. She had her long blonde hair all pulled back, kind of like Bo Derek in the movie "10," with the braided weaves. She looked amazing.

We started drinking, and boy, let me tell you, could she really put the alcohol down.

After a few rounds of tropical beverages, there was a live DJ there who started up a set of music. He was playing some pretty crazy dance music, and Missy just loved it. She started dancing around and I started dancing around with her, with both of my two left feet.

At some point, I picked her up and spun her around. Like some girls who like a strong man, she seemed to like the spinning around thing very much. I figured that this was the case because immediately after lifting her up the first time, she started making out with me almost instantly. Just like a dog learning a new trick, I picked her up and spun around again as many times as I could, hoping for the same result. Can you blame me? When we were finally done dancing, I picked her up, spun her around one last time and then sat her down on top of the bar. She put her arms around me and started kissing me, again. With both of us a little buzzed, I was slow to notice that something smelled weird.

What is that? ...Burning hair?

Man, oh man, in all the fun, we didn't notice that her hair had flipped back behind her, and one of her braids fell right down into a coconut candle!

To make matters worse, there must have been some kind of product in her hair that was also apparently flammable. The mousse, or gel, or Aqua Net, whatever the hell it was, immediately caused the fire to spread.

PUFFF!!!

A big flame puffed up in an instant.

"Holy shit!" I said.

Frightened, Missy jumped down off of the bar top. She started to run around the bar frantically like a chicken with its head cut off, looking for a way to put the fire out. She grabbed some drinks off a table and tried emptying the glasses behind her, but to no avail.

I quickly tried to help. I ran after her as fast as I could, dodging chairs and tables, but that didn't work either.

Eventually, the bartender had enough common sense to pull her back behind the bar. He spun her around and pushed her down, having her bob her blazing braids into the sink, where he was soaking a bunch of glasses.

Soaking the flames did just the trick. The fire was out.

"Thanks, brother," I said. "That was a close one."

Missy was pulling her braids forward to assess the damage. She wrinkled up her nose and smelled the tips of her blackened singed hairs. She stuck out her bottom lip and frowned.

"You knew just what to do, sir. It actually looked like you had done that before," I said.

"Happens all the time," the bartender joked, laughing.

Missy didn't see the humor in it. I thought at first that this was the end of the night for us. After almost catching her head on fire, I figured that she was not going to be at all in the mood for any romance. But I had no idea that the fire probably helped my chances.

Missy Hyatt was crazy. I think the danger had only turned her on more!

When I went to drop her off back to where she was staying, I leaned in for a kiss goodnight. She quickly pushed the door open and said, "Wait here for me."

I thought we were done and she was about to leave, but then I realized the night was not over. She went inside, grabbed a bag with some clothing in it, and came right back out to my car.

We went out to a few more bars. We continued to drink up a storm until we closed another bar down. After that, not trying to presumptuous I said, "Okay, now what?"

I had learned that you cannot just say the obvious to most girls. That never worked. You couldn't just say, "Let's go back to my place." You had to make the girl want it and say, "Let's go back to your place." If you wanted a really good time, it had to be her idea. So even though she had a beach bag of clothing with her to wear for tomorrow, and that idea in itself gave me a very big boner, I decided not to just state the obvious.

We went and found another bar that was only open another half an hour, or so. When they decided to close up shop and turn out the lights, we realized that was about it. And that is when she said it, "Let's go back to your place." So she ended up at my house.

We both continued to drink even more at the house, and then she had had enough. She attacked me. Missy was very aggressive, and I loved it. She wanted me to pull her hair. Who was I to tell her no? So while we were fooling around I was pulling and yanking her hair, but that wasn't enough.

"Pull harder!"

Eventually, I pulled a whole handful of her braids out of her head.

As we continued with the festivities at hand, she then negotiated some ass spanking. Again, who was I to say no?

"Spank me."

So I spanked that ass like there was no tomorrow.

After that, when it was about time for the moment of truth, she decided that it would be a good idea to role play.

"I want you to chase me like you want it."

Well, it was totally obvious that I already wanted it. The "little Beefer" was clearly not so little at that point in time. But hell, she wanted me to chase her like I wanted more, so that is just what I was going to do.

We were both completely butt-naked.

"Come and get it if you can." She ran around the table and said, "If you want more, you are going to have to chase me."

I am not sure if this is a regular game that she played with her lovers in the past, but she was really good at it. I could not catch her for the life of me.

As I was just about to catch her, she threw open the screen door and ran out onto the patio. Now, I lived in a pretty nice area, and I do not think they would have appreciated waking up and seeing these shenanigans at like 3:00 am in the morning. But Missy didn't seem to care. She was screaming, "Come and get me," and then she ran over to the front lawn of my neighbor's house.

It was on.

Running completely naked, I had to tackle Missy Hyatt in the grass before she made it to their front door and did, who knows what? I was afraid she was going to ring the bell!

I don't know if you have ever had to tackle someone completely naked with an erection before, but it was not easy. When I hit the ground, all of my weight landed on my penis. It felt like somebody hit me hard in the Jimmy with Hacksaw Jim Duggan's 2x4 – a definite "head" on collision.

I finally dragged her back to the house like a caveman to save us from a police visit. She loved the whole roleplay thing. She was kicking her feet and all. It was scary, but pretty funny at the same time. Missy was crazy.

Years later, she told me that she had broken things off with Jason Hervey, a big Hollywood producer, and who became partners in a production company with Eric Bischoff. She had since bought a Ferrari with the money that he gave her, and had a lot left that she had been saving for a big idea. She finally decided that she wanted to start up a subscription porn site featuring girls from wrestling.

"Can you think of any good places in Tampa where we could shoot pictures of a bunch of drunk naked girls," she asked.

I told her, "of course."

Then I called up a neighbor of mine, Loose Bruce Bernstein, who was a photographer and a big boat guy too.

"Have I got a gig for you!"

He was delighted. When I told him that she just broke up with a Hollywood producer and she bought herself a Ferrari with the money he left her, it didn't take long for him to grab his camera.

We were in the car, practically right after I hung up the phone!

The days of debauchery and alcohol that followed are now a big huge blur to me. All I remember was a bunch of drunken naked hoochie-mama girls. Another guy at the shoot, Mark Mancuso, told me he took the all the girls out to Madeira Beach, and he would have the girls go at it. Bruce was practically shooting soft porn scenes all over the island! It was all like "Girls Gone Wild" kind of stuff, but maybe even worse.

Missy had a few other female wrestlers there with not much fame and not much in the moral department either. Sunny was there too, but we didn't talk much. She was a mess. She was already drooling over a bottle of Vodka and drooling over her new flavor of the month, some indy worker named Jeff Starr.

I do remember that Missy was in her heyday. She looked really good and was the only one I was really interested in seeing naked. I'm pretty sure we were just as naked as the models were, most of the time.

She wasn't the only female wrestler, however, that I have been connected to…

CHYNA

Back in August of 1990, after my parasailing accident, Greg's wife was helping to watch over me some.

She knew this pretty cool aerobics instructor, who also was a waitress at the Dollhouse in Tampa. She thought it would be a good idea to introduce us. That is when I first met the woman who would eventually be known as, "The Ninth Wonder of The World."

Seven years or so before Chyna would debut standing outside of a WWF ring, Joanie Laurer was spending some time standing at my bedside. We met at a time where we had to have people there watching me 24/7, just in case my face were to fall off, or in case something bad would have happened to me.

Joanie was a great, great help to me at my worst of all times. She had a great bedside manner and was very helpful to me, both in a nurse-like fashion and for my spirits.

After things were looking better for me physically, Joanie went out on the town with me some. As a thank you for being there, I brought her to some of the best restaurants I could to really show her the best gratitude that I could for all she had done.

Joanie at this point was around 21. She was really into fitness then, but she was not at all what I would call "jacked" yet, as she would later look on WWF television with DX. She was still very femininely attractive, however. She had that "farmer's daughter" kind of look to her which I loved. We dated a bit.

She got in on a couple of road trips with me. I did some wrestling shows, and she immediately fell in love with the business. She got bit by the bug.

The next year or so, off and on, we would go out when I was in town. Sometimes she would stop over for some dinners with the Hogan family, and she still maintained her friendship with Julie and Greg.

She told me that she would go and visit her parents. Her dad owned an old marina in the Keyes. They would always ask her about her dinners with me, and her time over at Hogan's place. They were always very interested in what she had to share, but by no means, did they want her to get into wrestling herself.

When you tell a younger person that they cannot do something, usually they want to do it even more. Joanie eventually became more and more intrigued with the idea of professional wrestling. After she had another good three or four more month taste of Hulk Hogan's family and a behind-the-scenes peek of wrestling, she wanted it for herself. So finally, one day, she went off to the Keyes again to tell her father she had made up her mind.

"No way!" Her father said. "You need to go back to school, and make something of your life."

I remember her calling me, all upset that her family was not supportive of her training to become a wrestler. I gave her some contact info, and that was about it. She was off and I wouldn't hear from her again for a few years, anyhow. During that period of time, I had no idea that she actually used the number. That really was the last time I had seen of her for a long time. She went off to Boston to train with Killer Kowalski by herself.

I guess she moved somewhere up by New Hampshire and started training at Walter's school; the same place that was also training Triple H at the same time. She got really into weightlifting and the rest is history.

RICK RUDE'S SISTER, NANCY

"I remember being at a party one time at Terry's place. All the wives were there. Greg's wife Julie. Linda Hogan. We all got on this Scarab boat Terry had just bought. It was really fast. I didn't know why at the time the other wives wouldn't get on, but quickly figured it out. One of the Nasty Boys was all set to drive. Now, I'll admit, when I saw that, I was hesitant to get on, and I shouldn't have. The Ride was terrifying! I was barely hanging on, with my legs flying off the back behind me. After we finally docked again, I was so dizzy, I fell off the dock and hit my head. I busted right open. There was blood everywhere. Brutus came running over to help. When he saw how much blood there was, he almost barfed. I thought it was funny, because here he was, a big tough wrestler, but at the sight of a woman bleeding - he took off running! Anyhow, Brain Blair came over and said, 'We better go get you some stitches. I can see your brain.' We washed up my head, and when it was all nice and clean, Brutus drove me to the hospital."   - Nancy Rude

Another girl who was a little in and out of my life, due to the crazy schedule that the WWF demanded was Rick Rude's sister, Nancy.

Nancy played the role of Rick's ring valet under the stage name Raven. She started out managing her brother in Texas for Fritz Von Erich, replacing Missy Hyatt when she left in her feud with Sunshine. That whole family must have had the good-looks gene. In the eyes of a WCCW fan, replacing Missy would be tough, but Nancy pulled it off. Years later, Nancy was a showgirl in the Las Vegas Strip production of "Abracadabra."

Now Rick was probably just as much of a dog as I was. He knew the deal. So when he saw me hanging around with Nancy, he wanted absolutely no part of that happening. There was probably some kind of self-projection going on. I know for a fact that he was pretty rough in relationships, and probably just assumed that I would be also, seeing how I was also a wrestler like he was.

To protect the business, a lot of the times guys who were riding together would have to meet up in strange places after the show so that fans didn't see them leave together. You probably have heard the story of how Hacksaw Jim Duggan got pulled over with the Iron Sheik together, and getting charged with having weed on the dashboard, or something like that. One of the big things that made that an odd story was that they were facing each other in the ring that very same night. To avoid fan exposure of people riding together who really shouldn't, sometimes a wrestler would go drive a few blocks away from the arena, and then pick up their companion then. This is what I had to do with Nancy, to hide the fact that she was riding with me from her own brother.

One time, Nancy came to the arena to pick me up after a show. The whole back lot was filled with wrestling fans, so it was going to be very difficult for me to walk down the road a piece without being seen. We had to time it just right. I watched out the back door window. When she finally pulled up, she was about 50 feet from the door, and Rick was still lurking around backstage. I really think he may have known and was trying to catch us in the act. He just wouldn't seem to leave the area. When the moment was right, she reached back and opened the passenger door. I literally had to dive into her Buick so Rick didn't see us, getting into the car together. After that, one of the boys said Rick was looking for me when I had left.

We did this for a long time. Whenever I was in Cleveland, we always got together. Being a WWF Superstar sure was awesome, but it was lonely. Having someone around like her was the best at that time in my life. She was really fun to hang with and she could party just like one of the boys. She was down for anything. I could be gone for months, and it wouldn't matter to her. We would pick up where we had left off like nothing had happened.

The night before my big accident, we were all at the dock. We were throwing a little party to test out one of the new toys, and Nancy Rude showed up. She was always around. She jumped on the new Ninja Jet Ski, just like one of the boys. She chipped her tooth that night, but kept on going and didn't skip a beat. We became really good friends. After my accident, she was right there helping me when I needed it most.

After a while, I started becoming a little more accepted in her family. I met her parents, and I even had dinner sometimes with them. One night, I remember Nancy told me her father's analysis of me.

"You know, Nancy," he told her after meeting me at a dinner one morning after a show. "Brutus really is not supposed to be a big guy. I looked at his wrists and everything, his frame isn't really made to carry all that weight in muscle."

"Oh yeah?" she asked.

"Yeah. I mean, he ordered six breakfasts this morning, probably trying to keep all that weight on," he said.

A year or so later, Rick Rude knew we were kind of seeing each other, off and on. Just as he was starting to seem okay with it, a rumor started to pass around that I had banged Valentine's sister-in-law, Julie's sibling. When Rick had caught wind of this, boy, was he pissed.

I had no idea the rumor was even out there. If I had, I would have been looking around everywhere, behind closed doors, to make sure I didn't just run into Rick. But I had no idea. When I showed up to a show one afternoon, Rick was waiting for me.

When he saw me across the locker room, I knew something was up. He came running right at me.

"Get over here Beefcake!" he demanded. "Now!"

Rather than to walk right over and essentially toss myself into a fight with the raging Rick Rude, I decided to do what any decent and sophisticated man would do - *run*.

"Who else's sister do you want to fuck?" Rick yelled, chasing me around the outside halls of the arena.

"I don't know what you are talking about!" I said, running with him.

Okay, I will admit it. Yes, he was right. But I didn't bring Toni, Greg's sister-in-law around with me ever. I never brought her anywhere near the boys, and she really wasn't a companion of mine like Nancy was. Toni lived in Nashville and I would only really ever see her when I was in Nashville. Looking back now, when she moved to Florida, I didn't see her anymore anyhow, so it is true that she wasn't all that special to me. She wasn't any different to me than my California girl, Sam Kinison's wife's best friend who was a star from adult films, who will remain nameless.

This was all back in a different time, however, and I was still back in my party days. Anyhow, I will come clean for the sake of this book:

I dated Toni, Greg Valentine's wife's sister briefly, but then Knobbs got my leftovers and married it. (Just kidding!)

NOW... HAPPILY EVER AFTER

I was married a second time, but the only good thing that really came out of that was my daughter. My second marriage was a whole lot of sleeping on the couch and being hen-pecked. Some years later, I was pretty much separated from my second wife, but still under the same roof

A picture of a fan that approached me after a show many years ago.

because of our child. After all the coldness, I was ready to move on.

Before that bad second marriage, something happened on the road many years before that would eventually lead to "Happily Ever After."

After a WWF house show in Massachusetts back in 1997, a girl ran up to me, at the Boston Garden when I was leaving. I was late for my plane, so I was in a rush. I had just cleaned up, was soaking wet and still carrying my towel from the shower.

"Brutus," she said, running backwards directly in front of me as I was walking toward the garage. I looked down to see this girl barely out of high school, staring at me like a deer in headlights with big green eyes. "Oh my God, oh my God, oh my God!"

"Okay, darling. Where do I sign? Do you have a magazine or something?" I said, thinking that she wanted an autograph. She just pulled out a camera and snapped a shot of me. I laughed. I kept it moving, just trying to get to my car.

"I love you," she said.

I stopped. I was shocked and that took me by surprise. Women would scream that they loved me all the time from the stands. Hell, everyone did! But there was something about the way she said it. I mean, she sounded serious.

"You love me?" I asked.

"Yes."

"Well, thank you," I replied, not knowing really what to say other than that.

"Please. Can I have that towel?" She reached for the white terry cloth around my neck.

"I can't," I said. I wouldn't give it up. "What if I get cold?" I gave her a quick hug and figured that was close enough. Then, I walked off. I knew I was maybe breaking that young girl's heart over a hotel towel that didn't even belong to me, but I had already learned I couldn't give my stuff to fans. If I gave a towel to one fan, and my shirt to another, and a sock to the next, and so on and so forth, I would be totally naked by the time I made it to the airport. But in hindsight, I probably should have made an exception to the girl in Boston who said that she loved me.

It was funny how timing works. Once I was resolved to leave my second wife, I got a weird message on Facebook from someone who said she was a big fan. She asked if I remembered the girl with the "big green-eyes from Boston who said she loved me."

Fast forward a number of years later... I married that same girl from Boston. Now, whenever I come home from a road trip, I always bring back a little white towel from the hotel I was staying in to give to my wife. When I walk in the door, I hand it to her and tell her, "I love you, too."

A picture of us that Missy took before a show. She was fresh out of high school.

The actual shot of me with the towel that Missy wanted. She saved it all these years.

CHAPTER 21 - WCW

"Brutus was a great neighbor and all-around friend to have. He was only 4 min. and was a great barbecue man. Many a day I would cruise over to Beefer's place ana some shrimp, or lobster. But even more so, he knew pretty much everything about the ocea. His place was right on it. You could get out of his pool, and then you would only be 20 feet away from the sand of the beach.

One time, my girlfriend Heather called me. There was a huge storm coming and no one was supposed to be in the water by the coast. Everyone abandoned the island, and Heather was getting ready to leave, as well. She looked outside, and there was a man out in the raging water with the skies quickly turning black. Brutus in the water, looking like Aquaman. Hulk Hogan had one of his 32-foot boats out in the water, and Brutus was out there like a madman saving it. Incredible." - Bushwhacker Luke

Finishing off a great payday in Japan, I soon was fully immersed in the acting world.

Hulk Hogan was contemplating retirement. He had some heat with Vince McMahon because Vince kept trying to replace him, seemingly, with the Ultimate Warrior, and also there was the pending steroid trial coming up in which Hulk was going to have to testify. Because of this, Hulk decided to start looking at the offers that had been stacking up from Hollywood.

Eventually, he signed a movie deal with the creators of Baywatch, and we were off to film the first *Thunder in Paradise* television-movie, with the TV series to immediately follow.

Filming *Thunder in Paradise* was a great time for me. We shot it right in Florida and it was almost like Knight Rider with a boat instead of a racecar. Boats were right up my alley, so you know I was in heaven. We started filming the whole first season of 22 episodes. We were at Disney the whole year long.

The story itself followed the adventures of two ex-Navy SEALS; Hurricane Spencer played by Hulk Hogan, and Martin Brubaker (Hurricane's buddy) played by Chris Lemmon. They operated their underground crime-fighting operation out of their tropical resort headquarters hidden in the Florida's Gulf Coast. Using their futuristic, high-tech boat, nicknamed "Thunder", they traveled around the world fighting crime! However, Hurricane was forced to balance his dangerous undercover work with his middle-class responsibilities of having to raise his younger daughter Jessica.

The producers were smart. Since they knew that there would be the ,otential for a lot of crossover wrestling fans as an audience, they had no problem having the Hulkster book some of his friends who were familiar faces from the squared circle to also appear with him on the big screen. Some of the guys from the WWF crew included Jim the Anvil, Hercules Hernandez, and Terry Funk. Then, later we enlisted some WCW guys who were right nearby shooting in Orlando like Sting.

To make a huge impact, the first movie had a huge man, not unfamiliar to wrestling fans. Jorge González was a giant basketball player from Argentina. González had wrestled some in World Championship Wrestling under the ring name "El Gigante" from 1989 to 1992. Right after that, he worked for the WWF where I met him, as a Bigfoot-looking bastard named Giant González.

THE WCW TRANSITION

As I mentioned before, we were shooting in Orlando, the same place as Ted Turner's rival wrestling promotion, which was a major thorn in Vince McMahon's side.

The majority of WCW's television tapings were at MGM Studios. Thunder in Paradise would shoot at MGM on "Soundstage A" at the very same time on occasion that WCW was shooting at "Soundstage B." This was totally coincidental, but pretty cool. From time to time, I am not going to lie, I wandered over and said hello to a couple of the guys.

I came to find out from talking to some of the boys that WCW's business wasn't doing so hot. Ticket sales were the shits. The ratings were down. The WWF had pretty much dominated the entire wrestling scene everywhere by this point, and things didn't look good. There had been some serious talk that Ted Turner was considering shutting down the promotion and getting out of the business altogether.

THE BLACK SATURDAY BACK HISTORY

Before explaining why Ted Turner may have been willing to pay Hulk Hogan the big bucks to change his new-found focus on acting and consider a comeback to wrestling, it is important to know this backstory. Ted Turner hated Vince McMahon and often made some expensive and at times arguably unwise business decisions, in order to ultimately exact some kind of revenge.

Ted Turner had owned the television airing rights of Georgia Championship Wrestling since 1972, and he was very proud of the success of this show. The two-hour long program aired every Saturday night from 6-8 PM, or later from 6:05 to 8:05. Because of its growing fan base, it had become the main NWA, and also the first NWA territory to be carried by many cable and satellite providers across the country.

In 1982, Georgia Championship Wrestling changed its name to WCW - World Championship Wrestling. At this time, the promotion itself was being operated by Jack Brisco and Gerald Brisco, Jim Barnett, and Ole Anderson who was the head booker. WCW was a great alternative wrestling program for traditionalists who didn't like what Vince McMahon was trying to usher in. Many hardcore wrestling fans believed that McMahon's attempt to mainstream wrestling as a form of entertainment instead of a sport was horrible, because of an emphasis on cartoon-like gimmicks. WCW, in turn, emphasized a more athletic sports-based product. If you have ever heard Gordon Solie commentate, you will know what I mean. He was an NWA announcer who I knew from his days with Championship Wrestling from Florida. He also hosted programs for various other NWA affiliated promotions at the time and brought a sense of realism to WCW that was unparalleled.

In 1983, Vince McMahon began his master plan to expand the WWF to a nationwide audience by use of cable television. Many felt he was throwing away the gentlemen's agreement seemingly all wrestling promoters had by doing this. Before this, there were very well-defined borders of where promoters could run their matches. They would never cross the borders with their product. Everyone respected this tradition and worked together, subsequently. "You stay on your side of the fence, and I'll stay on mine – then everyone will be happy." However, Vince's first step was to ignore the old way of doing things. He wanted to get a national timeslot on cable television with the intent to do it as a commercial for his product – *then ultimately compete in every market.*

His first step was purchasing Southwest Championship Wrestling's Sunday morning timeslot contract on the USA Network. He replaced that programming with his own show, WWF's *All American Wrestling*. In addition to that, he created two more shows for syndication to reach other areas called, WWF Championship Wrestling and WWF All-Star Wrestling. Then he made a wrestling talk show called Tuesday Night Titans to also air on USA.

I am sure that Ted Turner saw what McMahon was doing. Rather than to secure his own new timeslots to feature his product, Turner felt he was buying out his competitor's to take their place and defeat competition at the same time. Eventually, McMahon decided that he wanted to control all nationally-televised professional wrestling in the United States by taking over WCW. However, when he made Turner an offer to buy the historic GCW/WCW time slot on Saturday night, Turner scoffed at the thought.

McMahon was a workaholic, however. I remember talking with him into the wee hours of the night with Hulk and him saying "sleep is your enemy." It is this "never say never" attitude that made Vince McMahon into the success that he is today. I don't think Ted Turner at the time knew that McMahon was going to do whatever he could to find a way to securing the last remaining national cable slot for the WWF.

While WCW had a loyal fan base and was very popular, Vince learned that things were not as great behind the scenes. Putting some feelers out there, Vince learned that Ole Anderson was locking horns with his fellow owners by the way he was operating the promotion. McMahon identified the weakness and decided to strike.

Knowing he couldn't buy the timeslot from Turner, Vince set up a secret meeting with the Brisco brothers and Jim Barnett. McMahon offered them roles in the WWF, as well as some good money and all three men agreed to sell their stock. This gave the WWF the controlling stake in WCW. Ultimately, by hook or crook, McMahon took over the Saturday night timeslot.

On July 7, 1984, was the end for a group of fans. That was when the last World Championship Wrestling episode aired. Many of them soon after that referred to July 14, 1984 as being "Black Saturday," the first week of WWF programming on TBS. First off, that initial WWF episode had no Gordon Solie. He had either resigned, or was terminated, but the staple voice of the program that everyone knew from that timeslot was gone. Then, the former show's co-host, Freddie Miller, introduced Vince McMahon who many felt stood for what was the direct opposite what the fan base wanted. McMahon promised the fans that they would love the new show more. The WWF's TBS show, however, was not live wrestling matches shot from the TBS studio, however. It was mostly a highlight show derived from using clips of their other programs, and some occasional house show footage.

Ted Turner was beyond pissed when he saw the new WWF product. On top of that, hate mail was flooding his office from angry WCW fans, often accusing him of being a sell-out and accusing him of being the catalyst of change in the programming.

Then, Vince's plan became evident. "WWF Georgia Championship Wrestling" on TBS quickly became an infomercial-like platform to promote the first WrestleMania. The purchase of GCW was all part of his big gamble;

he needed it for more exposure. On March 2, 1985, the WWF began airing in-studio squash matches commentated by Freddie Miller and new play-by-play commentator Gorilla Monsoon. These programs ran until March 30, 1985, the day before WrestleMania. After that, McMahon sold the slot to Jim Crockett, who had taken over WCW.

However, McMahon's purchase of the timeslot led to a rivalry between himself and WTBS owner Ted Turner. He had also purchased an enemy for life. Eventually, Ted Turner bought WCW from Jim Crockett Promotions, to run against the WWF - just to piss off Vince McMahon.

MEGA DEAL

For almost ten years, Ted Turner never really got the revenge he wanted by purchasing WCW. Vince's gamble paid off and all competition was minimal, at best. Ted Turner's wrestling company was doing poorly, but then, someone from within came up with an idea. One of the commentators saw Hulk Hogan as being the potential fix for the problem. That was Eric Bischoff.

Eric had Ric Flair go over to the set of Thunder in Paradise and had him introduce him to Hulk. Hulk had an idea what the introduction was for, and he was right. Eric offered him some kind of deal without real numbers, when he really didn't have the power yet to do anything of the sort, in the company.

Hulk hesitated on even the idea of going back to wrestling. We talked about it later that night. We both agreed that it would be only worth it if it were some real major cash. We also figured that if he held out, the number could possibly go up and up. We were right.

After ignoring a number of attempts from Eric Bischoff, Hulk eventually agreed to meet with Ted Turner. Eric had set up a rare face-to-face meeting between the two. Normally, a man of Ted Turner's stature would not have met with prospective talent for one of his shows, but he hated Vince and made an exception. Ted was willing to pay to snatch up Vince McMahon's former poster-child. Being somewhere in May 1994, I think, Ted offered Hulk $2.5 million dollars to finish out the year. He also agreed to pay out plus 25 percent of any additional revenue WCW PPVs would see featuring Hogan from whatever was earned in the previous year.

Hogan agreed.

The plan worked. Fans were finally able to see the dream match, Hulk Hogan versus Ric Flair that never panned out in the WWF. The feud continued and made big money for the promotion. Ted Turner was impressed and started to give Eric Bischoff more and more power. He loosened the purse strings and agreed to bring in some celebrities like Shaquille O'Neil and Mr. T for big paydays.

Then, deciding to "give it back" to McMahon, Ted Turner began to lure away important talent from Vince. Turner agreed to what would have previously been considered too expensive of a talent signing to consider. Eric Bischoff signed Macho Man Randy Savage for something like $400,000.

BROTHER BRUTI

In 1994, I too was set to debut in World Championship Wrestling. At first, I only made small appearances with Hulk Hogan for his promotional appearances. The first month or so was all just like press conferences and promos about Hulk finally coming to WCW. Hulk didn't even really know what to call me. Initially, I was part of his entourage and only in a few promos here and there. Borrowing from a nickname that Gorilla Monsoon had said from time to time on WWF programming, Hulk referred to me as "Brother Bruti," pronounced "Bru-Tie."

He had called me this back in the day when we were tag team partners in WWF, back in 1989 and 1993, so it made sense. But why not Brutus? Or Barber? Or Beefcake, one may ask? Yes, you guessed it. There were legal issues with the name.

When I checked into it, my trademark attorney said those three words were owned by the World Wrestling Federation. It didn't make sense, because I had gone through a copyright process in the past for the name. However, upon my exit from the company, they pushed some paperwork through upon my exit from the Federation, and my lawyer told me that they actually trademarked my name illegally.

"Once a trademarking is done, however, getting it undone from a huge company like the WWF is going to be tough," he said. "My professional opinion is it could cost you more than it is worth, and then you may not even undo it in the end."

So, yes, while I was leaving in 1993, someone in the office seemingly maliciously trademarked my name and likeness. They didn't need it, they just didn't want me using it somewhere else. That paperwork meant I couldn't wrestle with a name that sounded like my old name, and I couldn't even look like my old self. I also couldn't do any of the barber stuff that I had created.

"How long does it last?" I asked the attorney. "I mean, is it theirs forever?"

"No. The trademark is good for about seven years, so it's theirs until 2000," he replied.

I was screwed.

I went to Eric Bischoff. I learned that while they did consider me an asset, I wasn't really as valuable to them without the possibility of the scissors in hand. Unfortunately for me, I also learned that WCW wasn't interested in trying to challenge the WWF in court over the gimmick.

Hogan beat Flair in his first WCW match at the Bash at The Beach PPV on July 17. Then, at Clash of the Champions XXVIII, I attacked Hulk Hogan in his next match with Flair, but I was wearing a mask.

I didn't know exactly what I was going to be called at this point, but we did, however, know I was going to be part of Hulk's next feud after Flair took some scheduled time off.

So much for Hogan's retirement from the ring, or my focus on acting. I was still in and out of movie sets doing some stunt work, but it was clear, the wrestling bug had bitten us once again. For me, money had nothing to do with it. I guess it was just something that when it gets in your blood, it never leaves you.

THE BUTCHER & THREE FACES OF FEAR

To work me into a run against Hulk Hogan, Kevin Sullivan's slower brother Dave Sullivan first started to worship the Hulkster. The fact that David became a Hulkamaniac really bothered his brother. Kevin developed a jealous hatred of Hulk, and eventually beat up his own brother and disowned him. Then Kevin Sullivan began to concoct some evil devious plans against him.

Kevin was a short stocky son-of-a-bitch. He had a Boston accent, but don't let that fool you. He was one of the very great minds in the business and, therefore, subsequently was booking for WCW. In the prime of his career, he used religious beliefs to get over – by taping on the taboos of many wrestling fans. He outwardly called himself a devil worshiper to get heat. He brought snakes to the ring, performed satanic rituals, and engaged in evil spirit-evoking incantations. Knowing he was in the twilight of his career, he decided to give it a last go against one of the biggest names in the business to go out with a bang.

The main event of *Clash of the Champions 25* was supposed to be the new WCW World Heavyweight Champion Hulk Hogan defending his title against Ric Flair. However, right at the start of the show, we borrowed an angle from the news to shake things up a little and place the match in jeopardy.

A short time before this pay-per-view, there was a very widely-known scandal between two Olympic figure skaters. For those of you who don't remember, or are just too young to really know, there was an arguably semi-white trash skater named Tonya Harding, who was very much like a wrestling villain in her underhanded attempted to have her biggest threat eliminated from competition. What she did was put a hit out on the "odds-in-favor to win," Nancy Kerrigan, by having her thug friends baton her in the knee with a steel pipe.

To strike a chord with wrestling fans for our angle, Hulk Hogan was similarly attacked by a man wearing a spandex bodysuit and a black mask. The mysterious assailant nailed "The Master of The Leg Drop" Hulk Hogan knee's in a similar fashion with a big nasty metal pipe.

For those of you keeping track, the man under the mask was actually not me. If you go back and look on the tape, you will see the body in the suit was a little shorter and a little heavier. The hooded wrestler that night was not me, it was actually Arn Anderson! I was still making appearances as "Brother Bruti" and the plan was supposed to be to continue that. However, Arn Anderson was never supposed to be revealed as the attacker in black either. The original plan was to eventually lift the mask and reveal Curt Hennig. However, the plans changed before that was able to happen.

On multiple occasions throughout October 1994, Hulk Hogan tried to identify just who exactly was his mystery attacker. Finally at Halloween Havoc, following Hulk Hogan's big win over Ric Flair in a steel cage match, the mysterious man ran out once again to attack the Hulkster, but this time was different.

This time the hood was lifted, and it was I who was revealed to be the man in black.

We had to drop the Brother Bruti name. Brother was just too friendly sounding, and I was now to take on a role of Hogan's enemy. Soon after, they started calling me "The Butcher."

Needing to look more heel as a character being master-minded by Kevin Sullivan, The Butcher was always to be dressed all in black. Wearing the dark regalia was very different from my bright, flashy Brutus Beefcake gimmick. The funny thing about it is, I still had the black pants that I wore for my skunk-looking, run-in man gimmick we called Fur Face. I decided that they would be perfect for this brand new role for me. If you look at the

Butcher's tights from WCW, they are the same black leggings I used for my Fur Face gimmick with skulls on one leg, and a big ax on the other.

Shortly afterward, the Butcher and Sullivan were joined by another former WWF wrestler, the former Earthquake, now renamed Avalanche, and formed The Three Faces of Fear with the goal of destroying Hulkamania.

The Three Faces of Fear with Kevin Sullivan finally finished it off by adding their third member Avalanche, aka Earthquake. Avalanche's timing couldn't have been greater. For a period of time, he could not get out of his WWF contract. When he finally was released, they brought him right in to become the third member of the 3 Faces of Fear.

The Butcher's trademark tights in WCW were the exact same ones worn by The Run-In Man in WWF. (See page 279.)

The Three Faces of Fear was the initial run of Kevin Sullivan booking for Hulk Hogan. This was like a courtship, to some degree – a means of the both of them working together and building up trust. Because a top talent name like Hulk Hogan had a lot of creative pull when they were on top, it was always important to work well with the booker and/or producer and make sure everyone was happy with the direction that both the character and the storyline was moving in.

A lot of guys had a creative control clause written into their contracts back in these days. This clause was important where decisions about their characters had to always be a collaborative effort, and both sides had to agree on everything. That's just how the business was in that era. I had elements of the same type of thing written into my WWF contract. Back in the territorial days, this type agreement was the norm. Sure, a creative control clause made it harder to book shows for promoters, but it kept your brand alive and kept you marketable for future promotions. Wrestlers had an easier time finding work with other companies because of this clause, because they still looked strong when they left. You see, we could protect our image and stay valuable by controlling how fans viewed us on television, even when leaving a market.

To call a spade a spade, Hulk decided to book my participation in this and all of my future WCW storylines. This could be why I was never really written for by any of the regular WCW bookers/writers in any consistent manner. If Hulk had an idea for me, as part of his creative control, that's just what we went with.

At *Clash of the Champions XXIX* in 1994, The Three Faces lost to Hulk Hogan, Dave Sullivan, and Sting. Then in December at *Starrcade 1994*, I was managed by Kevin Sullivan for my big title match against Hogan for the WCW World Heavyweight Title. After losing that, Randy Savage appeared and teased a possible alliance with our Three Faces of Fear, but then actually joined the Hogan camp. The point to this was to set up a big tag team main event with Sullivan and myself versus Hogan and Savage at *Clash of the Champions XXX* later on in January 1995.

Everyone involved then went off in different directions and the Three Faces of Fear folded. That match ended the program between the Faces of Fear and Hulk Hogan, who went off to start his run with Vader. Avalanche began a feud with Sting. Sullivan started a run with me. Due to the "injuries" I sustained, they started up a storyline where I had lost my memory.

THE MAN WITH NO NAME

I then became known as "The Man with No Name." This was short-lived, however. At *Slamboree 1995*, I lost to Kevin Sullivan and then mysteriously disappeared off of TV.

I know everyone says that, in the commentary booth, they said I had been injured by Kevin Sullivan who attacked me, blaming me for dropping the ball at the end of the Hogan run and losing for our team. The commentators said I lost my memory from that beat down. The thing about it is that, at the time, I wasn't even initially informed that I was supposed to be the Butcher with amnesia, by the writers. In fact, to this very day, I don't even remember that even being the case.

I feel like everyone told me I was supposed to play "Man With No Name" as a different character completely. Maybe they did tell me about the amnesia element of my character, but if they did, I ironically can't remember it! Maybe with all the chairshots over the years and the accident and all, I lost my memory of how this really panned out!

CHAPTER 22 - ZODIAC & THE BOOTY MAN

"Brutus was a huge part of the 80s bombardment of professional wrestling into the mainstream. He is iconic and a crossover name all wrestling fans will always remember. One thing that always amazed me was he was able to transform himself to play whatever character was asked of him. He was always in top shape and always looked how a pro wrestler should have looked like. He is a real credit to the business."

— Kevin Sullivan, Prince of Darkness

It was the Summer of 1995. WCW writers hadn't come up with the idea of the nWo yet, and they still needed a major storyline to get back on the map to compete with the WWF who was killing it in the ratings. The time of Sting being the major babyface and Ric Flair being the major heel had gone, and was no longer effective in the ratings against Vince McMahon's product at that time. WCW needed something new.

Hulk Hogan was supposed to be the new ratings fix for the company, but he wasn't entirely being accepted by the WCW fans yet. This was probably in part due to the same reasons people didn't like the WWF taking over the WCW television timeslot for a short time before the first WrestleMania. Atlanta crowds were a different type of wrestling fan.

Because of this, Hulk Hogan was getting booed! Kevin Sullivan was a booker then, and he needed to come up with something to shake things up. He wanted something that would both work for Hulk Hogan and also work for the ratings.

The reason he created this crazy faction of 20 ridiculous characters was initially to build trust with Hulk Hogan for something very big down the road. Hogan wasn't a technical wrestler and needed a different storyline to compliment his wrestling style. At the same time, WCW's fan base was growing to the company's acquisition of Hogan. He just wasn't fitting into that style of wrestling that WCW was accustomed to.

In the past, Hulk Hogan had all of these massive feuds in the WWF with the kingpins of different manager's factions. These cornerstones were always really big characters like Andre the Giant, King Kong Bundy, Big John Studd, Big Boss Man, Earthquake, and Zeus. Kevin figured that if he could it would be easy for him to wrestle people he was comfortable with and end up ripping his shirt off, standing in the middle of the ring and posing.

"What would Vince do?" Kevin asked himself when sitting in front of a pen and paper, trying to come up with the next big thing for the show.

That is when it happened. The light bulb went off over his head. He was going to present an almost gang of evil cartoon-like characters that Hogan could easily work with, much like what he looked at in the WWF, but only worse. Hogan would take on each of the threats, and then defeat them one by one.

That is when he created the Dungeon of Doom.

The presentation was over-the-top. This storyline was to include wrestling storylines with doses of super-human powers like teleportation and magic. It was crafted to be tongue in cheek with bizarre sci-fi elements like monsters and spirits, lightning and thunder, and giants and leprechauns.

The members were a who's who of ridiculous gimmicks, and if they weren't ridiculous enough to be in the Dungeon, Kevin had them amp up their presentation even more.

For one, Avalanche was back, but this time his new name was "The Shark." The man formerly known as Earthquake in the WWF was also prior to this point known by the WCW audience as a former member of "The Three Faces of Fear." For this new role, he painted his face with teeth and tried to make himself look like a shark as much as possible. He talked about biting any Hulkamaniac that got in his way. Buying into the gimmick as much as he could, he even went so far as to have the big tattoo of a tiger on his arm lasered off and changed into a big great white shark.

Too bad for John Tenta and his investment in new body art, however. The gimmick didn't last as long as they had projected. It took a tattoo artist over 24 full hours to transform his tiger ink into a shark, but The Shark gimmick itself only lasted a few months for him, before they did away with his new character!

Haku was a dungeon dweller, too, renamed Meng. For his appearances, he wore some big crazy dragon head that made him look like a either a college football mascot, or something from Disney World.

We also had some actor-turned-wrestlers, as well. A familiar face, now known in WCW as "Z-Gangsta," made an appearance. Yes, my friend Tiny Lister was back; the same guy who was formerly known as Zeus from *No Holds Barred*. Another actor from the very same movie was also brought in. He was the 6' 4", 405 lb. Jeep Swenson. Possibly Jeep's best-known character was when he played Bane in the 1997 film, *Batman & Robin*. His name in the Dungeon was The Ultimate Solution. Hulk and I actually first met him while we were working in the AWA.

Some of the other DOD members included Kamala, One Man Gang, Barbarian, Big Bubba, Konnan, Jacqueline, Big Van Vader, Hugh

Morrus, Loch Ness, The Yeti (who was a ridiculous mummy,) and Braun The Leprechaun, (yes, a Leprechaun!)

The Dungeon of Doom set was built in my hometown of Tampa. It was set up in a studio where they shot a lot of local commercials. When we first started out shooting the initial introductions for the Dungeon, we were on set, all day for a total of five days. At the same time, we were also wrestling at Universal Studios. It was really busy. We would wrestle early on at the TV tapings in Orlando and then go back over at night to shoot even more in Tampa.

We had about a dozen vignettes all filmed, leading up to the last big one on the set; the introduction of one more major villain who would be playing a giant role in the Dungeon of Doom. He debuted breaking through a stone wall.

"The Giant" was played by Paul Wight, who would later be known to the world as "The Big Show."

Paul was actually initially a basketball guy that Hogan and I ran into one day and saw some promise in. It was a classic case for him of being in the right place at the right time. The first time we saw him, he was in Chicago, I believe. He was with Mr. T playing for a charity basketball game at some fundraiser. I remember thinking that he looked like Godzilla out there on the court just winging balls and shooting baskets. After the event, we just had to pull him aside and get his number. A few weeks later, we brought him into Florida and trained Paul White, with big plans for the seven-foot giant.

To get Paul used to bumping in the ring, we had to get him off of his feet. Being such a big guy, he wasn't all that keen on dropping to the mat at first. It really was against his nature. I remember I bodyslammed him one time when we were training. You should have seen the look in his eyes when he got up. "Holy shit," he said. Since then, he has gained a lot of weight and looks like a real giant. I am not sure I could still lift him over my head today, or if I would even want to!

The commentators did such a good job building him up and putting him over. To help make him be even more feared, they explained that he was the actual son of the late Andre the Giant. They did such a good job with all that hype that even to this very day, people still believe that this is true. Fans often ask The Big Show about, "his father Andre."

THE ZODIAC

So let's see… What was my custom character, again?

My role in the Dungeon of Doom was a character that underground hardcore wrestling fans still talk about to this very day, as well.

After wrestling as "The Butcher" when The Three Faces of Fear broke up in May of 1995, the commentators explained that I contracted amnesia. For a month or so, I didn't know who I was, so the commentators called me, "The Man with No Name." I will admit, that gimmick wasn't the greatest idea and really went nowhere. So after a little break off of TV, we decided to go back to the drawing board and reboot me with yet another character for my return.

Behind the scenes, Hulk wanted me to reunite with my master, Kevin Sullivan, and join his new faction. One primary reason he did this was so that he would have someone familiar there to work against.

For those of you who remember my character for this run, I was a crazy looking, insane character who wore black and white tights and black and white face paint. …And the only words anyone ever heard me say were, "Yes, no, yes, no!"

Yes. I was The Zodiac. (Yes. No. Yes. No!)

What many people do not know, however, the Zodiac was not a new gimmick at all. I actually plagiarized myself. Borrowing from a gimmick that was played on screen only a short amount of time in the opening credits of the movie Mr. Nanny, I decided to bring back to life a character that I figured probably nobody had remembered.

I was right.

Do you remember seeing the Zodiac in Mr. Nanny, two years before his debut on WCW television?

See, the inspirational character I played and lifted from Mr. Nanny was filmed for the big screen in 1993, but he wouldn't be fleshed out in the ring until 1995 – two years later. By this time, nobody was thinking about Mr. Nanny, and the new gimmick went completely unnoticed as being a former cameo from a movie.

For those of you who may remember Mr. Nanny, the film opened up with Hulk Hogan who (in a real stretch for him) was playing a retired professional wrestler. He fell asleep while fishing, remembering his glory days in the wrestling ring. The action then moved into a dream sequence that continued on playing throughout the credits. The dream then turned into a nightmare.

For this segment, the director wanted Hulk Hogan to pretty much just get destroyed by a bunch of wrestlers while the opening credits were rolling.

For the casting of these big bad wrestlers, Hulk booked a bunch of the scariest guys visually that he could find from the wrestling business to beat on him in front of the camera. He brought in Jim "The Anvil" Neidhart, Kamala the Ugandan Giant, George "The Animal" Steele, Afa the Wild Samoan, and one of the scariest wrestlers of all time… *me*.

Me? A scary wrestler?

When I showed up for that role on the set of Mr. Nanny and looked at the script, we immediately all agreed that it didn't make sense for Brutus Beefcake, who was a fan favorite, to join a group of thugs.

At that time, Hulk Hogan was always depicted as friends with Brutus on WWF television. Knowing that a number of wrestling fans would probably be interested in seeing Hogan on the big screen, we thought that it may be confusing for them to see me beating up on someone who was often billed as being my best friend.

However, I didn't hate the idea so much that I was willing to give up the payday.

The villains I was appearing with were very old-school. They especially didn't like the idea of Brutus Beefcake, a well-established babyface, joining in with a bunch of recognizable bad guys to beat up Hulk Hogan. It just didn't make sense. However, we decided that our union wouldn't make sense only to the fans *who recognized me*.

So then the question at hand became, how can we make me unrecognizable?

"Why don't you just put on a mask, or paint your face or something?" Hulk suggested.

So that is just what I did. What I decided to do was take Brutus Beefcake and make a nightmare version of him for the film. Essentially, I tried to make a heel version of Brutus "The Barber" Beefcake for the dream sequence, who was almost unrecognizable, insane and almost zombie-like to help set the hellish, underworld tone.

I put on a ripped pair of tights, and then I painted my face to try and match them. The face paint was intentionally made to look like a twisted mirror look of the black and white stripes from the zebra print pants. Next, I made my hair all crazy so it wouldn't really look like I was Brutus The Barber. Finally, I added more white tassels to the gloves to give it a mummy-like feel.

Two years later, I was asked to try and come up with a new gimmick I could do with Kevin Sullivan's new group of monster-like wrestlers. The Butcher was just too plain for me. Using this nightmarish zombie Brutus character immediately came to mind. It seemed like the perfect choice to me, when I was set to join the Dungeon of Doom. Nobody remembered the wrestler from the credits of Mr. Nanny – if you blinked you would have missed it. So it felt fresh to everyone.

When it came time to name it, I think we were thinking of a ying-yang, but for some reason, somebody said Zodiac. That also made you think of the Zodiac Killer. The letter Z seemed pretty twisted so we went with that.

COSMIC COOKIES WITH KING CURTIS

Kevin Sullivan took on the evil role of "The Task Master," or a manager-of-sorts of the Dungeon of Doom. However, he wasn't the only voice of the group. To really put it over the top, he contacted a wrestler he knew from his past to play his father "The Master" of the dungeon, King Curtis Iaukea.

A native of Hawaii, King Curtis played football in California out of the very liberal Berkeley. It was at that university that he started to experiment with recreational pharmaceuticals. He then took on football playing for Canada's CFL. He met up with a guy named Lord Blears, who also shared his love of surfing, and pulled him into the wrestling game. He got tired of whistles blowing in his ears on the field and took off to wrestle in Japan.

Curtis immediately became recognized as arguably one of the best talkers ever in the business. His scary facial expressions, his booming voice, and his ridiculous level of creativity made him an asset to any promotion.

The fact that he was into some weird drugs didn't hurt either. They added a strange mystical element of darkness to him. He was cryptic and scary with his delivery.

"Misssterrrr Francisss!" and "It's been seven long years…" were odd ways he would start his promos, and once he got started, he would continue to break all the rules. He would put his back to the camera, he would whisper. He would shout. No matter what he would end up doing, however, he would always hurl himself into an intense, lunatic-like interview with visceral words erupting from his gut like lava from a volcano.

King Curtis as a wrestler visually looked like one of the Samoans in the ring. He had big wild hair and was 250-300 pounds. He also was very, very known for those massive deep scars on his forehead from bleeding a lot.

King Curtis Iaukea doing what he did best; getting some good color.

One time, he told the boys in the back that he wanted them to come watch how to really get some good color in a match. Curtis pointed out the gross grooves and red etching above his eyes and said, "Sometimes, you need a little bit of red to make a little bit of green."

Curtis was working Rick Martel. When the finish came, Rick hit the big islander with a chair. Curtis then dug so deep into his forehead with a razor blade that it looked like open-heart surgery. The blood poured out so thick, that Rick Martel became instantly nauseous and wanted to puke.

"Oh, you sick son of bitch," Rick said, with the afterbirth-like ooze slugging down his forearms.

"Ewwwwww!!!" the front row said, barfing into their popcorn.

When he retired in the early 80s and turned to managing, King Curtis teamed up with Mark Lewin and Kevin Sullivan. Without ever using the word "Satan," Curtis became the mouthpiece for his cohorts, "guiding" them under the persona of an evil cult leader. Their faction of darkness feuded with rivals Austin Idol and Jumpin' Joe Savoldi and it seemed like something straight out of a horror movie. King Curtis really mastered his craft of being one of the scariest guys in the ring.

Come the mid-80s, Curtis Iaukea also took a manager role in the WWF. There he was known as the "Wizard." There he managed Kamala and later the unpredictable tag team of Kamala and Sika, acting as the voice for their promos. They too were all very dark, monster-like interviews. One had Kamala eating a chicken, and another had Sika eating a live lobster. His teaming with those guys and working as a manager in the WWF was among the best I had ever seen.

Now King Curtis' first real big run was in Australia back in the mid-60s, where he was a heel teaming with another crazy guy, Skull Murphy, and later more commonly known for being paired down under with Mark Lewin. He was huge in Australia back then working for Jim Barnett, who had a territory in Australia called WCW (no relation to Turner's promotion.)

Some 20 years later or so in the mid-80s, I was working with Curtis on a show in Australia. Coming from Hawaii, he had a certain love of nature that permeated his very being. Curtis was a legit legend in the Hawaiian Islands known for wrestling and football, and because of that, he had his connections.

I remember, around lunchtime before a show we were doing for the WWF in Australia, a bunch of us were sitting around at the hotel and we had a little time to kill before our show. Tama from the Islanders, aka The Tonga Kid, was eating some kind of bullshit cookies and Sika was laughing.

"You think those are good cookies? You should try King's cookies," Sika said.

"Oh yeah?" he asked, crunching away on whatever Keebler delight he had in his grubby little paws.

"Yeah, the cosmic cookie" he replied. "It's the best in the galaxy."

Now, I knew exactly what he was talking about, but Tama had no idea, so we all went up to find the hotel room of King Curtis.

Now, just for clarification, Tama was one of the Islanders; the one who tag-teamed with King Tonga, also known as Haku or Meng. Tama was not, however, the Fatu from the Headshrinkers - as people often confuse him for being. (I know, it is confusing, because there literally is like 300 kids in the Anoa'i line.) Tama's real name is Sam Fatu. He is the twin brother Solofa Fatu; the guy from the Headshrinkers; aka Rikishi (aka master of the stinkface.) It is funny because they are twin brothers, and they also both have twin boys each themselves, now.

Once we sat down, one of the Samoans (okay I don't really know which one it was) asked Curtis about something that was very sacred to him - something that Curtis was very known for behind the scenes with all the old school boys.

"So what is the deal with the cosmic cookie?" Tama said.

"Oh-ho-ho," Curtis said laughing. "I would let you try it, that is, if you think you can handle it."

"We are all grown up," I said, having heard about the legend of his cookie, myself and wondering what all the hoopla was about. Curtis loved to party, and the stories of his of "magic cookies" are still told by ring veterans who traveled with him in Jim Barnett's territory to this very day.

"I think we can handle it," the Wild Samoan said.

"Oh, but a cosmic cookie is a commitment," Curtis said. "It is so powerful, you can't even eat it."

"You can't eat it?" I said. "Well what the hell do you do with it then?

"You lick it."

Curtis said that if you indulge before a match, your timing would be all off. You will get hit with paranoia, the whole nine yards. Using the cosmic cookies as inspiration for his interviews was a different story. They could help him get to that crazy plane of existence that was perfect for where he wanted to go to for cutting promos. But a cosmic cookie before a match, was not recommended.

Like idiots, we insisted.

King Curtis reached in his suitcase and revealed a brown paper bag.

"One lick from the cosmic cookie brings power like one could not believe," he said, almost in his full wrestling character. "Seven years ago, a guy took an extra good, hard lick on a Sunday, his day off. Come Saturday, he was still hanging from the tree of woe!"

Tama reached for the bag, but Curtis batted his hand with his cane.

"That one extended lick kept that man loaded for 10 days and 10 nights! Now, any man who wants more than even the smallest of licks should caution," he said, raising the brown paper bag higher and higher above his head. "Hear my word! More licks than one will not bring a man any higher, but his mind is going to wander. …His mind is going to WANDER!!!"

That's right. Curtis cut a promo on us, right there in the hotel room. Sika was laughing his ass off, while Curtis kept his poker face.

"Okay, just one lick," I said, not even knowing what the hell a cosmic cookie even was. "We got it. Only one lick."

King Curtis smiled. He reached into the bag and started pulling out this very long string that looked like a bootlace. On the end of it was a round, cookie-like medallion of sorts. It, even more, looked like a big luminous sand dollar.

There was a long silence. We all gazed on all its beauty in a hypnotic moment of wonder.

"Behold!" he exclaimed. "…THE COSMIC COOKIE!!!"

You couldn't even write this shit. In the distance, I swear I could almost hear thunder.

We were memorized.

He passed it around. Slowly but surely, we accepted the trinket before us. Each one of us licked it, accordingly.

Just as I suspected. It's a rib. It was all a work. What a crock of ssshhh…

Just then, time froze.

It was the weirdest …sensation …I ever …experienced.

Minutes after the cosmic cookie circled around us in orbit, I was already seeing stars! Everything moved slowly. I felt like I was floating in space, and I wasn't alone. We each dropped off our chairs, one by one, docking our bodies with the floor at turtle-speed, all slow and creepy like a space-sloth. It was all beyond our control, involuntary, like the carpet had a gravity beam that was magnetically and majestically pulling us down.

Looking over at Sika making his way to the ground was like watching honey drip. We all were moving so slowly.

Eventually, we all ended up lying out on the floor, and we were laughing. We were laughing hysterically, and we didn't know why. The cosmic power of the cookie had won. It totally took over our bodies.

"Damn," Sika said, in a weird low and raspy voice. He took what felt like an eternity of time to gesticulate towards the end table. "Look at the clock!"

"Is it melting?" Tama asked.

"No," Sika said. "Not that. We have to get downstairs to the show!"

Sika was right. We must have been on the floor for three hours. We lost track of all space and time.

I tried to sober up, but I literally could not find the energy to even stand.

The show was actually in a huge hall arena, off the side of the hotel itself, so fortunately, we didn't have to drive. If we did, that would have just been impossible. We couldn't walk, we had so little energy. We could barely even crawl.

I'll tell you, it took us probably a half an hour to get up off the floor in the room just to make it to the elevator. We just kept laughing and laughing because we were so messed up on whatever the hell King Curtis had put into that cookie.

Eventually, we made it to the door. Sika and I practically crawled the whole way on our hands and knees, with Tama following behind us down the hall to the elevators. When we got there, Tama tried to hold the elevator door open for what seemed like an eternity, while King Curtis was still rolling his slow ass down the hallway to the elevator. The doors kept closing right on Tama, so I rolled forward to help him hold the door.

Somebody downstairs must have needed the elevator while we were holding the door, because it must've opened and then tried to close again, banging into our sides as we stood into the frame waiting for the King. It would then open back up again and try to shut maybe 50 to 100 times.

When we finally were all in the elevator, we all fell to the floor. We were laughing and could not stop. Everything felt like time was frozen, and it took so much energy to do almost nothing like pressing the button in the elevator to tell it which floor to go to.

There we were, four big huge professional wrestlers lying on the elevator floor, taking up almost the whole entire thing. None of us could manage to hit the button to our destination to make our way to the lobby, and subsequently, we ended up riding all over the place. Guests would come in and look down at us. They shriveled up their faces in disgust and then exited without speaking.

At one point, we randomly made it to our floor destination, but nobody had the energy to stand up and leave, so, we just laid there for what felt like hours. Eventually, we did make it to the show, however. I don't know how we wrestled that night, but we did. Man, that cookie was something else!

After years of blading, King Curtis' head looked like the surface of the moon.

THE DUNGEON MASTER

Kevin Sullivan, now in the late 90s, again, called up King Curtis again to this time play the role of The Master of The Dungeon. For this, Curtis wore a black flowing robe and made himself appear as ominous as ever. By this point, his bald head was viciously scarred-up from years and years of blading. It was arguably worse than Abdullah the Butcher's, if you have ever seen it. On top of that, Curtis' head was powdered up and painted all crackled to look almost like it was decaying. His gravelly voice was both disgusting and horrifying at the same time. He looked like a carnivorous, fat zombie. To get that sickly dead look, he just rubbed baby powder on his face and torso.

He was absolutely perfect for the role. The exchanges between Kevin and him, "My Father," and "Kevin, my son," are still scarred into my own head to this very day.

King Curtis wasn't at live WCW shows. He was really only around for television tapings. But whenever I could get a few minutes in to talk with King, I would.

A GIANT DUNGEON STORYLINE

The war between the members of the Dungeon and Hulkamania came off perfectly. Come Fall Brawl, Hulk Hogan teamed up with Randy Savage, Lex Luger and Sting against myself as Zodiac with my partners The Shark, Meng and Kamala. That Wargames match took place in a big double-ring cage. In the end, the babyfaces won. Hogan's team won, which also enabled Hogan to get 5 minutes alone with Kevin Sullivan inside the cage, meeting a special contractual stipulation. During this time, the Giant made his way into the cage and attacked Hogan, "almost breaking his neck."

The Giant was granted a world title match at the Halloween Havoc. Before they got in the ring to wrestle, however, they had this big crazy monster-truck competition. It was almost like a Sumo match competition in their vehicles, on the roof of the venue, Cobo Hall of Detroit, Michigan.

Hogan won the Monster Truck match. After that, Hulk and the Giant continued to fight it out on the roof. In the end, the Giant fell off the roof, disappearing into the Detroit River.

Of course in typical WCW writing fashion, when it came time for the main event, the Giant was ready for competition with no real mention as to how he survived the plunge of death from the rooftop.

In the end, the Giant won the match. What happened was Jimmy Hart (manager of Hulk Hogan) hit the referee with his megaphone and Hulk Hogan was subsequently disqualified. The next night, there was a big swerve reveal. Hart explained that he added a stipulation to the contract that allowed the championship to change hands on a DQ. He then defected from Team Hogan to become the manager of the Dungeon of Doom. His double-cross move rendered the Giant the new WCW champion.

In an even more funny twist in real life behind the scenes, we decided to play a trick on the Giant after he won the title. The next day after winning the championship, we told him that he needed to walk throughout the airport with the belt on, for all to see.

"Living like a champion is what WCW officials expected of you," we told him. "No matter where you go for the next week, you have that belt on you at all times, visible so people can see."

"That makes sense," he said.

The next day came, and sure enough, he complied. He was so new to the business that he really didn't know any better. So here he is, a 7-foot-tall real-life Giant, and he is walking around the airport wearing the WCW belt.

It was a ridiculous sight, to say the least.

He walked around the entire airport, and he wore the belt on the plane. He also wore the strap at the next airport after getting off the plane, as well. All the boys looked at him and laughed behind his back, knowing how green he was to go along with such a silly idea.

THE DUNGEON FIZZLES

The Dungeon of Doom feuded with Hulk Hogan for the remainder of 1995. The Zodiac was visually impressive on camera and also a pretty cool character, but didn't find a whole lot of success. It especially wasn't going to work outside of the zany world of The Dungeon of Doom. For me to transition out of the Zodiac character and into a different gimmick, it was revealed that Zodiac was actually a "double agent" for Hulk Hogan. Zodiac was secretly trying to take it down, and destroy it from within.

So once Hogan had me turn against my stable mates revealing me as a mole, I turned face once again. As the Zodiac gimmick dissolved, I once again became the tag partner for Hulk Hogan. This was something I knew how to do well.

For this run, I took on a new gimmick called "The Booty Man."

Kevin Sullivan also has said that The Dungeon of Doom was not a last-ditch effort to save Hogan's status as WCW's top hero. He knew all along that when the Dungeon of Doom run ended, he wanted to try and convince Hulk to turn heel for the first time in years.

"I knew that now was the best chance anybody had to convince Hulk Hogan to finally turn heel after his huge babyface run," he said. "After working with me so long with The Three Faces of Fear and The Dungeon, he finally trusted my booking. I convinced him to turn heel."

Eric Bischoff saw the NWO taking off, and replaced Ted DiBiase with himself, turning himself heel. Hulk Hogan was also not 100% opposed to also making the leap.

Hogan was getting heat from a bunch of the boys about the idea of working as a heel. A lot of us who had worked with him in the WWF knew that he was a big draw and that meant more money for the others around him. The boys always wanted to work on the same shows that Hulk Hogan was on because they had bigger gates and that meant more money to split with the locker room. So when people hear he might be turning heel, the other wrestlers worried that this could mean less money for them, in the event that he turned out to be a traditional villain that didn't draw.

Both Jimmy Hart and I had Hogan's ear at this time, as did guys like Macho Man Savage. I thought it could have been interesting to see what a modern day heel Hogan would look like, but Jimmy Hart did not. He absolutely thought it was a terrible idea, and he also thought it would hurt everybody's earning potentials in the WCW locker room.

In the past, wrestling fans always bought tickets to see the babyface get revenge and finally beat up the bad guy. Old school wrestling history would dictate that nobody would likely buy tickets just to see a bad guy they liked. However, times were changing.

The night before Hogan joined the nWo, Kevin Sullivan had him crash at his place because people were trying to talk him out of turning heel. Kevin was smart though, he wouldn't let him be persuaded and wouldn't let him out of his sight.

When the next night finally came, Kevin drove him right up to the arena directly before his run-in at Bash at the Beach 1996 was set to happen, almost right down to the very minute. Nobody saw him beforehand. With him joining forces with Kevin Nash, Scott Hall, and The 123 Kid, it looked like an invasion. In the eyes of the fans, it was finally the WWF versus WCW.

THE BOOTY MAN

As the nWo was about to kick ass, I was about to show mine off. This gimmick to say the very least was insane. After leaving The Dungeon of Doom, we decided to go with a gimmick that looked more like Brutus "The Barber," again, only of course without the scissors. Since we couldn't use the haircutting persona that made me famous, we decided to fall back on one of my other best ASSets… my butt.

Hey, what can I say? Girls had always told me I had a nice one, so I decided to try and make a little money off of it. Therefore, "The Booty Man" was born.

This gimmick, like a number of my other WCW gimmicks, did not last long.

Yes, this gimmick was that of a man infatuated with his own buttocks. It was very booty-centric. I would shake my tooshie on the way, point at it constantly, and slap myself on the ass on my way out.

The only way to play this ridiculous, over-the-top character was tongue-in-cheek, of course. My signature move was, therefore, a high knee… Get it? A heiney? Think that's bad? Look at the BACKSIDE of this book.

To put me over as a ladies man and rather not someone with a strange self-fascination fetish, we brought in Kimberly Page to play my valet. She became known as "The Booty Babe." To make it even more interesting, we feuded with Diamond Dallas Page, who at the time, was Kimberly's real-life husband.

I know. I know. I was face, then I was heel, then I was face, then I was heel again. Now, I was face again? I totally knew it looked bad for anyone to want to get BEHIND one of my characters. (Yes, pun intended again.) Unfortunately, I had very little direction, because of the writers not knowing what to do with me and because they would just "yes" Hulk Hogan to death. You see, Hogan would throw all these ideas at them so I at least would have something. His intentions were good, but he didn't honestly have the time to really develop anything, and the writers were too afraid to ever tell him that his ideas may not have been the absolute best to write around.

It was also very hard for me to complain, too. I just wanted a job. Of course, I didn't want to switch gimmicks every year, none of that was my decision. It wasn't up to me. It was up to them; the very unorganized WCW writing committee. If I had complained, however, I saw how the politics were playing out. If you bitched, then you basically would fall off the radar altogether and you wouldn't even have a story. So at the time, I was happy to have my gimmicks keep changing if that's how the cards fell, as long as I was still employed and collecting a paycheck.

Eric Bischoff was at this point frustrated with the different storylines and personas that Hulk was throwing my way. As soon as he saw an opportunity, he found a way to write The Booty Man off of television.

HOG WILD

The last ever Booty Man appearance was at the first ever *WCW Hog Wild* event. It took place on August 10, 1996, in front of 5,000 people at the famous "Sturgis Motorcycle Rally" in South Dakota. The concept was simple; a big portion of the fans would surround the ring and watch the show entirely from their bikes. It looked pretty badass on television, especially when they revved up their motors as a means to cheer.

Despite it being a visual success and translating well to the screen, a writer for the online website "Wrestlecrap" took a big shit on it. A guy named Art O'Donnell called the event a "financial blunder" saying that WCW had a yearly pay-per-view at a biker rally that collected zero at the gate, "…just because Eric Bischoff loved motorcycles." His accusation of selfishness from

Bischoff sounds about right, but I liked bikes too so the idea was totally cool with me, just as long as we were still getting paid.

Not charging for tickets isn't the only weird thing that happened at Hog Wild. Another funny piece of trivia is the oversight that happened in its advertising. The cover art poster for the show featured Hulk Hogan in his traditional yellow and red Hulkster colors, despite the fact that he had already joined the nWo a month before. He should have been donning his new black and white Hollywood gimmick. Also, after the first Hog Wild, they would end up changing the yearly event's name to "Road Wild" because of a trademark issue with Harley-Davidson's "Harley Owners Group." But anyhow, Hog Wild, or whatever you want to call it left quite an impression in my now somewhat-spotty memory.

First off, we flew into Denver to stay at a hotel a day or so before the event. Even though the motorcycle rally was still about 6 hours away from where they were putting us up, a number of us all showed up almost a full day early to prepare for the bike-centered gig.

Upon arrival, we all collected at the hotel bar to get drinks like we always did. By the time Hogan and the Nasty boys met up with me, I was already a few beers in the hole from hanging out with "The Giant" Paul White (aka The Big Show.)

"Hey, guys. Get this," Paul said, as the boys bellied up to the bar. "Lex Luger got here hours ago. He came down and said hi, but I guess he is too good to drink with us. He blew us off again, as usual."

"He sucks," said Hogan.

Lex had a little bit of a reputation for not always socializing when he could. Later that night as payment for not joining in on the fun, Paul decided to play a joke on old Sexy Lexy.

After surveying the hallway on Lex Luger's floor, Paul devised his genius plan. Using a giant-sized helping of charisma, he went back downstairs to try and convince a clerk at the hotel desk to give him a key to Lex's room.

"I need to drop some baggage off for him for the TV taping," he said.

Stupidly thinking everything was on the up and up, and also maybe not wanting to say "no" to a 7-foot giant, the staff member complied.

We followed Paul up to Lex's room and saw him crack open the door. With Lex already fast asleep, the stage was set perfectly. Paul came out, put a huge sausage finger up to his mouth and shushed us, and then he finally gave us all the thumbs up.

The big man then tiptoed a few doors down with all eyes glued to him. He stopped and then opened a little glass door in the wall that read "FIRE EMERGENCY." Behind the red letters was not a traditional fire extinguisher as one would have thought, however. It was rather one of those old-school gimmicks that housed an actual working fire hose. The Giant fiddled around with it for a moment and then began uncoiling the long tube. He pulled out the slack and tossed some of it over his shoulder. Once he had freed a significant amount of hosing, he headed back to the open door dragging the line behind him on the carpet.

Finally, we all snuck back into Lex's room, one-by-one. We circled around his bedside for the best view of "the big show" that The Giant was about put on for us.

I bit my lip and did everything I could to keep from laughing, when the Giant shoved that hose under the sheets and unloaded.

"ARRRGGGHHH!" Lex awoke abruptly. He put his hands up over his face and screamed like a bitch, as he rolled out of the bed and dropped into a puddle on the floor. Lex, the bed, and everything in the entire bedroom was soaked.

We all went running.

The real reason we got their early wasn't to fuck with Lex, however. You see, our bikes had also been shipped to Denver along with us, because we needed to get them ready for the show. The idea was that some of the wrestlers were going to actually drive their own motorcycles down the aisle to the ring as part of their entrances. Therefore, WCW paid to ship our bikes along with us for this one, but that meant we had to drive them from Denver, Colorado to Sturgis, South Dakota.

The thing about it was, there was no direct route to the venue from any shipping point. This was probably a 300-mile trip, and it was 55 degrees and raining. So the Hulkster, the Nasty's, and a handful of others got all leathered up and set out for a road trip to the show.

The "Beefcake Bike" at the time was super comfortable, so it wasn't so bad for me. I didn't care. I was cruising on a Softail Harley with all the amenities plus great suspension. It was just smooth as hell. You couldn't say the same thing for Hulk's custom nWo bike, however. What he was riding was nowhere as near as comfy as mine. On the other hand, his bike fit his wrestling persona perfectly; it was more about looking cool than how it actually worked.

We zipped down the road. Somewhere along the way, Hulk caught up with me and said, "Hey, Beefer. Let's trade."

I pretended like I didn't hear him at first, and raced off ahead. Not too long later, he pulled up and asked me again. I shook my head "no," made a face like I just smelled a bad shit, and then took off without looking back.

"Come on, brother," he said, after catching up with me a third time. "My ass is killing me!"

I shook my head no again and zipped away. It was pretty funny. Eventually, we pulled over to get something to eat. There, Hogan bitched and moaned the whole time about back pains, so I finally gave in.

However, the joke was on him. Not only was I the most experienced biker, but I was also the only one with the directions to Sturgis. Since the Hollywood Hogan nWo bike had no speedometer, I used it as an excuse to speed like a bat out of hell. They all kept trying to catch up with me the whole rest of the trip. I was driving like a lunatic and, at the same time, driving them crazy.

"Sorry guys," I would say, once someone had caught up. "With no meter, I really can't tell how fast I'm going!"

Yeah, right.

Then I zipped right off again.

Eric was right, though. Having our bikes there really was a great touch. It really helped make the show. At the end of the main event of the evening, the crowd really went crazy. The referee got distracted by Scott Hall and Kevin Nash, allowing Hogan to nail The Giant with the belt for the pin. After the match, I had a spot as The Booty Man. I ran down to the ring with an nWo T-shirt on trying to "join the club" so-to-speak. Hogan acted like Booty was to be the next to join the group, but it was all just a swerve. He beat me down right along with Hall and Nash. (Some of you may remember that was when he famously spray-painted "nWo" on the World Heavyweight Championship belt.)

As the office planned, right after the show we left Sturgis with a police escort through a ton of traffic. There were so many people trying to leave the area that it was very easy to break protocol and lose the cops so we could go have a little fun. At the very first turn, we were supposed to make, the police turned right, and we turned left. Just as we planned, we all ended up at a bar controlled by the Hells Angels.

Now, I can't remember a whole lot about what happened there. You are always thirsty after you wrestle a match, and there were a whole lot of drinks there. Now, most of the rest of the night is just a blur. However, I do remember someone had a nasal inhaler loaded with meth that the Nasty Boys were marveling at. They couldn't believe the time someone had put into creating such an idea.

An hour or so in, someone suggested that we head out to another party that promised to be even wilder and even more badass.

I don't remember where the second party was, but I do remember driving out to the boonies in the middle of the night through the woods. It was pitch black. I could barely see the road at times.

We were all following this one big burly biker who didn't talk. When we finally got there, he led me and the boys up to a big fancy gate. There were these two scary security guards dressed in black standing guard, holding AK47s. Without saying a word, they nodded and let us up into biker party number two.

We parked our bikes along a row of some of the most beautiful motorcycles I have ever seen, and then followed our guide into a huge fancy clubhouse.

A guy with a sweeter Fu Manchu mustache than Hogan answered the door in a leather vest. He patted us down and then showed us in. When he turned around, I finally got to see the name of which gang was hosting this shindig. This one was a group called, "The Sons of Silence."

Aligned with The Hells Angels, these guys were known for their love of weapons. The Sons of Silence claim that their need for firepower stems from a turf war that has been going on for decades. A 1999 police raid of one of their locations once revealed a crazy stockpile including machine guns, pipe bombs, and even hand grenades.

A few of the members where fans and immediately pushed drinks into our hands. In most cases, however, they had to set a gun on the table first to free up a hand. It seemed that everyone in the club was packing and showing off their pieces. Despite the fact that this group had guns everywhere, it surprisingly wasn't scary at all. They Sons sure knew how to throw a good party. Both their food and their women were delicious.

So, anyhow, at the end of Hog Wild, we did that angle where I attempted to join the nWo, but to no avail. There was no storyline after that. I wasn't set up to get revenge, or earn my way in. In the end, I was instead attacked by Scott Hall, Kevin Nash, and Hollywood Hogan.

Then, they wrote me off of TV.

Then, they fired me.

ERIC BISCHOFF, NO FAN OF MINE

Most people would think that since Hulk and I were friends, and since Hulk and Eric were friends, that would mean Eric and I should be friends, as well. That sounds logical, but that just wasn't the case. Eric was the money guy at WCW, and I think he always looked at me as being a waste of money.

Let's fast-forward a second to 2017. WrestleCon is a big fan-friendly, wrestling-themed convention that now kicks off WrestleMania weekend. While writing this book, my new wife, Missy, ran into Eric Bischoff at WrestleCon 2017. She was making the rounds a little, helping to produce the book some and get some quotes back to the ghostwriter Kenny Casanova. I didn't think she would bother Eric for a comment, but that's just not how Missy rolls.

She marched right up to his table.

"Eric, hi! How are you?" my wife asked, shaking the hand of my ex-boss, the former WCW Executive Producer.

"Hi, how are you?" he said, not knowing who she was, but seeing the "All Access" pass around her neck. He assumed she was someone important and he came off very warm and friendly.

"Good, I'm Brutus' wife, Missy," she said.

"Oh. Good to meet you," he said, possibly not really meaning it, but still sounding good-natured.

"Nice to meet you. I was wondering," she said. "We are in the process of writing Brutus' book, I was wondering if you have anything nice that you might want to say about Brutus?

"No, I don't actually. No, I don't."

"Wait, do you hate him?" she asked, not exactly knowing much about Eric, as we got married many, many years after I was all done with WCW.

"No, I don't hate him."

"You sure? Nothing you could say?"

"Pretty sure, yeah," he laughed. "No. Sorry."

"Nothing even nice you could say to me about my husband?"

"Sorry."

I hoped after all of these years, there may have been something there. She was just looking for a little bit of something nice he could have said and provided a quote for the book, but it didn't happen.

His response that day was the total of our WCW relationship in a nutshell. He didn't really have the time of day for me at WrestleCon, and he didn't have anything for me back then, either.

Eric Bischoff was Hogan's friend, but he was never mine. Yes, he would throw me a bone here and there, but not for me. He did that as a favor for his breadwinner. He never gave me even the slightest push to help make me mainstream, again. I think he just looked to me as an expense, as a means to keep Hulk Hogan happy. Later, he would also come to show signs that he didn't like me, perhaps, due to my *history with Missy Hyatt.*

See, back just before I started with Turner, they had a WCW guest appearance by an actor named Jason Hervey. Hervey befriended Eric Bischoff and instantly became an executive producer for WCW. He was there the whole time after that appearance, even until the company went out of business in 2001.

Some of you might remember Hervey as being the bitchy actor that Pee Wee steals his bike back from in *Pee-wee's Big Adventure.* (It's possible that he did so well in that role because he wasn't really acting.) Early in Hervey's career, he also appeared in *Back to the Future, Meatballs, Police Academy,* and *Different Strokes.* I think he was mostly known for being the older brother of Fred Savage's character in *The Wonder Years.*

During his time behind the scenes in WCW, he teamed up with Eric Bischoff and they created Bischoff/Hervey Productions. They have since worked on a number of projects outside of wrestling that were a little sports-related at times, and also a little reality show like, in construct. Their company had their hand in creating shows like Scott *Baio Is 45...and Single, I Want to Be a Hilton,* and *Hulk Hogan's Celebrity Championship Wrestling.*

I believe he also dated Missy Hyatt, someone who I also have been connected to in the past. After they eventually broke up, things became weird between them. Some people believe that Jason never really got over her. I don't know.

Before I showed up in WCW, during a match at *Starrcade '93*, there was a nip-slip. I guess Missy's breast popped out of her dress, accidentally, on TV at the big event. About a month later, she showed up for her spot at a show at the CNN center in Atlanta, Georgia. When she walked in, she was immediately reminded of the incident.

They say that a WCW cameraman isolated that still from Starrcade, and printed out a beautifully blown-up frame of her fresh nipple in high definition. The color glossy was a perfect shot of the wardrobe malfunction, with Missy's exposed breast and all. It was then conveniently taped up on the

CNN bulletin board in the lobby, right next to pictures of Wolf Blitzer and Larry King, for all to see as they entered. Even though Missy's tits were clearly nicer than the famous newscasters', there was no reason to prove it and embarrass her all over again.

Missy was irate. She immediately ripped the picture down and went straight to Eric Bischoff. Bischoff promised Missy he would handle things, but she said that nothing was ever really done. Not hearing anything anytime quick, Missy went above Bischoff's head to his boss about the incident. The very next day, I guess someone fired Missy. Now, don't get me wrong, but that seemed like a stupid thing to do, even if it was for something else. From the best of my knowledge, there was some kind of harassment lawsuit filed, and then Missy won.

It doesn't take a rocket scientist to figure out why Eric Bischoff doesn't seem to like me, back then and still today. First off, my history with Missy Hyatt is probably something that Eric Bischoff's partner, Jason Hervey, didn't care for. Next, you can also factor in Hulk Hogan getting me double my salary from Eric right after my next short-lived gimmick didn't pan out.

Let's fast forward a moment to years after my time in WCW, when I was brought in for a trial run at TNA Impact Wrestling for an Australian tour. The idea was that if things went well, they would hire me when we got back to the States. I worked out hard before the tour and got into really great shape. I was ready. The tour went well. I was working with Umaga, and we drew great money for the promotion. Our matches were great.

While Hogan certainly wanted me there to work with him there, it didn't take me long to realize my former WCW boss still wasn't too keen on the idea, or me overall for that matter. I believe it was Eric Bischoff who stooged me out to the TNA officials on an Australian tour and got into some trouble "because I went out and got all the boys pot."

What a hater.

Despite a good showing in the ring, when we came back to America, they stopped taking any of my calls and also didn't return any of them.

DOUBLE-OR-NOTHING

The pay for WCW wasn't great at all unless they really wanted you and were signing you to a deal. For me, my salary was pretty much in the dogshit category. At this time, I wasn't yet married to my second wife, and this was before I had a daughter - so I didn't care that much about the money. I just wanted to work and hoped to stay on TV and be somewhat relevant for a potential return to WWF one day.

Before my big Starrcade match against Hogan, I was only working on a pay-per-appearance deal. That meant each night, they would figure out what they were going to give me, and that was basically it. There was no longevity. There was no contract protecting me. There was nothing written in stone that I would even return the next night. I was pretty much living day to day.

After that bigger main event, I think they saw a little more in me, at least if only for a moment. Once my job kind of stabilized there in WCW and I seemingly had a spot, I signed a $100,000 deal. Then, I finally started receiving a regular check.

That job stability didn't really last, however. It was short-lived. It seemed that once I got married and really needed that job security - that was when they took it away from me. Immediately after I married my second wife, the "Man with No Name" gimmick had seemingly run its course in the minds of WCW officials. Hogan was off doing his thing with Vader and the writers had nothing else planned for me to do. Soon after that, Eric Bischoff faxed me at home and essentially fired me on a piece of paper.

As the story goes, I pulled into the driveway after a taping. I opened the door.

"Honey, I'm home," I said.

"…"

"Honey?"

When I came home the day of the fax firing, I came around the corner and heard sobbing. I looked down. My ex-wife's face was beet red. She was crying on the floor in the living room, holding a crumpled up sheet of paper in her hand.

"What are we going to do?" my ex-wife cried between sobs.

"Don't sweat it," I said. "I think I can fix it!"

I honestly didn't know. I was banking on the idea that Hogan might go to bat for me, but at the time, there were a whole lot of weird political things going on backstage at WCW. My fear was that the whole reason why I was being let go was out of a political move and that Hogan was not going to have the leverage that he had to help bring me in like he did initially.

The next day, Hulk Hogan, Randy Savage, and I had all planned to meet up for a road trip together. We thought we would go drive up to Cape Canaveral to see Jim Duggan, who had finally signed up with Turner. We were all going to crash a grand opening appearance for Jim Duggan, just to surprise him.

I figured that, at the right time, I would have the conversation with Hulk in person sometime that day. This way I could read body language and know exactly what he thought about the situation. For some reason, I really thought he must have had known before I had. Therefore, I wanted to skirt around the issue and feel him out.

Hulk spun by my place in his new V12 Mercedes. Randy and I jumped in, and we all took off for Orlando. I was driving.

It was supposed to be a fun ride to see and surprise our good buddy Hacksaw, but Hulk and Randy knew that something was wrong with me. You see, I didn't want to tell them yet that I had been fired, until maybe after the big surprise. I didn't want to shit on the fun until after, but I guess they could tell that something was up. Maybe it was a pouty look on my face, or maybe it was just the fact that I was cruising at almost 100 on the highway.

So of course, they pumped me for information, and I subsequently spilled my guts.

"No, no," Randy said. "This is bullshit."

I looked over at Terry. I had known him for a long time. I could tell when he was lying, and I could tell when he was sincere. He really had no idea what had happened.

"They don't want to fight for your name, and then they wonder why there isn't a bigger response when some of the audience doesn't know you?" Hogan said. "We will see about this."

Hulk made a call in the backseat to Eric Bischoff, right there while we were sitting in the car.

"What the fuck?" he said to start out the call to his boss. "Why are you firing Brutus?"

Excuses came on the other end of the line.

"Fuck you, bullshit!" Hogan said. "Letting it expire is the same as firing. You need to renew it."

Eric said something on the other line and Hulk wasn't buying it.

"NO!" he said. "I said, you need to renew it, and up it for more money. Give him a raise for that bullshit, you understand me?"

Hulk looked at me, smiled, and nodded "yes" in that very sweet way.

There was silence on the phone. Randy had his hand over his mouth and was actually laughing.

"Let me see what he wants," Hogan said. "What do you make now, Brutus?"

"100 grand," I said.

"And what do you want, Brutus?"

"200 grand!"

There was a little more talking, and then Hulk gave the thumbs up. Just like that, I went from being unemployed to Hulk having them double my salary.

And they did it.

The new contract was decent. It showed that I didn't have to work as many shows on the road, I was working mostly TV. I would then work every two or three weeks and do a few days of tapings. Then, I would collect a check for around $8 grand every two weeks. I was able to put a few hundred thousand into my house.

Upon securing my new deal, I didn't even have to go back to work right away. During the little break, I rebuilt my second house out by Treasure Island – or should I say, WCW rebuilt it. I added 4 or 5 bedrooms to it, overlooking the water. I did a lot of work myself, and it turned out really nice. If you know the area, it was over by Mediera Beach, by the last real street before you get to the pass where the Inner Coastal comes through, like 30 seconds to the Gulf of Mexico. It was right over a little canal, on a tiny island off the mainland. You could pull a yacht right behind my house. ...Thanks Eric!

Me, Hogan & Chrysler's Tony Carlini; the guy who designs all the cool cars.

Me, X-Pac, Kevin Nash, Scott Norton, & Scott Hall.

CHAPTER 23 - NWO RUN

Enter The Disciple…

The Booty Man gimmick did not last long at all. I was okay with it ending, however. At around this time, I had a new baby coming at home, and wanted to take some time off to get the house ready. For the storyline at WCW to write me off, what we did was have me attempt to join the nWo and instead get beat down by Scott Hall, Kevin Nash and Hollywood Hogan.

I left WCW for about a year or so after that to get things going at home for the baby. When I came back for the February 23, 1998 episode of Monday Nitro, a lot of people had absolutely no idea who I was. During my time off, I did a lot of work outside and got a pretty good tan going. I grew my hair out and did a lot of training in the gym. As the new personal bodyguard of Hollywood Hogan, they simply knew me as the new guy called, "The Disciple."

Just like when I showed up in the locker room for the first time as "Brutus Beefcake" and worked all the boys who didn't recognize me, about the same thing happened. I walked in and people had to really look at me to see who I was. Most said with the really full beard that I was totally unrecognizable, all together. This time around, I wanted to do it right. I wanted to be a new character that had no history behind me. I wanted to play the role of a big, mean guy that would kill anyone who got in my way. I didn't want any ties to the silly Zodiac creature I played, or any connections being made to a man who loved his own butt.

The new Disciple character's look was very much motorcycle gang-like. I had the long full beard and grown out sun-bleached hair. I was wearing dark sunglasses, sporting leather biker gear, and flashing the nWo-logo. For a few weeks, some of the most hardcore wrestling fans out there still had absolutely no idea that I was the guy they once knew as Brutus "The Barber" Beefcake. Many of the people watching at home on TV wouldn't even have known today, if it weren't for my secret identity being later blown by Roddy Piper while he was on the mic, during his feud with Hogan. I think the original intent was going to be the same as it was with the Zodiac. The Disciple was a new person. He was not the same person as who played the Booty Man or Zodiac, it was a new-comer. But that eventually didn't fly.

For this year and a half run or so, I was back with Hulk Hogan to the ring for all of his matches. It was kind of like old days, again. While I was technically there to "protect" him, I was more used as the assist in the beat down of some unsuspecting victim of team "Black and White."

For the new character, I developed a new finishing move I called, "The Apocalypse." Usually when determining a good finishing maneuver, you want to use or create a move that can be done on anybody. You don't want to select a finisher that cannot be applied to someone who is too big to muscle up in the air, for example. If the move can't be done on everyone, then it is no good. A finisher that can only be used some of the time is a waste. It gets less over because it is less recognizable with the fans.

After Hogan became the WCW World Heavyweight Champion in the Spring of 1998, I decided to do something I hadn't seen before then, and haven't really seen since. I made my finisher include a weapon. The weapon – the WCW title belt, itself. Essentially, the Apocalypse was a stunner with gold. You see, for my finisher, I would prop Hogan's belt over my shoulder, put their face on it, then hit the victim with the Apocalypse. That way, there would theoretically be the extra impact of the belt's golden center plate slamming into my opponent's face on the way down to the mat.

The fact that I was using a Diamond Cutter which was close to the stunner, it only made sense that I would work another program with Diamond Dallas Page.

TROUBLE WITH DDP

Years after working with Diamond Dallas Page as the Booty Man and before the Sturgis thing, I was booked to work with him again. This time, I would play the heel, the Disciple of the NWO.

We had a massive crowd leading up to what was to be a big Hogan versus Goldberg main event. Many argued that the Hogan/Goldberg match should have been a pay-per-view, but they decided to actually put it out there for free on live TV for Monday Nitro. Ratings were turning in the favor of WCW in the Monday night wars, and they figured a PPV quality event on TV could really help sink in the ratings.

I was supposed to come out and aid Hollywood Hogan with another member of the NWO, Curt Hennig. After that DDP would do a run in and take us out of the match as a potential factor. Before the taping, we talked out what we would do before the match. The booking instructions were relatively simple; it was all set up for me to get taken out with a steel chair, while standing out at ringside. Just like I had to tell IRS my head situation, I felt the need to explain to DDP that all was fine, but he just had to be careful.

"Listen," I said. "You can hit me as hard as you want on the back, but you can't hit me in the head no matter what. You got to watch out, is all. The wrong spot could literally kill me."

DDP told me not to worry. He said I could trust him, but come time for the show…

SMASH!!!

I got nailed in the back of the head with the chair.

I saw like the white flash of light and everything and went down. I hit the ground half-selling, and half really in pain because he hit me pretty hard. I reached up and touched the spot of impact, then brought my hand to my face. There was hard-way blood, in other words, I was bleeding for real with no help from a blade or anything.

What the hell?! Why did he do that? Was their heat for something I don't know about? Was he just being irresponsible? Was he just trying to look good? This is bullshit.

I went down. Blood literally spurted 10, 15, 20 feet into the first few rows. It sprayed right into the audience like Gallagher's "Sledge-o-matic" demonstration, and everyone in the general area was grossed out.

By the time I went back to the dressing room, I was seeing stars. That was one more concussion that I didn't need, I'll tell you that. I showed the EMT the cut. The good thing about it was, rather than having to go off to the hospital and the whole nine yards, the EMT went out to his car and got his own personal kit that he had just in case of an emergency. He came back in. We found a little room somewhere, and he sewed me right up.

I was pissed at first. When it was done, I went to find Dallas and see what the hell that was all about. I felt like he ignored my request to not hit my head with a chair, maybe just to look good on Nitro, at my expense. Paul Orndorff came with me, just in case. Dallas said he was sorry and it was an accident. I was heated and didn't want to hear excuses, so I quickly left the locker room.

Ever since then, I have been a little pissed at what happened. I frankly also never understood it.

GUEST PASSAGE – DIAMOND DALLAS PAGE ON THE DISCIPLE

For the sake of this story, Dallas was cool enough to try and settle the heat once and for all for that one spot. He did it the very moment we called him. He actually took time out from one of his DDP Yoga classes to give his take on what happened, to apologize and to help clear the air. Here is what Diamond Dallas had to say about the incident:

"I'm sorry for what happened. I've always been sorry.

I saw Greg Valentine recently at an appearance somewhere. We talked a bit and caught up. Towards the end of our conversation, I said, "Hey, how is Brutus?"

"He's still pissed at you," Greg said, laughing. "He still has heat over the chairshot!"

"Uggg!"

It still bothers me to this day to think I bummed him out like that. Brutus was the last person I ever wanted to hit in the head. With everything he had been through with the accident and all, it's too bad it happened like it did.

Like I've always said, I always loved Brutus, before I was even in the ring wrestling, myself. I first met him back in days when he was Brutus "The Barber." Man, he was a real superstar back then, but he didn't act like it to me, and I wasn't in the business yet.

I don't know if he remembers this or not, but the first time I met him we were both at a bar called "Macos" in Tampa Bay, or maybe it was Clearwater. I was a huge wrestling fan back then.

Whenever the wrestlers were in town, I always tried to meet up with them and network, in hopes that I could one day maybe get into it myself.

Brutus was a big superstar then, top of the card. He was super nice to me, and he didn't have to be. I think early on, he thought maybe I was actually a wrestler, myself. I tried to carry myself like one, and I certainly looked like one of the boys, but this was way before I had even gotten into a ring to train. Either way, he was down to earth.

When I first met Brutus, I had these sharkskin boots. He was a big boot guy, always wearing cowboy boots. He saw my boots and asked about them. I told him where I got them. The next time I saw him at the bar, he was wearing something very similar to the same pair that I had. We talked a bit, and he thanked me for the lead.

After that, whenever the WWF was in town, he always snuck me in to see wrestling shows in the back door. I would hang a little in the locker room. The boys also thought I was one of them, too. Then, I would go and watch the show, because I was a huge fan. I thought Brutus was cool, man. A really good guy. Everything was cool with us. The guy hooked me up!

Years later when I finally got to work with him in WCW, I did everything I could to help get him over with the Booty Man and Booty Babe gimmick. Then after that, I had to do this thing with him at the Georgia Dome.

It was huge. It was at the big Hogan vs Goldberg event, in front of 44,000 people. Basketball player Karl Malone and I had a run-in spot during a Scott Hall/Goldberg match. There, we were supposed to stop the nWo's Disciple and Curt Hennig from interrupting the match.

All of us got together and talked before the match. I was told I had to do a run-in and hit the Brutus with a chair, so I asked him if that was okay to do. Brutus told me a chairshot was no problem, but under no circumstances could it be in the head. Doctors said to always have him be cautious of that because, if it hit him just right, it could kill him. Therefore, the plan was I should nail him in the back.

"No problem," I said.

When the time finally came, the run down to the ring was no cake walk. It was pretty far away. It was a hike. And I was worried that by the time I got down there, "What if I missed my cue?" So, I am huffing and puffing, running down there all frantic to make it on time. By the time I got there, I was almost blowing up (out of air).

Now, they had all these extra mats everywhere. The extra mats on the floor were needed because, being a TV taping, they had all these wires and cables underneath them to hide them from sight. So as I'm just getting up to Beefer, I'm running and, all of a sudden, I trip on a bump from a big cable under the padding just before I get to him.

So there I am, running and tripping on a full gallop. I had to think on my feet, while I was still on my feet. Now, if I had fallen, the whole spot would have been ruined. The fans would have laughed like the time the Shockmaster fell, and it would have been ruined. The whole spot would have looked stupid. So knowing I was out of position and that I had to swing early before I fell, I thought I would just pull the shot some and like just touch his head with the chair. Then, he would sell it and go down.

He went down, but not because he was selling. He went down because I caught him good.

"Oh shit," I'm thinking to myself. "I split him wide open, and that really wasn't at all what I was trying to do!"

The whole thing was mistimed, and I felt horrible. I didn't even know what to say to him after that happened. How do you say anything? I just did exactly what I said I would not do.

Up to that moment, everything was cool. But after that, I know there has always been a little something.

I know he thinks I was irresponsible, but I hope he knows more who I am now with my positivity and trying to help people. As lame as it may sound, it was an accident - for real. I'm sorry for what happened at the Georgia Dome. I've always been sorry.

I don't like there to ever be heat with me and any of the boys. I'm not about that. I always try and fix that and hope this does that.

So when I saw Valentine, and he is saying, "Beefcake is still mad at you," of course it bothers me, brother. Brutus is a great guy and I hope this book does really well for him!" – Diamond Dallas Page

ONE WARRIOR NATION

The Disciple gimmick was unfortunately not all that eventful, either. It was mostly just standing around looking tough and during nWo interview segments, and a lot of ringside stuff. I was basically a supporting character, which got old fast.

What we decided to do was get me on the other side of Hogan so I could feud with him again, as we always worked well together. When the idea of teaming up with the Ultimate Warrior who just signed in came along, I figured that could be just what I needed.

To have it make sense in the storyline, they had me get abducted on TV by Warrior to join the Warrior's feud against Hulk Hogan. The thought was I must have been brainwashed by Hogan, and Warrior was going to un-brainwash me and help me see the light.

The abduction was in typical WCW style. They filled the ring with smoke and had me appear in the ring lying face down. The nWo came running to save me, but when they got there, the smoke came again and I mysteriously disappeared. Then, the commentators cut to Warrior way up in the rafters.

The footage revealed that the Warrior was holding my head with me on my knees, like a Baptist minister. The only thing is, it was not me, it was a body double. What really happened was I just ducked underneath the ring when the smoke went up, the same place I had been hiding all night.

After being un-brainwashed by The Warrior, I turned on Hogan and became the second member of Warrior's One Warrior Nation. But then, the nail in my coffin really happened. There was some kind of contractual negotiation fallout, and the Warrior left.

I hear he was a little hard to work with. One interview explained that Warrior would write pages and pages of storyline scripts on how he felt he should be used on television. Then, he would blow up Eric Bischoff's fax machine with his ideas, sometimes 50 pages deep.

After Warrior left WCW, any kind of push for me was gone. I had just turned on Hogan to become the "Disciple of the Warrior," but now there was no Warrior to follow. Because of the poor timing of it all for me, that was about it. Not being able to use "The Barber" gimmick was a curse that followed me throughout my days in WCW.

The wrestling business had changed. It wasn't working like it used to, back in the time when there were territories. There were really only two promotions. Early in '99 Hogan and I had a TV match against each other, and that was about it.

I didn't know it at the time, but that last big Hogan match ended my TV relevance on a national level. With nowhere to go really, I was stuck on the smaller, unimportant B and C cards for WCW. Being part of no storylines at all, I ended up just working my final days under my real name.

Even the commentators knew it was lame. They started ribbing me and would just talk about all the failed gimmicks I had in WCW. Jobbing out sucked and it obviously didn't pay well.

My last WCW pay-per-view match was on November 22, 1998, at the World War 3 big cluster battle royal. They pretty much emptied everyone in the locker room out for that one.

After a year of doing pretty much nothing, my last televised match aired on the November 6, 1999 episode of *WCW Worldwide*. I knew I was done so I wore gear that looked like my very early WWF days as Brutus Beefcake, even before the Dream Team. Nobody was really paying attention, but I had come full circle and went out looking like I did when I came in.

That night, I lost to my good friend, Hacksaw Jim Duggan.

After that, things started to really fall apart for me. I didn't have enough money to get a lawyer to try and fight for the rest of my contract money that WCW owed me. Without a job, I had two mortgages I still had to pay.

My wife at the time bailed from Tampa to go up to Boston. She had a lifelong friend she went up to help who had cancer up there. She said she was going to stay just for summer to help her out, but I know she only used that as an excuse to get out. With all those bills and no steady contractor job, there just was no way I could afford $4000 on the mortgage. I stuck around for a short time, then had to put the houses on the market.

At this point, we weren't divorced, but we were pretty much separated. The writing was essentially on the wall.

CHAPTER 24 - THE INDEPENDENTS

Years after the WCW, we sold the big house and downsized. I continued to wrestle. I accepted bookings everywhere and worked hard to be a headliner for a bunch of real small promotions.

It was tough not having all the people to help you organize your days, weeks, and months. WWF and WCW did all of that. They would hand you a big stack of plane tickets and you would be off. In the case of being the indy worker, you had to figure a bunch of that out all for yourself. You also had to try and be strategic about which bookings you accepted and where they were so that you weren't on the plane seven days out of the week.

INDY SHOCK

The transition for me to the indys was a little difficult. I mean, I had worked a lot of horrible shows during my territory days, but moving to the real of shoe-string budgets after my WWF and WCW days, was quite the difference. It was like night and day.

Now, don't get me wrong. Some independent promoters today are really learning from the past mistakes of the promoters. Some people say there is a big resurgence in wrestling on the horizon and that business is finally starting to pick up again. However, while there are some great promotions out there today, when I started digging my heels into the independent show scene in the late 90s and early 2000s, they were really horrible.

After the collapse of WCW, Vince had no competition. The writing was arguably lazy, and wrestling in general went right to shit. Almost all the promotions I was finding work with felt like the very worst days for any territory I had ever worked for before, but for every single show. There were never any good ones. It was then that I realized that all territories as they once existed were, in fact, dead. There really wasn't anywhere to go.

I can't tell you how many independent shows only had one or two rows of people in attendance. The days of selling 8,000 tickets and that being a "small show" in the WWF were gone. Most of the independent shows I saw were lucky to bring in a few hundred people. That had nothing to do with my or anyone else's drawing power, but more, rather, the ability of the promoter to get the word out.

The difference was alarming at first. I can see how a big name can fall into depression, after leaving the big leagues and making the lifestyle transition into working for independent promotions. You go from being pampered with great catering spreads, quality lodging, and all the amenities to virtually nothing. Rather than working in a nice clean wrestling ring with high-end lighting, video production, and sound, you would find yourself in an adapted boxing ring with no give, laced with a urine-soaked ring apron.

Though some indies are really starting to finally take off, many of these poor independents are still around today. If you have only seen WWF wrestling on TV, or something like it, it may be difficult for you to understand the differences – especially if you have never seen an independent show that is the drizzling shits. Most indy shows are in a lousy bingo hall, or an American Legion that smells like mildew and fish piss. The rings have all seen better days, with ratty ropes and sagging centers. The seating is laughable, and often a collection of barstools and mismatched lawn chairs. Nice guard rails are far and few between, but rather a "rope barricade" is sometimes provided crafted from a spool of yarn. Loudspeakers and pyrotechnics are nonexistent. Instead, wrestler theme music is played over a karaoke microphone held up to a cell phone. Some places didn't even have a ring bell. Instead, they used a glass of water hit on the side with a spoon.

This is what you deal with sometimes, but as a professional wrestler, we still do it for the love of the sport, *and the love of a paycheck.*

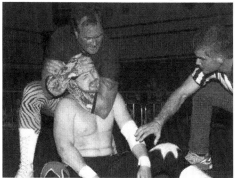

There really is nothing professional about many of at least some of these so-called "professional wrestling" promotions on the indy scene. If you are not a wrestler with TV experience, you cannot earn a living. Most local indy wrestlers like this guy, Chuck Deep (pictured), work for $50, a slice of pizza, a hotdog & a handshake, *or nothing.*

The differences between TV and independent promotions are vast – so much so that it often pissed us off. It felt like promoters were intentionally not providing us, former-WWF stars, with the same luxuries that we had become accustomed to. Therefore, we figured they were all cheap assholes. Early on, WWF names would take advantage of promoters, almost out of revenge for promoters not treating us to a level that we considered to be "fair."

Right after the Monday night wars and the collapse of WCW, independent shows went to crap. They had no real merchandise income. They had no real revenue other than house show attendance. They had horrible payoffs for their regular wrestlers and pretty much all of their budget went to the one "name wrestler" talent who has had some kind of television exposure. Therefore, there was no money left for anything else.

To further hurt the business, these independent promotions opened professional wrestling schools, as another means to generate income. Their "teachers" all had very little experience in front of any kind of real audience, and subsequently, they cranked out garbage talent that would work for free, lessening the quality of shows everywhere.

This became even worse because promoters didn't know how to promote. They would just post their show up in one place and think that everyone was going to see it, because of their stupid egos. They became more engrossed in writing a storyline than they did finding people to come see a storyline. Then, in the end, shows looked like crap and people stopped going.

Because of this, I stopped going quite a bit, too.

I do remember one show, however, where a promoter didn't want to pay anyone after the show. The show had a handful of decent wrestlers on it. It had Greg Valentine, Road Warrior Animal, myself and MVP.

At the end of the night, the shady promoter said he didn't have anything for anyone. He said the reason was, we as names didn't draw. He insinuated that we were too old and it was our fault that nobody came.

Joe (Animal), Greg and myself got into a corner in the locker room to figure out what we were going to do about this situation at hand. While we were still discussing the problem, out of nowhere, MVP went and charged the promoter.

We couldn't hear their discussion, but we didn't need to. We could see what was happening. The promoter said something similar to MVP and he wasn't hearing any of it.

MVP grabbed the promoter by the throat and lifted him three feet off the floor. Now, I am all about the Benjamins, too. When there is a discrepancy or an issue, I go write up to the promoter myself. I was about ready to, that is, when I saw MVP attack the shyster.

We thought about running over to stop MVP from killing the asshole, but I think we secretly wanted to see him do it. So we sat right there in the locker room and watched the after-show.

When MVP let go of his throat, the promoter dropped to his knees. MVP kicked him as hard as he could in the ribs and told him to empty his pockets and give him his pay. MVP shook the promoter down for everything he had on him, which amounted to about $600 and a Pizza Hut gift card.

Even though MVP took some of his payment in pizza like the rest of his guys did, at least he got some of what they had agreed on.

BEING ERASED

Once the TV wrestling money dwindled off, things changed. When my daughter was about four or five years old, my ex said she was going up to Boston. The idea was she wanted to visit a friend who had cancer, and she also wanted to visit her parents. The thing about it is, that visit never ended. She just never came back. While my ex seemed to love me while I was on the road wrestling and making the big money, after the gigs dried up, I think she became sick of me being around and having to struggle a little more than I had to before.

I waited about six months and realized she must have decided that our marriage was done. With only one income and being in semi-retirement from wrestling, it was hard to make the payments on the big house that we had. I tried to save it for about a year by renting out a room to help pay the mortgage. Eventually though, I had to sell the house and get an apartment.

At this point, selling the house we had made a family in felt like "the end." When our home was gone, I called my lawyer and filed for our divorce. Around the same time, I think my wife was also having problems paying bills in Boston on her own. She started sending me pictures of my daughter, Alana, who was on the floor having a temper tantrum. She was upset after being told that she would never see me again. Not wanting to see my daughter wasn't the case at all, and I was ready to prove her wrong.

I called up my lawyer and canceled the divorce.

Following my ex, I moved up to Boston to try and give my daughter normalcy. However, we did not by any means have a normal relationship after that. My ex had moved Alana into her bedroom with her. It was clear that I was not going to be sleeping in the same bed. Even though Alana had her own bedroom, that room was just for show for whenever her friends would come over. I lived up in this shitty room in the attic sleeping on a mattress on the floor like a hermit.

I felt like I was allowed to stay there only if I acted as a slave. I was pretty much Alice from the Brady Bunch. I did all the shopping. I did all the cleaning. I did all the cooking. I did all the laundry. I was the one who helped Alana with her homework.

My ex made me work every single lousy autograph signing, or independent wrestling show out there, for often as little money as possible. I argued that overexposure at horrible events was going to hurt my brand, but she didn't care.

So I lived up in the attic and every day, my ex would call me stupid, and call me an asshole for not being able to bring in the money like I had used to. Every day for years, she would fight with me and belittle me in front of my daughter. I was browbeaten.

I became depressed. I gained weight. I went from being on top of the world with the WWF …to working shitty jobs to make ends meet. I was in a horrible relationship. I will be honest, I often thought about ending it all. I pictured taking a gun and blowing my brains out. The only thing that stopped me was thinking about how that would scar my daughter forever.

STABS AT A NINE-TO-FIVERS

Five years or so of nothing but independent wrestling was just too much for me, at the time. I wanted something regular. In February 2004, I took on a job working for Boston's MBTA station. The idea was I wanted to eventually drive the trains themselves, however, making it through those certification classes never happened. First, they stuck me in a lousy collecting booth. The place was disgusting. There were always big nasty rats running around, and it was a dirty mess. To make matters worse, I also had to work some with a real miserable girl who pretty much hated all men, let alone a guy like me.

Down in the drafty subway, I got horrible headaches - killer headaches, even worse than ever. They used to come and go quite a bit after my parasailing accident, but because of the damp conditions in there, I think the headaches were even worse. One of the Nasty Boys, I think Knobbs, suggested that I try taking this fast-acting crushed aspirin that his father took, some old timer shit powder. I started using this BC Aspirin powder, and he was right. It worked really fast to overcome the hellish migraines.

One day, I had left some BC my drawer, and of course, the girl went through my stuff. It poofed in a gust of air and somehow got some on her black sweater. She freaked out screaming, thinking it was anthrax because the hot news story at the time had a madman sending people anthrax in the mail. She pointed the finger at me as being the anthrax guy. Subsequently, her "drama queen" bullshit caused an anthrax scare that shut down the trains for hours and hours. It really had nothing to do with me, and I wasn't even there when it happened.

Now, I was already gone and done for the day, but apparently, police and my work were trying to call me at home to see if I knew what the substance was. I was at the gym and never answered. This pissed everyone off. Some rumors hit the news that anthrax closed down the subway. Other rumors circulated that since a wrestler was involved, it probably wasn't anthrax, but rather cocaine – *neither were right!* The girl got upset over a hot topic news story, when in reality, she was afraid of something that was the medical equivalent of Bayer.

Eventually, I was interviewed by the police, and never charged with anything. The dirt sheets picked up on it and pushed the idea it was drugs. *I was a party man back in my wrestling days, so it had to be cocaine, right?!* The unfair part of the whole thing was that nobody ever read the actual report. The team tested for powder. It wasn't anthrax, and it wasn't coke. If it was either, the cops would have charged me, and I would have gone to jail. That never happened.

Now I'm no angel, and my wife at the time knew that. I partied a lot. When she heard the rumors, she didn't want to take any chances and started beating me up for everything. So I checked into a rehab anyhow, despite the fact that my partying and the subway incident were two totally different things.

The subway people didn't have my back so we parted ways.

Five years or so of nothing but independent wrestling was just too much for me, at the time. I wanted something regular. I took on a nine-to-five job working for a big pool company back in 2005. It was a major distributor for New England pool companies. We handled all kinds of retail outlets in Upstate NY, New Hampshire, and Massachusetts - big company.

I took a little time off and worked for my neighbor designing in ground pools with a pool kit. When I came back, my sales job had already been filled, so the pool company put me into their accounting department. At first, I was worried. I knew I was horrible at math. After all, I only had a high school education.

However, I got lucky at first. Some other company owed some ridiculous amount of money like $870,000 dollars to our company after a big fire, and a bunch of inventory had been destroyed. Somehow, I was able to collect $740,000 back with no real experience in this line. This got me over big with the company, and I kept trying to make it happen again for them.

In the end, I was maybe a little too aggressive trying to collect money for them, and they didn't like the way I worked. I started calling people who owed us money every day, and they lost their minds. I cut promos on them, and they didn't know what to do.

Eventually, the owners had enough. In order to keep the people who owed them money happy – in hopes that they would eventually pay out, they fired me. It was like a good cop, bad cop thing. To save face for my promos, they told the people I had called that they had fired me.

No real worries, however. Brutus Beefcake was not really supposed to be a nine-to-fiver, anyhow.

CELEBRITY WRESTLING & NAME RIGHTS

In 2007, Terry called me up to work on his new half reality, half wrestling show. Eric and Hervey were producing it. Though they were more Hogan fans than they were of mine, they didn't seem to have any real issue with me being a judge on it, if I could use my old "Brutus Beefcake" name to help ratings.

When they put the info out there about the upcoming show in 2007, they credited "Brutus Beefcake" as being a special coach, because the copyright to that name had ended 8 years ago. However, the WWF immediately sent Eric a cease and desist letter, claiming rights to the Brutus Beefcake name. Honestly, truth be told, I didn't care either way what they called me on the show. I just wanted a payday.

Jason Hervey's brother is a huge attorney in Hollywood, California. Eric gave him a call to help the show's potential ratings. He set up an appointment so I could have a talk with him. He gave me some homework to do, but I got it done. I ended up giving him over 100 different documents where, in the past eight years, I had wrestled all over the world as "Brutus Beefcake" and "Brutus 'The Barber' Beefcake." Those instances were all since the WWF copyright had expired.

He shook my hand and said, "I believe they currently have no legal trademark and no legal right to that name."

We went to court, but it was over before it started. With no legal standing to say I couldn't use my name, the courts upheld the cease and desist order and made a decision that ultimately helped me get my name back. At that point, the WWF no longer had any legal standing to my name.

Now, that lawsuit might have been why WWF never called me to do anything with them over the years following that court case. I wasn't included in any "Legends Contracts" that some of the boys were being offered. I also wasn't in any of the video games, or any promotions for the WWE Network.

Now, some of you collectors might note that, during this time, there were some Brutus Beefcake action figures. They came out under the WWF logo by Jakks Pacific. However, my participation with that was done with a deal directly through the toy company, and not with the WWE. It seemed that I was doomed. It was great that I owned my name, but my dream of returning to the company in some capacity wasn't going to happen.

The whole time I was doing all those silly fly-by-night gimmicks that didn't work well at WCW, was because I didn't want to directly rip off the Beefcake gimmick in a cheap knockoff form and upset WWF. I secretly hoped that one day WWE might want to bring me back. While it did take a while, finally, it paid off. I am proud to say that Triple H is the man. He really is one of the boys after all, and I believe he played a big part in welcoming me back home with open arms. Now, I am under a Legends Contract, I am in a video game, and also have a few new action figures out there.

Now, back to the *Celebrity Wrestling* show story…

We were all staying in these apartments not too far away from each other for the shooting of the series. I was able to hang out with pretty much everyone, and they all seemed relatively ok. There was me, Brian Knobbs, Todd Bridges, Butterbean, and Tiffany. I remember also going to a party being thrown by another one of the people on the show, Erin Murphy, who played the daughter of Samantha and Darrin on *Bewitched*. It was a nice little house in the valley. Everyone was there except Dennis Rodman. She was super nice.

Also on the show was Danny Bonaduce from the Partridge Family, who was, at the time, a DJ for an LA radio show. He was the only guy who wasn't really great to be around. He was really a mess during the filming of that show. He was still shooting up steroids, eating pain pills, and showing up to the set "half in the bag."

The training was good fun. We got in there and treated the stars the same way that we would have taught any person who wanted to be a wrestler at any training camp, or wrestling school. We beat them up pretty good, and blew them up the best we could.

It was pretty difficult to train people who never wrestled or really ever wanted to, but, it was rewarding to see how some of them did come along. Now, Todd Bridges came in with an excellent attitude, and he really was great to work with. He tried really hard and did a good job. He even got into some of the training and fitness aspect of things after it was all done.

Danny Bonaduce, on the other hand, was the opposite side of the spectrum from Todd Bridges when he started out. He was a diva and pretty much an arrogant prick. I will say, however, Bonaduce did greatly improve by the end of the run.

Years after *Celebrity Wrestling*, I caught up with Butterbean. He was another guy I really liked working with from the show. We had a wrestling match together in New Jersey, and it was funny to see him using some of the tips that I showed him in the ring still.

Being a worker at heart, he is the same as me. He is still out on the road looking for gigs. It's in his blood. Being a big guy is tough on a fighter, however. He has a really bad back now, and he could barely walk. He told me that he can't fly in planes much anymore, either.

"I literally can't fit in those coach seats," he confided. "And you know promoters. They just won't pay first class. If I ask $1000 for an appearance, the plane ticket also costs $1000."

He said he has to drive everywhere, now in order to find work. He mentioned he drove all the way to New Jersey with his wife for that show. The thing is, he is from Mississippi!

CELEBRITY BOXING

At one point, I planned a return to the ring, but this time boxing, and not your everyday regular boxing… *Celebrity Boxing*.

Sometimes for these events, promoters would have a difficult time booking. For one, a lot of real celebrities would have no interest in getting in the ring and messing up their money-makers. The other reason was often just that the promoter couldn't afford to get names that people gave a damn about, or sometimes even heard of before. Therefore, they would often pit a decent name against some B-level celebrity or lower, maybe like G-level; G for *God-awful*.

For this particular endeavor back on July 24, 2009, I was competing at an event called "Celebrity Boxing 10" out in Philly. My opponent was a hometown hero. He was famous competitive food-eater named "El Wingadore" Bill Simmons. Admittedly, I had never heard of this local legend before, and from what I heard, his best years of stuffing wings down his gullet were already behind him before getting in the ring with me.

In his prime, they say that Simmons had an uncanny superpower of being able to eat a massive amount of meat. In particular, he had a mutant wing-eating ability. In 2005, he won the contest by eating 162 chicken wings. This pig-like skill led him to win the Wing Bowl on five separate occasions.

Simmons used to strut into these big competitive eating events, acting his very hardest to look like a pro-wrestler. If you saw him, you would swear he was trying to steal my gimmick. It only made sense then, I guess, that they pair him up with me.

The celebrity boxing event I competed in was not a shoot. It was like a spar. The hits were somewhat real, but many sequences and finishes were all predetermined to some degree. There were actors involved, and the entire show had professional wrestling-like elements of storytelling.

Right from the start, I should have known there was going to be trouble. The first red flag was that Oakland Baseball player, Jose Conseco, took the promoter's deposit and decided that he wasn't going to the show.

My match was supposed to go the duration and end in a draw. The night of the show, I showed everyone in attendance that I was the superior athlete. I was not going to let the "King of Wings & Blue Cheese" outperform me. He just stood there in the middle of the ring like a big lump, and I was running circles around him. I think he realized that he couldn't keep up, and it bruised his ego.

It was a classic case of the promoter putting a mark in the ring with me, who didn't understand that things were a work. That was always a bad thing. Rather than to go with the predetermined plans, marks believe it is real, and often decide they have something to prove. Simmons did the same thing. The competitive eater decided he wanted to try and offer some real competition, so he thumbed my eye intentionally.

I couldn't see. Knowing from past experiences that marks are not good to work with, I fell back to the corner and said, "Screw this. I'm done." That's not me being chicken of the chicken wing man, that's the wisdom that comes with age. Sure, I could have taught the mark a lesson. Sure I could have beat the living buffalo sauce right out of that jabroni, but risking getting hurt wasn't worth it. If I did, I could have missed appearances in which I couldn't wrestle, and then I would not have been able to provide for my family. That's just common sense.

As smart as I may be, I wasn't smart enough to turn down yet another celebrity boxing payday some two years later. On May 28, 2011, they pitted me against Todd "The Punisher" Poulton, yet another mark for himself with something to prove.

Todd was basically a boxer that Celebrity Boxing promoters used to make the celebrities look good. In later years, however, The Punisher became a little more known in the public eye, being spotted at Trump rallies during his campaign. He took on a role of security in some venues at Massachusetts and New Hampshire. He also beat the crap out of hecklers. He then declared himself the "unofficial bodyguard" of the Republican frontrunner for the presidential nomination.

The same thing happened again a few years later in yet another celebrity boxing match. In our match this time, I was really taking it to Poulton and, perhaps, looking better than he thought I would.

So then he started punching back in the face, when we were clear that face shots were off the table. Regardless, to make matters worse, the ring started bouncing strangely underneath our footing during the fight. It turned out that the promoter, of course, had deep pockets like most. He had some kind of cheap, unstable ring. When I went for a killer roundhouse, the ring shifted. The swaying underfoot somehow caused my quad to tear right above the knee.

One second I was hitting the guy, and the next second I was hitting the mat.

With literally no real offense from my opponent, I went down. I couldn't move my leg, and they had to announce me as the loser, though that wasn't in the original plans. I couldn't stand, let alone finish the fight.

When I got backstage, the medic looked at my leg and immediately put me in an ambulance. They brought me to the hospital which, fortunately, was right across the street. I thought that I had blown my knee out altogether, but then found it was, in fact, a tear in my quad tendon. They shot me up with morphine and sent me home. Fortunately, the injury wasn't all that bad. It only really meant a month or so out of action.

My ex-wife and I weren't happy at all. I felt like she didn't care about me. I felt like she only wanted me to go out and make more money so she could just spend it, whether I was injured or not. She wanted a new bag, or she needed a new outfit, or whatever. I felt like it was always about her buying stupid crap that she didn't need. That was the story of my life.

So while I was still injured, she harassed me until I actually wanted to leave the house to get away from the torment. A few weeks later, I just taped up my leg and was off to wrestle for some more bad independent promotions with a bad wheel.

I was hobbling around like a peg-leg pirate, but that didn't matter to her. She wanted a new Coach purse. I wanted a divorce, but I also wanted to stay with my daughter. I'm glad I did. I know I taught her good study habits and like to think I helped her tremendously. I did the right thing by staying in a broken marriage, to help with my kid. It helped her quite a bunch, and it was worth suffering through the bad relationship.

It was always my plan to leave when Alana graduated from high school and left for college, but that idea got cut off about two years early. I finally met my new wife who loves me dearly. She pulled me out of depression and made me feel alive again. After getting caught talking to her on the phone with her one night up in my crappy room in the attic, I finally left. I roughed it out until Alana was just getting into her junior year of high school.

My new wife has since taught me how to be happy again. She explained how she idolized me when she was younger, and she made me feel important again. She reminded me that I am "Brutus The Fucking Barber Beefcake," and how "that really is something." It is my new wife that *really is something.*

After I left, it seemed like my ex began to try and erase me in the eyes of my daughter. I felt like she was filling her head with lies. My guess is that she told Alana that I wanted nothing to with her, but that was the furthest thing from the truth. Many, many times, I would call to try and spend time with my daughter, but I think my ex would just conveniently never pass on any of the messages.

After moving back down to Tampa with my new wife, I set up a meeting with my daughter while she was about to start college. I bought a plane ticket. I rented a car. I set up hotel reservations - the whole thing. When I landed in Boston, my ex texted my wife, Missy, and said that Alana wouldn't be meeting with me today, or ever. Then she went online laughing and tweeting about the whole thing.

Being a WWF Superstar was great. If you can make it there, you really are made of rockstar material. You travel the world. Fans everywhere scream your name. For me, it was quite the experience. However, with all of the fame goes all of the spoils. Like other wrestlers, I sacrificed some of my love life for the love of wrestling. I only want my daughter to know that despite whatever she was told, and whatever was hidden from her, I do love her. My love for her is not erased.

GUEST PASSAGE – HACKSAW JIM DUGGAN ON BEEFER & INDIES

I continue to make occasional appearances at independent shows, today. Finally, the money has improved to some degree, and it is always great to see the boys, again.

Hacksaw Jim Duggan recalled a show we did together where we felt the promoter was being entirely too cheap. Here's what he had to say:

"…When we started taking independent dates after the WWE days were over, we would just like take over in the locker room. I remember me and the Beefer staking claim over a big bin of chicken wings that the promoter left in the locker room for all of the wrestlers.

What we did was we would stand on opposite sides of the table, naked, on our way to the showers. We were really gross, dripping the sauce all down on our chests and all. Then, we would eat the entire thing. Ha ha! Nobody wanted any of that food, or any part of the two big wrestlers pounding wings, for fear of getting a chicken wing submission put on them instead.

It was a different time. When a promoter tried to screw us, we would often have an "us versus them" mentality. When guys like me and Beefer would get together, we would just like take over like they owed us. It's not so bad now, though, and we were different people back then, too."

– Hacksaw Jim Duggan

**Speaking of nudity, Jimmy Hart looks on as his client rips
his pants and does some Struttin' & Buttin'**

The Dream Team... still "Bad Ass" in semi-retirement.

CHAPTER 25 - STILL GOT IT

Not so long ago, I got up early one morning. I put on the news. I was making myself some coffee when the phone rang. I heard a familiar voice on the other end of the receiver.

"Hey Brutus," he said. "It's Peter."

"Hey man! What's up?" Calls from my agent Peter were always great. I would listen with dollar signs in my eyes.

"It looks like we got Mr. T a pretty good paying appearance gig in Spain. Big payday for some media event," he said. "They said that they were looking for some more American TV names, so I mentioned you. That is, if you want to travel to Spain?"

"Sure, Peter, that's really what we wrestlers do," I said. "We do more time on the road than actually in the ring. Thanks, man. That would be great!"

Mr. T, by the way, was represented by the same company I was, the Sovereign Talent agency. We also shared the same agent; a nice guy by the name of Peter Young. Peter handled my movie endeavors and all. From time to time, he would also find me some good appearances gigs.

I spoke with the promoter in Spain. He said he wanted another American to come so his attraction could have a tag team feel to it. I called Greg, and he was in. We booked the flights, and when it came time, we flew out of Tampa airport with business class tickets.

The gig itself was really weird. It wasn't really a wrestling show. It was some big event for one of the most popular television shows at the time in Spain. For that event, however, they did feature a, kind of wrestling sideshow, for one of the nights, in what was to be a week-long affair.

For our show, they had us go into the audience, way up in the cheap seats. We were surrounded by lots of little Spaniards who were going nuts and hugging us, only because we were Americans like they saw on TV. They interviewed us way up in the crowd on live TV, and we didn't know at all what they were saying.

When our match finally came, we got in the ring. Then all of a sudden, all of these Luchadores started storming the barricades running at us from all different directions. We had had an idea that this was the plan, but we didn't know for sure. We didn't speak Spanish well, and they didn't really speak English. Anyhow, probably a dozen Spanish guys dressed as Mexicans charged us, and we didn't care. We just started launching them out of the ring. It was crazy.

Later that night, we went to dinner. The Spanish promoter loved it and bought us the most amazing Spanish food I have ever had in my life. Spanish food is not like Mexican. You should really try it if you ever get the chance. After that, we walked around the street a little, then went back to the airport.

For those of you who may not know, most often wrestlers go everywhere but see nothing. We fly all over the world, but when we get there, it is always rush, rush, rush to get to the arena, then the same thing to get back to the airport. In the wrestling business, very seldom do you ever get very much downtime where you can actually enjoy seeing a far away and distant land to really appreciate much of the diversity and culture that they have to offer.

Back at the airport, Greg showed his passport to customs, paid his tax and walked right through to head off to the plane. When they got to me, they looked at my passport and shook their heads. I looked at the paper.

The son-of-a-bitch expired!

"Sir, I just flew in the day before yesterday," I argued, but the customs guy wouldn't hear it.

"I am sorry, we cannot let you board, he said in broken English.

I was pissed. I mean, I know I should have looked to see when the passport was going to expire before I had left, but come on! You would think someone at the airport in America would have mentioned that the expiration date was coming up the same as when the guy tells you your inspection is about due when you get an oil change.

After that, I sat down to watch Valentine take off, before making my way to the American Embassy. I was screwed. I knew that I was looking at a lot of top quality bullshit in my future. I was going to have to stay more days. I was going to need more hotel time, which was super expensive where we had been staying. I was going to need a rental car.

As I was sitting down watching the plane I was supposed to be preparing to fly away, I noticed an American Airlines lady come by. She was rushing to get on the same airplane, herself. I had recognized her from the flight up, thinking about what a mile-high club membership would have been like with her. I rushed to her side and flagged her down.

Time for some of the old school "Love-em and Leave-em Leslie" charm.

I poured it on thick. After I told her my whole story, I thought I had her sympathy, so I went for the finish with something like this:

"Look, is there anything you can possibly do for me? This is totally my fault, but nobody missed the fact it was expiring when I left the USA," I said with puppy dog eyes. "Help me get back and I will deal with it when I get home in Miami?"

Yep. I still got it!

It worked! I totally charmed her. She snuck me around the back way, and I got on the plane. One of the best things about that whole interaction was somehow, I managed to miss customs altogether. I had around $20,000 grand cash on me in my pocket, and anything over $10,000 was supposed to be declared. I walked with it all, duty-free!

When I got back to the airport in Florida, I really didn't want to have to sort everything out. I wanted to get off the plane and go home. International flights are so long and everything, who wanted to go work on paperwork. Someone on the plane had mentioned to me, too, that there was going to be a pretty big fine to pay for having an expired passport. I was not looking forward to that either.

I mean, this is coming from the same guy who had the same suitcase since the 80s. The bag I bring to indy shows is so old, it's actually older than half of the guys I am working with on the card. That should show that I don't like to spend money.

I got off the plane and headed down the ramp towards customs.

Man. I hope they miss the date. MAN! I HOPE THEY MISS THE DATE!

As I headed towards the US Customs line, I saw that there were three agents there. I was in the front of the crowd coming and knew I had a choice.

There was an old woman. There was a man from the Mideast. There was a short little guy with a military haircut.

I calculated. I crunched the numbers. I ran the three subjects before me through my titanium-laced fan-radar scanner to see who would be the best option. The results came back to me with outstanding probability: *SHORT LITTLE MILITARY GUY.*

"Hey," I said to the agent.

I saw how he looked at me. I had seen that look before, at least I thought.

"Passport please."

"Oh, sorry," I said, putting down my bag. "Forgive me. I'm a little beat up still from the WRESTLING show I'm coming back from."

I put the bait out there and waited. I knew that if he was a wrestling fan and he had heard of me, there was a chance I would be saving myself all kinds of hassle. All I needed was for him to be in the same club as me. If he was from my world, I would be golden.

This was the same technique that often found me a free dinner at the diner after a show. This was the same technique that could often find me a room in a "sold out" hotel. Fan fishing is something very real. I had learned that when I dangled the wrestling carrot and put it out there, it could be a very powerful thing - more powerful than any Diners Club Card, or any Backstage VIP pass.

If I can only just make the connection… Be a fan. Be a fan!

Pro wrestling can connect very different people like nothing else in the world can.

There is an argument that sports, in general, does this as well, but not to the degree that wrestling can. Some sports fans are just fans of their hometown teams simply because they are from that area. Others may actually select a remote team. However, with wrestling, there is so much more to be a fan of. You can like the heroes, the villains, the announcers, the storylines, wrestling styles, wrestling personas, particular divisions, particular promotions, particular eras, and the list goes on and on.

Talking to a stranger about a particular match, for instance, can instantaneously transport them back to another age, another era. I think this is because wrestling can strike a chord with every emotion. When you are a wrestling fan, the combination of sports and entertainment make wrestling relatable to the inner soul of everyone on a storytelling level.

Some people look at sports entertainment as being cheesy or silly, but the ones who don't realize that it is so much more than that, and that is what makes everyone in the know more special. It connects us all in the know, because it's a way of life.

There has never been a time when this connection has been more important. Thousands of people who do not know each other will go to an arena and relate to each other for three hours. An old woman will sit down next to a young boy. A black person will sit down next to a white person. A far-right conservative Republican will find their seat next to an extremely liberal Democrat. They don't see how they are different. All they see is the common love of the game. They will then cheer together for the same wrestler, show their shared disapproval for another, and sit on the edge of their seats at the same instant.

If you don't believe that wrestling is a connection, the next time you see a kid in the supermarket or a guy at the gym wearing a wrestling t-shirt, walk by them and do the John Cena "U Can't See Me" thing, waving your hand in front of your face. Believe me, they will see you, and you will have instantly made a connection that shows you are from the same universe, stronger than any worker handshake.

"Wrestling?" he asked.

"Yeah," I said, trying to downplay for realism. "Had a show in Spain."

The short little military-looking guy looked at me with different eyes. My fan-radar was right.

"Oh my god, Brutus?!" he asked, as if he had finally met up with his long lost friend. "Brutus Beefcake?"

I nodded. I continued to downplay everything, but inside, I was high-fiving myself. Fireworks were going off and a marching band was dancing by me with all the bells and whistles.

"Wow, man," he said. "I just want to shake your hand, and tell you thank you so much for making my childhood so special!" He grabbed my hand and hugged me like a long-lost brother. "You were legit one of my favorites ever."

"Thanks brother, that means so much to me," I said. Later in life, I really did learn to appreciate true words like that, more so than I ever had in the past.

The next thing I knew, I was posing for a picture with him and signing an autograph. I almost felt bad that I was using my "Wrestling Club Membership" to try and ask for a special favor from someone who was that happy to have met me.

"Uh, about the passport," I said, taking it out of the front zipper of my bag. Before I could give him my story, he was already cutting me off.

"Oh, yes," he said grabbing my paperwork from me. "Of course."

I winced a little. He opened up the little booklet and thumbed to the front page.

"ED LESLIE," he read through star struck eyes. "That's right. Ed Leslie!" He flipped through my passport and stamped it.

"Man, thanks again. You made my day," he said with a smile.

Now, I just don't know. Maybe he saw the expired date and ignored it because we both had wrestling in common. Or, maybe he just didn't notice it at all because he was blinded because one of his childhood heroes had just taken a picture with him. Either way, it worked. I worked him. I went right through! I walked calmly away from the customs line, then I ran around a corner and immediately did a happy dance!

I caught my layover, and maybe an hour later we landed in Tampa. That whole flight home, I wondered if they had figured anything out after I had left, or not. Paranoia set in pretty hard. I know there was at least one person who knew my situation, and she said she was going to call my destination to make sure I made good on my promise to settle up the expiration issue. I would be lying if I said I wasn't worried about that conversation.

At the Tampa airport terminal, when I went to get my bags, I by chance ran right into my old friend, my face doctor, Dr. Habal.

"Brutus!" he said. "It's so good to see you, again."

"Oh, you too!" I hugged him. The man truly saved my life, and I couldn't blow him off, no matter how freaked out I was. "You are the best, doc."

"You are a miracle," he said. "I'm so happy all has worked out for you."

Looking over his shoulder, I saw a few guards walking our way down the hall.

"You really are the best, doc." I looked him right in the eye so he would know I wasn't brushing him off. I surveyed the guard situation. They were moving a little more quickly and still heading in our direction. "Listen. I really have to get out of here. I'm really late!"

"Oh no," he said. "You go and we can catch up later."

"Thanks doc!"

I ran out of baggage claim, just as two guards perambulated up to where I had been standing with the good doctor. However, I was long gone. I jumped in my car and hauled ass out of there. Want to know why barbers always make the best drivers? Because they always know all the shortcuts!

Most books have some kind of definitive ending, but I can't do that yet because it's not over for this barber quite yet. I'm still out there, struttin' and cuttin' my way into different cities and hopefully now into your heart.

Thanks for taking a chance with my book!

CREDITS

AUTHOR:
Brutus Beefcake

COAUTHOR/GHOSTWRITER:
Kenny Casanova

EDITOR & LEGAL STUFF:
Marty Carbone

RESEARCH CONSULTANTS:
Todd Bovair, Rob Rosen, &
Bert Williams (aka Head Researcher)

WOHW WEB/SOCIAL MEDIA:
Beth Kempf

BEHIND THE SCENES HELP:
Maria Bevan
Kerri Bevan
Mike Johnson
Shockwave The Robot
Scott Wilder

QUOTES & CONTENT:
Wade Boggs (Foreword)
Bruno Sammartino
Brain Blair
Marty Jannetty
Diamond Dallas Page
Lanny Poffo
Jerry Jarrett
Koko B Ware
Hacksaw Duggan
Honky Tonk Man
Outlaw Ron Bass
Kevin Sullivan
Dusty Wolfe
Bushwacker Luke
Greg Valentine
Nikolai Volkoff
Don Muraco
"Typhoon" Fred Ottman
Bill Apter
King Kong Bundy
Kamala

PHOTO COLLECTION CONTRIBUTIONS:
Chris Swisher
Howard Lapes
Dr. Mike Lano
Missy Leslie
Carmine Despirito

MORE PHOTOS:
Adam JWC (182)
Wrestling Revue Archives (132)
Andrea Kellaway (369)
George Napolitano (191)
John McKeon (182, 214, 230)
Rodney L. Freeman (285)

HELPFUL RESOURCES:
WOHW.com
KennyCasanova.com
KamalaSpeaks.com
BrutusBeefcake.com
VaderTime.com
PWInsider.com
InsideTheRopesVIP.com
MemphisWrestlingHistory.com
Slam Canoe Wrestling
ObsessedWithWrestling.com
BETwrestling.com
Steve Austin Show Podcast
Konnan's Keepin' it 100 Podcast
Sean Mooney's Prime Time Podcast

VERY SPECIAL THANKS FROM KENNY CASANOVA:
...To my lovely wife, Maria, for putting up with me & dealing with the countless hours spent on this project! ...To Marty for the pages and pages of errors and edits. ...& To anyone else who supports these wrestling books to keep the legend alive!

KENNY CASANOVA
CO-AUTHOR/GHOSTWRITER OF THIS BOOK...

Kenny is a ring announcer, pro wrestling manager, wedding DJ, English teacher, and Fulbright Scholar. As the organizer of this project and other ones like it, his recent mission has been helping wrestlers like Brutus Beefcake & Kamala get their stories out there for the appreciation of future generations.

Please email questions or promotional inquiries to Kenny himself at **ken@kennycasanova.com,** or find him on all social media platforms.

Also, check out **Walking on Hot Waffles** at **WOHW.com** for more books like this one including *Kamala Speaks, Mr. X: The Real Life Story of Dangerous Danny Davis, SABU: Scars, Silence, & Superglue, and Vader Time.*

Made in the USA
Columbia, SC
18 October 2022